Microsoft®

Internet Information Server

Resource Kit

Property of

Tim Lee

Microsoft Press

PUBLISHED BY
Microsoft Press
A Division of Microsoft Corporation
One Microsoft Way
Redmond, Washington 98052-6399

Library of Congress Cataloging-in-Publication Data
Microsoft Internet Information Server Resource Kit / Microsoft
    Corporation.
            p.   cm.
        Includes index.
        ISBN 1-57231-638-1
        1. Microsoft Internet information server.   2. Internet (Computer
    network)--Computer programs.   3. Web servers.   I. Microsoft
    Corporation.
    TK5105.875.I57M534   1998
    005.7'13769--dc21   97-48754
                                                                       CIP

Printed and bound in the United States of America.

4 5 6 7 8 9   WCWC   3 2 1 0 9

Distributed in Canada by Penguin Books Canada Limited.

A CIP catalogue record for this book is available from the British Library.

Microsoft Press books are available through booksellers and distributors worldwide. For further
information about international editions, contact your local Microsoft Corporation office. Or contact
Microsoft Press International directly at fax (425) 936-7329. Visit our Web site at mspress.microsoft.com.

Acquisitions Editor: Casey D. Doyle
Project Editor: Maureen Williams Zimmerman

Special thanks to the IIS Champs

Contributing Writers

Seth Manheim ("Introduction," Chapter 1, "Internet Information Server Overview," Appendix A, "Using the IIS Resource Kit CD"); Jim Morey (Chapter 2, "Managing Content"); Jon Singer (Chapter 3, "Capacity Planning," Chapter 4, "Performance Tuning and Optimization"); John Sudds (Chapter 5, "Developing Web Applications," Chapter 6, "Data Access and Transactions," Appendix C, "Debugging Applications and Components"); Shawn Bice, Paolo Branchesi, and John Butler (Chapter 7, "ISP Administration"); Michael Howard (Chapter 8, "Security"); John Meade (Chapter 9, "Accessing Legacy Data and Applications," Appendix B, "ASP Standards"); Glenn Scott, Bill Colburn, and Jorge Arturo Hernández Serrano (Chapter 10, "Migrating Web Sites and Applications")

Resource Kit Program Manager: Jim Laurel

Documentation Managers: Sue Turner, Robert Davis

Writing Manager: Seth Manheim

Lead Editor: Alexander Price

Technical Editor: Karen Carter-Schwendler

Contributing Editors: Rick May, Rebekka Stahl

Production Manager: Nick Leggett

Production Lead: David Fleischman

Production: Lisa Black

Indexer: Frank Maier

Lead Graphic Designers: Michael McDevitt, Bob Cottington

Design Support: Gary Goodrich

Lead Software Developer and Tester: Prashant Luthra

Production Support Liaisons: Cathy Pfarr and Kat Reynolds

Technical Consultants:

J Allard, Bruce Baker, Aaron Barth, Dina Berry, Sachin Bhatia, Dave Browning, Kresimir Bozic, Barry Butterklee, June Blender Cahn, Tom Campbell, Philip Carmichael, Patrick Coston, Howard Davidson, Kris Dinkel, Bill Duemmel, Matthew Dunn, Peter Durham, Jeff Fink, Dan Fisher, Gordon Garb, Scott Gate, Scott Guthrie, Mary Haggard, Basil Halhed, Doug Hebenthal, Janice Hertz, Brad Huggins, Stu Klingman, Paul Kreemer, Murali Krishnan, Paul Larsen, David Lee, Eric Lee, Rich Lowry, John Ludeman, Richard Maring, Christy McCoy, Robert McMurray, Mike Moore, Dan Morrow, Paul Morse, Mark Mortimore, Jamie Myxter, Susan Nellis, Eric Niebler, Mark O'Brien, Jee Fung Pang, Sam Patton, Jonathan Perera, Seth Pollack, Jeff Prothero, Saveen Reddy, George Reilly, Joseph Roberts, Dmitry Robsman, Rob Sanfilippo, Paul Schafer, Darren Stalder, Kavi Singh, Luc Talpe, David Treadwell, Todd Wanke, Bob Watson, Gary Watts, Todd Weeks, Audrey Wehba, and Mark Whidby.

Contents

Introduction

Welcome to the *Microsoft Internet Information Server Resource Kit.*

The *Internet Information Server Resource Kit* consists of this book and one compact disc (CD) containing samples, tools, and utilities for Internet Information Server version 4.0.

The *Internet Information Server Resource Kit* provides detailed information on Microsoft® Internet Information Server (IIS). This information is intended as a supplement to the online documentation included with IIS version 4.0. It does not replace that documentation as the primary source for learning how to use the product's specific features.

About the Internet Information Server Resource Kit

This book contains the following chapters:

Chapter 1, "Internet Information Server Overview," describes each of the technology components included with Internet Information Server 4.0. This chapter presents a "technology map" that shows where the elements of IIS and associated products included in the Windows NT® 4.0 Option Pack fit into different usage scenarios.

Chapter 2, "Managing Content," concerns the creating, deploying, and testing of Web page content.

Chapter 3, "Capacity Planning," discusses issues involved in planning Web server capacity.

Chapter 4, "Performance Tuning and Optimization," discusses issues involved in optimization and tuning your IIS-based Web server and covers some of the tools you can use for accomplishing these goals. It also provides some guidelines to help your server recover from bottlenecks.

Chapter 5, "Developing Web Applications," presents the features and benefits of the many pieces of underlying technology in IIS, stressing the important functionality that can be obtained by creating Web applications.

Chapter 6, "Data Access and Transactions," introduces key components of Web data access, and discusses how to harness the power of a data-driven approach for Web content publishing.

Chapter 7, "ISP Administration," is a guide to running and maintaining an Internet Service Provider (ISP) operation in the context of Windows NT Server and Internet Information Server.

Chapter 8, "Security," discusses Web server security issues.

Chapter 9, "Accessing Legacy Data and Applications," discusses how to employ the Web to make legacy data and applications easily accessible (via the Internet or the company intranet) to customers and members of the internal organization using Web browsers. This chapter describes how you can use IIS for efficient utilization of legacy data and applications in Web solutions based on IIS.

Chapter 10, "Migrating Web Sites and Applications," discusses the issues involved in migration of your Web servers from Netscape Enterprise Server (NES) to IIS 4.0.

Appendix A, "Using the IIS Resource Kit CD," is an overview of the samples, components, and utilities included on the compact disc included with the *IIS Resource Kit*.

Appendix B, "ASP Standards," is an intranet standards planning guide that provides corporate guidelines for Active Server Pages usage.

Appendix C, "Debugging Applications and Components," discusses how to connect to running applications, and step through the source code. The section includes tips for making Web applications easier to debug.

Glossary of Internet-related terms used in this book.

Resource Kit Compact Disc

The IIS Resource Kit CD includes a variety of tools, components, and utilities to help you work more efficiently with IIS and Active Server Pages. Sample applications as well as the source code to the utilities are included that demonstrate how to write components and IIS filters and applications. Appendix A, "Using the IIS Resource Kit CD," provides an overview of the tools provided on the CD. Complete documentation for each tool is included when you install from the CD.

Resource Kit Support Policy

The software supplied in the *Internet Information Server Resource Kit* is not officially supported. Microsoft does not guarantee the performance of the *Internet Information Server Resource Kit* tools, response times for answering questions, or bug fixes to the tools. However, we do provide several ways for customers who purchase Internet Information Server or the *Internet Information Server Resource Kit* to report bugs and receive possible fixes for their issues. You can submit feedback on the *Internet Information Server Resource Kit* by sending e-mail to Rkinput@microsoft.com. This e-mail address is only for Resource Kit–related issues. For more general feedback on Microsoft Internet Information Server as well as Resource Kit issues, send e-mail to Iiswish@microsoft.com.

C H A P T E R   1

Internet Information Server Overview

1

Microsoft Internet Information Server (IIS) is a file and application server for the Internet and for private intranets. IIS 4.0 is part of the Windows NT Server 4.0 Option Pack, which includes a number of useful server technologies that can be used in conjuction with IIS to establish a powerful Web computing platform.

This chapter provides an overview of IIS 4.0, including its major new features. It also describes other components of the Windows NT 4.0 Option Pack, and discusses their integration with IIS.

In this chapter:

- What's New in Internet Information Server 4.0
- IIS Architecture
- Resources

What's New in Internet Information Server 4.0

As part of the Windows NT 4.0 Option Pack, IIS 4.0 is integrated with Windows NT as well as with a suite of Internet and intranet products. This section discusses the new features included with IIS 4.0.

Industry-Standard Internet Protocol Services

IIS now includes support for the following industry-standard protocols.

HTTP 1.1 Support IIS support for HTTP 1.1 includes the following features:

- **Pipelining** Pipelining allows clients to send many requests before receiving a response from the Web server, thereby providing a performance boost.

- **Persistent Connections (Keep-Alives)** When a browser connects to a Web server and requests a page, a connection is established with the server. Establishing and tearing down connections is an expensive operation for the Web server, client, and network. By using persistent connections, a client can use a single or reduced number of connections for multiple requests.

- **HTTP PUT and DELETE** With the PUT and DELETE directives, users can post and delete files to and from a Web site using any HTTP 1.1 compliant browser.

- **Transfer Chunk Encoding** Active Server Pages (ASP) now supports the transfer encoding header, which lets the browser know if a transformation has been applied to the body of the page being sent.

SMTP Mail IIS now includes a Simple Mail Transfer Protocol (SMTP) mail service that can send and receive SMTP mail messages. For example, the server could be programmed to send a confirmation e-mail message to a customer who submitted a registration form.

A Web server can also receive messages sent to it. For example, if an e-mail message sent by the Web server cannot be delivered, the non-delivery receipt can be returned to the Web server's mailbox. A Web administrator could also use the server's mailbox to collect customer feedback messages regarding a Web site.

NNTP Discussion Groups IIS now includes a Network News Transport Protocol (NNTP) service with which you can host local discussion groups on a single server. Because this feature uses the NNTP protocol, any standard news reader client can be used to participate in these discussion groups. The IIS NNTP service does not include support for news feeds or replication. If, for example, an organization wanted to host an Internet news group such as comp.os.windows, they would need to purchase a product like Microsoft Exchange Server, which provides support for both news feeds and replication. The same solution applies if a user wanted to replicate this discussion group across geographically distributed sites.

RFC 1867 Support Allows programmatic control of file uploads, such as uploading content from a browser to the Web server. Like the HTTP 1.1 PUT directive, it provides a way to post files to a remote Web server from a Web browser.

HTTP Redirects Allows administrators to redirect requests for files to a different Web site, directory, or file; requests can also be redirected to applications. This gives administrators the means to ensure that browser requests are always fulfilled even when content has been removed or moved, or when the name of a virtual directory has changed.

Web Application Development

IIS offers a number of new technologies to make it easier to create more robust, scalable Web applications.

Transactional ASP Pages An ASP page and any components it calls can now be part of a transaction managed by Microsoft Transaction Server. If any portion of the script fails, the entire transaction is aborted. Information in multiple distributed databases can be updated without risking the integrity of the data.

Process Isolation ASP and Internet Server API (ISAPI) applications can now run in processes separate from the main server process. This process isolation prevents the possibility of an error in one application affecting other applications on a site—or the server itself. If an application crashes, it is automatically restarted with the next request, without an administrator manually restarting the application or the server.

Message Queuing IIS is now integrated with Microsoft Message Queue Server (MSMQ). An ASP application can send a MSMQ message to a remote source for deferred processing. MSMQ messages can be grouped with other transacted work (SQL updates, other MSMQ messages, and so on). This greatly enhances a developer's ability to build scalable, fault tolerant applications on IIS.

Microsoft Script Debugger You can use Microsoft Script Debugger to interactively test ASP applications written in any Active Scripting language, such as Visual Basic® Scripting Edition (VBScript) or JScript™.

IIS Admin Objects IIS Admin Objects (IISAO) are components that expose the administration properties of IIS. Developers can use the same programming model to create customized administration utilities that can run either from a command line, as a Windows® application, or in a browser, as a Web application.

COM Logging Interface Developers can write Component Object Model (COM) components that access IIS logging capabilities to provide custom logging.

Failover Clustering Support Failover clustering support in IIS provides integration with the clustering feature of Windows NT 4.0 Enterprise Edition. Using this failover capability, two separate Web sites can be hosted on two separate servers, with failover support for both sites. If one server fails, the other takes over.

Updated Java Virtual Machine Provides developers with a high-performance virtual machine for creating and running Java components on the server. It integrates an industry-standard, scalable implementation for building and deploying Java-based applications.

Component Load and Unload Provides Web developers with the ability to dynamically load and unload Web application components that run out of process without having to stop and restart the Web server. This feature also makes it easier to develop Web applications.

Server Administration

IIS provides the following new administration features:

Multiple Web Site Support With support for HTTP 1.1 host header names, Web site operators, per-Web-site bandwidth throttling, and enhanced HTML administration, IIS enables organizations to host multiple departmental intranet sites and enables ISPs to provide hosting services to multiple public Internet sites.

- **Host Header Name Support** Through the use of HTTP 1.1 host header names, multiple Web sites can share the same IP address. For older browsers that do not support host header names, IIS implements a cookie-based solution. For browsers that do not support cookies, the IIS Resource Kit CD offers the Cookie Munger utility, which provides cookie-like functionality for browsers that do not support cookies.

- **Web Site Operators** Web site Operators are a special group that have limited administrative privileges on individual Web sites. Operators can administer properties that affect only their sites. They do not have access to properties that affect IIS, the Windows NT Server-based computer hosting IIS, or the network. An ISP that hosts sites for a number of different companies could assign delegates from each company as the operators for each individual company's Web site.

- **Bandwidth Throttling** Organizations and ISPs running more than one site on IIS can throttle the bandwidth available to each of the sites individually. Throttling bandwidth on individual sites assures that bandwidth is available for all the sites sharing the network bandwidth.

- **Remote HTML-Based Administration**   IIS provides a Web-based administration tool so that administrators can manage their Web sites remotely using a standard Web browser.

- **Command-Line Administration**   Using the Windows Scripting Host (WSH), administrators can automate the administration tasks on the server using any scripting language supported by Active Server Pages . For example, an administrator can write a Microsoft Visual Basic script to create a new virtual directory, and then with WSH, run the script file from the command line to create a new virtual directory on the Web site. Administrators can write a single script to target multiple Web sites, or multiple physical servers, to provide effective grouped server administration.

Microsoft Management Console Microsoft Management Console is a new host environment for "snap-in" administrative tools. IIS includes a snap-in to administer IIS and a snap-in to administer Microsoft Transaction Server.

Total Content Control In earlier versions of IIS, most of the configuration information was set on a per-server basis. With IIS version 4.0, you can set most properties on a per-file, per-directory, or per-site basis, as well as globally for the server. Properties set at a higher level are inherited by a lower level. For example, properties set at the site level are inherited at the directory and file level.

Security and Authentication

The Windows NT Server security model is the same across all operating system functions. The same features available for file servers and database servers are available to the IIS Web server. New users can be given limited access to private network resources such as HTML pages, Web applications, shared files and printers, corporate databases, and legacy systems on all servers, all of which can be protected using the same user account and passwords.

Client Authentication Secure Sockets Layer (SSL) 3.0 provides a secure way to exchange information between clients and servers. Unlike previous SSL implementations, SSL 3.0 provides a way for the server to verify or authenticate who the client is without the user having to log on to the server. In IIS 4.0, client certificates are exposed to both ISAPI and Active Server Pages, so that programmers can track users through their sites. Also, although it is not enforced, IIS can "map" a client certificate to a Windows NT user account, so that administrators can control access to system resources based on the client certificate.

Certificate Server With the integrated Certificate Server, organizations can set up certificate authorities and issue standard X.509 digital certification to clients. This provides a mechanism for organizations to issue industry-standard X.509 certificates and manage the authentication of users on that basis.

Domain Blocking Using IP Address and Domain Restrictions, administrators can grant or deny access to any specific content based on the domain name of the requester. This feature provides a way to allow only users from a specified domain access to information on the server.

For information on IIS security issues, see Chapter 8, "Security."

Content Management and Control

IIS 4.0 provides an assortment of tools to manage and control the content of Web servers.

Integrated Indexing and Searching With Microsoft Index Server, IIS provides full-text indexing of HTML, Text, Microsoft Office, Adobe PDF, and other file formats. Using Active Server Pages, ActiveX® Data Objects, and SQL, organizations can build custom search pages to provide users with the ability to search for information on an IIS Web site.

Content Ratings Administrators can add rating labels to Web page headers. The default ratings are based on the Platform for Internet Content Selection (PICS) ratings developed by the Recreational Software Advisory Council (RSAC). Content is rated according to levels of violence, nudity, sex, and offensive language. Administrators can also choose a content rating system provided by another organization.

Content Expiration Content expiration labels give administrators the ability to control the life of the content in the browsers' cache. Administrators can use this feature to prevent stale or time-sensitive content from being stored for longer-than-necessary periods on the client's system cache.

Document Footers Administrators can include footer information in an HTML file that can be appended to the bottom of specified documents.

Custom HTTP Headers Administrators can add a custom HTTP header to a document or group of documents. This would, for example, allow a client browser to cache a particular page, but prevent a proxy server from caching it.

One-to-One Content Replication Provides content managers with the ability to select an entire content tree from one server and, with a single click of a button, propagate the content to another server.

Custom Errors Using this feature, administrators can return a custom page or run an application when a user encounters an error. Custom errors provide administrators with an easy-to-use interface for returning more context-sensitive error messages from the Web server.

Microsoft Site Server Express Microsoft Site Server Express provides a subset of the functionality available in Microsoft Site Server. Site Server provides a comprehensive set of features and management tools for enhancing, deploying, and managing intranet, Internet, and commerce sites. Site Server Express includes a site analysis tool, Content Analyzer; a usage analysis tool, Usage Import and Report Writer; and a content publishing tool, Posting Acceptor.

IIS Architecture

This section describes how the many different components of IIS work together. It begins with an overview of IIS as a whole, followed by discussions of its administrative and programmability architectures.

Architecture Overview

IIS is a core product, which means that it is designed to work closely with many other products, including the products that accompany it on the Windows NT 4.0 Option Pack. Figure 1.1 shows the relationship between IIS and other products installed as part of the Windows NT 4.0 Option Pack.

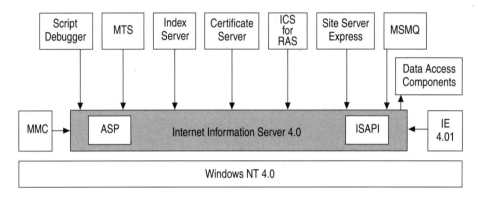

Figure 1.1   IIS architecture

The standard Internet services (FTP and Web servers) reside in a process called Inetinfo. In addition to the Internet services, this process contains the shared thread pool, cache, logging, and SNMP services of Internet Information Server. File Transfer Protocol (FTP) is the protocol used to transfer files between two computers on a network that uses Transmission Control Protocol/Internet Protocol (TCP/IP). FTP was one of the earliest protocols used on TCP/IP-based networks and the Internet. Although the World Wide Web has replaced most functions of FTP, FTP is still a reliable way to copy files from a client computer to a server over the Internet.

Internet Information Server is integrated with Microsoft Windows NT Server. IIS uses the same directory database (user accounts) as Windows NT Server. Using the same directory database eliminates the need for additional user account administration. Internet Information Server administration also uses existing Windows NT Server tools such as Performance Monitor, Event Viewer, and Simple Network Management Protocol (SNMP) support to maintain similar administrative procedures.

In addition, the following products are tightly integrated with IIS.

Microsoft Management Console   Microsoft Management Console (MMC) provides a framework for various network administration programs. The console hosts programs, called "snap-ins," which administrators use to manage their servers. MMC provides a common framework in which various snap-ins can run, so that administrators can manage their network products with a single integrated interface. In addition to providing integration and commonality of administrative tools, MMC also enables console customization; administrators can pick and choose specific snap-ins to create management consoles that include only the exact administrative tools they need. For IIS, MMC hosts Internet Service Manager as a snap-in. Microsoft Transaction Server includes an MMC snap-in for administration of its transaction packages. Future releases of Windows NT and all BackOffice® products, as well as third-party networking products, will include MMC snap-ins as their administrative programs.

Microsoft Transaction Server   Microsoft Transaction Server (MTS) 2.0 is a transaction processing system for developing, deploying, and managing distributed server applications. A transaction is an operation initiated by an application that succeeds or fails as a whole, even if the operation involves many steps (for example, ordering, checking inventory, and billing). Transaction processing is crucial for distributed business applications that require accuracy, data consistency, and security. With MTS you can work with transactions effectively, and even package components within transactions. You can develop a transactional application for a single user and then use simple scripting commands to scale it for use in a production environment. MTS components are activated when needed and deactivated when not, thereby conserving server resources and increasing the number of users who can run your application concurrently. MTS applications can also be run in separate memory spaces so that their operational status will not affect other applications; this is called process isolation.

MTS defines a programming model, and provides a run-time environment and graphical administration tool for managing enterprise applications. MTS is much more than a transaction-management server, it is also an object manager for distributed network objects and environments. MTS provides the following:

- Distributed transactions
- Automatic management of processes and threads
- Object instance management
- A distributed security service to control object creation and use
- A graphical interface for system administration and component management

Figure 1.2 shows the graphical interface for the MTS snap-in to the Microsoft Management Console. The installed packages are shown; using this interface you can add or delete packages or configure MTS as needed.

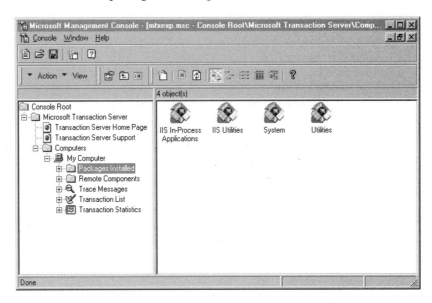

Figure 1.2   Microsoft Management Console

Active Server Pages and Microsoft Script Debugger   Active Server Pages (ASP) is a server-side scripting environment that you can use to create dynamic HTML pages or build powerful Web applications. ASP pages are files that can contain HTML tags, text, and script commands. The script commands execute on the server and return HTML pages to the requesting browser. ASP pages can call ActiveX components to perform tasks, such as connecting to a database or performing a business calculation. With ASP, you can add interactive content to your Web pages or build entire Web applications that use HTML pages as the interface to the user.

Microsoft Script Debugger is designed to help you quickly locate bugs and interactively test your ASP server-side scripts. Script Debugger, which works with Windows Internet Explorer version 3.0 or later, includes just-in-time (JIT) debugging. When a run-time error interrupts execution of your ASP script, the Script Debugger automatically starts, displays the .asp file with a statement pointer pointing to the line that caused the error, and generates an error message. With this type of debugging, your computer suspends further execution of the program. You must correct the errors with an editing program and save your changes before you can resume running the script.

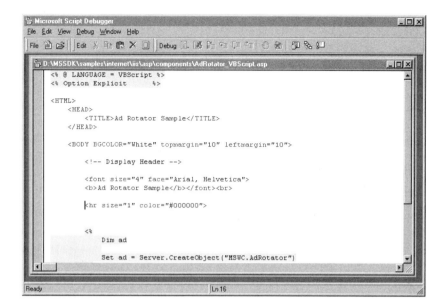

Figure 1.3   Microsoft Script Debugger

Microsoft Index Server Index Server is the Microsoft content indexing and searching solution for IIS. Index Server indexes the full text and properties of documents stored on an Internet or intranet Web site. Users can formulate queries by filling in the fields of a simple Web query form. The Web server forwards the query form to the query engine, which finds the pertinent documents and returns the results to the client formatted as a Web page. With Index Server, an administrator (or any user familiar with Web documents) can create simple query forms. Index Server indexing services can search corporate intranets as well as sites on the Internet.

In addition to indexing Web pages in HTML format, Index Server indexes documents formatted by applications such as Microsoft Word and Microsoft Excel. Using this feature, you can add documents to a Web site without having to convert them into HTML format.

Microsoft Certificate Server Microsoft Certificate Server is a general-purpose, customizable server application for managing the issuance, revocation, and renewal of digital certificates. Certificate Server generates certificates in standard X.509 version 3 format. Digital certificates are used for public-key cryptography applications such as server and client authentication under the Secure Sockets Layer (SSL) or Private Communication Technology (PCT) protocols. With Certificate Server, organizations can perform authentication on a corporate intranet or across the Internet through the use of these certificates.

Internet Connection Services for Remote Access Services   Microsoft Internet Connection Services for Remote Access Services is a collection of software applications designed to help corporations and ISPs build comprehensive Internet access solutions, including dial-up Virtual Private Networks (VPNs). Whether you are building an Internet service or managing a corporate network, Internet Connection Services helps you implement a custom remote access network. With Internet Connection Services, you can provide your subscribers or your employees with seamless connection capabilities, a global dial-up service, and secure connections over the Internet to a private network. With Internet Connection Services you can also centrally manage remote access to your network.

Site Server Express

IIS provides a number of new features that make it easier to manage content and analyze usage on a Web server. Microsoft Site Server Express, included with IIS, enables organizations to analyze log file data, crawl a Web site to map content and check for broken links, and publish content from a browser to a server running IIS.

Site Server Express offers a subset of the functionality found in Microsoft Site Server. It includes Content Analyzer, Usage Import and Report Writer, and Microsoft Posting Acceptor.

- Content Analyzer provides you with the Web site visualization and link-management tools you need to view and manage your Web site. Webmasters, content authors, and Web-server administrators can use Content Analyzer to find broken links, analyze site structure and object properties, manage local and remote sites, and perform a variety of other Web site management tasks. Visualization tools include both Cyberbolic and Tree views. The Tree view provides a linear hierarchical view of the map. The Cyberbolic view depicts the map items in a web-like structure that emphasizes their interconnected nature. Link management tools enable you to ensure that your site's links go where you want, when you want.

- Usage Import and Report Writer makes it easy to collect and analyze IIS log files from a single server. Nine pre-defined reports give you insight into the actual requests, users, and organizations that interact with your site. By extracting this usage information, you can identify trends and gain valuable insights for making more informed Internet business decisions.

- Microsoft Posting Acceptor is a server add-on tool that Web content providers can use to publish their content using HTTP POST (RFC 1867). Posting Acceptor allows IIS and Microsoft Personal Web Server to accept Web content from Microsoft Web Publishing Wizard and Netscape Navigator 2.02 or later through any standard HTTP connection. In conjunction with Microsoft Content Replication System (CRS), Posting Acceptor can also distribute content to multiple servers simultaneously.

Microsoft Message Queue   Microsoft Message Queue Server (MSMQ) enables application programs to communicate with other application programs quickly, reliably and asynchronously by sending and receiving messages. MSMQ features ActiveX support, security controls, administration tools, and integration with other strategic Microsoft products such as IIS, MTS, and Certificate Server make MSMQ the message queuing product of choice for applications running on Windows 95 and Windows NT. MSMQ is also interoperable with other important platforms and products via the MSMQ connector.

Microsoft Data Access Components   Microsoft Data Access Components provides programmatic access to all types of data. Data driven client/server applications deployed over the Web or an intranet can use these components to integrate information from a variety of sources, both relational (SQL) and non-relational. Microsoft Data Access Components consist of ActiveX Data Objects (ADO) and Remote Data Service (RDS), the Microsoft OLE DB Provider for ODBC, and Open Database Connectivity (ODBC) which are released, documented, and supported together.

ActiveX Data Objects (ADO) can help you write applications to access and manipulate data in a database server through an OLE DB Provider. The primary benefits of ADO are ease of use, high speed, low memory overhead, and a small disk footprint. ADO supports key features for building client/server and Web applications.

ADO also features the Remote Data Service (RDS), a high-performance client-side data caching technology that brings database connectivity to Web applications. You can use Remote Data Service to build intelligent Web applications that let you access and update data from any OLE DB Provider, including ODBC-compliant database management systems (DBMS). Because you can implement RDS with familiar technology—off-the-shelf visual controls, HTML, and Microsoft Visual Basic Scripting Edition (VBScript)—Remote Data Service integrates seamlessly with existing Visual Basic applications, so you can transport them to the Web.

Microsoft Data Access Components also includes Open Database Connectivity (ODBC) and the Microsoft OLE DB Provider for ODBC. Used in conjunction with an appropriate ODBC driver (see the list in the "Microsoft Data Access Components Overview" section of the IIS online documentation), these components provide access to several popular database management systems, including Microsoft SQL Server, Oracle databases, Microsoft Access, and several other desktop databases.

Administrative Architecture

IIS provides a comprehensive set of tools for managing the Web server and its components. Administrators are able to use the tools provided by IIS to manage the Web server or an independent Web site. In addition to these management tools included with IIS, customers can create their own custom interfaces using the IIS administration objects that ship with IIS.

Figure 1.4 illustrates the administrative tools provided with Internet Information Server and how they interact with the IIS Admin Objects (IISAO).

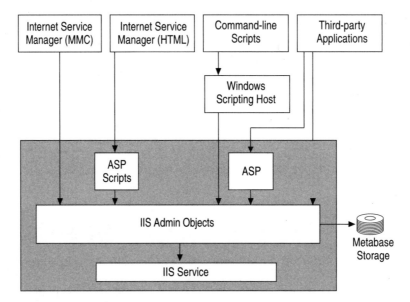

Figure 1.4   Administrative architecture

The IIS Admin Objects are programmable COM objects that an ASP script or custom application can call to change IIS configuration values stored in the IIS metabase. For example, file and directory access permissions used by IIS are stored in the metabase. You can efficiently set these permissions for one or many files and directories with a simple ASP script. The Internet Service Manager snap-in to the MMC, the HTML-based version of Internet Service Manager, the Windows Scripting Host, and third-party administration applications use the IIS Admin Objects to manage IIS.

Internet Service Manager With Internet Service Manager, a snap-in for the Microsoft Management Console, administrators can manage many Internet Information Server sites from a single location anywhere on the Internet. IIS also includes a browser-based version of Internet Service Manager, shown in Figure 1.5. Using Internet Service Manager (HTML), an administrator can configure IIS from almost any computer on the Internet or on a private intranet.

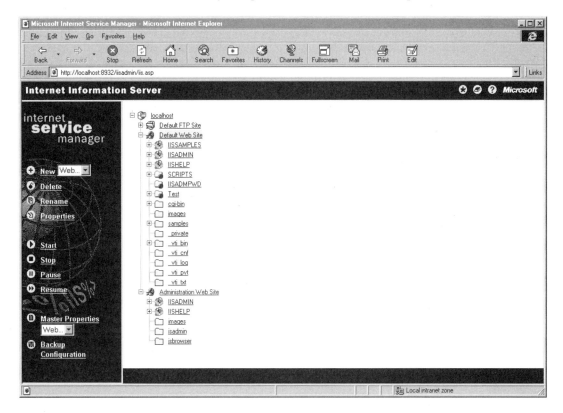

Figure 1.5   Internet Service Manager (HTML)

Windows Scripting Host The Windows Scripting Host (WSH) is a language-independent scripting environment for 32-bit Windows platforms. Microsoft provides both VBScript and JScript scripting engines with the Windows Scripting Host. Third-party companies provide ActiveX scripting engines for other languages such as Perl.

Programmability Architecture

Web applications are maturing to become mission-critical, line-of-business applications. Before the Web, most applications were written and executed on stand-alone computers as single-user applications, and most shared server code was written and executed within databases. Web applications are deployed in a distributed, disconnected environment often running on many different servers and accessing information from many different data stores. IIS adds the necessary technologies to the Windows NT Server platform so that organizations can develop and deploy reliable and scalable multiuser Web applications.

Figure 1.6 illustrates the programmability architecture of IIS and the components described in this section.

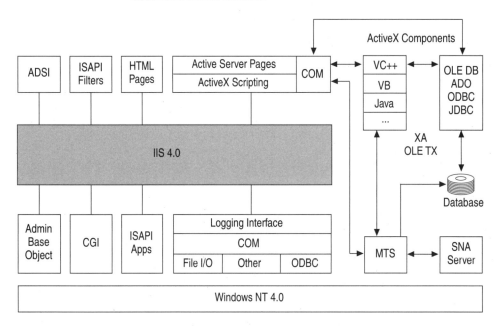

Figure 1.6   Programmability architecture

Developing Web applications involves many of the same complexities as developing multiuser server applications. For instance, when creating a multiuser application, developers must invest time building complex routines for managing server process pools, thread pools, database connections, user context, and transactions usually associated with server applications. IIS and the Windows NT 4.0 Option Pack eliminate much of this complexity by providing new server technologies. Along with Windows NT Server 4.0, these features provide developers with a platform for developing Web applications.

For more information on developing Web applications, see Chapter 5, "Developing Web Applications," and Chapter 6, "Data Access and Transactions."

ADSI Administration Scripts   Using the ADSI administration scripts and the Windows Scripting Host, you can administer a Web site from the command line. The IIS Resource Kit includes a set of sample scripts that you can run to perform many of the common tasks involved in maintaining an ISP or a Web site. For more information, see Appendix A, "Using the IIS Resource Kit CD."

ISAPI Filters and Applications   ISAPI is an API for developing extensions to the IIS server and other HTTP servers that support the ISAPI interface. ISAPI filters are DLLs that allow pre-processing of requests and post-processing of responses, permitting site-specific handling of HTTP requests and responses. ISAPI applications are DLLs that can be loaded into the same memory space occupied by the Web service, and perform some server-side tasks as an interface between the user and IIS. The IIS Resource Kit CD contains a number of sample ISAPI filters and applications.

Admin Base Object   The IIS Admin Base Object is a fully-distributable COM object with methods that enable your application to manipulate IIS configuration keys and data in the memory-resident metabase. You can use the IIS Admin Base Object to write applications, such as server administration or Web authoring tools, that check and update the server's configuration by manipulating keys and data in the metabase. You can also use the IIS Admin Base Object to store your IIS-related custom application configuration data in the metabase (with faster access) without filling up the Windows NT system registry.

Logging   By using IIS logging, you can track which users access your site and when they access your site. Tracking users helps to identify security and performance issues. Logging can be directed either to a log file that can be processed offline and offers faster performance, or to an ODBC Data Source Name (DSN) for dynamic evaluation.

IIS provides several logging features that allow customization of the logging information from an IIS Web site: customized extended logging and resource logging.

- **Customized Extended Logging**   IIS supports the new industry-standard W3C extended logging format. The W3C format is a customizable ASCII format that provides administrators a variety of different fields (items) to record. Administrators can gather detailed information while limiting log size by omitting unneeded fields. These fields include about 20 different items, including date, time, client IP address, and browser type.

- **Resource Logging**   As with most configuration settings in IIS, logging can be set on a per-file basis. With resource logging, the administrator can choose which resources are logged, thus improving performance, reducing log file size, and making it easier to interpret the log files. For example, to reduce the log file size, the administrator could put all the image files in one directory and choose not to log the files in that directory.

- **COM Logging Interface**   Developers can create custom modules to log information regarding the Web site. Each module is responsible for processing request events and writing to a SQL Server data source or its own log file format. IIS logging capabilities can be extended by "plugging in" additional logging modules that developers or third-party software vendors create.

ActiveX Components   Using development tools such as Visual C++®, Visual Basic, or Java, you can develop ActiveX components that can be embedded on a Web page, adding a higher level of interactivity to the page. ActiveX components can be run on the server, on the client, or both. The IIS online documentation, for example, uses an ActiveX Control called HTML Help in the left-hand frame of the browser for its table of contents. Interfacing with OLE DB, ADO, or other database access methods to access information stored in a Microsoft Access or SQL Server database, you can write ActiveX components in any ActiveX-compliant language such as Visual Basic, C++, or Java.

Active Server Pages   ASP applications can add functionality to your Web pages as well. An ASP page is an HTML page that includes server-side script. After the server-side script on an ASP page runs, the results are returned to the client browser in the form of a standard HTML document.

CGI   The Common Gateway Interface (CGI) specification is a widely used method for creating executable programs that run on your Web server. Remote users can start these executables by filling out an HTML form or by simply requesting a URL from your server. Arguments following the question mark in the URL are passed to the CGI application as an environment string, which is parsed and acted upon.

Resources

The following Web sites contain further information and useful resources for IIS and the Windows NT 4.0 Option Pack.

http://www.microsoft.com/IIS/
   The IIS product Web site. Among other things, it provides developer news and samples, and updates on Internet Information Server.

http://www.microsoft.com/intranet/
   The Intranet Solutions Center is a comprehensive Web site designed to provide everything needed to plan and build an intranet. You can download white papers, FAQs, case studies, and free intranet solutions written by Microsoft Solution Providers.

http://www.microsoft.com/workshop/
   Microsoft's Site Builder Network home page, a useful resource for
   Webmasters and Web application developers.

http://www.microsoft.com/workshop/server/
   The Active Server Pages area of the Site Builder Network.

http://www.activeserverpages.com/
   A good Active Server Pages resource. The site contains ASP-related articles,
   ASP FAQs, tutorials, tools, and free ASP component downloads.

http://www.microsoft.com/merchant/
   Microsoft's Internet commerce Web site, including information on Site Server,
   Commerce Server, and the Microsoft Wallet.

http://mspress.microsoft.com/
   The Microsoft Press® Web site. Microsoft Press publishes a number of books
   and training materials about Microsoft's products and related technologies.

CHAPTER 2

Managing Content

Regardless of the type of content you put on your site, knowing how to *manage* the creation, staging, and deployment of that content is critical to your success.

Publishers and managers who have been given the responsibility of managing Web site content should find this chapter especially useful. It includes guidelines regarding the assembly of a Web team, the creation of a hand-off procedure, the management of creative collaboration, and suggestions for choosing tools to make the content management process more effective. A case study of Microsoft's Investor site is included to demonstrate how the content management strategies presented in the chapter can be put into practice.

In this chapter:

- What Is Content Management?
- Creating Content
- Staging Content
- Deploying Content
- Case Study: investor.com
- Resources

What Is Content Management?

Content management is the administration of the overall process of taking your Web site from its inception to its final distribution on the Internet or your intranet. This includes tasks such as defining the vision for the site, assembling a team to make that vision a reality, and managing creative collaboration, team communication, and scheduling.

Internet vs. Intranet: The Most Important Differences

The most important differences between the Internet and an intranet are bandwidth, purpose, security, and hardware.

Bandwidth   Internet users typically have slow modems and require a lot of time to download large pages. On an intranet, however, connection speeds can be in millions of bits per second. This means that large files, high-resolution graphics, true-color photo files, and multimedia can be supported easily.

Purpose and security   Unlike information on the Internet, intranet sites are intended to be seen by selected users within an organization. In order to regulate who has access to your intranet information, you can build security into your site and network connections by using a firewall application such as Microsoft Proxy Server. You can also include internal file management security to ensure that sensitive information can be viewed only by selected individuals.

Hardware and software uniformity   The Internet community uses a wide range of hardware and software. Intranet hardware and software is much easier to regulate. You can implement corporate standards to construct an intranet that includes one type of computer platform, one operating system, and one Web browser. This simplifies design and testing issues because it alleviates cross-platform and cross-browser issues.

The Content Life Cycle

There are processes for all business endeavors. In print publications, information is created, edited, and then printed. In manufacturing, an item is engineered, tested, and fabricated. In the case of a Web site, content must be created, staged, and deployed. The following graphic illustrates that this process, referred to as the *content life cycle*, is continual and ongoing because your Web site content is dynamic.

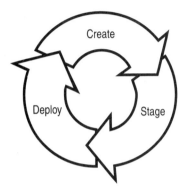

The content life cycle involves three main phases:

Creation encompasses all elements of your Web pages, including text, graphics, and sound.

Staging refers to the phase in which you test and refine your site to ensure that it appears and functions as you intended.

Deployment consists of making your site available to visitors, ensuring that they can find it, and monitoring how it is used.

What Makes a Web Page Successful?

Most successful Web pages include design features that enable *malleability*, *extensibility*, *dynamic content*, and *interactivity*.

Malleability   In print media, once a page is printed, the content is static. In order to change that content, you must print a new version. With a Web site, you can create or alter content and publish it whenever you want. Depending on the goals of your site, you may choose to update the content of your site monthly, weekly, or even daily. You can also update different parts of your site on different schedules.

Extensibility   A good Web site is also extensible, so that you can add and delete new pages and features with ease. If the entire architecture of your site is fluid, you can change it at any time to include new technologies and new features.

Dynamic content and interactivity   Web content can be both dynamic and interactive. Dynamic content, such as a stock ticker tape, can change constantly. Interactive content allows the visitor to compete in online contests, order products, or chat with others visiting the site.

Elements of a Web Page

A typical Web page contains elements that can be divided into two groups: 1) those that provide information; and 2) those that provide functionality. To provide information to your readers you can use a combination of HTML tags, text, graphics, and multimedia. To provide functionality (in other words, dynamic content), you can use scripting and ActiveX components.

Active Server Pages (ASP) applications, cascading style sheets, dynamic HTML, and channels are new technologies that blur the distinction between these two categories in that you have greater control over the format and functionality of your Web pages with them than with HTML alone.

Note   Although all Web browsers support HTML, they do not all currently support the Web page elements described here, nor do they implement these elements in the same way. Microsoft Internet Explorer, version 4.0 and later, supports all of these features.

Following is a picture of a typical Web page with callouts for several elements, and brief descriptions.

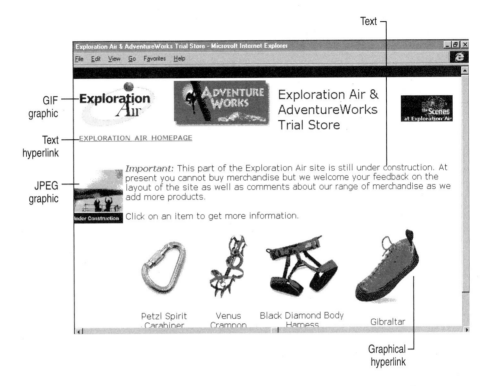

Figure 2.1   The Exploration Air sample site showing common Web page elements.

Hypertext Markup Language (HTML)

HTML is a formatting language used to create Web pages. It consists of tags, or formatting commands, that are set apart from the page content by the less-than and greater-than symbols (< >). These tags tell the client's browser how to render the page's content. They control formatting of text, images, and other page elements.

Text

HTML allows a variety of fonts and styles to be displayed. Just like a printed page, a Web page can have various formatting, including different fonts, text colors, font weights and attributes, spacing, columns, and more. Tables and frames allow even further text-formatting features.

Graphics

There are many types of graphic files, but the most common are GIF and JPEG. The GIF image format is typically used for line drawings or diagrams. The JPEG image format is typically used for photographs.

Hyperlinks

Hyperlinks are text or graphics that, when clicked on, take a visitor from one page to another on your site, and to other sites.

Multimedia

Multimedia can provide your visitors with a rich and memorable journey through your site. You can provide streaming audio-video by using products such as Microsoft NetShow™ to convey content that words alone may not. For example, you can advertise new products or services on the Internet, or train employees over an intranet. The "Getting Started" section of the online documentation for Internet Information Server provides good examples of streaming multimedia.

Scripts

Scripts are small pieces of programming code written into your Web page that add functionality. They can be written in languages such as JScript or VBScript, and can be run on the server or the visitor's browser. Scripts written for the browser are browser-specific. For example, the Netscape browser object model differs from the one for Internet Explorer 4.0.

Active Server Pages (ASP) Applications

Active Server Pages applications are basically HTML pages with scripts enclosed by ASP delimiters (<% and %>). These special delimiters tell the server that these scripts are to be run on the server; they are not even displayed on the client's computer. After the scripts are run and the operations have been accomplished, the server returns the results to the client in the form of an ordinary HTML document.

ASP applications can be used to send dynamic content to a visitor of your Web site regardless of the browser that is used. ASP can perform a variety of tasks such as interfacing with a database and returning the data to the client. Forms can be incorporated into the page to allow the user to access information or functionality on the server. For more information, see Chapter 5, "Developing Web Applications."

ActiveX Components

ActiveX technology can also add functionality to your site. ActiveX components are self-sufficient and self-contained. They can be run on the server, on the client or on both. Components have been made available that can perform almost any task, from showing an AVI movie in a Web page to setting up a Web-distributed interactive schedule and calendar. Components can be written in any ActiveX-compliant language such as Visual Basic. You can create components for specific tasks and export them over the Web.

Cascading Style Sheets

This standard give you the ability to control the look of your entire site, or sections of it, by using a single page of HTML called a style sheet. Style sheets define the function of the various HTML tags in your Web pages. For example, you can define all of the <H1> tags to format text as Arial 18-point italic, bold font. By placing these definitions in one place and calling or invoking them in each Web page, you can achieve a consistent look for your entire site without having to define and redefine each Web page separately. When you want to change the look of your site, all you have to do is alter the style sheet, and the changes apply to your entire site.

Dynamic HTML (DHTML)

DHTML is a new technology that builds upon cascading style sheets so that you can use scripts to control every aspect of HTML tags and their content. With scripts, you can precisely control the layout, appearance, and function of your page. Whereas cascading style sheets are used to define format statically, dynamic HTML can be used to define format dynamically. You can add interactivity, dynamic content, dynamic styles, special-effect transitions between pages, and have graphics or text sections that appear to fade in and out, all without further requests to the server. You can also import custom fonts to the client so that your pages appear exactly as you intended.

Channel Definition Format

Channels are a new technology that allow you to inform regular visitors that the content of your site has been updated. Users who "subscribe" can display pieces of their favorite Web sites on their desktops and choose to have them updated automatically, or manually. Once the content is loaded, they can browse those portions of the site without maintaining an Internet connection.

Creating Content

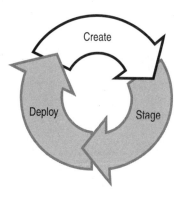

Successful Web sites are the outcome of collaboration and careful planning. In order to plan and manage your site's content, you need to begin by assembling the right team.

Choosing the Right Team

The members of your Web team must be more than just experts in their fields. They must also understand how their contribution fits into the overall vision for your site.

The following is a list of the staff you might need, and some of the qualifications you might want to look for when hiring team members. Depending on your plans and situation, you may create a team that differs from the one listed below—what follows are simply guidelines.

Producer

For small projects, the producer is usually the driving force behind the look, feel, and functionality of the site. He or she guides how the content will be arranged, how the graphics will look, and how the scripts interact with content and media. For larger projects there may be more than one producer: one for multimedia, another for scripting, and so on. In this case, each producer would specialize in one area of expertise and be responsible for managing specific tasks.

There is no definitive job description for a producer—it will vary depending upon the size and tone of your site. In general, however, the producer should be able to focus on the "how" (implementation) while you concentrate upon the "what" (content) of your site. This person should have knowledge and experience in one or more of the following areas:

- Web site structure and design, including server configuration, scheduling, versioning, and testing procedures. It would also be desirable for the producer to be familiar with scripting, as well as server administration.

- Knowledge of and experience in the management of Web page content and layout.
- Ability to manage people in a fast-paced environment.
- Knowledge of release strategies and workflow models, and the ability to determine what sort of plan is appropriate for a given project.

Editor

The editor helps to set and maintain the site's style and integrity, is responsible for the correctness and flow of the text, and sometimes the multimedia content of your site. Determining and enforcing the schedule is also part of an editor's responsibilities. The following qualifications are desirable:

- Attention to detail: The editor is last in the chain of correctness.
- Understanding of the site's tone, and ability to guide writers and multimedia staff toward it.
- Understanding of hand-off procedures.
- Working knowledge of trademark and copyright laws.
- Skill in solving scheduling problems.

Writer

Writers must be concerned with technical accuracy and adherence to stylistic standards, proper word usage, spelling, and grammar. You may want the writer to have HTML experience, but this is not always necessary due to the availability of HTML authoring tools such as Microsoft FrontPage®.

Of all the staff you will need, the writers are the ones most likely to be available from other departments in your company. You may even be able to "borrow" a writer who could produce special versions of their "for print" work to be put up on the site.

Scripter

The scripter will develop and debug scripts, ActiveX components, and other interactive Web elements, and should have the following programming-related skills:

- Working knowledge of HTML, ASP scripting, JScript (or JavaScript), and VBScript.
- Ability to determine schedule information relevant to programming.
- Knowledge of how to develop, debug, and streamline scripts and Web applications.

- Familiarity with programmatic issues of Web site directory structure.

- Knowledge of issues involved in determining the best level of interactivity.

- Ability to write browser sniffers to determine how to present the content to various browser types.

- Familiarity with ActiveX Controls, programs that run on browser to add interactivity or multimedia.

If you are gearing up for the latest technology, you'll want a scripter with knowledge of dynamic HTML, XML (extensible HTML), and Channel Definition Format. Knowledge of IIS is a plus.

Graphic Artist

The graphic artist may not only create the graphic files for your site, but may also need to create sound and movie files. When hiring a graphic artist, it is important to find someone who is aware of the distinction between creating graphics for print and for the Web. A good Web artist will know how to make great-looking art that takes up little bandwidth. The following skills are desirable:

- Intimate knowledge of high-level graphics platforms.

- Artistic ability—knowing what looks great on a Web page.

- Knowledge of how to balance appearance and bandwidth considerations.

- Experience developing and testing cascading style sheets.

Note Bandwidth is defined as the amount of data per second that can be transferred from one computer to another. This can be either over a local area network (LAN), a wide area network (WAN), or over the Internet. Bandwidth is important to consider because it is a measurement of how long your visitors will have to wait for your Web pages to load.

Hardware Technician

You may want to consider hiring a hardware technician, especially if you have multiple servers. This person would set up, configure, test, operate, and maintain your computers, printers, and other machinery necessary to run and maintain your site. For smaller sites, these tasks may also be performed by the producer. A hardware technician should have a strong knowledge of:

- Computer hardware repair, configuration, and troubleshooting.

- MS-DOS®, Windows 95, Windows NT, and other operating systems, as well as server administration.

- Internet and intranet networking and connection technologies, such as TCP/IP, routing, and firewalls.
- Network security and system backup procedures.

The hardware technician should also be proficient in the mechanical and electronic repair of computer and other electronic equipment.

Testing Technician

If you have a large or complex site, you may also want to hire a testing technician, or in some cases, a testing team. For smaller sites the producer and hardware technician can fill this role. The tester will have many skills in common with the scripter and the hardware technician, including knowledge of the following:

- Testing strategies, programs, and technologies.
- Computer hardware repair, configuration, and troubleshooting.
- MS-DOS, Windows 95, Windows NT, other operating systems, and Internet Information Server.
- Internet and intranet networking and connection technologies, including clustering.
- HTML, ASP scripting, JScript (or JavaScript), VBScript, OCX controls, and the latest Internet technologies.
- Good knowledge of network security and system backup procedures.

Hand-off Procedure

Once you have assembled your Web team, it is important to establish a hand-off procedure for site-related tasks. By deciding who handles each task and how each part of the project is passed from one team member to the next, you ensure repeatable success, consistent quality, and a reduction in the impact of personnel turnover. For an example of a successful hand-off procedure, see the case study at the end of this chapter.

Tools for Creative Collaboration

Microsoft has several tools that can help you manage the collaborative efforts of your team. This topic discusses tools for versioning, group communication, remote authoring, HTML editing, and overall site management.

Versioning

As content for your site is being created and edited, you need to be able to track changes that occur in files, when they were made, and who made them. It is important to ensure that only one person can work on a file at a given time, and that corrections by each team member are made to only one version of a file. Consider using Microsoft Visual SourceSafe™ for versioning.

Visual SourceSafe

A typical Web site can be organized as a main directory, with a starting page, supporting pages, and subdirectories stored in a directory tree on the Web server. Copy and paste this folder structure into the Visual SourceSafe Explorer and then add your Web files to the SourceSafe project tree. The following figure shows an actual screen from Visual SourceSafe Explorer, showing the database used by the Visual SourceSafe Web team.

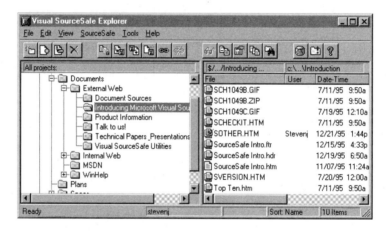

Figure 2.2   Visual SourceSafe Explorer showing Web site directory structure.

Under External Web (which represents the main URL root directory) is a SourceSafe sub-project called "Introducing Microsoft Visual SourceSafe." This subproject contains overview information about Visual SourceSafe: white papers, descriptions of version control advantages, and other materials. As the screen illustration shows, one file—SOTHER.HTM—is currently checked out by a user named Stevenj. When Stevenj clicked "Check Out" for this file, a copy was made in his local working directory on his computer. He is now editing this file locally. When he completes his changes, he will check the file back into Visual SourceSafe, thus making the revised file available to the rest of the team.

Visual SourceSafe allows you to share files between projects. For instance, the file "SWHITE.htm" is used on both the External and Internal Web sites. In both cases, the file exists in subdirectories called Techinfo. In Visual SourceSafe, the file is shared between the "Techinfo" subprojects under both the "External Web" and "Internal Web" projects. Visual SourceSafe stores only one copy of the file internally—so whenever a change is made to this file in either project, that change is automatically reflected in the other project as well. The benefit is that the SourceSafe developers, in general, do not have to worry about multiple Web sites. They can change a file once, and know that the change will propagate to both Web sites if it should, and will affect only one Web site if the file is used only once—automatically.

Visual SourceSafe 5.0 includes a feature to check your hyperlinks, to give you an easy way to test for broken hyperlinks before you publish your content to the server. The Check Hyperlinks feature works against your working directory or the shared project on the server, providing you with a concise report outlining any internal broken hyperlinks.

Visual SourceSafe 5.0 gives you a way to publish your updated content to a test server, or a live Web server, by using the Deploy command. The Deploy command is capable of working across corporate proxy servers (firewalls), such as Microsoft Proxy Server, or deploying Web content to several different Web servers at once. The Visual SourceSafe administrator configures the Deploy path and other related variables from the Visual SourceSafe Administrator program. Inside the Administrator program, you can tag a Visual SourceSafe project as representing a Web site. Once this association has been established, your administrator can set other options that apply to the target Web server directory, proxy server settings, and so on. After the appropriate settings have been established, authorized users can publish content with the click of a button from within Visual SourceSafe.

The Shadow Directory feature in Visual SourceSafe is often used to publish content to an internal staging or test server. Once set by the Visual SourceSafe administrator, a shadow directory is a central directory on a server that always echoes the contents of a project. Whenever a developer updates a file in a Visual SourceSafe project, that file is automatically copied out to the shadow directory.

Group Communication

Throughout your project, it is essential that all the team members be in constant communication. Microsoft Outlook™ is a premier communication platform that can be used to keep your team informed. It may not be practical or even possible to have regular meetings, so e-mail or group Web pages are communication options to consider. With IIS and FrontPage you can easily and effectively build Web pages that can be used to broadcast information to your team regardless of their location.

Remote Authoring

In today's world, with the speed of Internet connections and computers rising almost daily, the definition of "team" is also changing. Before the advent of e-mail, the Internet, and the tools to administer them, the thought of having authors on your team who lived and worked on the other side of the globe was untenable. Now, you can have a writer who works for your Los Angeles–based magazine from home in New York. You can have a multimedia expert in New Zealand creating graphics or a scripter working from a laptop computer in Glacier National Park.

The promise of remote team members using Posting Acceptor, which comes with the Windows NT 4.0 Option Pack, adds flexibility to the way businesses can operate. Posting Acceptor is a feature that you install and configure on your server that allows remote authors to directly contribute to your site. They can create and edit Web pages and post them directly on your Web site using the HTTP Post protocol. Using the ActiveX Upload control, contributors can use drag-and-drop to move files to your Web server. This way, your production team does not have to convert text files into HTML files—the remote author can send HTML files directly to your server. Security options can be set so that a password is required before information can be posted.

HTML Editors

Much of the work involved with creating and editing Web content involves working with HTML tags. This task can be made much easier by using an HTML editor with a variety of features that can make the writing and editing process much easier. Microsoft FrontPage is a tool that has features every team member can use to speed production and minimize incompatibility. It utilizes a WYSIWYG ("what you see is what you get") editor as well as a full-featured HTML editor. FrontPage Server Extensions in IIS make it possible to integrate FrontPage documents with your site.

Overall Site Management: Content Analyzer

Content Analyzer provides comprehensive site visualization, content analysis, link management, and reporting capabilities for managing Web sites. Web administrators, content authors, and Web server administrators can use Content Analyzer to find broken links, analyze site structure and object properties, manage local and remote sites, and perform a variety of other Web site management tasks.

At the heart of the Content Analyzer reporting capability is the WebMap, a compact information base that represents the content and structure of a Web site and includes a wealth of helpful information about the site's resources. WebMaps show your entire Web site in an easy-to-understand, visual format. A WebMap includes graphical representations of the resources in your site, such as HTML pages and graphic images; audio, video, and program files; Word files; and Internet services, such as FTP.

You can choose to see either the Tree view of the map or the Cyberbolic view, or both. The Tree view provides a linear, hierarchical view of the map. The Cyberbolic view depicts the map items in a Web-like structure that emphasizes their interconnected nature. As you work more with the program, you will discover which view you prefer, and you can switch back and forth as you perform different tasks or work with different maps.

As you work on your Web site—editing HTML files, moving files, and so on—hyperlinks can break. Using Content Analyzer, you can quickly find the broken links in your site and restart the applications you need in order to edit the source files.

Content Analyzer also helps you keep track of changes made to your site. You can remap your site after each major revision, and, depending on the remap options you choose, can retain any annotations from the old map, review a new set of HTML site reports, and see which areas of the site are new, "orphaned," or changed. Comparing different versions of your site can be especially useful if you want to track the various stages of your site's development.

Content Analyzer can be used as a unifying hub for all the applications you need to create and modify. You can configure as many as nine helper applications for each resource type. If you need to make changes to a page or other object, simply select the object in the map and launch your chosen application to edit the source file. Using Content Analyzer in conjunction with helper applications seamlessly integrates all the desktop tools you use to maintain your Web site.

Staging Content

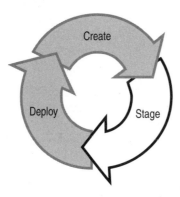

Once the content for your site is created, you need to stage it in preparation for deployment to the Internet or your intranet.

Staging consists of two parts: testing and refinement. Testing involves running your site under various circumstances to ensure that it performs properly. Refinement involves solving any problems found during the testing phase, and can also prepare the site for subsequent rounds of testing.

Testing

If there are problems with your site, it's important to identify them during testing. There are two basic types of testing: appearance testing and performance testing.

Appearance Testing

Appearance testing involves making sure that your site will look as intended on different types of computers, processors, monitors, and different versions of popular browsers. Different browser types and versions will have various page element compatibilites. Some will not run graphics or ActiveX Controls. Consequently, it is necessary to test your page on browser types and versions on which you think your site will be rendered.

To test appearance, have remote testing partners access the site using different browsers and hardware. For example, have one tester use a PC compatible computer using Internet Explorer version 3.0, another using 3.02, and still another using 4.0. Other testers could test with other popular graphical and text-based browsers.

Performance Testing

Performance testing is the process of ensuring that your site performs as you intend it to and that it can handle the expected request load.

Establishing Criteria

It is important to establish performance criteria for your site in order to ensure reliability and consistent quality. A few issues to consider:

- Estimate the amount of traffic your site will experience daily. Consider the number of simultaneous users, requests per second, requests per day, and total data requested and downloaded in megabytes.

- Try to determine any periods of usage "spikes" that might take place, such as after a new feature is added or after a new advertising campaign. These spikes will have to be handled by your server and connection.

- Establish an acceptable failure rate for your site. The failure rate is the number of requests that are not answered or completed per total requests. IIS and Windows NT have built-in performance counters for this purpose.

- Establish which operating systems and browsers you are willing to support. Browsers may request and receive data in various ways and this will affect your server.

- Monitor your site from the very start. Information about usage is invaluable in re-engineering your site and content, and can tell you where any bottlenecks might be and help you to balance hardware, software, and network bandwidth.

- Test your site rigorously; test it to the point of failure—know how much your site can take, and push it to the limit. If real usage outpaces testing, then your testing procedure needs to be scaled up.

WCAT: Web Capacity Analysis Tool

The Microsoft Web Capacity Analysis Tool (WCAT) tests monitor the response of an Internet or intranet server to the demands of its clients in a controlled experimental setting. WCAT is included on the IIS Resource Kit CD. WCAT tests your server by running simulated workloads on client-server configurations. Using WCAT, you can test how your Internet Information Server and network configuration respond to a variety of different client requests for content, data, or (HTML) pages. The results of these tests can be used to determine the optimal server and network configuration for your computer running Microsoft Windows NT Server version 4.0 with Microsoft Internet Information Server (IIS) version 4.0. WCAT is specially designed to evaluate how Internet servers running Windows NT Server and Internet Information Server respond to various client workload simulations.

You can test different server and network configurations by using the prepared WCAT content and workload simulations. When you change your hardware and software configuration and repeat the prepared tests, you can identify how the new configuration affects server response to the simulated client workload. You can use WCAT to test servers with single or multiple processors and to test servers that are connected to multiple networks. The Web Capacity Analysis Tool provides the following features:

- Prepared, ready-to-run workload simulations to test the most common aspects of server performance. These simulations provide World Wide Web content files of varying sizes to test your server's response to different workloads.

- Prepared workload simulations to test the response of your server to Active Server Pages (ASP), Internet Server Application Programming Interface (ISAPI) extensions, and Common Gateway Interface (CGI) applications. You can run these simulations even if your server does not currently run any ISAPI extensions or CGI applications.

- Prepared workload simulations to test the response of your server to Secure Sockets Layer encryption.

- Prepared workload simulations to test the response of your Hypertext Transport Protocol (HTTP) service to HTTP Keep-Alives. HTTP Keep-Alives are an optimizing feature of servers and browsers; an HTTP Keep-Alive maintains a client connection after the initial request is satisfied. HTTP Keep-Alives are part of the HTTP version 1.1 specification.

- The ability to create and run your own client-server workload simulations.

- The ability to use cookies, a technology supported by some Web sites. Cookies are a means by which, under the HTTP protocol, a server or script can maintain state information on the client workstation. Cookies are usually used to provide Web site customization features.

- The ability to test servers connected to more than one network.

A WCAT test includes four primary components: a server, a client, a controller, and the network. During a WCAT test, each of these components runs a different WCAT program.

The *WCAT server* is a computer configured with Windows NT Server and Internet Information Server. The WCAT server uses prepared sample content files of varying lengths that simulate those that a server might provide its clients. A particular set of prepared content files is associated with a particular WCAT test. In a WCAT test, the server responds to requests for connections; establishes, manages, and terminates connections; receives requests for Web content; and processes client requests and sends responses.

You can investigate server performance by subjecting the server to a wide variety of client demands by varying which prepared test is run. Alternatively, you can test the effectiveness of changes to server hardware and software by repeatedly running the same prepared test after hardware and software changes are made.

The *WCAT client* consists of one or more computers running the WCAT client application. The prepared tests provided with WCAT are configured to run with one client computer.

The WCAT client application runs in a single, multithreaded process. Each thread in the process represents a *virtual client*. Each virtual client simulates one connection and page request to the WCAT server. This design enables each client computer to simulate more than one client. In a WCAT test, you specify what level of client demand the server is subject to, including the number of client browsers in the test; the size and type of pages the clients request; the rate at which clients send requests; the relative frequency at which different specific pages are requested; the duration of the test.

The *WCAT controller* is a computer running the WCAT controller application. The controller is provided to minimize the effect of test administration on test results; it does so by separating the computer administering the test from the computers being tested. The controller hardware and software are not monitored as part of a WCAT test. Once the test is complete, the controller application collects the test results and writes output files showing the test results.

The input files provide complete instructions for a WCAT test and are stored on and interpreted by the controller computer. You can either run WCAT with the controller input files provided with WCAT or design your own tests by creating new or modified input files.

During a test, WCAT collects statistics on the activity of the clients and the response of the server and produces detailed reports for later analysis. The statistics are collected by the WCAT controller in the output files. The controller writes the output files based on data gathered by the controller and clients. WCAT produces two types of output files:

- A log file, which includes reports and analysis of the statistical data gathered during the test. The log file is a comma-separated, variable-length file designed for use as input for a spreadsheet or data processing program. You can also use any text editor or word processor to view and edit the log file.

- A performance results file, which presents the data collected from Performance Monitor counters on the server computer during the test.

WCAT version 4.13 is included on the IIS Resource Kit CD.

Testing Your Site in Stages

In establishing your testing strategy, it is advisable to follow an approach that has been used successfully in the software industry. You can release your site for testing to increasingly large groups. For example, if you want to test an Internet Web site, release it in the following stages:

- Internally
- Externally, to a specific testing group
- To a larger testing group
- To the whole Internet community

During these release stages you can continue to test appearance and performance. The initial internal release can be done throughout the creation and staging process. If you have a company intranet available, release your site there as you develop it. Viewers on the intranet can review your site, offer feedback, and participate in performance testing. You may even want to release your site to the Internet without advertising its location publicly—let your testing group know where the site can be found, but do not register it with search engines or other services. This way your testing group can try out the site under realistic conditions.

Budget and Audience

The budget needs of the testing process are usually driven by one consideration—the breadth of your target audience. Although you cannot determine who will visit your Web site, the technology choices you make will have an effect on who stays there. For example, if your site uses graphics for navigation or some other necessary feature, those without graphics-capable browsers will not be able to use your site. On the other hand, if you are too technologically conservative, you will lose audience members who want to see the latest Web features.

Deploying Content

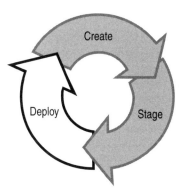

Deployment involves publishing your site on the Internet or your corporate intranet. During this phase you should make a backup copy of your site, propagate your site to the Internet, register it with search engines and other services, advertise it, and keep your site up-to-date. Below are a few suggestions for managing the deployment phase of your project.

Choosing a Release Strategy

One of the things you must decide upon during the deployment phase is what type of release strategy to use. Here are two options:

Progressive Release

In this strategy, the entire site is released in progressive stages in which the complexity and size of the site increase with time. One advantage of this strategy is that you can use the lessons that you may have learned in the early releases in subsequent stages. The other advantage to this approach is that you can break up the final deadline date into smaller milestones.

Complete Release

In this strategy, you release your entire site when it is finished and complete. By this time, it is likely to be complex, so thorough staging is critical. Keep in mind too that this release strategy does not allow you to "learn as you go," so you will have to plan your site very carefully and have an exacting hand-off procedure.

Backing Up Your Site

The only thing worse than discovering that your server has crashed, is finding out that there is no current backup copy of your site.

There are several common ways to make backups.

Automated backups   With some versioning tools, such as Visual SourceSafe, you can shadow your files to another computer, thus providing an automatic backup. As files are added and changed in your VSS directory, the changes are automatically propagated to the shadow directory.

You can also use Microsoft Content Replication System to set up automated replications of your site to another computer or computers.

Manual backups   To back up your files manually, you can copy them, along with your IIS metabase, to a stable medium such as a removable hard disk or a read/write CD-ROM disk. If your server or source computer is on a network, you can drag-and-drop copies of your files to another computer by using Windows Explorer.

Deploying Content

Before you can go online with your site you must obtain an Internet connection, or in the case of a corporate intranet, you must establish a network and start IIS.

Your producer and hardware technician will know more about what type of connection you need and how much bandwidth you'll require. For more information on connection types and speeds, see Chapter 3, "Capacity Planning."

When you are ready to put your site online, there are two strategies possible: 1) connecting directly to the Internet; or 2) collocation through an Internet service provider (ISP) (this means that your server is located, or collocated, at the service provider's facility).

Connecting Directly   This requires that you function as your own Internet service provider. This strategy is most appropriate for large sites that require a direct connection to the Internet backbone where high connection speeds can be achieved.

Connecting Through an ISP   This involves hooking your server up at an Internet service provider. With collocation you can simplify administration, but you are also limited to a maximum of three T1 connections. This may not be suitable for large sites or those that anticipate a great deal of traffic.

Publicizing Your Site

There are three main ways that users can learn about the location of your site:

Word of mouth   Internet users often e-mail their favorite URLs to other users.

Advertisements   You can advertise your site through print media, television, radio, or even over the Internet itself. Many sites include rectangular banners—usually at the top of the page—that rotate between different advertisements. These ads include clickable links to the advertised sites.

Search engines   Register with several of these to ensure that your site's URL will be returned when an Internet user searches for topics or keywords.

Monitoring Your Site

You can use Usage Import and the Report Writer (which comes with the Windows NT 4.0 Option Pack) to collect and analyze IIS log files from a single server. This feature provides 21 predefined reports that can give you insight into the users and organizations that interact with your site. You can also create customized reports to manipulate usage data in ways that best fit your needs. By extracting this usage information, you can identify trends in your viewer-market and make informed Internet business decisions.

Case Study: investor.com

Microsoft Investor has the attributes of a successful site as described in this chapter—it is *malleable* in that it includes content that is updated at various times (weekly, daily, and multiple times a day); it is *extensible* in that it is constantly being adapted to reflect changes in technology, team views, and reader feedback; it incorporates *dynamic and interactive content* including a chat-room, a stock ticker, and applications for tracking and analyzing stocks. Of particular interest to content managers is the fact that beneath this complex site lies a fairly simple content-management process.

Note   As with all online projects, the Investor team is constantly looking for ways to improve and further automate their processes and procedures. This case study applies to the content-management practices for versions 3 and 4 of the site.

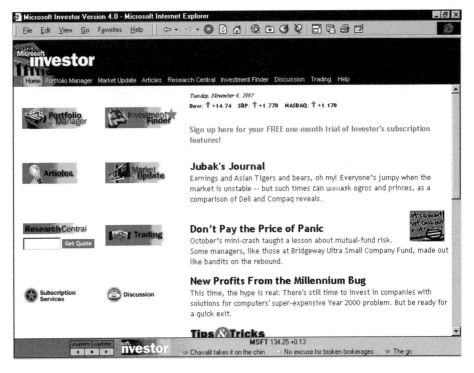

Figure 2.3   The Investor home page as it appears in Internet Explorer 4.0, in full screen view. The stock ticker at the bottom of the window offers continual stock quotes and news items.

Overview of Features

Microsoft Investor has approximately 750,000 different visitors each month, and *Barron's* recently referred to it as "the best all-round site for investors on the Web today." The site offers the following features:

Portfolio Manager   An interactive application that allows you to build and maintain an online investment portfolio. This application can chart and track investments, set up alert messages that will notify you when a stock reaches a certain price, customize how your investments are displayed and analyzed, and much more.

Market Update   Includes up-to-date summaries of what is happening in the market today. This feature provides a bird's-eye view of the total market with links to individual articles and stock analyses in the Research Central section.

Articles   Provides access to regularly-updated columns, including weekly interviews with leaders in the field. Each article offers an in-depth analysis of a specific aspect of the market.

Research Central   Has interactive applications for charting investment changes, such as price and value, up-to-date market summaries, stock quotes, and analyses of the S&P 500, Dow Jones, and NASDAQ, and much more.

Investment Finder   A search engine that you can use to find information about more than 8,000 stocks and bonds.

Discussion   Here you can share trading tips and advice with other investors. This section includes discussion groups centered around specific investments and investment types as well as a chat room where you can engage in online conversations.

Trading   Here you can sign up and trade online with an investment broker.

Help   An extensive online Help system that includes a text-based list of topics, frequently asked questions (FAQ), a brief tour of the site and its features, a glossary of investment terms, a summary of membership services, a graphical site map with links to each page, a systematic product-support guide with a link to online product support, a page where readers can send in their suggestions, and an overview of the Investor team.

This site offers two levels of features. Subscribers who pay a monthly fee have access to the entire site, including features marked with a gold star. Non-paying visitors do not have access to these subscription features.

Note   Investor is optimized for Internet Explorer version 3.0 and later. Some features of the site, such as the stock ticker at the bottom of the home page, may not be available with other browsers.

To create this site, the Investor team uses various combinations of the Web page elements discussed in this chapter. The articles combine text, GIF, and JPEG image files, as well as hyperlinks. The interactive applications, including the stock ticker, are ActiveX components. These applications—when viewed in browsers other than Internet Explorer—are ASP applications that use HTML forms to interact with users. The navigation controls consist of scripts running in an HTML page.

Team Overview

Investor currently has 39 full-time staff and from 15 to 20 freelance writers. The full-time staff can be divided into these categories:

Editorial The editorial staff includes editors, writers, production staff, and graphic artists. The editors and writers have strong backgrounds in financial publications and journalism. The production staff is primarily responsible for HTML coding.

Program Management This group guides the development of the product, overseeing the Web site as a whole. Each manager has his or her own area of responsibility.

Marketing The marketing team is involved in both the advertisements that appear in the site and the marketing of the site itself.

Development The development team is experienced in software development and Web site creation. This group is involved in all phases of the content life cycle.

Testing The testers are responsible for the staging phase of the content life cycle.

The Investor team also includes two positions that were created specifically to deal with tasks resulting from features of the site:

Community Manager This person processes user input from e-mail, newsgroups, and other online sources. This information is used to adapt to and reflect trends in the Internet market and Investor's users.

Usability Engineer This team member tests how users interact with the Web pages that make up the site. This way the usability of the site can be assessed and adapted to offer visitors and subscribers the richest experience possible.

Hand-off Procedure

In the case of article development, the hand-off procedure used by the Investor team is process based. For example, articles pass from one team member to the next in a linear fashion, as on an assembly line.

1. An editor assigns an article to a writer, based on that writer's suitability. At the same time, the graphic artists are informed of the general contents of the article so that they can begin to plan artwork, and the producer begins planning the coordination of Web-page elements including text, graphics, and scripts.
2. The writer submits the completed article to the assigning editor via e-mail, as a Microsoft Word document attachment. The file is placed into a shared folder named Raw Copy, located on a computer at the Investor main office.

3. The managing editor assigns a new name to the file, using a naming convention that includes part of the author's name and the date that the article will appear on the site. The article is then copied into a folder named New Copy. The file in the Raw Copy folder is retained as a backup.

4. At this point, the assigning editor performs an initial (developmental) edit on the article.

5. Once the developmental edit is done and the appropriate artwork is created, the article is given a full edit. It is then copied to a file named The Rim.

6. From here, the article is copyedited, and a headline is created. The file is then moved to the Ready To Post folder.

7. The production manager moves the file from Ready To Post to another hard disk, and codes the HTML. When this is done, an e-mail message is sent to the editorial and testing teams with a link to the file.

8. The finished file is then proofread by the editorial team, and the links and scripts are checked by the testers.

9. After testing and proofreading are complete, the production manager corrects any errors that are found. The file is then replicated and placed on the staging server.

10. Deployment is done automatically using the Microsoft Content Replication System. The contents are replicated to the deployment server and made available to the public at 2 a.m.

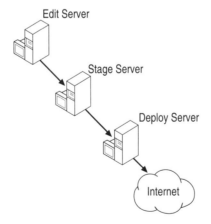

Figure 2.4   The Investor Web site release uses three server computers: one for editing, another for staging, and a third for deployment.

Staging

The staging/testing phase of the site involves three main elements: editorial passes, page-level testing on completed HTML files, and full site-level testing for all aspects of content. The text of the articles is reviewed during the editorial process and again later when the HTML is coded, to ensure that no mistakes were introduced during the editing and production processes. Additionally, each individual page (including text, graphics, links, and scripts) is tested to make sure that it appears as intended. Testing is performed on Windows NT and Windows 95 operating systems running Internet Explorer version 3.0 and later and Netscape Navigator version 3.0 and later. These browsers are also used on the Macintosh platform for testing.

Because some browsers may be incompatible with certain features used on the site, the Investor team creates multiple versions of selected portions of the site. For example, Research Central is created in two different versions—one for ActiveX-compatible browsers and another for those that are not. An ASP application detects the capabilities of a visitor's browser and redirects them to the appropriate version of the pages requested.

Deployment

To deploy the site to the Internet, two main steps are taken. First, the completed site is transferred to a server where final testing and editing take place. Second, the site is replicated to the deployment server by using the Microsoft Content Replication System. This dual-server scheme creates a built-in backup of the site.

Resources

The following resources provide additional information relevant to content management.

Web Links

http://www.microsoft.com/sitebuilder
The Microsoft Site Builder Network includes tips, tricks, and tools for Web designers, producers, programmers, and more.

Books

Windows NT Server 4.0 Resource Kit (Microsoft Press, 1996-1997).
Network building and maintenance, security issues, Windows NT features that help with information management, and more.

C H A P T E R 3

Capacity Planning

3

Capacity planning for a Web server involves determining the future needs of the server to whatever extent possible. Because there are so many variables and intangibles, and because needs change so rapidly, capacity planning is more of an art than a science, and requires an iterative approach.

This chapter offers ways to determine server needs, discusses options for meeting those needs, and presents a set of guidelines to use with Performance Monitor so you can effectively monitor your server. Finally, it provides a real-life example of capacity planning and performance monitoring.

In this chapter:

- Determining the Server's Requirements
- Meeting the Server's Requirements
- Monitoring the Server
- A Case Study: www.microsoft.com
- Resources

Determining the Server's Requirements

Server requirements are primarily determined by the amount of traffic the site or sites hosted by the server will be required to sustain, and by the reliability and security required.

Traffic

Traffic is a mixture of incoming requests and outgoing responses. Not surprisingly, there is a direct relationship between the amount of traffic and the network bandwidth needed. The more visitors a server receives and the larger the pages it provides, the more network bandwidth it will require.

To start with a simple example, consider a server that displays HTML text-only pages that average 5 KB in size (a full page of text is about that size). The server is connected to the Internet via a DS1 or T1 line, which can transmit data at 1.536 megabits per second (Mbps). (A DS1 line is rated at 1.544 Mbps, but a small amount of the bandwidth is lost to inherent overhead.) How many 5-KB pages per second can the server send out under optimum conditions?

To send out a page, the server must first receive a request from a browser. The browser must establish a TCP connection with the server before it can send a request. Once the connection is made, the browser sends the request (for example, GET http://microsoft.com/default.htm), which typically amounts to a few hundred bytes. After the server receives the request, it begins to send the requested page. Requests and responses are split into packets and each of these packets includes header information and other network-protocol overhead. For a small, 5-KB file, protocol overhead is significant, amounting to about 30 percent of the file's size. As files increase in size, overhead accounts for a smaller percentage of file transfer traffic. For example, overhead for the 53-KB file examined later in this section amounts to about 14 percent.

The following table shows the traffic generated by a typical request for a 5-KB page. Note that all of the figures for overhead are estimates. The precise number of bytes sent varies with each request.

Table 3.1   Traffic Generated by a Request for a 5-KB Page

Traffic type	Bytes sent
TCP Connection	172 (est.)
GET Request	256 (est.)
5-KB file	5,120
Protocol overhead	1,364 (est.)
Total	**6,912**

The total number of bytes sent over the network is 6,912. To find the number of bits sent, 6,912 bytes is multiplied by 8: 6,912 x 8 = 55,296. A DS1 line can send 1.536 megabits per second. Thus, the number of 5-KB pages that can be sent over a DS1 line per second is 1,536,000/55,296 or about 28 pages per second.

The following table illustrates the relative speeds of several connection types, using the hypothetical text-only page from this example. Some of these connection types are discussed in more detail later in this chapter.

Table 3.2   Comparative Connection Speeds

Connection Type	Speed	5 KB Pages Sent per Second
Dedicated PPP/SLIP via modem	28.8 Kbps	0.5
Frame Relay or fast modem	56 Kbps	1
ISDN	128 Kbps	2
ADSL	640 Kbps	11
DS1/T1	1.536 Mbps	28
10-Mbs Ethernet	8 Mbps (best case)	136
DS3/T3	44.736 Mbps	760
OC1	51.844 Mbps	880
100-Mbs Ethernet	80 Mbps (best case)	1,360
OC3	155.532 Mbps	2,650
OC12	622.128 Mbps	10,580
1-Gbs Ethernet	800 Mbps (best case)	13,600

Now suppose you add a small graphic to the 5-KB page. An image, in the form of a JPEG file that appears on screen as perhaps a one-inch square (the actual size depends on monitor settings), takes up about as much disk space as the original text file. Adding one such picture to each page nearly doubles the average page size, which reduces the number of page requests that the server can send to the Internet on the DS1 line to about 14 per second, regardless of how fast the computer itself runs. If there are several such pictures per page, if the pictures are larger, or if the pages contain other multimedia content, they will take considerably longer to download. There are only two ways to serve more of them per second: either remove the pictures from the pages, or connect to the network using a faster (and more expensive) connection.

A site that serves primarily static HTML is much more likely to run out of bandwidth than to run out of either processor cycles or the ability to sustain large numbers of simultaneous connections. A site that performs a lot of dynamic page generation, on the other hand, uses more processor cycles, and can create bottlenecks at the processor, memory, disk, or network level. There are no hard-and-fast rules that apply to all sites, though the general relationship between bandwidth and CPU utilization for static versus dynamic pages of a given size is shown in Figure 3.1.

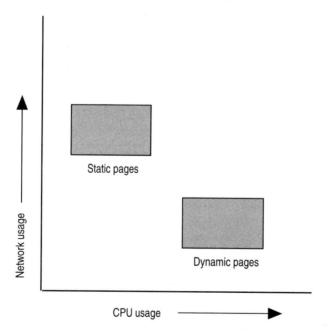

Figure 3.1   The relative demands of static and dynamic content.

Browser Download Time

The number of pages a server can send is one half of the bandwidth equation. The other is the time it takes a browser to download a page.

Consider how much time a browser needs to download a page that, including overhead, amounts to, say, 90 KB. (Pages of that size are not at all unusual.) That's 720 kilobits, which takes 25 seconds to download through a 28.8 Kbps connection if everything is working perfectly, ignoring latencies, which typically add a few seconds. If there is any blocking or bottlenecking at the server, if the network is overloaded and slow, or if the user's connection is slower than the full 28.8 Kbps because of poor line quality, downloading takes longer.

It takes about 52 connections at 28.8 Kbps to saturate the capacity of a DS1 line. If no more than 52 clients simultaneously request the hypothetical 90-KB page, and if the server can perform the processing required to keep up with the requests, the clients will all receive the page in the 25 seconds calculated in the example (again, ignoring latencies). If 100 clients simultaneously request the same page, however, the total number of bits to be transferred is 100 times 737,280; it takes between 47 and 48 seconds for that many bits to travel down a DS1 line.

A DS3 line carries nearly 45 megabits per second, about 30 times as much capacity as a DS1 line, and it takes almost 1,520 clients at 28.8 Kbps to saturate its bandwidth. At 2,000 simultaneous connections, it still takes less than 33 seconds to download the page. Figure 3.2 shows this relationship.

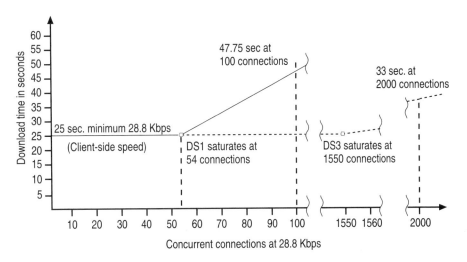

Figure 3.2   Download time of a 90-KB page

Because users only spend a fraction of their time downloading, the actual number of users a connection can support is larger than these figures indicate.

Perceived Latency

It is important to remember that page latency as users perceive it is not precisely identical to measured latency, nor to the time it takes for a page to display fully. If the first thing the user sees upon reaching a given page is a set of buttons allowing further navigation, for example, it may not make much difference if the rest of the page takes over a minute to download, because the user need not wait for it. If, on the other hand, the buttons don't appear until after the rest of the page, the user must wait until the page is fully displayed. The amount of latency that is acceptable to users depends to some extent on the kind of information provided by the page, but is appreciably less than 30 seconds under most circumstances.

Timescale

A timescale between one second and several minutes is appropriate for calculating or measuring the network bandwidth required or used by a server at times of peak traffic. If your server uses its entire network bandwidth for more than a few minutes a day, consider upgrading to a faster connection to the network. Longer-term measures are also important, because you need a wide distribution of data when you are performing monitoring to establish a baseline. See the section "Monitoring the Server," later in this chapter, for more information about baseline logging.

A Deeper Look at Traffic and Content

The 5-KB page discussed earlier in this chapter is representative of a text-only page, but relatively few pages contain only text. The example was deliberately simplified to provide an overview of network bandwidth usage. This section examines what happens when a server receives a request for a typical Web page that includes links to several graphics files. The page is Samples.asp, the Windows NT 4.0 Option Pack samples home page (the page is installed with the Windows NT 4.0 Option Pack and can be viewed at http://localhost/iissamples/default/samples.asp). It is a simple ASP page that returns ordinary version 2.0 HTML and contains six graphics, as shown in Figure 3.3.

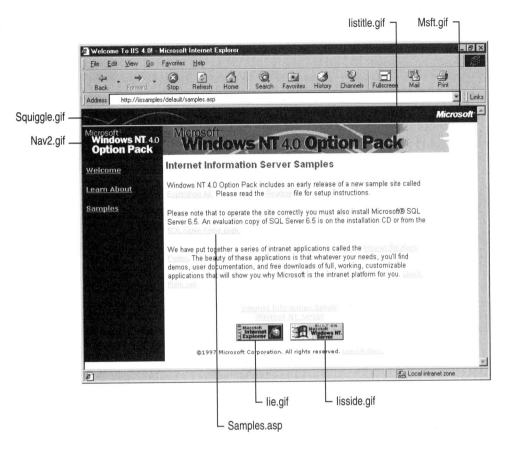

Figure 3.3   Samples.asp

The following series of events occur when a browser requests this page:

- First, the client requests a connection, which is started on TCP port 1357. (TCP port numbers above 1023 are chosen at random for use by various services.)
- Next, the client issues a GET request, for Samples.asp.
- When that file has been transferred, the client issues a GET request for Squiggle.gif.
- Almost immediately, before Squiggle.gif has been fully transferred, the client requests another connection, which is started on the next port, 1358.
- As soon as the second connection has been set up, and before the download of Squiggle.gif resumes, the client issues a GET request for Msft.gif, on port 1358.

The process continues, with transfers interleaved between the two connections, as shown in the Table 3.3.

Table 3.3   Details of a Request for Samples.asp

Action	Total Packets	Connection Port	Data Size	Total Size
1357 Setup	3	1357	0	172
GET Samples.asp	10	1357	5,228	6,495
GET Squiggle.gif	4	1357	2,471	3,199
1358 Setup	3	1358	0	188
GET Msft.gif	2	1358	338	1,011
GET Nav2.gif	4	1358	1,911	2,235
GET Iistitle.gif	27	1357	21,318	23,126
GET Ie.gif	13	1358	8,609	9,751
GET Iisside.gif	19	1357	14,687	16,134
Total	85		54,562	62,311

The Total Packets column lists the number of TCP packets that were required either to set up a connection or to transfer a file. The Data Size column lists the size of the file transfered. The Total Size column lists the size of file with network overhead included; the difference between the number in the Data Size column and the one in the Total Size column is the network overhead incurred during the download (network overhead includes IP, TCP, and HTTP protocol overhead). Overhead amounted to 7.5 KB—about 14 percent of the download.

By using HTTP 1.1 Keep-Alive headers, the browscr needed only two TCP connections to transfer seven files (Samples.asp and its associated graphics files). Without Keep-Alives, another kilobyte or so of overhead would have been needed to set up the additional connections—a relatively small amount. The real cost of the added connections is the round-trip time required to set up a connection (the browser contacts the server and waits for its response; the server then waits for the browser's acknowledgement of the server's response).

For static objects like GIF files, the object size is reported by the server, using a "Content-Length:" header entry. (These sizes are automatically determined by IIS.) This allows the browser to determine approximately how long the active connection will be used, which affects the browser's connection strategy. A browser such as Internet Explorer creates a new connection only when an existing one is "blocked." Because of the small size of the files linked to Samples.asp and the high speed of the connection, the browser was able to download the page with a small number of concurrent connections. If the order of requests were changed so that the larger GIF files were downloaded first, or if the connection speed were slower (the page was downloaded over an intranet), more connections might be necessary.

Figure 3.4 illustrates how, once the browser has opened a second connection to the server, it interleaves the two connections to download more than one file at the same time. The diagram's vertical lines represent packets.

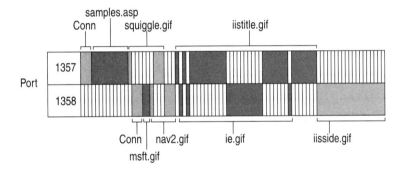

Figure 3.4   Packet distribution during the download of Samples.asp and linked files

Tip When HEIGHT and WIDTH attributes are included with an image link, the browser is able to determine in advance how much screen space the image requires, which allows the browser to render other content more quickly while the image is being retrieved.

Refreshing a Page

Now consider what happens if, after having downloaded Samples.asp, the user clicks the browser's **Refresh** button. The resulting network traffic is shown in the following table:

Table 3.4   Details of a Refresh Request for Samples.asp

Action	Total Packets	Connection Port	Data Size	Total Size
1576 Setup	3	1576	0	172
GET Samples.asp	12	1576	5,228	6,495
GET Squiggle.gif	2	1576	0	612
1577 Setup	3	1577	0	188
GET Msft.gif	2	1577	0	608
GET Nav2.gif	2	1576	0	608
GET Iistitle.gif	2	1576	0	612
GET Ie.gif	2	1577	0	646
GET Iisside.gif	2	1576	0	649
Total	30		5,228	10,590

As before, the browser creates two connections, but this time it retrieves only Samples.asp. The other files were not retrieved because they hadn't been modified since the previous request, and were stored in the browser's cache. When the browser requests a file in its cache, it includes the file's date stamp with the request, using the If-Modified-Since header. The Web server then determines whether the file has been modified since the time indicated by the date stamp. If not, the server replies with a brief "Not Modified" packet.

Although nothing on the page changed, the browser still retrieved Samples.asp. By default IIS sets HTTP cache-control to prevent browsers from caching ASP pages, because there is no way to guarantee that an ASP page will be the same the next time it is requested. A static HTML page, on the other hand, is not retrieved during a refresh if it is has not been updated. As a result, just changing a file's extension from .htm to .asp, without putting any script on the page, causes refreshes to take longer. You should only use the .asp extension for files that actually contain scripts.

As this example demonstrates, browser (and proxy) caching can dramatically reduce the expense of retrieving objects on a page. Some publication processes copy files that haven't been modified, which gives them new time stamps and thus "updates" them as far as the system is concerned. Resources are wasted because client-side caching is eliminated.

Adding Secure Sockets Layer

Now consider what happens when a browser requests Samples.asp using Secure Sockets Layer (SSL). (A table to show the details of the request isn't included here, because the traffic generated by an SSL request is encrypted, which makes it difficult to see what happens during the request.)

When a browser makes an SSL request for a page, a delay occurs while the server encrypts the page. When the server send Samples.asp and the six graphics files linked to it, SSL adds additional network overhead. The server sends 64.6 KB with SSL, instead of 60.8 KB without it—an increase in overhead to 21 percent with SSL from 14 percent without it (Samples.asp and related files add up to 53.3 KB).

Once the browser has received the requested files, the user must wait while the browser decrypts them. SSL also disables proxy and browser caching, so the considerable performance gains they allow are lost.

The delays introduced by SSL are not trivial. In a test download of Samples.asp over a single-hub local network, the request using SSL took almost 10 times longer than the request without it.

All of which is to say that SSL should be used only when necessary—for example, to ensure the security of financial transactions. SSL has a significant effect on CPU capacity and a noticeable effect on network capacity as well.

Web Application Performance

If Web applications are an important part of your site, the performance of those applications is critical in determining the site's capacity. Testing is the only way to find out the capacity and performance of a Web application. The WCAT utility included on the IIS Resource Kit CD is a useful testing tool. Before writing an application, however, it's useful to have a sense of the performance capabilities of different Web application types. In IIS, ISAPI applications running as DLLs in the IIS process generally offer the best performance. Next is Active Server Pages (ASP), followed by CGI.

For most applications, the recommendation is to use ASP scripting to call server-side components. This strategy offers performance comparable to ISAPI performance with advantage of more rapid development time. For more information on Web application development strategy, see Chapter 5, "Developing Web Applications."

This section provides some comparative performance data between ISAPI, ASP, and CGI. Three representative tasks were chosen: pulling data from a database, instantiating a COM server-side component, and accessing server variables. For each task, an equivalent script or program was written in ASP, ISAPI, and Perl (for the CGI case). Here is a more detailed description of the tasks, which were given the names DataGrab, GetObject, and ServerVars:

- **DataGrab** Pulls data from a database using a database-access COM component (written in Visual Basic). The component object provides a method that can be used to connect to a small Access database, send a SQL query string, and return the query result.

- **GetObject** Instantiates a simple COM component, calls a method provided by that COM component, and sends the result of the call to the client. (The particular method implemented by the component returns the username by calling the Windows API function **GetUserName()**.)

- **ServerVars** Accesses 18 server variables (such as PATH_INFO and SERVER_SOFTWARE), and sends the results to the client.

The scripts and executables were tested using the Web Capacity Analysis Toolkit (WCAT). The tests were run with five clients, each running 20 threads, for a total of 100 virtual clients. The virtual clients fired requests at the server and recorded how many of the requests were served—how many pages per second the server was able to serve. The Perl scripts were tested using ActiveState's Perl for Win32 and Perl for ISAPI packages. Perl for Win32® runs Perl scripts as CGI applications. Perl for ISAPI runs scripts as DLLs within the IIS process. Perl for ISAPI generally offers a performance advantage over Perl for Win32 because each request to a Perl for ISAPI DLL does not generate a new process, as is the case with CGI applications (Perl for Win32).

Table 3.5 shows the relative performance of the different application types for different tasks. Note that the figures are *relative*. They do *not* record how many pages per second were served, only the relative ability of different scripts or executables to serve pages. The worst performing script (GetObject CGI) was set to 1; all of the other figures are relative to that figure. So, for example, the ServerVars CGI offers performance that is relatively 33.16 times better than GetObject CGI. (DataGrab CGI could not be tested, so no figure is provided.)

Table 3.5 Relative Performance of Dynamic Pages

	ISAPI	ASP	Perl for ISAPI	CGI
DataGrab	69.37	57.19	29.04	Not available
GetObject	209.14	169.64	38.09	1
ServerVars	560.07	195.97	109.89	33.16

An important point brought out by these figures is that the relative performance of different application types depends greatly on the application's task. For example, ISAPI offers almost three times better performance than ASP for the ServerVars task; for the GetObject and DataGrab tasks, however, ISAPI provides only about a 20 percent performance advantage over ASP.

Reliability

Some sites can afford to fail or go offline; others cannot. Many financial institutions, for example, require 99.999 percent or better reliability. Even if your requirements are less rigorous, you may want to consider using RAID arrays for disk drives and clustering your servers. You might also consider creating a "Web farm"—multiple servers hosting a single site. In addition to allowing for very large sites, Web farms introduce greater reliability, since a site's fate is no longer tied to a single server.

Clustering

The term "failure" commonly brings to mind the idea of a system crash, but in fact many failures are deliberate: the administrator brings a server down for routine maintenance or for hardware installation or upgrade. Clustering makes it possible to take a server down for maintenance or service without causing the site itself to fail, and also provides reliability in the event of an unscheduled failure.

There are three commonly used cluster configuration types for Web service:

- In active/active clustering, there are no redundant servers. If one computer in the cluster fails, the other computers take on the increased workload. The delay or latency of the failover ranges from about 15 to about 150 seconds, and depends in part on what software packages are running on the servers.

- In active/standby clustering, one computer is designated to take over in the event that another computer fails. If an active node in such a cluster fails, the standby node takes over. Failover times are about the same as for active/active clusters.

- In fault-tolerant clustering, computers are also paired, but both computers perform all tasks simultaneously. Failover times are typically less than one second.

Windows NT Enterprise Edition Clustering

By using Windows NT Enterprise Edition clustering, an active/active clustering solution, you can set up applications on two servers (nodes) in a cluster and provide a single, virtual image of the cluster to clients. If one node fails, the applications on the failed node become available on the other node. Failover times range from 20 seconds to 2 minutes.

To use the Windows NT clustering feature, you must have two servers that are connected by a high-speed private network. Each of the servers must have at least one shared SCSI bus, with a storage device, and at least one storage device that is not shared. For best reliability, each computer should have its own uninterruptible power supply.

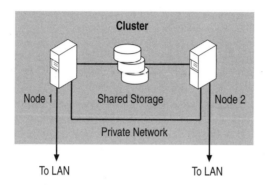

Figure 3.5   A Windows NT Enterprise Edition cluster.

DNS Round-Robin Distribution and Load Balancing

Domain Name System (DNS) round-robin distribution is a technique used for load balancing servers. Consider a scenario in which there are four IP address entries for the same host on a DNS server:

```
copperhead.glennwo.microsoft.com A 157.55.106.88
copperhead.glennwo.microsoft.com A 157.55.106.193
copperhead.glennwo.microsoft.com A 157.55.107.62
copperhead.glennwo.microsoft.com A 157.55.107.220
```

If a client sends a query, the DNS server returns all four IP addresses, but typically the client uses only the first one it receives. The next time the DNS server receives a query for this host the order of the list is changed in round-robin fashion (the address that was first in the previous list is last in the new list). When the client chooses the first IP address in the list, it chooses a different server. This technique distributes incoming requests evenly among the available IP addresses, but does not fully balance the load because it is not interactive. That is, the DNS server does not check the loading of an IP address to be sure it is ready to handle a request.

Interactive Load Balancing

In interactive load balancing, the list of IP addresses returned by the DNS server is ranked by load. The address with the lowest load is placed first in the ranking. There are many ways to determine the load level on a given computer, most of which are sufficiently complex that they are not yet in common use.

Loadbal.dll is an ActiveX component that repeatedly gathers Performance Monitor counter data on a user-specified list of servers and returns a ranked list each time it cycles. The Loadbal component is an Automation server, and can be used by any Automation client. Loadbal is included on the IIS Resource Kit CD.

Loadbal includes a "manual read" capability, so that you can programmatically scan a list of servers to check their relative loadings.

There are, in addition, third-party load-balancing solutions; in considering purchasing one of these, you should be sure that it is compatible with Windows NT and IIS.

Meeting the Server's Requirements

There are a wide variety of options available to site administrators when they build or upgrade Web servers. This section discusses some of the hardware and network options available. It does not discuss software, because it is assumed that you are using Microsoft Windows NT as your operating system and IIS as your server software.

Hardware Options

The following sections describe the hardware requirements of IIS and some of the hardware issues involved in server performance.

Minimum and Recommended Hardware Configurations

The following hardware configurations are suggested for Internet Information Server 4.0:

Table 3.6   Hardware Recommendations for IIS

Item	Minimum	Recommended
Processor	66 MHz 486	90 MHz Pentium or higher
Level 2 Cache		Maximum possible
RAM	32 MB	128 MB or more

The amount of hard disk space required for IIS installation depends on the options you choose in Setup. The following table lists approximate requirements.

Table 3.7   Disk Space Requirements for IIS Installation

Setup Option	Approximate Disk Space Required
Minimum	30 MB
Typical	50 MB
Full	100 MB

Data Latency and Transfer Rates

Everything that happens in a computer takes time. There are two clocks that measure this time: the CPU chip's master clock, and the master clock of the system bus. Most of the usage of time occurs in three areas:

- Data latency, which is the delay before data appears (and could actually be considered time that is wasted rather than time that is used).

- Transferring data from source to destination once the flow of data starts.

- CPU processing.

The clock cycle of a CPU chip is a few nanoseconds long. Other parts of a computer are typically much slower. When the processor needs information that must be retrieved from disk, for example, it may have to wait as long as several milliseconds, a *million* or more of its clock cycles, before any data reaches it. When the system runs short of RAM it uses virtual memory, which means that it writes some contents of memory to disk. This has a serious impact on performance.

Any time the server gets its data from RAM, of course, it avoids disk latency. Adding to main memory helps your server avoid using virtual memory and also increases the size of both the IIS cache and the system file cache. In addition, if your server has many pages that are visited frequently (too many to fit in the cache area of main memory), using a disk controller with a large onboard RAM cache is also likely to enhance performance. On the other hand, if your server hosts many Web sites or a large database, such a cache probably won't improve performance much.

RAM also exhibits latency. For example, the internal clock cycle of a 266-MHz CPU chip is just under 3.8 nanoseconds long. When such a processor reads data from RAM that has a 60 nanosecond access time, many processor clock cycles pass before the RAM places any of its contents on the bus. If the processor can get the same information from cache memory, which is faster, some of that delay is eliminated. Level 1(L1) cache actually runs at processor speed, but the amount of level 1 cache cannot be increased except by changing the processor, because L1 cache is contained within the CPU chip. Many new processors have Level 2 (L2) cache on the CPU, to help compensate for the fact that the CPU clock runs much faster than the system bus clock; on-chip L2 cache can run at full CPU clock rate. L2 cache outside the CPU is usually on a special fast bus; such external L2 cache is faster than system memory, but slower than L1 cache. In addition, different types of RAM used in system memory have different characteristics. For further discussion, see the section "Memory," later in this chapter.

Data transfer rates are also important. Hard disks continue to improve, and some can transfer data at tens of megabytes per second, but they still transfer data much more slowly than processors can handle it. In addition, drives cannot transfer data at the maximum rate if files are fragmented; it's a good idea to check for fragmentation often, and correct it before it becomes a serious issue.

The system bus also exhibits latency. When a peripheral requests the use of the bus, the interval before control is granted is on the order of 20 microseconds, which amounts to several thousand processor clock cycles, and dozens of bus clock cycles.

All of these issues contribute to overhead, and any of them can cause or contribute to a bottleneck. For example, if requests come in to a Web server that doesn't have enough RAM to sustain a suitably large file cache, the pages must be retrieved from disk; the result is slow service. If the requests come in so rapidly that the pages cannot be retrieved from disk fast enough to meet them, a bottleneck develops as the server falls farther and farther behind.

The Processor

The importance of processor performance is sometimes exaggerated. For a site that consists primarily of static HTML pages, older processors are quite capable of making full use of any but the fastest network connections. It may, in fact, be pointless to purchase a computer with several fast processors, if the chances are that it will be limited by its connection to the network. A server farm built of older computers, for example those with 486 or slow Pentium processors, can be a good solution, particularly in corporations or workgroups that have some unused computers available and anticipate only light traffic.

On the other hand, processor performance is a significant concern for large sites, for sites that generate much of their content dynamically, and for sites that run memory-intensive applications in addition to IIS.

Given the choice between buying, say, two mid-range servers or one high-end server, how do you decide? Generally, the decision comes down to how dynamic or static the site is. If the bottlenecks are in throughput (either disk or network), as tends to be the case with static content, upgrade the disk or network pieces as needed and purchase multiple computers. If the issue is raw processing power, as it can be with dynamic content, a more powerful computer will provide better throughput and a more cost-effective solution.

Adding Processors

Because all processors in a single computer use the same system resources, adding processors does not enhance performance in a linear way. Going from one processor to two can give IIS a roughly 50 percent performance increase, and going from two to three processors is likely to produce an additional 25 percent increase; beyond three processors, IIS performance does not significantly improve. On the other hand, if you are doing dynamic page generation, running applications under Microsoft Transaction Server, or if your Web server also hosts SQL Server, adding processors can be effective.

Many computers sold as small servers today have two processors, with capacity for four to six. Larger servers may have several motherboards, each with several processors.

The Bus

All computers have some sort of main system bus for moving data among the various hardware components. In addition, some computers have a separate bus that runs at processor clock rate, which is used for devices that require faster data transfer rates. Such a bus is called a local or processor-direct bus.

Today, most computers intended for use as servers are based on the PCI system bus, which currently operates at 50 to 66 MHz; future implementations are expected to operate at 100 MHz or more. With 64-bit-wide data paths, current versions of the PCI bus can transfer data at rates in excess of 500 megabytes per second (MBps). That's faster than most devices attached to the bus, including all but the fastest currently available RAM.

Many PCs also have an ISA or EISA bus, for peripherals that use it. The data paths on these buses are narrower, and the clock rates slower, than those on PCI buses.

Memory

Level 2 cache memory, which is small in comparison with main memory, uses SRAM (Static RAM), which is faster than DRAM (Dynamic RAM) but is considerably more expensive. If your server supports external L2 cache, it should probably have as much as it can handle. Pentium Pro processors, on the other hand, have a fixed amount of L2 cache, which is actually part of the CPU chip. Although this design limits the amount of L2 cache (to a maximum of 1 MB, as this book goes to press), it enables the cache to run at the full clock speed of the processor.

Main memory in PCs is DRAM. Typical DRAM access times are measured in tens of nanoseconds. There are several types of DRAM, which operate at different effective speeds. The first access from a bank of RAM may take 60 nanoseconds or so (if that's the rated speed of the chips), but subsequent reads, particularly those within the same small region of memory, can be faster. Just how much faster depends on the RAM type, as shown in the following table.

Table 3.8   RAM Type Comparison

RAM type	Comment
FPM (Fast Page Mode)	Provides modest acceleration on subsequent access.
EDO (Extended Data Out)	Can keep up with PCI bus clock; transfer rates that can exceed 500 MBps.
SDRAM (DRAM that is synchronized with the processor's clock)	Supports burst access as fast as 10 nanoseconds.
RAMBUS (proprietary DRAM solution)	Fastest current implementations allow up to 600 Megabits per second transfer rate.

Slow RAM can cause a bottleneck, as can narrow data buses that limit data transfer speed. Pentium systems use 64-bit-wide data paths; 72-pin SIMMs use a 32-bit-wide data bus. Thus, most Pentium systems require that SIMMs be installed in pairs. (Even if the system is capable of using odd numbers of SIMMs, you should always add SIMMs in pairs, because twice as many memory accesses are required to retrieve the same amount of data from a single SIMM as from a pair; performance is impaired.) Systems based on the 486 processor tend to use 32-bit-wide data buses. Even if they are capable of running at the same bus-clock rate, these systems transfer data between memory and processor more slowly than Pentium-based systems. If your server performs a lot of dynamic page generation or frequently serves pages from its cache in RAM, slow memory or a narrow bus can be a problem.

In addition, different motherboards support different levels and varieties of memory. Some, for example, can make full use of FPM and EDO but not SDRAM; some support interleaving, while others do not. Interleaving is a technique that divides memory into two (or, rarely, more) banks, and permits simultaneous reads from those banks. Instead of the usual arrangement, which would have all data words in order in a single linear array of memory, interleaving arranges the data with all the even numbered words in bank 0 and all the odd numbered words in bank 1. When the processor needs a pair of words, it can read them at the same time by accessing both banks simultaneously. Usually only identical memory types can be interleaved. Interleaving does not change the number of wait states for memory access, but does improve the data transfer rate.

How Much Is Enough?

In general, so long as your server's capacity is not limited by its network bandwidth, the more RAM the server contains, the better it will perform. One way to determine how much RAM you need is to sum the sizes of all the applications and services you expect to run, add the sizes of all the commonly used files, and add the RAM required by Windows NT and IIS, remembering the 4 MB that the operating system keeps clear—but this is not always practical. Another way is to monitor the system's actual performance, and add RAM as necessary. For more information, see "Monitoring Memory Usage" in Chapter 4, "Performance Tuning and Optimization."

Control of the Working Set

The operating system controls the memory available to each process (the process's working set). It can reduce a process's working set when it needs to. It does so by writing some of the working set to disk, and then allocating the newly freed RAM to the process that needs it. Typically, the data that was written to disk must later be copied back to RAM. These transfers, which are very slow, constitute a large source of overhead, and can contribute to bottlenecking. It is important to be aware of the fact that the operating system tries to keep 4 MB of memory free, and starts reducing the working sets of processes long before it actually "runs out" of RAM. You must include this "extra" 4 MB if you construct a memory budget for your server.

A server administrator has some control over the way Windows NT allocates RAM. If you're running IIS, it's a bad idea to set Windows NT to maximize throughput for file sharing, for example, because at that setting all available memory is used for the file system cache. For more information, see "Suggestions for Optimizing Memory on an IIS Server" in Chapter 4, "Performance Tuning and Optimization."

Paging to disk is not, in and of itself, an indication that something is wrong or that performance and capacity are bottlenecked. Parts of the operating system, for example, are specifically written to be paged, so paging is a routine occurrence. It's better to think of it in the other sense: if the performance of your server is impaired, it is possible that too much paging is occurring.

The Swap File

If you are more concerned with performance than with fault tolerance or correction, you can put the paging (swap) file on a different drive from the Windows NT system folder to minimize the interaction between system accesses and swapping accesses. You need to be aware, however, that doing so destroys your system's crash-dump capability. If the operating system crashes, it writes the contents of memory into the swap file, but it can only do so if the paging file is on the same disk spindle as the Windows NT system folder and if the swap file is large enough to accommodate that much data. (The swap file must be at least twice the size of memory.) If you are willing to sacrifice this capability in a tradeoff between performance and reliability, you can move the swap file to a different drive or make it much smaller.

Hard Drives and Controllers

Older IDE controllers and drives are too slow for most Web servers, and are not recommended for Windows NT. IDE is limited to two or four disks per controller, whereas SCSI is limited to seven or 15, depending on the standard.

Among SCSI controllers, which are preferred for Windows NT, there is a wide range of available characteristics, including controllers that support RAID in hardware, controllers with large RAM caches, and so on. The SCSI standard has evolved into several forms, which are listed in the following table:

Table 3.9   SCSI Standards

Standard	Data path width, bits	Maximum transfer rate, MBps
SCSI-1 (de facto)	8	5
SCSI-2	8	5
Fast SCSI-2	8	10
Fast/Wide SCSI-2	16	20
Ultra SCSI-3	8	20
Ultra Wide SCSI-3	16	40

Make sure that your disk drives are matched to your controller or controllers. It is pointless, for example, to put a drive that supports high data transfer rates on a controller that doesn't. In addition, it's a bad idea to connect fast and slow devices to a single bus; it can result in errors.

If you have large or diverse storage requirements, you can use more than one controller, or a controller that supports multiple buses, to spread the workload and improve performance.

For more information on SCSI and IDE performance, see the Microsoft TechNet paper, "SCSI Hardware Performance Considerations for Microsoft Windows 95/Windows NT," available on http://www.microsoft.com/.

Beyond the space required for operating system and server software, each site has its own storage requirements. A site that maintains a large database or that serves large amounts of multimedia content, for example, may require dozens of gigabytes of disk space, while a site that provides only static HTML with only a small number of images may be able to get by with a single, smaller drive.

If your site must store and access a lot of data, and particularly if your site has high reliability requirements, you should consider RAID arrays, particularly some recently developed proprietary RAID levels that offer multiple redundancy. (See sidebar.)

RAID

RAID stands for *Redundant Arrays of Independent Disks.* It is a set of protocols originally developed at the University of California at Berkeley. Support for RAID can be implemented either in software or in hardware in the disk controller. A software implementation is usually undesirable because it imposes considerable loading on the processor. The Windows NT Disk Manager supports RAID levels 0, 1, and 5 in software.

RAID levels start at 0, which involves data striped across drives without redundancy, and is therefore not fault-tolerant. Because it is not redundant, level 0 is sometimes not considered to be RAID. What RAID 0 does is equalize use across a volume set, filling all of the disks in the set at the same rate. It also improves performance. One workaround, which is expensive but offers advantages in performance, is a combination of levels 0 and 1: mirrored striped arrays, usually described as "RAID 10."

RAID levels continue as follows:

RAID 1 is the simplest kind of redundancy: mirroring. Data written to a given drive is copied to a shadow or mirror drive, which can be slightly faster than "RAID 0," if overlapping reads and parallel writes are possible. Provides immediate fallback in case of drive failure: the system just keeps running. Although you can mirror a partition or drive in any partition or drive of equal or larger size, it is best to use disks of the same size and model. In a level 1 array there is no speed penalty even with a single failed drive, an advantage this level has over levels 3, 4, and 5.

RAID 2 uses multiple extra check disks to hold information for Hamming code error-correction. (Because SCSI drives almost always have onboard error-correction, and because it requires many drives, level 2 is rarely used.)

RAID 3 parity information is stored on one drive in a multidrive array; data is striped across the other drives at the byte level. Read performance is the same as "RAID 0," but write performance is degraded because parity information must be calculated, and because all disk accesses must be synchronized in order to maintain the correspondence between the data and the parity information. Large writes and long sequential write series are fairly fast. If one disk in a level 3 array fails, it is possible to recover the information from the other disks along with the parity disk. This typically involves shutting the system down to replace the drive and reconstruct the data.

RAID 4 data is striped across drives at the block or track level, with parity on a single drive as in level 3. Read performance is the same as "RAID 0"; write performance can be limited by contention for the single parity disk. If one disk in a level 4 array fails, the information can be recovered from the other disks along with the parity disk. As with level 3, this typically involves shutting the system down to replace the drive and reconstruct the data.

RAID 5 like level 4, but with parity distributed among drives along with the data. Small writes, especially in multiprocessor systems (in which there would otherwise be contention for the parity disk), are slightly faster than in level 3 or 4 systems because there is no single parity disk to act as a bottleneck. But there is a performance penalty for updates caused by the fact that parity and data must be read, and parity recalculated, for each update operation.

Various RAID controllers support different levels. There are also newer (primarily proprietary) variants of RAID with other level numbers, many of which offer multiple levels of redundancy for enhanced fault tolerance. For example, many new controllers support "RAID 10," which is a combination of striping ("RAID 0," not in itself redundant) and mirroring (RAID 1). This combination offers excellent performance, at some penalty in price.

It is important to be aware of the performance penalties inherent in all RAID levels except RAID 0 and RAID 1. If you are concerned about performance but cannot afford the added expense of "RAID 10," a level 0 array and frequent backups may be an option.

None of the original RAID levels offers more than a single level of redundancy, and none is an excuse for failure to perform backups. If more than one disk fails in a level 3, 4, or 5 array, or if both disks of a mirrored pair in a level 1 array fail, data is irretrievably lost.

Network Options

A network involves hardware and devices that are external to the Web server, which makes it less susceptible to analysis and control. You can set up a Web server that is fully capable of doing everything you need it to do, but network crowding or incompatible network hardware may prevent it from achieving its full capacity and performance.

Although the number of optical fiber connections is increasing, most computers still connect to networks via wires. These may be analog telephone lines, digital telephone lines, or coaxial cables. The wires or optical fibers plug into network interface cards in the computers. (Some computers have Ethernet or other network interfaces built in.)

Network Adapters and Other Hardware

Don't use an 8-bit network adapter in your server or even, for that matter, a 16-bit adapter, unless your server is very inactivite or is connected to the network via a very slow connection. The narrower the data bus on the network interface, the slower the data travels through the card and onto the network. Use modern 32-bit adapters and avoid the older PIO and coprocessor adapters.

Although the hubs, routers, and cabling that are part of your network are not themselves part of your server, they are indeed part of your site, and they have a direct influence on the performance and capacity of the network. For example, you may have TCP/IP set to deliver packets that cannot be fragmented. Some older routers, however, may need to fragment packets; if such a router is present on your network, packets travel out, are bounced back, and must then travel out again with a bit flipped so they can be fragmented. In the worst case, where all packets must pass through the router, this problem triples your network traffic. Thus, what would ordinarily be an improvement in performance becomes a bottleneck. It is important to match settings to the available equipment.

In addition to hardware, network connections involve software both in the form of drivers to enable the computers to talk to the network interfaces, and protocols for transporting data. Networking hardware options operate at a wide range of data rates, and more or less directly determine the bandwidth of the connection, though the precise amount of overhead may vary, depending on the protocol or protocols in use.

Connection Types

Hardware for network connection ranges from modems that are used in conjunction with telephone lines at speeds of a few thousands of bits per second, to optical fiber networks, some of which are as fast as several gigabits per second. For a table of connection types, see the section "Traffic," earlier in this chapter.

Software involves layered protocols that interact to permit a wide variety of devices and connecting links to function together reliably. Networking protocols and their interactions are too complex for complete coverage here.

Local Area Networks

Many sites connect both to one or more local area networks (LANs), and to the Internet or other wide area networks (WANs). These connections are likely to be of different types, but there are areas of overlap. For example, many LANs use the same TCP/IP protocol that the Internet uses. One characteristic of LANs is that in many cases clients have access to the same network bandwidth as servers. This is not as often the case on the Internet, for example, where many clients connect via modem.

LANs typically operate at high speed, in part because the wiring is in short runs (and therefore inexpensive), and is locally owned. That is, the lines are not usually leased from a telephone company or other common carrier. In some cases, a building may already be wired for LAN connectivity when an organization acquires or rents it.

Ethernet and Token Ring

The Ethernet and token ring protocols are widely used for local networking. In principle they operate at high speed, but they are both shared resources, which means that when any one computer on an Ethernet or token ring is transmitting, none of the other computers can do so. (When only two computers are present, this is the equivalent of a half-duplex connection: either computer can send at any given time, but not both.)

There are several ways to implement the Ethernet protocol in hardware, none of which affects the rated speed of the network. Standard Ethernet networks, regardless of whether they move signals on "thick" coaxial cable, "thin" coaxial cable, or twisted pair, provide a specified bandwidth of 10 megabits per second (Mbps). Overhead makes it impossible to realize the full capacity; 8 Mbps is a reasonable expectation.

Switches that split an Ethernet into subnets are available. These switches have several ports, each of which is a network that is separate from the others. The switch routes frames between networks as necessary. Some switches are store-and-forward devices, and must receive and hold an entire frame before routing it to its destination network; others perform cut-through switching, which eliminates the latency associated with store-and-forward operation.

Fast Ethernet involves a backbone that runs at a specified bandwidth of 100 Mbps, but is otherwise similar to standard Ethernet. It's advisable to test adapters in both server and client computers, because performance may vary by more than a factor of two. There is also an emerging 1-gigabit per second Ethernet standard, which transfers packets on optical fiber or, for short distances, copper wire. It operates at speeds well in excess of 700 Mbps.

In principle, token ring networks perform better under load than Ethernet networks, but older token rings run at only 4 megabits per second stated bandwidth, and as with Ethernet, the stated bandwidth is never realized in practice. Newer token ring networks operate at 16 Mbps, and can provide performance that is similar to or slightly better than that of standard Ethernet networks.

Network Segmenting

An Ethernet network is a shared network, so no single server can use all of the available bandwidth. For example, if there are 25 servers on a 100 Mbps Ethernet network, and they are all about equally active, the average bandwidth available to each computer is 100 megabits divided by 25: 4 Mbps.

A bandwidth of 4 Mbps is enough for a Web server connected to the Internet by a DS1 line rated at 1.5 Mbps. But what if the Web server needs a larger connection, say a DS3 link rated at 45 Mbps? In that case, the solution is to segment the Ethernet network so that the Web server has part of the network to itself and can use the full 100 Mbps of available bandwidth. With 100 Mbps of bandwith, the Web server can make full use of the DS3 link.

The network topology in Figure 3.6 illustrates how a server running IIS is segmented from the rest of the network. Connected to the server running IIS are two servers that provide services to IIS, one running SQL Server, the other running Microsoft Exchange. Each server includes two network cards, so that the servers can be linked together and each server can use the full 100 Mbps of bandwidth to communicate with the other servers. Also, Internet traffic does not share bandwidth with traffic to and from the servers running SQL Server and Exchange. The server running IIS is connected the rest of the network and to its link to the Internet through an unshared Ethernet switch.

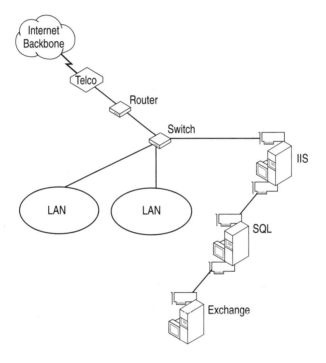

Figure 3.6   Appropriate technique for connecting a server to the Internet

Now consider the network topology shown in Figure 3.7. Although this topology looks similar to the one shown in the previous figure, it is considerably inferior. First of all, note that the server running IIS is connected to the rest of the network through a hub, which, unlike the switch in the previous figure, is shared. The IIS server appears to have its own segment, but its connection through the shared hub means that it shares bandwidth with the rest of the network. Secondly, because the server running IIS has no direct connection to the servers running SQL Server and Exhange that service it, Internet traffic competes for bandwidth with traffic to and from the servers running SQL Server and Exchange.

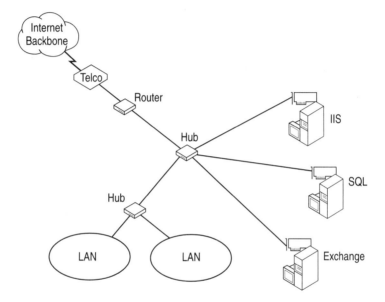

Figure 3.7   Poor technique for connecting a server to the Internet

Fiber Distributed Data Interface

Fiber Distributed Data Interface (FDDI) is a 100-Mbps variant of the token ring network, and is viable for larger sites despite being considerably more expensive to install. It is inherently immune to electromagnetic interference because the signals travel as pulses of light rather than of electricity. This makes FDDI particularly attractive in electrically noisy environments.

Other High-Speed Optical Fiber

Optical fiber interconnections at speeds in excess of 1 gigabit per second are available, but are still quite expensive, and are not yet in common use. Such fiber interconnects can be used with 1-gigabit Ethernet, ATM, and so on.

WAN/Internet Connections

There are many ways to connect to WANs and the Internet. Because the network connection is the most likely source of bottlenecking, you should investigate connection methods that are faster than what is necessary to meet current needs.

Modem

Many users connect to the Internet via modem. Unless it's a small site, a modem typically is not a viable way to connect a Web site to the Internet, because of the serious bandwidth limitation.

ISDN and Frame Relay

ISDN and Frame Relay provide bandwidth ranging from 56 Kbps to 128 Kbps, and are suitable for small servers. They use specialized telephone lines, and may not be available in some areas. Both are suitable for small sites.

ADSL

Asymmetric Digital Subscriber Line (ADSL) is an emerging technology that sends information at relatively high speeds over ordinary (copper wire) telephone lines. It promises to offer clients connection bandwidths in excess of 500 Kbps at reasonable cost, but is too new to be widely available at this time. ADSL has been described as an interim solution to fill the gap between existing modems and forthcoming optical fiber telephone service. ADSL, if it is available in your area, is suitable for small to midsize sites.

DS1/T1, DS3/T3, OC1/3/12/48/192

DS1/T1 and DS3/T3 are high-speed telephone line standards. They provide full-duplex 1.544 Mbps (DS1) or 44.736 Mbps (DS3) bandwidth, and are suitable for midsize to large sites. The Microsoft Web site, discussed in "A Large Site Example," currently uses eight DS3 lines.

OC1 is a 51.844 Mbps standard, equivalent to DS3 bandwidth, implemented on SONET (Synchronous Optical NETwork) fiber optic networks. OC3, OC12, OC48, and OC192 are extensions that carry 155.532, 622.128, about 2488.5, and about 9954 Mbps, respectively.

ATM

Asynchronous Transfer Mode (ATM) is not actually a connection type. Rather, it is a transfer mode in which the information is organized into cells that contain 48 bytes of data and 5 bytes of header information, rather than packets of arbitrary size. (Some SONET networks, for example, carry their data in IP packets that have been mapped into ATM cells.) Because the cells are of fixed size, it is possible to design relatively inexpensive high-performance routers and switches for use on networks that operate in this mode.

Connection Implications

Some servers connect only to intranets, which are smaller and less complex than the Internet, and are usually less subject to major variations in behavior. Even on intranets, however, traffic varies with time, and network loading can cause changes in capacity. For servers connected to the Internet, Internet traffic can have a huge influence on throughput and thus on users' experience.

Monitoring the Server

Monitoring is integral to site management, both for capacity planning and for troubleshooting and tuning. When you are setting up a Web server, you should stress test it and monitor it to discover whether its capacity matches your site's requirements. When it is in operation, you should monitor it to discern trends. When a server is in trouble, you monitor it first to track down problems and then to see whether corrective actions are having the expected results.

Monitoring a Web server is much the same as monitoring a file and print server or an application server, though there are a few more Windows NT Performance Monitor objects and counters to consider. Use Performance Monitor to make an extended baseline log file, covering up to, say, a week of operation. Log relevant counters for the seven most important objects: Processor, Memory, Disk, Network, IIS Global, Web Service, and Active Server Pages. Use a polling interval that is short enough to give you a good picture of activity at your site, but long enough to keep Performance Monitor from taking up too many CPU cycles and too much space on disk for the log file. If you change the configuration significantly, for example by adding more RAM, you need to generate a new baseline log file, because the existing one no longer reflects your server accurately. (You can and probably should keep earlier baseline logs for comparison. Long-term trends may not show up when you view your site at a shorter timescale.)

In addition to maintaining an up-to-date baseline, you need to continue to monitor your Web server on a daily or weekly basis to find trends and to catch impending bottlenecks.

What to Check

A Web server is similar to a file server in the sense that it takes relatively short requests and dispenses larger sets of data. It differs in the sense that it must do more processing than a file server, so you need to watch processor overhead more carefully. Here are some things to look out for:

Processor Depending on how much dynamic page generation your server performs, and on whether your site is subject to spikes, as most are, you need to keep tabs on processor usage.

Memory The IIS cache and the file system cache are good candidates to follow here. To find out whether you are running out of RAM, or experiencing memory leaks, however, watch disk activity.

Disk Among the things you can check for are hard page faults. An excessive number of hard page faults indicates that your server needs more RAM. You must specifically enable disk counters if you want to monitor disk performance. Just running Performance Monitor, however, won't provide any disk activity data. To enable disk counters, invoke a command line and type **diskperf -y** or, if you have a RAID array under hardware control, **diskperf -ye**. Then restart your server before running Performance Monitor.

You must decide whether it is more appropriate for you to monitor logical drives or physical drives. If you have a single large drive, monitor the physical disk. If, on the other hand, you have a large array with several partitions, it may be useful or important to monitor each partition separately.

Network You can add the Network Monitor agent for its counters, and the Network Interface object for its counters. In addition, all protocols have objects, so NetBEUI, TCP/IP, and IPX/SPX all have their own counters. Remember that you must install the SNMP agent to see TCP/IP counters, which are important for IIS. Network usage correlates directly with traffic; if it shows signs of reaching a limit during periods of peak traffic and thus compromising your server's capacity, consider increasing network bandwidth.

Note that Network counters may give unreliable results on symmetrical multiprocessor (SMP) computers.

IIS Watch the cache to be sure that IIS has enough memory. If Cache Hits % is low, especially if your site serves many static HTML files, you may need to increase cache size beyond the 10 percent of RAM that it defaults to.

Relevant Counters

The following table lists Performance Monitor counters that are useful for monitoring your server. If you find problems, you will need to use these and other counters to zero in on them. For example, if you see evidence of a memory leak (a slow rise in committed bytes or pool nonpaged bytes), you should monitor processes and their threads. One thread or one process will probably show a continuing increase in memory usage. Similarly, if you see evidence of a disk bottleneck, you can examine reads and writes separately as you begin to track down the problem. See the next chapter for specific information on tuning and troubleshooting.

Table 3.10   Performance Monitor Counters for Baseline Logging

Object:Counter	Ideal Value
Memory: Pages/ sec	0-20 (if over 80, indicates trouble).
Memory: Available Bytes	At least 4 MB.
Memory: Committed Bytes	Not more than about 75 percent of physical memory size.
Memory: Pool Nonpaged Bytes	Steady (slow rise may indicate a memory leak).
Processor: % Processor Time	Less than 75 percent.
Processor: Interrupts/ sec	Depends on processor. Up to 1,000 for 486/66 processors; 3,500 for P90; more than 7,000 for P200). Lower is better. If the value is too high, try moving some hardware devices to a different server.
Processor: System Processor Queue Length	Less than 2
Disk (Logical or Physical): % Disk Time	As low as possible
Disk (Logical or Physical): Queue Length	Less than 2
Disk (Logical or Physical): Avg. Disk Bytes/Transfer	As high as possible
Internet Information Server Global: Cache Hits %	As high as possible
Web Service: Bytes Total/sec	As high as possible
Web Service: Bytes Total/sec	As high as possible
Active Server Pages: Request Wait Time	As low as possible
Active Server Pages: Requests Queued	Zero
Active Server Pages: Transactions/Sec	As high as possible

Your Mileage Will Vary

Every server has its own performance and capacity issues. The values listed in Table 3.8 are guidelines, not absolutes. Also, when you optimize one area you may interfere with performance in another area. It's usually safe to add capacity, but careful monitoring and comparison with past performance is necessary when you change settings. If you need to run several applications that make intensive use of one system resource, consider moving applications to another server if you can.

Although it can be useful to track trends, any one trend won't necessarily be helpful at indicating impending bottlenecks. If your server supports 50 users at average 10 percent processor loading and 100 users at average 25 percent processor loading, it's tempting to assume that it could easily support, say, 300 users. But the processor load measure doesn't tell you how close the server is to filling up its available network bandwidth. Even 100 users could be too many for the current network connection, depending on what those users are doing.

One useful way to approach the issues of both management and planning is to look for places where the flow of information is impeded. Under ordinary circumstances, the most likely place is the connection between a server and the Internet. In order to find bottlenecks in existing sites, you need to take measurements. Almost any server can saturate a 10-Mbps or even 100-Mbs Ethernet connection.

The importance of close monitoring cannot be overstated. There is no substitute for hands-on experience of a site and its operating conditions.

A Case Study: microsoft.com

One of the largest and most active sites on the Web, microsoft.com receives over 150 million hits per day and hosts more than 12 gigabytes (GB) of content. Building a high-traffic Web site of this kind involves careful planning and constant monitoring to achieve a balance between user demand and the site's key components: hardware, software, and network infrastructure. These components need to be in balance to efficiently handle the content on the site, the number of hits to the site, and "spikes" of intense usage.

Despite the size of microsoft.com and the special needs that follow from its size, the processes the Microsoft team follows to plan, deploy, and maintain the site are relevant to many sites, and are worth examining even if your Web server is connected only to a small intranet.

A Snapshot of the Site

The Microsoft Web site is currently hosted on 65 PCs, with a total of 26.75 GB of RAM and more than 7 terabytes of disk storage (some of which is not shown in Table 3.11). The site has far more server hardware and bandwidth than necessary for day-to-day use, but all available capacity is needed for the inevitable spikes when thousands of concurrent users download, register, or participate in some type of online activity. Software running on the servers includes:

- Microsoft Windows NT Server
- Microsoft Internet Information Server
- Microsoft Index Server
- Microsoft SQL Server

Hardware

The following table shows the size and number of servers used for each service available on microsoft.com:

Table 3.11   Hardware Configuration of the microsoft.com Web Site

Service	Servers	CPUs per server	MB RAM per server	GB Disk per server	Comments
www.microsoft.com	18	4 P6	512	50	250,000 pages of HTML, ASP, and ISAPI; plus 250,000 other related files
search.microsoft.com	6	4 P6	256	30	150 requests per min., per server
http download servers	3	4 P5	256	28	2.5 GB of downloadable software each
FTP servers	3	4 P5	512	16	2.5 GB of downloadable each
SQL servers	6	4 P5	512	160	750 applications, averages 300 concurrent connections
home.microsoft.com	13	4 P6	512	50	
msid.microsoft.com	4	4 P5	256	28	
premium.microsoft. com	3	4 P6	256	30	
support.microsoft.com	3	4 P6	256	30	
activex.microsoft.com	2	4 P6	256	30	
register.microsoft.com	2	4 P6	512	50	
backoffice.microsoft.com	2	4 P6	256	28	

Network Infrastructure

To provide greater internal network capacity, the site architecture distributes servers among four FDDI rings, which run at 100 Mbps. GIGAswitches distribute incoming traffic among the four rings and outgoing traffic among eight DS3 (44.736 Mb per second each) lines to the Internet. Only three of the four rings have HTTP download servers, so one ring is always available to service requests for Web pages, even if a spike of downloads uses up the other rings' total capacity.

Prior to moving to this configuration, the microsoft.com team debated whether to add only two routers and four hubs and forgo the expensive GIGAswitches. Even though the network capacity would have been the same in either scenario, the new design provides better failover protection and scalability by including an intermediate switching device and moving the hubs upstream.

The following diagram illustrates the servers and infrastructure of microsoft.com currently implemented at the Redmond data center. (There are also Japanese and European data centers, and various FTP and other servers in other locations worldwide.)

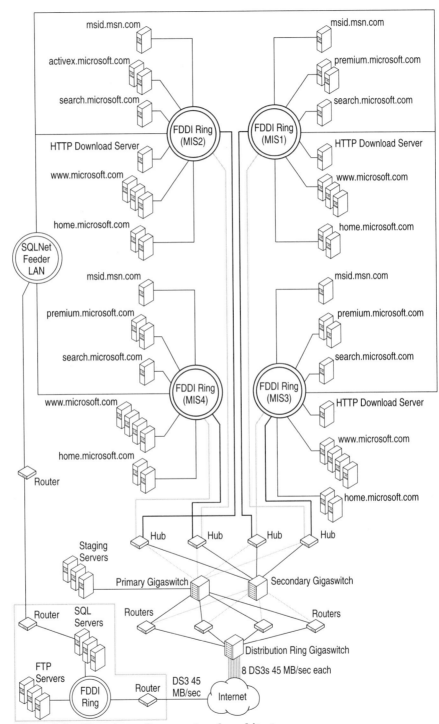

Figure 3.8   The microsoft.com network architecture.

Planning for Spikes

The site's involvement in the Windows 95 launch led to a surge of activity inside Microsoft as product and marketing groups added content. During 1996 the number of hits per month on the site grew from 118 million to over 2 *billion*. The product groups' increased focus on Web-based marketing has fed the ramp-up as more content is accessed by more users.

Beyond the continuing growth and the regularly occurring periods of peak usage, irregular spikes and special events place much larger burdens on many Web sites and servers. For Microsoft, many of these coincide with software releases. The release of Internet Explorer 4.0 in October, 1997 is a good example: In one week, more than 2 million users downloaded an average of 18 MB each. Peaks exceeded 6 terabytes per day.

Microsoft's site has special requirements, but companies of every size need to plan for spikes, which can occur when they launch a new ad campaign, appear in a news article, or are linked to a popular Web site. Even a single Web server connected only to a small LAN can experience spikes in its activity, although if it serves only a small number of clients, and their needs are not urgent, the impact won't be catastrophic. But if it is important to the enterprise that even a few of those clients be able to access the Web server without delay under all circumstances, the site manager must build in the relevant capacity.

When Planning Is Not Enough

Spikes are not the only pitfalls. The continued expansion of day-to-day operations and the ongoing change in orientation from static HTML to dynamically generated pages and increased interactivity led to unforeseen difficulties at microsoft.com. Toward the end of 1996, for example, problems began to emerge at home.microsoft.com as users found error messages appearing on their browsers. By May 1997 the servers had begun to show signs of blocking as thousands of delayed access requests backed up. Performance of the Internet Start page went downhill gradually for two or three weeks, then suddenly took a nosedive. The site's existing hardware and software technology was simply unable to keep pace with demand.

Working Toward a Resolution

Because the Internet Start page at home.microsoft.com is the default home page for the Microsoft Internet Explorer browser, the hit rate at the site is continually increasing. Each of the servers handles between 2,000 and 4,000 viewers per second. In May, as access to home.microsoft.com became increasingly difficult, a task force was formed and given the charter to find a solution. The group met daily for six weeks, working to return the site to nominal performance.

The first step was to examine the hardware, beginning with the servers—Internet connection bandwidth was not saturated, and therefore could not be the central issue. With the number of viewers increasing rapidly, the servers were adding viewer requests to the queue faster than they were delivering responses. More servers were added to handle the load, but that alone was not sufficient. The task force began probing the connections among servers, databases, and viewers to find and eliminate possible signal breakdowns or bottlenecks. They also initiated a process of streamlining the site's HTML and ASP code to make it as lean and efficient as possible. By mid-June some progress had been made, but it was clear that something else was wrong.

A Case of External Dependency

The task force began to look at the objects—text files, graphics, and other files that make up individual Web pages—that were being called by the servers. Some of those objects are housed in the Microsoft Properties Database (PD), which receives and stores individual user preferences: news headlines, personalized home-page options, and stock quotes, for example. Through a process of elimination, the task force came to suspect the PD of being the main culprit in the ongoing slowdowns and failures. All of the servers were drawing on the same central repositories or databases for page elements, like wells drawing on a common aquifer. In other words, the problem was external to the servers themselves, and adding more of them only made it worse.

Part of the solution was to cut down the number of requests to that particular set of databases. New, less demanding ways of personalizing pages were developed, and the server software was adjusted to work better for the rapidly increasing numbers of viewers using the site. In addition, the database servers were moved physically closer to the Web servers in order to allow the team to eliminate intervening routers and other hardware. Meanwhile, the team continued to examine the entire process of creating Web pages and serving them to visitors.

A Case of Internal Dependency

A new Internet Explorer download page was deployed just before the release of Internet Explorer 4.0. This page was complex, and the path to it led through two other processor-intensive pages, one of which was the www.microsoft.com home page. Almost immediately the site began to suffer processor bottlenecks. Analysis showed that a large number of clients were following a single path into the site, straight to the Internet Explorer download page, and that there were serious inefficiencies along that path. Streamlining the ASP code was not sufficient to resolve the problem. Nor was adding hardware the answer: site engineers estimated that even an order-of-magnitude increase in the number of servers wouldn't be enought to handle the demand. Instead, temporary measures were put into place:

- Pages involving frames, other than the site's home page, were reduced to single panels.

- The download page and both pages leading to it were redesigned as static HTML, rather than dynamic, pages.

This solution demonstrates another way to deal with spikes: Reduce the load by temporarily reducing functionality, thereby reducing overhead. Once the load returns to normal levels, the original functionality can be restored.

Finding a Balance

Building an Internet or intranet site requires balancing server hardware, software, and network resources, and then maintaining that balance as site traffic grows. It is important for site managers to be on the lookout for hidden assumptions and external dependencies that interfere with the balance. The visible or obvious parts of the balance are hardware, software, network, and content; constant monitoring keeps the balance in view.

The Hardware

Hardware is a necessary part of site capacity and performance, and it is important to select hardware that can be scaled or upgraded easily when demands increase. The microsoft.com team continually reviews its hardware to be sure that capacity is staying ahead of demand. The current CPU utilization for microsoft.com is as high as 40 percent per server; it is purposely kept well below capacity so that the site can handle spikes.

The Software

In addition to the Microsoft software used to run the site, the microsoft.com team has developed a few internal content management utilities by using Visual Basic and Microsoft Access. For example, a content-tracking tool scans the site each day and fills a database with information about each of the 250,000 HTML and ASP pages, including where the links on each page point. When a page is to be deleted, a check of the database shows other pages that point to that page. Links on the other pages can be changed before the page is deleted, so someone viewing them won't find broken links.

Another document management tool keeps track of who is responsible for each page and when the page was sent to the servers. Even with thorough testing, problems—such as errors in ASP pages—sometimes get through and are difficult to pinpoint among a quarter-million pages of content. The tool provides a list of pages sent to the servers shortly before the problem appeared, narrowing the number that have to be investigated.

The Network

In another move to increase network capacity at Microsoft, system engineers installed two network interface cards in each server. One card is for the FDDI ring that carries Internet traffic, and the other is for the corporate network, which handles administration and content replication. With this arrangement, administrative traffic doesn't take bandwidth away from Internet traffic.

The Content

Just as the microsoft.com team constantly reviews its hardware capacity to ensure quick response for the user, it also studies the way it configures its servers to manage content. Currently, the content is updated eight times a day, with 5 to 7 percent of the total content changing each day. Because each of the 18 www.microsoft.com Web servers contains a complete copy of the site's content, each set of changes has to be replicated to every server. The team is investigating an alternative approach: segmenting content among several clusters of servers based on product groups. While this would make it possible to adjust the number and size of servers based on the popularity of the content they dispense, it would also increase internal network loading and require tracking what content is on what machine. In late 1997, the trade-offs were still being studied.

Ongoing Changes

Groups producing content for microsoft.com want to use the latest Web publishing features to make their content more eye-catching and interesting to users. The result is a tug-of-war between content providers, who want users to have the richest experience possible, and the team running the Web site, which wants to increase download speeds and the site's capacity. The site currently has a size limit of 100 KB per page, including graphics, and prefers that each page be smaller than 60 KB. The bottom line is that content needs to strike a balance between being visually interesting, and being as small as possible so as to improve download performance. Bigger pages take longer to download, which consumes server time and network bandwidth and, most importantly, irritates users.

The User Experience Counts

The amount of content a site delivers does not necessarily indicate user satisfaction. To monitor the user download experience the microsoft.com team periodically tests the access, search, and download times for specific pages, using 28.8-Kbps modems stationed in various U.S. cities. The January 1997 test showed that users averaged 50 seconds per task. A more recent test of download times indicated a 20-second improvement to 30 seconds per task, thanks in part to the new network design.

Summary

Microsoft.com team members are hard-pressed to define a formula for how much server power, software, and network bandwidth is needed to build a high-traffic Web site. Instead the team relies on constant monitoring, worst-case planning, and powerful servers. Their experience and recommendations can be summarized in four rules of thumb:

- Learn as much as you can about your audience, potential content, marketing plans, and future initiatives, and then take your best guess.

- When in doubt, choose bigger and faster. You may overbuild today, but you'll likely need the extra capacity sooner than you expect.

- Once your site is in operation, watch it closely. Find out which of the three components—hardware, software, and network bandwidth—is lagging behind, and bring it into balance with the others.

- Know that nothing will stay static for long. Keep an eye on growth and usage trends, and be prepared to react (that is, to add or shift hardware, software, or network capacity) quickly.

Resources

The following Web sites and books provide additional information relevant to Web server capacity planning.

Web Links

Web site information is current as of the date of publication, but is, of course, subject to change.

http://esdis.gsfc.nasa.gov/msst/A5_01P.html
NASA paper on optimizing RAID performance with cache.

http://tebbit.eng.umd.edu/nasa/node12.html
Discussion of ATM networking latency.

http://www.canadacomputes.com/tc/Nov96/Cwb.html
Overview of memory types.

http://www.ots.utexas.edu:8080/ethernet/gigabit.html
Description of Gigabit Ethernet, with links to other sources of information on Ethernet.

Books

Professional Web Site Optimization (Wrox Press Ltd., 1997).

WebMaster in a Nutshell (O'Reilly and Associates, 1997).

Web Server Technology: Advanced Guide for World-Wide Web Information Providers (Morgan Kaufman Publishers, 1996).

CHAPTER 4

Performance Tuning and Optimization

4

Performance tuning and optimization involve monitoring and testing your site, and changing parameters, settings, and hardware to help your site deliver content to users more efficiently. This chapter discusses memory, processor, network, security, and Web application issues. It describes some of the available tools for monitoring and testing and provides some guidelines to help you recover from bottlenecks.

In this chapter:

- Using This Chapter
- Monitoring Memory Usage
- Preventing Processor Bottlenecks
- Monitoring Bandwidth and Network Capacity
- Security and Performance
- Monitoring Web Applications
- Resources

Using This Chapter

This chapter suggests several approaches to monitoring and improving the performance of a site running Internet Information Server (IIS) with Windows NT 4.0 Server. It is intended as a technical guide for network administrators, but should also be useful for anyone running IIS.

The chapter includes the following five sections:

- *Monitoring Memory Usage*

    Memory is discussed first because memory shortages often manifest themselves as poor performance in other components, especially processors and disks. It is important to rule out a memory shortage before investigating other components.

    This section presents an overview of some techniques for determining whether a computer has adequate physical memory to be an efficient Internet server. It discusses how IIS uses physical memory, including the IIS object cache and the file system cache, and includes suggestions for tuning some server parameters to improve memory use.

- *Preventing Processor Bottlenecks*

    This section presents a brief discussion of tools and strategies for monitoring processor use in single-processor and multiple-processor computers running IIS, and for preventing the processor from becoming a system bottleneck. It provides information about the role of the processor in servicing client connections and requests. It includes tips on tuning to balance processor load.

- *Monitoring Bandwidth and Network Capacity*

    This section is an overview of some techniques for measuring how much data a network configuration is able to transmit during periods of average and peak use. It includes some suggestions for capacity planning based on the number of files and connections the server is expected to handle.

- *Security and Performance*

    A brief discussion of some techniques for monitoring the performance overhead associated with some common security strategies, such as Windows NT Challenge/Response authentication and the Secure Sockets Layer (SSL) protocol.

- *Monitoring Web Applications*

  Applications can be responsible for poor performance and inefficient processor and memory use. This section builds on the monitoring techniques discussed in the memory and processor sections. It suggests some ways to monitor the basic aspects of application performance. It discusses static and dynamic applications, and explains why some applications perform better than others on IIS. It also includes some suggestions for mitigating the effects of poor application performance.

Monitoring Memory Usage

There are four major areas to look at when monitoring IIS memory usage:

- Overall server memory usage.
- Memory used by the IIS working set—as well as the working sets of any out-of-process applications.
- The IIS object cache. Is it as large as it needs to be? Is it configured in the most efficient way?
- The file system cache.

Memory Requirements of an IIS Server

A server running Internet Information Server should have sufficient physical memory to keep the following items in physical memory:

- *Program code for IIS services.* This code occupies about 2.5 MB with all services running simultaneously. This code is part of the *working set* of the IIS process, Inetinfo.exe, and can be paged to disk. (Without ASP code, the working set is roughly 2 MB with all services running.)

  Note Each connection adds about 10 KB to the working set. Thus, if there were, say, 1,000 simultaneous connections, they would cause the working set to expand by about 10 MB.

- *Frequently accessed Web page files.* The number and size of these files varies widely with the installation. These files are stored in the *file system cache*, an area of physical memory reserved for frequently and repeatedly used pages. The remaining files are stored on disk until needed.

- *Frequently used objects.* These are objects that are costly to retrieve and are frequently reused by the service, such as file handles, file directory listings, and so on. These objects are stored in the *IIS Object Cache*, a cache maintained by the IIS service. The IIS Object Cache is also part of the working set of the IIS process, Inetinfo.exe, and can be paged to disk.

- *IIS log files.* IIS maintains one memory-mapped file for each site that has logging enabled. These files are mapped in 64-KB chunks. The mapped segments of the log files are part of the working set of the IIS process. Logged data also appears in the file system cache because data is cached when the file-mapping objects are written to disk.

- *TCB table.* TCP maintains a hash table of transmission control blocks (TCBs) to store data for each TCP connection. A control block is attached to the table for each active connection. The control block is deleted shortly after the connection is closed. The TCB table is part of the operating system's *nonpaged memory pool.* As such, the TCB table must remain in physical memory; it cannot be paged to disk.

- *HTTP connection data structures.* HTTP maintains pageable data structures to track its active connections. When these data structures are in physical memory, they are counted as part of the working set of the IIS process.

- *Pool threads.* The threads that execute the code for the services are stored in the *nonpaged pool* in physical memory, along with other objects used by the operating system to support IIS. Threads in the nonpaged pool must remain in physical memory; they cannot be paged to disk.

You can measure your server's physical memory and measure the amount of physical memory used directly or indirectly by Internet Information Server. You can also log the data over time to identify patterns of memory use.

Monitoring Overall Server Memory

Like most well-designed user-mode processes, IIS services derive much of their benefits from the Windows NT operating system architecture, including the Windows NT security model, RPC communication, messaging, the file systems, and other operating system services. Thus, monitoring memory for IIS begins with monitoring overall server memory, particularly on a multipurpose server.

Monitoring the physical memory of a server running IIS involves measuring the size of the areas in physical memory used by IIS and assuring that enough space is available to contain the elements IIS needs to store. The physical memory space should be sufficient for normal operation and for routine peaks in demand; but your site may also encounter occasional spikes. If it does, you must decide how much degradation in performance (if any) you will allow at those times. Routine peaks on most sites are about twice the average amount of utilization, whereas spikes can easily be a full order of magnitude beyond the average.

The Windows NT virtual memory system is designed to be self-tuning. The Virtual Memory Manager and Cache Manager adjust the size of the file system cache, the working sets of processes, the paged and nonpaged memory pools, and the paging files on disk to produce the most efficient use of available physical memory. Similarly, the IIS service regulates the size of the IIS Object Cache. Therefore, the primary purpose of monitoring memory in a Windows NT–based server running IIS is to make sure that the server has enough physical memory, not to adjust the size of each memory component, as might be the case with other operating systems.

How to Monitor Overall Server Memory

This section is a brief review of the most important memory monitoring techniques. Many performance monitoring tools measure system-wide and per-process memory use. These tools include the Windows NT administrative tools Task Manager and Performance Monitor, as well as various tools included with the *Windows NT Workstation Resource Kit*, including Process Monitor (Pmon.exe), Process Viewer (Pviewer.exe), Process Explode (Pview.exe), and PerfLog (Pdlcnfig.exe and Pdlsvc.exe). PerfLog and Performance Monitor can measure memory use over time.

Here are a few guidelines for using Performance Monitor and PerfLog to monitor overall server memory use:

- *Monitor available memory*. Compare the total physical memory available to Windows NT to the available memory remaining when you are running all server services. To gather more reliable data, log this value over time, making certain to include periods of peak activity. The system attempts to keep available bytes at 4 MB or more, but it is prudent to keep at least 5 percent of memory available for peak use.

   To track available memory, use Performance Monitor or PerfLog to log the Memory: Available Bytes counter.

- *Monitor paging*. Continuous high rates of paging indicate a memory shortage. *Paging* occurs when code or data requested by an application or service is not found in physical memory and must be retrieved from disk.

Paging is measured in several ways:

- *Numbers of page faults.* Page faults occur when the system cannot find a requested page in the working set of the process that requested the page. The system also counts a page fault on a file access if the requested page is not found in the file system cache.

  To measure page faults on working sets and on the file system cache, use Performance Monitor or PerfLog to log the Memory: Page Faults/sec and Memory: Cache Faults/sec counters.

- *Disk reads due to page faults.* All page faults interrupt the processor. Only *hard faults*, those that require reading from disk, seriously delay system response. Monitor hard faults and compare the ratio of hard faults to all page faults. In general, a sustained rate of more than five hard faults per second indicates a memory shortage. To measure hard faults, use Performance Monitor or PerfLog to log the Memory: Page Reads/sec counter. Use the Memory: Page Faults/sec counter as an indicator of all page faults.

- *Monitor the file system cache.* The file system cache is the working set of the file system. This cache is a reserved area in physical memory where the file system stores its recently used and frequently used data. By default, the system reserves about 50 percent of physical memory for the file system cache, but the system trims the cache if it is running out of memory. A large and effective file system cache is vital to servers running IIS, which function like specialized file servers. This topic is discussed in more detail in the "Monitoring the File System Cache" section later in this chapter.

- *Monitor the size of the paging files.* The paging files on disk back up committed physical memory. The larger the paging file, the more memory the system can commit. Windows NT creates a paging file on the system disk. You can create a paging file on each logical disk, and enlarge existing files.

  To monitor the paging files, use Performance Monitor or PerfLog to log Process: Page File Bytes: Total.

- *Monitor the size of the paged and nonpaged memory pools.* The system's memory pools hold objects created and used by applications and the operating system. The paged pool holds items that can be paged to disk. Items in the non-paged pool must remain in physical memory. The contents of the memory pools are accessible only in privileged mode. On servers running Internet Information Server, IIS threads that service connections are stored in the nonpaged pool, along with other objects used by the service, such as file handles.

  To monitor the pool space for all processes on the server, use Performance Monitor or PerfLog to log the Memory: Pool Paged Bytes and Memory: Pool Nonpaged Bytes counters. To monitor the pool space used directly by Internet Information Server, log the Process: Pool Paged Bytes: Inetinfo and Process: Pool Nonpaged Bytes: Inetinfo counters for the Inetinfo process.

These general monitoring techniques are useful for any computer running Windows NT. The following sections discuss techniques for monitoring components specific to the IIS service.

Monitoring the Working Set of the IIS Process

A server running IIS must have enough physical memory to support the IIS process. The physical memory visible to a process is called its *working set.* If the working set of the Internet Information Server process is not large enough, IIS is not able to store its code and frequently used data in physical memory. Therefore, the IIS services are delayed by having to retrieve code and data from disk.

The system continually adjusts the size of the working set of a process as the process runs. The amount of space the system provides to the working set depends on the amount of memory available to the system and the needs of the process.

This section suggests methods for monitoring the size of the IIS working set over time and explains how to determine whether the working set of the IIS process is large enough to enable IIS to run efficiently.

About the Inetinfo Working Set

IIS runs in a pageable user-mode process called Inetinfo.exe. Active Server Pages and the Web, FTP, and SMTP services run in the Inetinfo process, and share the threads of the process. Each of the current connections is also given about 10 KB of memory in the Inetinfo working set.

For IIS to run efficiently, it must be able to maintain all of its code and the most frequently used files in its working set. In addition, the working set of the Inetinfo process should be large enough to contain the IIS Object Cache, data buffers for IIS logging, and the data structures that the Web service uses to track its active connections.

There is no fixed optimal size for the Inetinfo working set. The requirements of the working set vary depending upon the number of connections maintained, the number and size of files, and the use of other supporting services, such as security features and logging.

You can monitor the IIS process as it runs on your server to determine whether its working set is large enough to support the IIS services.

Using Performance Monitor to Monitor the IIS Working Set

You can use the following Performance Monitor counters to monitor the working set of Inetinfo.exe. IIS and its component services run in the context of the Inetinfo process. (You can monitor the IIS Object Cache separately. For more information, see "Monitoring the IIS Object Cache" later in this chapter.)

Table 4.1   Performance Monitor Counters for the IIS Working Set

Counter	Indicates
Memory: Available Bytes	The amount of physical memory remaining and available for use, in bytes. This counter displays the amount of memory not currently used by the system or by running processes. This counter displays the last observed value, not an average.
	The operating system attempts to prevent this value from falling below 4 MB. The system often trims the working sets of processes to maintain the 4 MB minimum available memory.
Process: Working Set: Inetinfo	Size of the working set of the process, in bytes. This counter displays the last observed value, not an average over time.
Process: Page Faults/sec: Inetinfo	Hard and soft faults in the working set of the process.
Memory: Page Faults/sec	Hard and soft faults for all working sets running on the system.
Memory: Page Reads/sec	Hard page faults. This counter displays the number of times the disk is read to satisfy page faults. This counter displays the number of read operations, regardless of the number of pages read in each operation.
	A sustained rate of 5 reads/sec or more might indicate a memory shortage.
Memory: Pages Input/sec	One measure of the cost of page faults. This counter displays the number of pages read to satisfy page faults. One page is faulted at a time, but the system can read multiple pages to prevent further faults.

You should log this data for several days. You can use bookmarks in the Performance Monitor log to identify times of unusually high and low server activity.

Analyzing the Working Set Data

The following sections describe how to use data about the Inetinfo working set to determine if the server has enough memory to support IIS efficiently.

Available Bytes and the Inetinfo Working Set

If the system has sufficient memory, it can maintain enough space in the Inetinfo working set so that IIS rarely needs to perform disk operations. One indicator of memory sufficiency is how much the size of the Inetinfo process working set varies in response to general memory availability on the server.

You can use the Memory: Available Bytes counter as an indicator of memory availability and the Process: Working Set: Inetinfo counter as an indicator of the size of the working set of the Internet Information Server process. Be sure to examine data collected over time, because these counters display the last value observed, rather than an average.

Page Faults and the Inetinfo Working Set

When available bytes fall below about 4 MB, the system attempts to provide more available bytes by taking memory away from the working sets of processes. This strategy increases the rate of page faults because each process must now retrieve data that was once in its working set from disk or from elsewhere in memory. When the rate of page faults for a particular process rises, the system attempts to expand the working set of that process to lower the page fault rate. The sizes of the working sets fluctuate accordingly.

The page fault counters for a process are incremented when the process requests code or data that is not found in its working set. The data might be found elsewhere in memory, such as in the file system cache or in the working set of another process; or in transition to disk. The system might also have to read the data from disk.

There are two kinds of page faults. The page faults that affect performance significantly are *hard faults*, which require reading from disk to retrieve a referenced page. *Soft faults*, which are page faults resolved when the page is found elsewhere in physical memory, interrupt the processor but have much less effect on performance. Unfortunately, the Process: Page Faults/sec counter includes both hard and soft faults; there are no counters for measuring the hard faults attributable to each process separately. However, Memory: Page Reads/sec and Memory: Pages Input/sec are good indicators of hard faults for the whole system.

Compare your data on the size of the Inetinfo working set to the rate of page faults attributed to the working set. Use the Process: Working Set: Inetinfo counter as an indicator of the size of the working set. Use the Process: Page Faults/sec: Inetinfo counter to indicate the rate of page faults for the IIS process. When you have reviewed data on the varying size of the Inetinfo working set, you can use its page fault rate to determine whether the system has enough memory to operate efficiently. If the system is not able to lower the page fault rate to an acceptable level, you should add memory to improve performance.

Monitoring the IIS Object Cache

The IIS service maintains the IIS Object Cache, a cache of objects that Active Server Pages and the Web, FTP, and SMTP services use frequently.

The Object Cache is also used for objects that are hard to retrieve. The IIS Object Cache is designed to improve the performance of IIS by keeping these objects readily available to the process. The primary components of the IIS Object Cache are open file object handles and directory listings, but the cache also stores other service-specific objects.

The IIS Object Cache is part of the working set of the IIS process in physical memory. The Object Cache can be paged to disk if memory is not sufficient to support a large enough working set for the IIS process. It is important to provide enough physical memory to maintain the Object Cache in the working set.

You can measure the size and effectiveness of the IIS Object Cache by using Performance Monitor.

Using Performance Monitor to Monitor the IIS Object Cache

Performance Monitor includes a set of extensible counters you can use to monitor the IIS services. These counters are installed in Performance Monitor when you run IIS Setup.

For descriptions of the IIS counters, select **Add to Chart** from the **Edit** menu in Performance Monitor; then select the counter name and click the **Explain** button. Note that many of the IIS counters display the last observed value or a cumulative count, not an average value or rate.

Performance Monitor includes five performance objects for measuring IIS performance:

- Internet Information Services Global
- Web Service
- Active Server Pages
- FTP Service
- SMTP Server

The following table lists the counters recommended for monitoring the IIS Object Cache. You should log the counters over time to record trends in the size, content, and effectiveness of the IIS Object Cache.

Table 4.2   Performance Monitor Counters for the IIS Object Cache

Counter	Indicates
Internet Information Services Global: Cache Hits Internet Information Services Global: Cache Misses Internet Information Services Global: Cache Hits %	A measure of the efficiency of the IIS Object Cache. These counters demonstrate how often data sought in the IIS Object Cache is found. Internet Information Services Global: Cache Misses indicates how often the system must search elsewhere in memory or on disk to satisfy a request. The first two of these counters display totals since the service was started. Internet Information Services Global: Cache Hits % displays an instantaneous value, not an average over time.
Internet Information Services Global: Cache Flushes	How many times an object was deleted from the IIS Object Cache, either because it timed out, or because the object changed.
Internet Information Services Global: Objects Internet Information Services Global: Cached File Handles Internet Information Services Global: Directory Listings	The number of objects currently stored in the IIS Object Cache.

Monitoring a Remote Computer

When you are monitoring a server remotely, the Internet Information Services Global, Active Server Pages, Web Service, FTP Service, and SMTP Server performance objects and counters appear in Performance Monitor only when the related IIS service is running on the computer being monitored. If you do not see these objects in the **Add to Chart** dialog box, close Performance Monitor on your computer, start the IIS service on the computer being monitored, and then start Performance Monitor again.

Note   If the objects and counters still do not appear in the **Add to Chart** dialog box, or if they appear intermittently, make certain that no one else is using Performance Monitor to monitor the remote computer. All remote users must restart Performance Monitor after the IIS service is started for any of them to see the IIS counters. Also, check the Event Viewer application event log for errors. Errors in the service or in loading the counters can also prevent Performance Monitor from displaying the counters.

Analyzing the IIS Object Cache Data

The Performance Monitor counters for IIS monitor three different aspects of the IIS Object Cache: its contents, its size, and its performance. This section explains how to interpret the data you collect by using the Performance Monitor IIS counters.

Analyzing IIS Object Cache Contents

You can use the Performance Monitor counters to reveal the contents of the IIS Object Cache. The Objects counter counts all objects. The Cached File Handles and Directory Listings counters are subsets of the Objects counter. At any given time, the difference between the total number of objects and the sum of Cached File Handles and Directory Listings is equal to the number of other objects stored in the cache. The Directory Listings counter is most important to servers running the FTP service.

When interpreting the counters, remember that they show the most recently observed value, not a long-term average, unless they specify otherwise.

Analyzing the Performance of the IIS Object Cache

Cache performance is judged by how often objects sought in the cache are found there. Frequent cache misses harm performance if they result in disk I/O. There are no fixed standards for cache performance, although a value of 80 to 90 percent for Cache Hits % is considered to be excellent for sites with many static files. If Cache Hits and Cache Hits % are very low or Cache Misses is quite high, the cache could be too small to function effectively. Adding memory increases the cache size and should improve its performance.

Cache flushes can also affect the performance of the IIS Object Cache. Cache flushes are regulated, in part, by an internal timer. The timer activates the *object-cache scavenger,* which deletes expired objects. Objects are flushed from the cache if they change or if they time out before they are reused. If the timer is too quick, objects can be flushed from the cache too frequently. If the timer is too slow, objects can be wasting precious physical memory space.

To measure cache flushes, compare the number of cache flushes over time to the number of cache misses and to the rate of page faults of the IIS process (as indicated by the Process: Page Faults/sec: Inetinfo counter. It is important to observe these values over time. Like the other global IIS counters, Cache Flushes displays an instantaneous value, not an average. If a high rate of cache flushes is associated with elevated cache misses and page faults, it is possible that the cache is being flushed too frequently.

If you suspect that cache flushes are occurring too often or not often enough, you can change the rate at which unreferenced objects are flushed from the IIS cache. Make sure you have ample memory before increasing the time between flushes. The cache flush time defaults to 30 seconds; to change it, add the **ObjectCacheTTL** key to the registry if it is not already present. Put this key in:

```
HKEY_LOCAL_MACHINE\System
        \CurrentControlSet
                \Services
                        \Inetinfo
                                \Parameters
```

Monitoring the File System Cache

The *file system cache* is an area of physical memory reserved for frequently and repeatedly used file system data. This cache is maintained by the Windows NT Cache Manager for use by all processes. This section explains how IIS uses the file system cache, how to monitor the size and efficiency of the cache, and how to interpret the data you collect.

How IIS Uses the File System Cache

The IIS services rely on the operating system to store and retrieve frequently used Web pages and other files from the file system cache. The file system cache is particularly useful for servers of static Web pages, because Web pages tend to be used in repeated, predictable patterns. Files read repeatedly are more likely to be placed in the cache.

Also, IIS always reads sequentially. Sequential reading takes advantage of a Windows NT Cache Manager feature called a read ahead. A *read ahead* occurs when the Cache Manager's predictive algorithms detect sequential reading and begin to read larger blocks of data in each read operation. Read aheads can provide a significant performance boost to a process.

The IIS services use the file system cache and the IIS Object Cache. Sometimes, the caches are used together. When a thread of an IIS service needs to open a file, the thread requests a file handle from the operating system. When the thread receives the handle, the thread uses the handle to open the file. Then, if space permits, the thread stores the handle in the IIS Object Cache and the system stores the file data in the file system cache. Later, if that thread, or any other thread, needs the file, the file handle can be retrieved from the IIS Object Cache and the file contents can be retrieved from the file system cache.

Using Performance Monitor to Monitor the File System Cache

Performance Monitor includes several counters in the Memory and Cache performance objects that monitor the size and effectiveness of the file system cache. The following table lists these counters.

Table 4.3   Performance Monitor Counters for the File System Cache

Counter	Indicates
Memory: Cache bytes	The size of the cache, in bytes. This counter displays the last observed value; it is not an average.
Memory: Cache faults/sec	How often data sought in the file system cache is not found there. The count includes faults for data found elsewhere in memory, as well as faults that require disk operations to retrieve the requested data.
	This counter displays the number of faults, without regard for the number of pages retrieved in response to the fault.
Cache: MDL Reads/sec	How often the system attempts to read large blocks of data from the cache.
	Memory Descriptor List (MDL) Reads are read operations in which the system uses a list of the physical address of each page to help it find the page.
	MDL Reads are often used to retrieve cached Web pages and FTP files.
Cache: Pin Reads/sec	How often the system attempts to read recently accessed blocks of data from the cache. This counter is more accurate for ASP content than the MDL Reads/sec counter is.
	Pin counters display reads of cache data that is held because it has just been read or written. They reflect cache data that is used repeatedly.
Cache: MDL Read Hits %	How often attempts to find large sections of data in the cache are successful.
	You can use the Cache: MDL Read Hits % counter to calculate the percentage of MDL misses. Misses are likely to result in disk I/O.

continued

Counter	Indicates
Cache: Pin Read Hits %	How often attempts to find recently accessed sections of data in the cache are successful. This counter is more accurate for ASP content than the MDL Read Hits % counter is.
	You can use the Cache: Pin Read Hits % counter to calculate the percentage of misses. Misses are likely to result in disk I/O. Pin counters display reads of cache data that is held because it has just been read or written. They reflect cache data that is used repeatedly.
Cache: Data Maps/sec	How often pages are mapped into the cache from elsewhere in physical memory or from disk.
	To measure the percentage of data maps from elsewhere in physical memory, use Cache: Data Map Hits %. The inverse of Cache: Data Map Hits % indicates data maps from disk.
Cache: Read Aheads/sec	A measure of sequential reading from the cache. When the system detects sequential reading, it anticipates future reads and reads larger blocks of data. The read ahead counters are a useful measure of how effectively an application uses the cache.
Memory: Page Faults/sec	Hard and soft faults in the working set of the process. This counter displays the number of faults, without regard for the number of pages retrieved in response to the fault.
Memory: Page Reads/sec	Hard faults in the working sets of processes and in the file system cache.

You should log this data for several days. You can use bookmarks in Performance Monitor to note times of unusually high and low server activity.

Analyzing the File System Cache Data

You can use the data you collect in Performance Monitor to evaluate whether your server has enough memory to support an effective file system cache. This evaluation consists of the following three steps:

- Determine how the size of your server's file system cache varies over time.
- Determine the extent to which the performance of your server's cache varies with the size of the cache.
- Verify that the server has enough memory to support an effective cache even when the server is most active.

The following sections provide information to help you with this evaluation.

Analyzing Cache Size Data

The Windows NT Cache Manager adjusts the size of the file system cache based on whether a computer is a workstation or a server, the amount of physical memory in the computer, and the applications and services the computer is supporting. In general, it is counterproductive to override the Cache Manager and manipulate the cache size directly. If the cache is too small to be effective, it is best to increase the amount of physical memory on the computer, or to redistribute memory-intensive applications to other servers.

The Performance Monitor Memory: Cache Size counter is a useful indicator of the size of the file system cache. Task Manager also displays the size of the file system cache in the **File Cache** field under **Physical Memory** on the **Performance** tab.

You can use also use Performance Monitor or PerfLog to log the Memory: Cache Size counter. A log of cache size reveals how the size of the file system cache changes over time. Compare this data to a measure of general memory availability, such as data from the Memory: Available Bytes counter. In general, when memory is scarce, the system trims the cache and when memory is ample, the system enlarges the cache.

Note the points in the log when the cache is smallest. Keep track of how small the cache gets and how often the cache is small. Also, note how much system memory is available when the cache size is reduced. This data is useful when associating the size of the cache to its performance.

Analyzing Cache Performance Data

You can use the Performance Monitor data to evaluate the performance of the file system cache on your server. A *hit* is recorded when requested files are found in the cache. A *miss* or *fault* is recorded when requested files are not found. Misses and faults indicate how often the system needs to do extra work to retrieve files from somewhere other than the cache.

To evaluate the performance of your server's file system cache, chart a Performance Monitor log of Cache: MDL Read Hits %. The file system cache is performing well when this value is highest. Values near 100 percent are not uncommon on IIS servers with ample memory. Subtract the percentage of hits from 100 to determine the number of misses. Misses on MDL Reads usually require disk operations to find the requested data.

MDL Reads are the most common type of read used for retrieving many contiguous pages. Typically, MDL Reads are the most common read operation on servers running Internet Information Server. To determine which type of cache read is most common on your server, create a Performance Monitor report of the rates of different types of cache reads. Include the Cache: Copy Reads/sec, Cache: Data Maps/sec, Cache: Fast Reads/sec, Cache: MDL Reads/sec, and Cache: Pin Reads/sec.

You can also use the Memory: Cache Faults/sec counter to indicate how often data sought in the file system cache is not found there. This value should be as small as possible. The Memory: Page Faults/sec and Memory: Page Reads/sec counters are included to help you relate the fault rate of the cache to the fault rate in the system as a whole. Memory: Cache Faults/sec is a component of Memory: Page Faults/sec. The ratio of Memory: Cache Faults/sec to Memory: Page Faults/sec indicates the proportion of faults occurring in the cache as opposed to the working sets of processes.

A high rate of cache faults can indicate a memory shortage. But it can also indicate a less than optimal organization of data on disk. If the files used in sequence are stored on the same logical partitions of the same disk, they are more likely to benefit from the Windows NT Cache Manager's optimizing strategies, such as read aheads. The Memory: Read Aheads/sec counter displays the rate of sequential reading from the cache.

Comparing Cache Size and Performance Data

You can determine the extent to which the performance of the file system cache varies with the size of the cache. Compare the size of the cache over time to the rate at which data sought in the cache is found there.

Use the Memory: Cache Bytes counter as an indicator of the size of the cache. Use Memory: Cache Faults/sec as an indicator of the rate of cache misses, and Cache: MDL Read Hits % as an indicator of the rate of cache hits.

If Memory: Cache Faults/sec rises and Cache: MDL Read Hits % falls when the file system cache is smaller, the cache might be too small to be of much benefit to the server. A less effective file system cache is likely to degrade the performance of an IIS server significantly, especially if the size of the cache is often reduced due to a general memory shortage.

If cache performance is poor when the cache is small, use the data you have collected to infer why the cache size is reduced. Choose a period when the cache is small and note the available memory on the server and the processes and services running on the server, including the number of simultaneous connections supported.

When you add physical memory to your server, the system allocates more space to the file system cache. A larger cache is almost always more efficient. In addition, defragmenting your disks makes it more likely that related pages are copied into the cache together and this improves the hit rate of the cache. It is also a good idea to use the NTFS (rather than the FAT) file system. Finally, consider reducing the workload on the server by moving some of the load to another server.

Suggestions for Optimizing Memory on an IIS Server

Servers running IIS, like all high-performance file servers, benefit from ample physical memory. Generally, the more memory you add, the more the servers use and the better they perform. IIS requires a minimum of 32 MB of memory; at least 64 MB is recommended. If you are running memory-intensive applications, your server could require a much larger amount of memory to run optimally (for example, most of the servers that service the microsoft.com Web site have 512 MB of memory).

Here are a few suggestions for optimizing memory performance without adding memory:

- *Improve data organization.* Keep related Web files on the same logical partitions of a disk. Keeping files together improves the performance of the file system cache. Also, defragment your disks. Even well-organized files take more time to retrieve if they are fragmented.

- *Try disk mirroring or striping.* The optimum configuration is to have enough physical memory to hold all static Web pages. However, if pages must be retrieved from disk, use mirroring or striping to make reading from disk sets faster. (See the section on RAID in Chapter 3, "Capacity Planning.") In some cases, a caching disk controller may help.

- *Replace or convert CGI applications.* CGI applications use much more processor time and memory space than equivalent ASP or ISAPI applications. For more information on ASP, ISAPI, and CGI applications, see the section on "Monitoring Web Applications," later in this chapter.

- *Enlarge paging files.* Add paging files and increase the size of your paging files. Windows NT creates one paging file on the system disk, but you can also create a paging file on each logical partition of each disk.

- *Retime the IIS Object Cache.* Consider lengthening the period that an unused object can remain in the cache (use the **ObjectCacheTTL** setting in the registry).

- *Change the balance of the file system cache to the IIS working set.* By default, servers running Windows NT are configured to give preference to the file system cache over the working sets of processes when allocating memory space. Although IIS-based servers benefit from a large file system cache, the **Maximize Throughput for File Sharing** setting often causes the IIS pageable code to be written to disk, which results in lengthy processing delays. To avoid these processing delays, set Server properties to the **Maximize Throughput for Network Applications** option.

▶ **To change Server properties:**

1. Double-click the Network icon in Control Panel.

2. Click the **Services** tab.

3. Click **Server** to select it, and then click the **Properties** button.

4. Click **Maximize Throughput for Network Applications**, and then click **OK**.

5. Restart the computer.

- *Limit connections.* If your server is running out of memory, limiting the number of connections on the server might help because some physical memory (about 10 KB per connection) is consumed by the data structures the system uses to keep track of connections. To limit connections, right-click the service in Internet Service Manager, then click **Properties**; change the value in the **Limited To** box on the main tab for the service. By default, the FTP service is limited to 100,000 connections; the Web and SMTP services are not limited by default.

- *Eliminate unnecessary services.* Windows NT provides some services that are not required by IIS; all services use memory, so you can conserve memory by turning off those that your system is not using. See the sidebar "Windows NT Services and IIS" for details.

Windows NT Services and IIS

The list below outlines the Windows NT services you need to successfully run IIS. Note that the requirements below are for IIS itself. Your particular configuration, especially on an intranet, may have different requirements. For example, on some intranets you may require WINS and DHCP. Moreover, the fact that a particular service is not required says nothing about whether it is useful—you must determine that based on your configuration and particular needs.

Be cautious when disabling Windows NT services; services may exhibit complex interdependencies. The following listings are intended only as guidelines.

Required

- Event Log
- License Logging Service
- Windows NT LM Security Support Provider
- Remote Procedure Call (RPC) Service
- Windows NT Server (or Windows NT Workstation)
- IIS Admin Service
- MSDTC
- Protected Storage
- Server
- Workstation

May Be Required

- RPC Locator. Required for remote administration from this computer.
- Server Service. This can, if necessary, be turned off, but User Manager requires it, as do some other services.
- Telephony Service. Required if access is via dialup.

Typically Not Required

The three services listed here are not required unless the administrator wants to use the Find All Servers option in Internet Service Manager.

- NetBIOS Interface.
- NWLink NetBIOS.
- WINS Client (TCP/IP). May be required for intranet use, particularly if no DNS server is present.

Not Required

- Alerter.
- ClipBook Server.
- DHCP Client. Not required as long as all Network interfaces use a single IP address.
- Directory Replicator. This is, however, a common service to use on large multiserver Web installations, to synchronize content among the servers.
- Messenger.
- Net Logon. Recommended, but not required if no Windows NT domain or remote logons are needed.
- Network DDE & Network DDE DSDM.
- Network Monitor Agent.
- Plug & Play. Recommended, but not required.
- Simple TCP/IP Services.
- Spooler.
- TCP/IP NetBIOS Helper.
- Uninterruptible Power Supply (UPS).
- WINS Client (TCP/IP).
- Network Monitor Agent.
- NWLink IPX/SPX Compatible Transport (unless you lack TCP/IP or another transport).

Starting or Stopping Services

To start or stop a service, double-click the Services icon in Control Panel; select a service and click **Start** or **Stop**. To disable a service so that it does not start again when Windows NT is restarted, click **Startup** and select **Disabled** under **Startup Type**.

Preventing Processor Bottlenecks

Servers running IIS rely on the speed and efficiency of their processors. The IIS code is multithreaded for efficient scaling on single-processor and multiprocessor computers, and is largely self-tuning. Nonetheless, processor bottlenecks are a potential problem on very active servers.

A *processor bottleneck* occurs when one or more processes occupy nearly all of the processor time of all processors on the computer. In a bottleneck, the ready threads of processes must wait in a queue for processor time. All other activity comes to a halt until the queue is cleared. Processor bottlenecks can occur on multiprocessor computers even when only a single processor is fully loaded, if the work in the queue cannot be or is not distributed to the other processors. By definition, adding or improving other components of the computer, such as memory, disks, or network connections, does not overcome the performance problem, and can make it worse if those components increase processor loading.

This section discusses strategies for long-term monitoring of processor activity and processor queues; describes how IIS uses server processors, and how you can monitor and measure processor activity; and concludes with suggestions for preventing processor bottlenecks.

Monitoring Server Processors

The processors in a server running Internet Information Server must support the operating system and processes unrelated to Internet services, as well as IIS processes. The processors must also support applications related to Internet services, such as those that assemble data from SQL Server databases or generate dynamic Web pages.

You have a choice of several tools you can use to monitor processor performance. Task Manager, Microsoft Web Capacity Analysis Tool (WCAT, available on the IIS Resource Kit CD), PerfLog, and Performance Monitor are commonly used to monitor processors on Windows NT–based servers. Remember that all tools use system resources. Monitor the processor use of the process in which the tool runs. Then, before you analyze your data, subtract the processor time of the tool process from the data.

Using Performance Monitor to Monitor Processor Activity

You can use PerfLog to log data from the following counters automatically on a regular or periodic basis, or use Performance Monitor to log the System and Processor objects.

Table 4.4   Performance Monitor Counters for Processor Activity

Counter	Indicates
System: Processor Queue Length	Threads waiting for processor time. If this value exceeds 2 for a sustained period of time, the processor may be a bottlenecck.
System: % Total Processor Time	The sum of processor use on each processor divided by the number of processors.
Processor: % Processor Time	Processor use on each processor. This counter reveals unequal distribution of processor load.
Processor: % Privileged Time	Proportion of the processor's time spent in privileged mode. In Windows NT, only privileged mode code has direct access to hardware and to all memory in the system. The Windows NT Executive runs in privileged mode. Application threads can be switched to privileged mode to run operating system services.
Processor: % User Time	Proportion of the processor's time spent in user mode. User mode is the processor mode in which applications like the IIS services run.
Process: % Processor Time	The processor use attributable to each processor.

You can use the preceding Performance Monitor counters to monitor general processor performance.

Paging and Processor Bottlenecks

The most common cause of an apparent processor bottleneck is a memory bottleneck. If the system does not have enough physical memory to store the code and data programs needed, the processor spends substantial time paging. Before adding or upgrading processors or disks, you should monitor the memory in your server. For more information about monitoring memory, see "Monitoring Memory Usage," earlier in this chapter.

Analyzing Processor Activity Data

Of the counters listed, the System: Processor Queue Length counter is the most important for analyzing processor activity data. This counter displays the number of ready threads in the single queue shared by all processors. Sustained high rates of processor activity, which leave little excess capacity to handle peak loads, are often associated with processor bottlenecks. Processor activity in and of itself indicates only that the resource is used, not that maximum use of the resource is a problem. However, a long, sustained queue indicates that ready threads are being kept waiting because a processor cannot handle the load assigned to it.

A sustained processor queue length of two or more threads (as indicated by the System: Processor Queue Length Counter) typically indicates a processor bottleneck. You might consider setting a Performance Monitor alert to notify administrators when the processor queue length reaches an unacceptable value.

The Processor: % Processor Time counter is most often used as a general measure of processor activity on both single-processor and multiprocessor computers. System: % Total Processor Time is included for monitoring system-wide processor use on multiprocessor computers. On single-processor computers, System: % Total Processor Time always equals Processor: % Processor Time. On multiprocessor computers, System: % Total Processor Time represents the active time of all processors divided by the number of processors.

If the server workload is shared equally among all processors, System: % Total Processor time is an excellent measure of processor activity. However, this counter hides bottlenecks resulting from unequal processor loads. (If one processor is 100 percent busy and three other processors are idle, the % Total Processor Time is 25 percent.)

Windows NT is designed for efficient scaling and includes several strategies for balancing processor load. An application, however, can create an imbalance by setting a processor affinity, which binds a process to a single processor. For detailed processor monitoring, you need to chart Processor: % Processor Time for each processor on the computer.

It's not unusual to encounter the following challenges in analyzing processor data:

- A large processor queue when all processors are busy. Create a histogram of Process: % Processor Time for each process. The histogram shows the processor time consumed by each process.

- A single bar rises above all of the others. The process represented by the bar might be consuming a disproportionate share of processor time and causing a bottleneck. Consider replacing the application running in the process, or moving the process to another server.

- The processors are being shared equally by several processes. Consider upgrading or adding processors. Multithreaded processes benefit most from additional processors.

For more information on processor use by applications related to Internet Information Server, see "Monitoring Web Applications," later in this chapter.

Monitoring Connections

It is important to determine how your server responds when it is managing different numbers of connections. When you have collected data on connection trends, you can associate data about general server performance with the number of connections being served.

This section discusses why connections have performance overhead, how you can use Performance Monitor and other tools to measure the overhead, and how to interpret the data you gather.

The Performance Overhead of Connections

Each connection that an IIS service establishes consumes some processor time. The network adapter card interrupts the processor to signal that a client has requested a connection. Further processing is required to establish and maintain the connection, to fulfill client requests sent on the connection and, when the connection is closed, processing is required to delete the structures that serviced the connection. Each time a connection is established, the load on the server increases.

One aspect of connection overhead is the time it takes to search the Transmission Control Block (TCB) table. TCP creates and maintains transmission control blocks (TCBs) to store data about connections. This might include data about the precedence of the connection and its local and remote socket numbers. The TCBs are stored in a hash table for efficient control. The hash table is stored in the operating system's nonpaged memory pool.

IIS includes several features to optimize its handling of connections. Among these features are HTTP Keep-Alives.

HTTP Keep-Alives maintain a connection even after the connection's initial request is complete. This feature keeps the connection active and available for subsequent requests. Keep-Alives are implemented to avoid the substantial cost of establishing and terminating connections. Both the client and the server must support Keep-Alives. Keep-Alives are supported by IIS version 1.0 and later, Internet Explorer version 2.0 and later, and Netscape Navigator version 2.0 and later.

HTTP Keep-Alives are different from and independent of TCP/IP Keep-Alives. TCP/IP Keep-Alives are messages sent to determine whether an idle connection is still active.

HTTP Keep-Alives are enabled in IIS by default. Although Keep-Alives significantly improve bandwidth performance on most servers, you can modify or eliminate them if they are not needed. You can also measure their effect on the performance of your system. To test their effect on the server, you can disable them, but it is recommended that you re-enable them when the test is concluded, to maintain the performance of the server.

In the Internet Service Manager, you can disable Keep-Alives by right-clicking a site, clicking **Properties**, selecting the **Performance** tab, and clearing the **HTTP Keep-Alives Enabled** check box.

Using IIS Logging to Monitor Connections

You can use IIS logging to monitor the number of connections your server makes and to track patterns of client demand for your server. For more information about configuring and interpreting IIS logs, see the IIS online documentation.

Using Performance Monitor to Monitor Connections

Performance Monitor can monitor the number of simultaneous connections to the IIS services and the processor use of the process in which the IIS services run. The following table lists the Performance Monitor counters that monitor connections to IIS.

Table 4.5   Performance Monitor Counters for IIS Service Connections

Counter	Indicates
Web Service: Current Connections FTP Service: Current Connections	The number of connections maintained by the service during the most recent sample interval.
Web Service: Maximum Connections FTP Service: Maximum Connections	The largest number of connections maintained simultaneously since the server was started.

Because these counters display the last value they observe, and not an average, you must log these values over time to collect reliable data.

Also, these counters are likely to exaggerate the number of simultaneous connections because some some entries might not yet be deleted even though the connection is closed.

Note The Active Server Pages, Web Service, FTP Service, and SMTP Server counters collect data at the Open Systems Interconnectivity (OSI) Application Layer. Counts of TCP/IP connections might not equal HTTP, FTP, and SMTP connections if any connections were blocked, rejected, or reset between the Transport and Application layers. For details on monitoring connections at lower layers, see the section on "Monitoring Bandwidth and Network Capacity," later in this chapter.

Analyzing Connection Data

By monitoring numbers of connections you can identify patterns of client demand for your server. Classify the data in your Performance Monitor logs into intervals by the numbers of connections served during the interval. Observe the length of the processor queue and the processor use on each processor during periods of small, moderate, and large numbers of connections. This data shows how your configuration responds to each load level.

You can identify a processor bottleneck at each interval by:

- A long, sustained processor queue (more than two threads).

- High use rates on one or more processors.

- A curve in the graph of the Current Connections counter on any IIS service performance object that reaches a high value and then forms a plateau. This pattern often indicates that additional connections are being blocked or rejected.

To prevent processor bottlenecks, make certain that a lengthy processor queue isn't forming when you serve large numbers of connections. Typically, you can avoid a bottleneck during peak time by setting the connection limit to twice the average value of Current Connections. If the processor regularly becomes a bottleneck when servicing large numbers of connections, you might consider upgrading or adding processors, or limiting the maximum number of connections on the server. Limiting connections might cause the server to block or reject connections, but it helps to ensure that accepted connections are processed promptly.

Adminstrators can use Internet Service Manager to limit the number of connections for Web and FTP, and SMTP services. Right-click the service, click **Properties**, and then change the **Limited To** value on the site or service tab.

Monitoring Threads

IIS runs in a multithreaded process designed for efficient scaling on single-processor and multiprocessor systems. *Threads* are the sequences of execution in each process that run the process code on the processor.

In the IIS process, there is no simple association between threads and connections or threads and requests. Nor is there an easily quantifiable relationship between the optimum number of threads in the process and the number of files served, the number of requests filled, or the number of connections maintained.

The relationship between threads, connections, and requests is complex because IIS uses the *worker thread* model, rather than the simpler, but less efficient, *thread-per-client* model. Instead of dedicating a thread to each connection or request, IIS dedicates one set of threads, the *worker threads*, to the task of accepting and monitoring all connections. This frees other threads to do the remaining work of the application, such as authenticating users; parsing client requests; locating, opening, and transmitting files; and managing internal data structures.

Even though you cannot associate individual threads and connections or requests, you can:

- Count the number of threads in the IIS process.
- Measure the amount of processor time each thread gets.
- Associate the number of threads (and processor activity) with the number of current connections, number of files served, and other measures of server activity and performance.

Several tools monitor the threads in a process, including Process Viewer, Process Explode, PerfLog, and Performance Monitor. Individual threads are difficult to monitor, especially if they frequently start and stop. Threads are also costly to measure. Be sure to monitor the overhead (by using Process: % Processor Time) of the process in which your tool runs, and subtract it from the data you collect.

Using Performance Monitor to Monitor IIS Threads

You can use Performance Monitor to monitor the threads in the IIS process. The following table lists the Performance Monitor counters that monitor threads. You can add to this list any counters you use to associate numbers of threads with performance, such as Web Service: Current Connections, Web Service: Bytes/sec, or Server: Logon/sec.

Table 4.6   Performance Monitor Counters for Monitoring IIS Threads

Counter	Indicates
Process: Thread Count: Inetinfo	The number of threads created by the process. This counter does not indicate which threads are busy and which are idle.
	This counter displays the last observed value, not an average.
Thread: % Processor Time: Inetinfo => *Thread #*	How much processor time each thread of the Inetinfo process is using.
Thread: Context Switches/sec: Inetinfo => *Thread #*	How many times the threads of the IIS service are switched onto and off of a processor. This counter is an indicator of the activity of the threads of the IIS service process.

Analyzing the IIS Thread Data

You can chart the Process: Thread Count: Inetinfo value over time to see how many threads the Inetinfo process creates and how the numbers of threads vary. Then, observe the processor time for each thread in the process (Thread: % Processor Time: Inetinfo => *Thread #*) during periods of high, medium, and low server activity (as indicated by the other performance measures).

You should also observe the patterns of *context switches* over time. Context switches indicate that the kernel has switched the processor from one thread to another. A context switch occurs each time a new thread runs, and each time one thread takes over from another. A large number of threads is likely to increase the number of context switches. Context switches allow multiple threads to share the processor, but they also interrupt the processor and might interfere with processor performance, especially on multiprocessor computers. As long as processor utilization is under 70 percent, however, this is not an issue.

Optimizing Thread Values

By default, the IIS process creates up to 10 threads per processor. IIS continually adjusts the number of threads in its process in response to server activity. For most systems, this tuning is sufficient to maintain the optimum number of threads, but you can change the maximum number of threads per processor, if your system requires it.

If the threads in the IIS process appear to be overworked or underutilized, consider these tuning strategies:

- If nearly all of the threads of the IIS process are busy nearly all of the time, and the processors are at or near their maximum capacity, consider distributing the workload among more servers.

  You can also add processors, but do so cautiously. Unnecessary or underused processors will degrade performance, not improve it.

- If nearly all threads appear busy, but the processors are not always active, consider increasing the maximum number of threads per processor. Do not increase the maximum number of threads unless you have processors with excess capacity. More threads on the same number of processors cause more interrupts and context switches, and result in less processor time per thread.

To adjust the maximum number of threads in the IIS service process, use a registry editor to add the **MaxPoolThreads** value entry to the registry. **MaxPoolThreads** does not appear in the registry unless it is added. It must be added to the following:

HKEY_LOCAL_MACHINE\System
    \CurrentControlSet
        \Services
            \Inetinfo
                \Parameters

MaxPoolThreads is calculated in units of threads-per-processor. If this value entry does not appear in the registry, Internet Information Server allocates a maximum of 10 threads per processor. Do not set this value below 5 or above 20.

Continue monitoring the system carefully to make sure that changing the number of threads achieves the desired effect.

Monitoring Interrupts and DPCs

One of the processor's tasks is to service interrupts and *deferred procedure calls* (DPCs) from all of the computer's subsystems. On a busy server running IIS, much of the processor's time can be spent servicing interrupts and DPCs, especially from the disk subsystem and the network adapter cards.

This section describes some methods of measuring how much time your server's processors are spending handling interrupts and DPCs from the network adapter cards. It discusses how network card interrupts and DPCs are distributed among processors in multiprocessor computers, and suggests some methods of tuning DPC distribution to improve processor performance.

Describing Interrupts and DPCs

Interrupts are very high-priority signals that halt the processor's activity and prepare the processor for a new activity, if only very briefly. Interrupts consume processor time and disrupt the processor's work, but they are essential to a preemptive multitasking system.

Client connections involve many interrupts. The network adapter card generates an interrupt when it receives a new packet or completes a transmission. The system collects some very basic information and then adds one or more DPCs to the queue to handle the next steps in the process.

DPCs are similar to interrupts except that they have a lower Interrupt Request Level (IRQL). (IRQL is the priority scale used for objects like interrupts. It is different from the priority scale that the microkernel uses to schedule processes and threads.) Unlike interrupts, DPCs can be delayed, allowing the processor to complete higher-priority work. When the DPC gets processor time, the work of establishing the connection can proceed.

Interrupts and Processor Performance

Commonly used server processors, such as the Intel Pentium and Pentium Pro, and RISC processors, can handle thousands of interrupts and DPCs without being consumed by the task. An active server running IIS at high bandwidth, however, can interrupt the processor often enough to impede performance.

To help improve processor performance, some newer network card drivers provide an advanced feature known as *interrupt moderation*. When the driver detects a high rate of interrupts from the network adapter card, the interrupt moderation code disables interrupts and accumulates the interrupts in a buffer instead of sending them to the processor. When the processor has completed its work, the interrupts are re-enabled.

Monitoring interrupts and DPCs is an important part of monitoring processor performance (and network adapter card performance) on a server running IIS. On a single-processor system, a very high level of interrupts can indicate a problem with the network card or disk adapter, as well as an overworked processor. On a multiprocessor system, data about interrupts and DPCs might also reveal a poor distribution of workload among processors.

Using Performance Monitor to Monitor Interrupts and DPCs

You can use Performance Monitor to monitor the interrupts and DPCs in the IIS process. The following table lists the Performance Monitor counters that monitor interrupts and DPCs.

When monitoring, chart these counters along with standard measures of processor time, such as System: Processor Queue Length and Process: % Processor Time: Inetinfo. If you are monitoring a multiprocessor computer, be sure to include Processor: % Processor Time. This counter displays the processor use of each processor over time. You might also include Processor: % Privileged Time because interrupts and DPCs are processed in privileged mode.

Table 4.7   Performance Monitor Counters for Interrupt and DPC Monitoring

Counter	Indicates
Processor: % Interrupt Time	How much time the processor is spending processing interrupts. Interrupts are generated when a client requests a connection or sends data.
	If processor time is more than 90 percent and this value is greater than 15 percent, the processor is probably overburdened with interrupts.
Processor: Interrupts/sec	The rate at which the processor is handling interrupts.
Processor: % DPC Time	How much time the processor is spending processing deferred procedure calls (DPCs). DPCs originate when the processor performs tasks requiring immediate attention, and then defers the remainder of the task to be handled at lower priority. DPCs represent further processing of client requests.
Processor: DPCs queued/sec	The rate at which DPCs are added to the processor's queue. (This counter does not measure the number of DPCs in the queue.)
Pentium: Interrupts/sec (Pentium, but not Pentium Pro, processors)	Only INTR and NMI hardware interrupts are counted.
Pentium: Hardware interrupts received/sec (Pentium Pro processors only)	The rate at which hardware interrupts are detected by the processor's internal counters.

Note The Pentium performance object includes counters that display data on interrupts and DPCs. Pentium counters are extensible Performance Monitor counters designed to monitor Pentium processors. The counters are included on the *Windows NT Workstation Resource Kit* CD in the Performance Tools group. You must install the Pentium counters before you can use them. For detailed instructions, see P5Perf.txt on the *Windows NT Workstation Resource Kit* CD.

Analyzing Data on Interrupts and DPCs

When you have collected data on interrupts and DPCs that is representative of the general activity on your server, you can use the guidelines in this section to help you interpret the data.

Analyzing Interrupt and DPC Rates

You can observe the rates of interrupts and DPCs during periods of high, medium, and low server activity. Note the rate of interrupts and DPCs when processor use is very high, especially when a processor queue is developing.

A very high rate of interrupts can indicate a problem with a component that generates interrupts, such as the disk subsystem or a network adapter card. Test your components and rule out a hardware problem before proceeding.

Analyzing Processor Time

You should observe the proportion of the processor's time that is spent servicing interrupts and DPCs. Compare the values of the Processor: % Interrupt Time and Processor: % DPC Time counters to Processor: % Processor Time.

If a busy processor is spending the majority of its time servicing interrupts and DPCs, the processor probably cannot function effectively and a processor bottleneck is likely to develop. Consider upgrading or adding processors to handle the workload.

Alternatively, if the processor has some excess capacity (that is, if the value of Processor: % Processor Time is less than 85), or if it is spending a relatively small amount of its time servicing interrupts and DPCs (if the value of Processor: % Interrupt Time and Processor: % DPC Time are less than 20), you probably do not have a problem with interrupts and DPCs.

Analyzing the Distribution of Interrupts and DPCs on Multiprocessor Computers

The most common interrupt-related problem on multiprocessor computers is not the rate of interrupts and DPCs, but their distribution among processors. To determine whether you have a distribution problem:

- Observe the proportion of time each processor is spending servicing interrupts and DPCs.

- Observe the rate of interrupts and DPCs for each processor.

- Note whether interrupts and DPCs are distributed equally among all processors or whether one or more processors are servicing all of the interrupts or DPCs.

A busy processor that is servicing all of the system's interrupts or DPCs is likely to become a bottleneck. The source of the problem is not the number of interrupts or DPCs but the way that interrupts and DPCs are distributed among the processors.

The following sections describe common strategies for distributing interrupts and DPCs on Windows NT–based servers.

Interrupt Distribution

Different processor platforms use different methods to distribute interrupts. The distribution of interrupts from network adapter cards is controlled by the Hardware Abstraction Layer (HAL) for each processor platform. The interrupt scheme implemented by the HAL depends on the capability of the processor. Some processors include interrupt control hardware, such as the Advanced Programmable Interrupt Controller (APIC) on some Pentium and Pentium Pro processors. The APIC allows processors to route interrupts to other processors on the computer.

You cannot control or modify the distribution of network card interrupts on your computer. The information in this section is included to help you interpret the interrupt data you collect and, in particular, to explain one of the reasons why one processor can be busier than the others. Monitoring the processor that services the majority of interrupts can help you anticipate or prevent a bottleneck.

There are many different strategies for distributing interrupts on multiprocessor computers. Common strategies are:

- *No distribution.* The traditional method for managing interrupts is to send all interrupts from all network cards to a single processor, usually the first (lowest-numbered) processor. If your data shows that all interrupts are being serviced by a single processor, your system may be using this method.

- *Static distribution.* Some systems distribute network card interrupts among processors statically, that is, the distribution doesn't change. These systems associate each network adapter card with a processor. The interrupts generated by the network card are always sent to the network card's associated processor, regardless of whether the processor is busy or idle.

  Typically, these systems associate the first (lowest-numbered) network card with the first (lowest-numbered) processor and each subsequent network card with each subsequent processor. If there are more network cards than processors, the system begins its assignments again with the first processor.

  If your data shows that interrupts are distributed rather evenly among processors, your system could be one that provides static distribution. If one of the network cards is idle or not used, static distribution results in unequal distribution of interrupts.

- *Dynamic distribution.* Some systems distribute interrupts to processors dynamically based on one or more elements of system data, such as processor activity. The interrupts generated by a network card can be sent to any one of the processors.

  If your data shows that interrupts are almost always distributed evenly, you probably have a system that provides dynamic distribution.

Distribution of interrupts to all processors, whether static or dynamic, is commonly known as *symmetric interrupt distribution*. Symmetric interrupt distribution is designed to improve scaling and to prevent a single processor from becoming a bottleneck while other processors have excess capacity. It is available on the Microsoft Windows NT 4.0 HAL for Pentium and Pentium Pro processors. For specific information on the distribution method used for your processor platform, consult your system vendor.

Strategies for producing the most efficient interrupt distribution systems are evolving. You cannot change the interrupt distribution scheme on your computer, but you can coordinate the distribution of DPCs with the distribution of interrupts.

DPC Distribution

The distribution of DPCs generated by network cards is a function of Ndis.sys, the Windows NT implementation of the Network Driver Interface Specification (NDIS). Ndis.sys is a wrapper that shields the details of the network adapter card from the rest of the operating system. Ndis.sys controls DPC distribution on all network cards that use miniport drivers, which includes nearly all varieties of network cards.

Ndis.sys attempts to balance the processor workload generated by interrupts. By default, Ndis.sys associates each network card with a processor and directs all DPCs from a network card to the processor associated with that network card. Ndis.sys attempts to compensate for the burden placed on the lowest-numbered processor by associating the first network card with the highest-numbered processor. Each subsequent network card is associated with the next processor in descending order of processor number.

On many systems, this strategy balances the load. If a server that does not distribute interrupts has two processors and one network card, Processor 0 services the interrupts and Processor 1 services the DPCs.

Unfortunately, this distribution strategy doesn't always work as planned:

- DPCs evolve from interrupts. When a DPC is generated from an interrupt, the DPC must be switched to another processor. The switch requires an interprocessor interrupt from the sending processor to the receiving processor. These very high-priority interprocessor interrupts consume additional processor time.

- Information gathered when the interrupt is processed is stored in the processor cache. When the DPC generated from the interrupt is switched to another processor, the data in the cache of the sending processor is flushed and must be collected again by the receiving processor.

- On many platforms, interrupts are distributed among all processors. Leaving the DPC on the processor that handled the interrupt reduces the number of interprocessor interrupts and allows the DPC to use data stored in the processor cache when the interrupt was serviced.

Fortunately, if DPC distribution is a problem in your system, you can improve system performance by optimizing DPC distribution.

Optimizing DPC Distribution

The solutions to poor DPC distribution differ depending on whether the system distributes interrupts symmetrically:

- *No distribution.* If you are administering a multiprocessor server that does not distribute interrupts symmetrically, monitor the highest-numbered processor carefully. If the processor frequently operates at capacity (that is, if Processor: % Processor Time = 100) and more than half of its time is spent servicing DPCs (if Processor: % DPC Time > 50), you can improve the performance of your system by one or more of the following methods:

  - Upgrading to a system that distributes interrupts.

  - Adding network adapter cards so that you have one network adapter card for each processor. Ndis.sys then distributes DPCs to all processors. Generally, you should only add a network adapter card if you also need the bandwidth because each additional network card has some intrinsic overhead.

- *Symmetric distribution.* If you are administering a multiprocessor server that distributes interrupts to all processors, whether statically or dynamically, you can improve performance by setting the value of the **ProcessorAffinityMask** entry in the registry to zero. If the value of **ProcessorAffinityMask** is zero, network cards are not associated with processors, and DPCs remain on the processor that handled the interrupt. **ProcessorAffinityMask** is located in:

HKEY_LOCAL_MACHINE\System
    \CurrentControlSet
       \Services
          \NDIS
             \Parameters

Suggestions for Improving Processor Performance

The IIS services run in a multithreaded process designed to operate efficiently on single-processor and multiprocessor computers. An Intel 486, Intel Pentium or Pentium Pro, or RISC processor should be sufficient to handle more than a thousand simultaneous connections. Servers with more activity benefit from multiple processors.

If your data on processor performance indicates that processor queues are developing regularly or while servicing large numbers of connections, monitor the memory of your server. Rule out a memory bottleneck or add more memory before (or in addition to) adding or upgrading processors.

In addition, consider the following suggestions for improving processor performance:

- *Redistribute the workload.* If nearly all of the threads of the IIS process are busy nearly all of the time, and the processors are at or near their maximum capacity, consider distributing the workload among more servers, or redistributing tasks among servers. You can also add processors, but do so cautiously. Unnecessary or underused processors will degrade performance, not improve it.

- *Add processors.* If the workload is distributed evenly, and all threads in the IIS process continue to be busy nearly all of the time, or if a processor queue forms when the number of connections rises, add or upgrade processors. You can avoid a processor bottleneck during peak use by calculating the processor use on your system when the number of current connections is at its average, and allowing enough processing power to handle twice the average number of connections. If it is important to maintain service through spikes of intense activity, you should consider allowing even more processing power, perhaps enough to handle ten times the average number of connections.

- *Upgrade the L2 cache.* When adding or upgrading processors, choose processors with a large secondary (L2) cache. File server applications, such as Internet Information Server, benefit from a large processor cache because their instruction paths involve many different components. A large processor cache (2 MB or more if external, up to 1 MB if on-chip) is recommended to improve performance on active servers running IIS.

- *Improve DPC handling*. Platforms that distribute interrupts to all processors do not benefit from the Windows NT default DPC affinity. If you are administering a multiprocessor computer that distributes interrupts symmetrically, such as an Intel Pentium or Pentium Pro (P6) system for Windows NT 4.0, set the value of **ProcessorAffinityMask** entry in the registry to zero. DPCs will be handled by the same processor that handled the interrupt from which the DPC evolved.

- *Add network adapter cards*. If you are administering a multiprocessor system that does *not* distribute interrupts symmetrically, you can improve the distribution of the processor workload by adding network cards so that there is one network card for every processor. Generally, you only add network cards when you need to improve the throughput of your system. Network cards, like any additional hardware, have some intrinsic overhead. However, if one of the processors is nearly always active (that is, if Processor: % Processor Time = 100) and more than half of its time is spent servicing DPCs (if Processor: % DPC Time > 50), then adding a network card is likely to improve system performance, as long as the available network bandwidth is not already saturated.

- *Upgrade Network Adapter Cards*. If you are adding or upgrading network adapter cards, choose cards with drivers that support interrupt moderation. Interrupt moderation prevents the processor from being overwhelmed by bursts of interrupts. Consult the driver manufacturer for details.

- *Limit Connections*. If you cannot upgrade or add processors, consider reducing the maximum number of connections that each IIS service accepts. Limiting connections can result in connections being blocked or rejected, but it helps ensure that accepted connections are processed promptly.

  To limit the number of connections for a service, right-click the service in Internet Service Manager, click **Properties**, and then change the **Limited To** value on the site or service tab. Reduce the number of allowed connections until the server can handle twice the average number of connections without developing a long processor queue.

- *Redesign the Web Site*. You can improve performance and reduce the processor workload by optimizing database use, optimizing ASP script design, calling compiled components from ASP scripts, using ISAPI instead of ASP (and ASP or ISAPI instead of CGI), substituting static Web pages for dynamic pages, eliminating the use of SSL except where it is necessary, moving trusted out-of-process applications into the Inetinfo process, and eliminating large bitmapped images or optimizing them to reduce their size. (For more information on optimizing ASP scripts, see Appendix B, "ASP Standards.")

- *Adjust the Maximum ASP Queue Length.* If the ASP queue grows too long, processing time for ASP requests may be unacceptably long. If the maximum queue length is too short, on the other hand, the server returns "too busy" errors. For more information on setting this parameter, see the section "Tuning Your Web Server's ASP Queue and Thread Pool," later in this chapter.

- *Adjust the Maximum Number of Threads.* IIS tunes the number of threads in its process dynamically. The dynamic values are usually optimal. In extreme cases of very active or underused processors, however, it may help to adjust the maximum number of threads in the Inetinfo process. If you change the maximum number of threads, continue careful testing to make sure that the change has improved performance. The difference is usually quite subtle. For more information, see the section "Tuning Your Web Server's ASP Queue and Thread Pool," later in this chapter.

Monitoring Bandwidth and Network Capacity

The primary functions of IIS are to establish connections for its clients, to receive and interpret requests, and to deliver files—all as quickly as possible. The pace at which these vital functions are performed depends, in large part, on two factors: the effective bandwidth of the link between the server and the network, and on the capacity of this link and the server to support network resources.

This section examines bandwidth and network capacity on a server running IIS and suggests methods you can use to measure and improve transmission rates and connection handling on your server. It is not intended as a comprehensive guide to network monitoring. Instead, it is a limited presentation of the network-related issues that are important on servers running IIS.

Defining Bandwidth and Network Capacity

Bandwidth refers to the rate at which data is transmitted and received over a communication link between a computer and the network. Bandwidth is measured in several different ways:

- The rate at which bytes are transferred to and from the server.

- The rate at which data packages are sent by the server. Data packages include frames, packets, segments, and datagrams.

- The rate at which files are sent and received by the server.

Effective bandwidth varies widely depending upon the transmission capacity of the link, the server configuration, and the server workload. The values for a single server also change as it operates, in response to demand and to competition for shared network resources.

Network capacity is a broader term that refers to the ability of the server and the communication link to carry network traffic and support multiple resources. Network capacity is measured, in part, by the number of connections established and maintained by the server.

The following sections describe in more detail the methods you can use to measure bandwidth and network capacity on your server.

Monitoring Transmission Rates

The simplest measure of the effective bandwidth of a server is the rate at which the server sends and receives data. Performance Monitor displays counts of data transmissions that are collected by many components of the server computer. The components that collect data each reside in different Open Systems Interconnectivity (OSI) layers:

- Counters on the Web, FTP, and SMTP server performance objects measure data transmitted at the OSI Application Layer.
- Counters on the TCP object measure data transmitted at the Transport Layer. (TCP stands for Transmission Control Protocol.)
- Counters on the IP object measure data at the Network Layer. (IP stands for Internet Protocol.)
- Counters on the Network Interface object measure data at the Data Link Layer.

As a result of their different positions in the OSI stack, the counters display different data. For example, the counters at the Application Layer count the bytes sent before the data is divided into packets and prefixed with protocol headers and control packets. Counters at the Application Layer measure data in this way because the data is in this form when the application sends it. Counts at the Application Layer also do not include retransmitted data.

In addition, the counters display the data in units native to the component measured. For example, the Web Service object displays data in bytes, and the TCP object displays data in segments.

The next section lists and describes the Performance Monitor counters you can use to measure data sent and received by your server. The following section also offers help in interpreting the data you collect.

Using Performance Monitor to Monitor Transmission Rates

The following tables list and describe some of the Performance Monitor counters that can be used for measuring transmission rates. The counters in this table display the transmission rate observed during the last sample interval. They do not display a rolling or cumulative average of the rate. Also, the counters that represent sums of other counters, such as IP: Datagrams/sec, are simple sums of the other counters' values. They are not weighted sums.

For more information about how counter values are calculated, check the counter type. A counter type determines how Performance Monitor calculates and displays that particular counter.

Note   You must install Simple Network Management Protocol (SNMP) to activate the counters on the TCP, IP, and Network Interface performance objects in Performance Monitor. To install SNMP, double-click the Network icon in Control Panel, select the **Services** tab, and click **Add**.

The following table lists and describes counters at the Application Layer.

Table 4.8   Performance Monitor Counters for Measuring Transmission Rates at the Application Layer

Counter	Indicates
Web Service: Bytes Sent/sec	The rate at which the HTTP server application is sending data, in bytes.
Web Service: Bytes Received/sec	The rate at which the HTTP server application is receiving data, in bytes.
Web Service: Bytes Total/sec	The rate at which the HTTP server application is sending and receiving data, in bytes; the sum of Web Service: Bytes Sent/sec and Web Service: Bytes Received/sec.
FTP Service: Bytes Sent/sec	The rate at which the FTP server application is sending data, in bytes.
FTP Service: Bytes Received/sec	The rate at which the FTP server application is receiving data, in bytes.
FTP Service: Bytes Total/sec	The rate at which the FTP server application is sending and receiving data, in bytes; the sum of FTP Service: Bytes Sent/sec and FTP Service: Bytes Received/sec.
SMTP Server: Bytes Sent/sec	The rate at which the SMTP server application is sending data, in bytes.
SMTP Server: Bytes Received/sec	The rate at which the SMTP server application is receiving data, in bytes.
SMTP Server: Bytes Total/sec	The rate at which the SMTP server application is sending and receiving data, in bytes; the sum of SMTP Server: Bytes Sent/sec and SMTP Server: Bytes Received/sec.

The following table lists and describes counters on the TCP object.

Table 4.9   Performance Monitor Counters for Measuring Transmission Rates at the Transport Layer

Counter	Indicates
TCP: Segments Sent/sec	The rate at which TCP segments are sent by using the TCP protocol.
TCP: Segments Received/sec	The rate at which TCP segments are received by using the TCP protocol.
TCP: Segments/sec	The sum of Segments Sent/sec and Segments Received/sec.
TCP: Segments Retransmitted/sec	The rate at which segments are transmitted that contain one or more bytes TCP recognizes as having been transmitted before.

Segments Retransmitted/sec is a proper subset of Segments Sent/sec and Segments/sec. To determine the proportion of transmissions caused by failed transmission attempts, divide Segments Retransmitted/sec by Segments Sent/sec.

The following table lists and describes counters on the IP object.

Table 4.10   Performance Monitor Counters for Measuring Transmission Rates at the Network Layer

Counter	Indicates
IP: Datagrams Sent/sec	The rate at which IP datagrams are sent by using the IP protocol. This counter does not include datagrams forwarded to another server.
IP: Datagrams Received/sec	The rate at which IP datagrams are received from IP by using IP protocol. This counter does not include datagrams forwarded to another server.
IP: Datagrams/sec	The sum of IP: Datagrams Sent/sec and IP: Datagrams Received/sec.
IP: Datagrams Forwarded/sec	The rate at which IP datagrams are forwarded to their final destination by the server.

The sum of IP: Datagrams/sec and IP: Datagrams Forwarded/sec represents the rate at which all IP datagrams are handled by the server.

The following table lists and describes counters on the Network Interface performance object.

Table 4.11   Performance Monitor Counters for Measuring Transmission Rates at the Data Link Layer

Counter	Indicates
Network Interface: Bytes Sent/sec: NIC#	The rate at which bytes are sent over each network adapter (that is, over each network interface card, or NIC). The counted bytes include framing characters.
Network Interface: Bytes Received/sec: NIC#	The rate at which bytes are received over each network adapter. The counted bytes include framing characters.
Network Interface: Bytes Total/sec: NIC#	The sum of Network Interface: Bytes Sent/Sec and Network Interface: Bytes Received/sec.

The Network Interface counters display data about the network adapters on the server computer. The first instance of the Network Interface object (Instance 1) that you see in Performance Monitor represents the loopback. The *loopback* is a local path through the protocol driver and the network adapter. All other instances represent installed network adapters.

Analyzing Transmission Rate Data

The data provided by these counters is collected by different methods, is displayed in different units, and represents the view of different system objects. Some guidelines for interpreting the data follow:

- The IIS service counters display the number of bytes transmitted on behalf of each service that server provides. To calculate the total number of bytes sent or received by all IIS services, sum the values for each service. You can determine the proportion of bytes transmitted by each service by computing the ratio of bytes for one service to the sum of bytes for all services, or for the network.

- Data collected by the IIS service counters underestimates the total number of bytes actually being transmitted to the network by the IIS services. These values are collected at the Application Layer, so they measure data only. They do not measure protocol headers, control packets, or retransmitted bytes.

  In general, the bytes counted by the services represent approximately 60 to 70 percent of the total number of bytes transmitted by the services on the network. If the sum of bytes for all services accounts for two-thirds or more of total network bandwidth, you can assume your network is running at or near the total capacity of its communications link.

- Counters on the TCP and IP performance objects display the rate at which data is sent and received on a Transmission Control Protocol/Internet Protocol (TCP/IP) connection at the Transport and Network layers, but they do not count in bytes. Counters on the IP performance object display data in datagrams, and counters on the TCP performance object display data in segments. It is difficult to convert segments to bytes because the bytes per segment can vary from 8 KB to 64 KB; the number of bytes per segment depends upon the size of the TCP/IP receive window and the maximum segment size negotiated when each connection is established.

- Counters on the Network Interface performance object display the rate at which bytes are transmitted over a TCP/IP connection by monitoring the counters on the network adapter at the Data Link Layer. The values of these Network Interface counters include all prepended frame header bytes and bytes retransmitted. These values provide a relatively accurate estimate of the numbers of bytes transmitted over the network, but they do not measure the bytes transmitted to a specific IIS service.

Despite the difficulty of comparing these counters to each other, they can all be related to other performance measures, such as the total number of connections served at a given bandwidth, or processor use at different throughput rates.

Monitoring File Transfers

Each successful request to IIS results in the transfer of at least one file. Most static Web pages include multiple files, such as a file of text and one or more files of graphics.

Performance Monitor includes counters for each IIS service. These counters display the number of files sent and received by the Web Service and the FTP server. The SMTP server is slightly more complex; its counters indicate messages sent and messages delivered, as well as messages received.

The file counters are listed and described in the following table.

Table 4.12   Performance Monitor Counters for IIS File Transfers

Counter	Indicates
Web Service: Files Sent FTP Service: Files Sent SMTP Server: Messages Sent Total	The number of files or messages sent by the service since the service was started.
Web Service: Files Received FTP Service: Files Received SMTP Server: Messages Received Total	The number of files or messages received by the service since the service was started.
Web Service: Files Total FTP Service: Files Total	The number of files sent and received by the service since the service was started. Files Total is the unweighted sum of Files Sent and Files Received. The SMTP service lacks this counter.

The file counters for a particular service can be used as indicators of the network activity of that service. They can also be associated with other performance measures to determine the effect of high and low rates of file activity on server components.

Note, however, that the file counters for an IIS service display cumulative totals on all traffic since the service was started, regardless of when Performance Monitor was started. The counters do not display current values or the rate at which files are transmitted.

To calculate file transmission rates, you can use Performance Data Log Service (PerfLog) to log the file counters. PerfLog automatically logs the time at which measurement is taken. After you have generated a PerfLog log, you can use the PerfLog output files as input to a spreadsheet that associates the time of the measurement and the file count to derive the transmission rates.

Monitoring TCP Connections

If the bandwidth of your server is insufficient to handle its workload, it is likely that clients will be aware of it before the server is. Client requests to the server will be rejected or will time out, or response will be delayed. On the server side, the indicators are less clear. The server will continue to establish connections, receive requests, and transmit data.

Bandwidth shortages are not uncommon. You can detect a bandwidth shortage on your server (perhaps even before clients do) by monitoring the success and failure of connections established and rejected by TCP. When the bandwidth is ample, the server can establish and serve connections before they time out. If bandwidth is not sufficient, the connections fail.

The following section describes the Performance Monitor counters recommended for monitoring the success and failure of connections on your server.

Using Performance Monitor to Monitor TCP Connections

The counters on the TCP object are the best indicators of the success of connection requests.

The counters on the Web Service and FTP Service performance objects monitor connections maintained by each IIS service. The counters on these objects display only successful connection requests. They do not display failed attempts to connect to these IIS services. Like all counters at the Application Layer, they do not have information about connections until the connections are established. Performance Monitor counters that display the number of simultaneous connections maintained by IIS are discussed in the section "Preventing Processor Bottlenecks," earlier in this chapter.

The following table lists and describes the Performance Monitor counters that monitor the success and failure of connections to TCP.

Table 4.13   Performance Monitor Counters for Monitoring TCP Connection Successes and Failures

Counter	Indicates
TCP: Connections Established	The number of simultaneous connections supported by TCP (at last observation). This counter displays the number of connections last observed to be in the ESTABLISHED or CLOSE-WAIT state. It displays the last observed value only; its value is not an average.
TCP: Connection Failures	The number of connections that have failed since the service was started (regardless of when Performance Monitor was started). TCP counts a connection as having failed when it goes directly from sending (SYNC-SENT) or receiving (SYNC-RCVD) to CLOSED or from receiving (SYNC-RCVD) to listening (LISTEN).
TCP: Connections Reset	The number of connections reset since the service was started (regardless of when Performance Monitor was started).
	TCP counts a connection as having been reset when it goes directly from ESTABLISHED or CLOSE-WAIT to CLOSED.

Analyzing TCP Connection Data

At the TCP level, you should monitor the TCP: Connections Established counter regularly. You might notice a pattern in which the counter value often reaches, but rarely exceeds, a maximum (that is, the graphed line rises and then reaches a plateau). If so, the peak value is likely to indicate the maximum number of connections that can be established with the current bandwidth and application workload. If you observe such a pattern, the server probably cannot support any greater demand.

Failure to support current or increasing demand also might be evident from the number of connection failures and resets. The counters that monitor failures and resets show cumulative values, but you can set Performance Monitor alerts on the values or use PerfLog to log values over time. You can then use a spreadsheet to calculate the rates at which connections are rejected and reset. An increasing number of failures and resets or a consistently increasing rate of failures and resets might indicate a bandwidth shortage.

Be cautious when interpreting the number of reset connections shown by the TCP: Connections Reset counter. Resets do not always indicate dropped or failed connections. Many browsers try to minimize connection overhead by routinely closing connections by sending a TCP reset (RST) packet, rather than by closing the connection with a normal close operation. The TCP: Connections Reset counter does not distinguish between connections reset because they are dropped and those reset to close connections abruptly.

Using Network Monitor to Monitor Bandwidth

Network Monitor is a tool you can use to monitor the data sent and received by the local computer. Network Monitor can:

- Capture or trace data and filter it based on different attributes.
- Monitor throughput based on bytes or frames.
- Monitor bandwidth based on the percentage of the network used.
- Monitor errors, a possible consequence of an overloaded network.

The Windows NT Server CD includes Network Monitor as an optional Windows NT tool.

▶ **To install Network Monitor**

1. Double-click the Network icon in Control Panel.
2. Click the **Services** tab, and then click **Add**.
3. In the **Network Service** box, double-click **Network Monitor Tools and Agent**.

For an overall view of bandwidth, use the **Network Monitor Frames Per Second** and **Bytes Per Second** status bars. Use the **% Network Utilization** status bar to view monitor network capacity used. The **# Frames Dropped** field indicates the number of frames that are not processed because the buffers on the network adapters are full. Frame-dropping occurs when the processor cannot handle the traffic generated by the network.

Limiting Bandwidth

If the bandwidth on your server is not sufficient to handle the load imposed by Internet Information Server, you can limit the amount of bandwidth Internet Information Server uses for static HTML pages (files with .htm or .html extensions). This setting affects all services that route directly through IIS, but not those that are sent to other engines or applications (ASP, ISAPI, CGI, and SQL, for example).

Remember that per-instance bandwidth throttling is not supported for the FTP service.

▶ **To enable bandwidth throttling**

1. In Internet Service Manager, right-click a site, then click **Properties** and select the **Performance** tab.

2. Select the **Enable Bandwidth Throttling** check box. In the **Maximum network use** box, type the maximum amount of bandwidth you want IIS to use for static HTML pages, in kilobytes per second.

You do not need to restart the server or the service to activate bandwidth throttling; it is enabled dynamically.

Monitoring Bandwidth Throttling

When you enable bandwidth throttling, IIS activates a set of Performance Monitor counters to monitor it. You can identify these counters by the presence of the phrase "Async I/O" in the counter name. These counters are active only when bandwidth throttling is enabled. (If bandwidth throttling is not enabled, the counters appear in Performance Monitor, but they always have a value of zero.)

The Async I/O counters are part of the Internet Information Services Global performance object. They represent totals for all of the IIS services. Bandwidth is not measured for each service. The following table lists and describes the Async I/O counters.

Table 4.14   Performance Monitor Counters for Monitoring Bandwidth Throttling

Counter	Indicates
Internet Information Services Global: Current Blocked Async I/O Requests	The number of requests blocked (that is, held in a buffer until bandwidth is available) by bandwidth throttling as reported during the most recent observation.
Internet Information Services Global: Total Allowed Async I/O Requests	The number of requests allowed by bandwidth throttling since the service was last started.
Internet Information Services Global: Total Blocked Async I/O Requests	The number of requests blocked (that is, held in a buffer until bandwidth is available) by bandwidth throttling since the service was last started.
Internet Information Services Global: Total Rejected Async I/O Requests	The number of requests rejected by bandwidth throttling since the service was last started.
Internet Information Services Global: Measured Async I/O Bandwidth Usage/Minute	The number of bytes sent per minute as indicated by a sample taken by bandwidth throttling.

Analyzing Data About Bandwidth Throttling

The bandwidth setting determines whether IIS accepts or rejects a request for a static HTML page, based on periodic samples of the rate at which bytes are sent on the server.

- If the bandwidth used (as indicated by the sample) approaches the maximum set by the user, bandwidth throttling blocks read requests but allows write requests and transmission requests. Read requests are blocked first because they are likely to result in further requests.

- If the bandwidth used exceeds the maximum set by the user, bandwidth throttling rejects read requests, blocks large write requests and transmission requests, and allows small write requests and transmission requests.

To determine how many requests are being blocked and rejected, monitor the Async I/O counters. These counters display cumulative totals, so it's best to use PerfLog to log the counter values. Alternatively, you can use a spreadsheet to calculate the rate over time. You can also set a Performance Monitor alert to notify administrators when the number of blocked or rejected requests exceeds a threshold.

No rule exists that sets a threshold or appropriate number of blocked and rejected requests. Tolerance for client delays and rejections is a business rule, not a performance measure. However, you can use the Async I/O counters to enforce your business's standards, at least for static HTML pages.

Suggestions for Maximizing Bandwidth

If the bandwidth on your server is not sufficient to support demand, you can solve the problem by increasing overall server bandwidth. You can also solve the problem by increasing the effective bandwidth of existing communication links. Some suggestions on how to do so follow. Many involve tuning parameters that can only be modified by editing the Windows NT registry.

Adjusting the Length of the Connection Queues

You might effectively increase existing bandwidth by increasing the length of the connection queues. Requests for connections to the IIS services are held in queues until the service is available to respond to the request. A separate queue exists for each of the IIS services, but all queues have the same maximum size. By default, each queue can hold up to 15 connection requests. If the queue to a service is full, any new connection requests are rejected.

The default queue length of 15 connection requests is sufficient for most servers. However, if your server is rejecting many requests when the services are most active, you can increase the maximum number of items in the queue. If you change the queue length, be sure to monitor server processor use, server memory use, and the connection counters to avoid creating a system bottleneck.

To change the maximum number of connection requests in the queue for each IIS service, add the **ListenBackLog** key to the registry. Set the value of **ListenBackLog** to the maximum number of connection requests you want the server to maintain. You must place **ListenBackLog** in the registry at:

HKEY_LOCAL_MACHINE\System
       \CurrentControlSet
           \Services
               \Inetinfo
                   \Parameters

Although there are separate queues for each IIS service, the maximum length for all three of the queues is identical and is determined by this value entry.

Using HTTP Keep-Alives

To ensure optimal bandwidth, you can also verify that HTTP Keep-Alives are enabled. HTTP Keep-Alives maintain a connection even after its initial request is complete. HTTP Keep-Alives are enabled by default, but can be disabled. To disable them, right-click a site in the Internet Service Manager, then click **Properties**; select the **Performance** tab and clear the **HTTP Keep-Alives Enabled** check box.

Working with "Black Hole" Routers

Another way to add effective bandwidth is by detecting and properly responding to "black hole" routers, which do not send an "ICMP Destination Unreachable" message when they cannot forward an IP datagram. Instead, they ignore the datagram. Doing so causes the connection to be reset. Typically, the reason an IP datagram cannot be forwarded is because the datagram's maximum segment size is too large for the receiving server and the Don't-Fragment bit is set.

To respond effectively to black hole routers, you can enable the Path MTUBH Detect feature of TCP/IP. Path MTUBH Detect recognizes repeated unacknowledged transmission and responds by turning off the Don't-Fragment bit. After the datagram in question is transmitted successfully, it reduces the maximum segment size and turns the Don't-Fragment bit on again.

Path MTUBH Detect is disabled by default, but you can enable it by adding the **EnablePMTUBHDetect** key to the registry and setting its value to 1. **EnablePMTUBHDetect** is an optional entry that does not appear in the registry unless you add it. You must place it in:

HKEY_LOCAL_MACHINE\System
        \CurrentControlSet
            \Services
                \Tcpip
                    \Parameters

You can disable Path MTUBH Detect by deleting **EnablePMTUBHDetect** from the registry or by setting its value to 0.

Optimizing Graphics File Sizes

Graphics can consume significant bandwidth and result in noticeable network delay. You can increase effective bandwidth (and improve user experience) by changing your graphics format to reduce the size of graphics files. Different graphics formats use different methods of encoding the data. Try different formats for your graphics, and choose the format that produces the smallest file size.

For example, the Joint Photographic Experts Group (JPEG) format usually produces the smallest file for a photograph. Graphic Interchange Format (GIF) usually produces the smallest file for a computer-drawn illustration graphic.

Security and Performance

Performance is not usually a primary consideration when designing a security strategy for servers running IIS, nor should it be. The intrinsic benefits of protecting your installation and its code and data from unwarranted access override performance concerns. Nonetheless, effective security features have performance overhead—sometimes quite significant overhead—so it is important to measure the overhead and provide enough excess capacity to accommodate it.

This section describes some techniques for measuring the effects of security strategies on server performance.

The Challenge of Measuring Security Overhead

Measuring the performance overhead of a security strategy is not simply a matter of monitoring a separate process or threads. The features of the Windows NT security model and other IIS security services run in the context of the IIS process; they are integrated into several different operating system services. You cannot monitor security features separately from other aspects of the services.

Instead, the most common way to measure security overhead is to run tests comparing server performance with and without a security feature. The tests should be run with fixed workloads and a fixed server configuration so that the security feature is the only variable. During the tests, you probably want to measure:

- *Processor activity and the processor queue.* Authentication, IP address checking, SSL protocol, and encryption schemes are security features that require significant processing. You are likely to see increased processor activity, both in privileged and user mode, and an increase in the rate of context switches and interrupts. If the processors in the server are not sufficient to handle the increased load, queues are likely to develop.

- *Physical memory used.* Security requires that the system store and retrieve more user information. Also, the SSL protocol uses long keys—40 bits to 1,024 bits long—for encrypting and decrypting the messages.

- *Network traffic.* You are also likely to see an increase in traffic between the IIS-based server and the domain controller used for authenticating logons and verifying IP addresses.

- *Latency and delays.* The most obvious performance degradation resulting from complex security features like SSL is the time and effort involved in encryption and decryption, both of which use lots of processor cycles. Downloading files from servers using the SSL protocol can be 10 to 100 times slower than from servers that are not using SSL.

If a server is used both for running IIS and as a domain controller, the proportion of processor use, memory, and network and disk activity consumed by domain services is likely to increase significantly. The increased activity can be enough to prevent the IIS services from running efficiently.

You can run a test that monitors processor, memory, and network activity by using the Microsoft Web Capacity Analysis Tool (WCAT). You can run WCAT alone or in conjunction with other tools, such as Performance Monitor. WCAT and its documentation are included on the IIS Resource Kit CD.

Using WCAT to Measure Security Overhead

WCAT is a script-driven, command-line–based application that tests your server configuration using a variety of predetermined, unvarying workloads. You can use WCAT to test how your server responds to different workloads or test the same workload on varying configurations of the server.

The WCAT toolkit includes a folder of prepared test workloads. You can also use WCAT to create your own workloads. WCAT also includes a special option, ssl.*testname*, which adds SSL protocol settings to any workload test.

Components of a WCAT Test

A WCAT test simulates clients and servers communicating over a network. WCAT ordinarily requires at least three computers for each test:

- At least one computer simulating a client, which runs one or more *virtual clients*.
- One computer acting as a *server*.
- One computer, called a *controller*, which initiates and monitors the test.

Both client and controller can run on one computer. (In fact, all three functions can run on a single computer, but this produces skewed results.)

To produce a realistic test, it is best to associate four or more client computers, each running several virtual clients, with each server. The processors in the client computers should be at least as fast as the processors in the server computer. If the client processors are not as fast as the server processors, more client computers should be associated with each server computer. WCAT works best if the network that connects the computers has little or no traffic that is not related to the test. It is preferable to use a link dedicated only to the test. A 100 Mbps or faster network is recommended.

Designing a WCAT Test of Security Features

To test a security feature, first run a WCAT test with the feature, then run the same test without the feature. It is important to run the "with feature" and "without feature" versions of the test on varying workloads. WCAT includes over 200 MB of prepared workloads ranging from 12 files to 1,600 files. You can create additional tests of workloads with 2,000 or more files.

WCAT has many options for collecting data on the tests:

- You can use WCAT's log of performance data. The WCAT log can be used as input to spreadsheet and charting applications. The WCAT user guide explains how to interpret a WCAT log.
- You can run IIS logging in conjunction with WCAT to count logons and file accesses.
- You can run Performance Monitor with WCAT. The WCAT **run** command includes a **-p** switch that activates Performance Monitor. You can select Performance Monitor counters by entering the names of counters in a script file. WCAT even includes a sample Performance Monitor counter file, Server.pfc.

WCAT provides test results in several formats. You can view the test results in a spreadsheet or charting program, or in Performance Monitor. You can use the same method to analyze the data of a WCAT test as you use to analyze other Performance Monitor data on processors, memory, disks, network, and applications. You should repeat each test several times and average the results to eliminate unintended variations of the test conditions. Then, compare the results of the "with feature" and "without feature" tests.

Consistent differences in the results of the tests are likely to indicate the overhead associated with the security feature. You can use these results to plan configuration changes to handle the security overhead.

WCAT is the primary tool used for monitoring security overhead. Performance Monitor also includes a set of counters you can use to monitor one specific aspect of security: authenticating users.

Using Performance Monitor to Track Anonymous and Non-Anonymous Connections

Performance Monitor includes counters that display the number of anonymous and non-anonymous connections to each IIS service. These counters are included in the Web Service and FTP Service performance objects.

The term *non-anonymous* is used instead of *authenticated* to account for custom authentication schemes that require data from the client other than, or in addition to, the user name and password.

By themselves, these Performance Monitor counters help you determine the number and proportion of each type of connection. You can also use the counter values to project the estimated effect of changing how you handle anonymous and non-anonymous users. For example, if the vast majority of connections are anonymous, prohibiting anonymous connections has a more significant impact than if most connections are non-anonymous.

Combining data from these counters with general measures of server performance, such as data on processor time, the processor queue, memory, disk reads and writes, and throughput, is even more useful. Using the combined data, you can associate varying numbers and proportions of anonymous and non-anonymous users with their effect on the performance of system components.

Anonymous and Non-Anonymous Connection Counters

The Performance Monitor counters that display the numbers of anonymous and non-anonymous connections are called Current Anonymous Users and Current Non-anonymous Users. These counters actually display connections, not users. Users who connect more than once are counted once for each time they connect.

The following table lists the Performance Monitor counters for anonymous and non-anonymous connections. These counters are part of the Web Service and FTP Service performance objects.

Table 4.15   Performance Monitor Counters for Anonymous and Non-Anonymous Connections

Counter	Indicates
Web Service: Anonymous Users/Sec Web Service: Non-Anonymous Users/Sec	How many anonymous and non-anonymous users connect to the IIS service during each second.
Web Service: Current Anonymous Users FTP Service: Current Anonymous Users Web Service: Current NonAnonymous Users FTP Service: Current NonAnonymous Users	How many anonymous and non-anonymous users are currently connected to the IIS service.
Web Service: Maximum Anonymous Users FTP Service: Maximum Anonymous Users Web Service: Maximum NonAnonymous Users FTP Service: Maximum NonAnonymous Users	The maximum number of anonymous and non-anonymous users that have been connected simultaneously to the IIS service since the service was last started.
Web Service: Total Anonymous Users FTP Service: Total Anonymous Users Web Service: Total NonAnonymous Users FTP Service: Total NonAnonymous Users	A running total of anonymous and non-anonymous connections to the IIS service since the service was last started.

The anonymous and non-anonymous user counters display the number of anonymous and non-anonymous connections to the IIS service when the values were last observed. They do not report averages or rates. These counters might exaggerate the number of connections because closed connections might not yet be deleted when the counter is displayed.

The Current Anonymous Users and Current Non-anonymous Users counters operate based on the following definitions:

- The *anonymous user* counters display the number of connections whose requests either did not contain a user name and password or whose user name and password were ignored because authentication is not permitted on the server. If anonymous connections are not permitted on the server, the value of all *anonymous user* counters is always zero.

- The *non-anonymous user* counters display the number of connections whose requests contained a valid user name and password, or whatever authentication is required by a custom authentication scheme. If authentication is not enabled on the server, and none of the applications that run on the server request or require authentication, then the value of all *non-anonymous user* counters is always zero.

The *anonymous user* and *non-anonymous user* counters count successful connections only. If a client request for an anonymous connection is rejected and the client responds with valid authenticating data, the connection is counted as non-anonymous.

Using Performance Monitor to Count Not-Found Errors

The Web Service performance object in Performance Monitor includes a counter that displays not-found errors. *Not-found errors* are client requests that could not be satisfied because they included a reference to a Web page or a file that did not exist.

Many not-found errors occur because Web pages and files are deleted or moved to another location. However, some can result from user attempts to access documents that they are not authorized to have.

You can use the Web Service: Not Found Errors/sec counter to track the rate at which not-found errors are occurring on your server. You can also set a Performance Monitor alert to notify the Administrator when the rate of not-found errors exceeds a threshold.

Following is a brief description of the Web Service: Not Found Errors/sec counter.

Table 4.16   Performance Monitor Counter for Not-Found Errors

Counter	Indicates
Web Service: Not Found Errors/sec	The number of client read requests that could not be satisfied because the URL did not point to a valid file. An increase in not-found errors may indicate that a file has been moved without its link being updated. However, it can also indicate failed attempts to access protected documents, such as user lists and file directories.

Capacity Planning to Support Security Features

After you have collected data on the effect of adding security features to your server configuration, you can use the results to plan configuration changes to handle the addition workload required to support security features. The following approaches are recommended:

- *Upgrade or add processors.* Security features are often very processor-intensive. In particular, the SSL protocol consumes a significant amount of processor time. Because Windows NT security features are multithreaded, they can run simultaneously on multiple processors. Thus, adding processors improves performance significantly and prevents the processors from becoming a bottleneck.

- *Upgrade the processor cache.* For best results, choose a processor with a large (up to 2 MB) secondary (L2) cache. When encrypting and decrypting data, the processor spends much of its time reading and writing small units of data to and from the main memory. If this data can be stored in the processor cache instead, the data can be retrieved much faster.

- *Add memory.* If security features cause increased paging or shortages in virtual memory, adding more memory will help. The physical memory used to support the security service consumes space that can be used otherwise to cache files. To accommodate peak use, you should allow for twice as much memory as is required during times of average use while still maintaining 10 MB of available memory.

- *Do not add disk space.* Any increased disk activity associated with security features is likely to be the result of a shortage of physical memory, not a need for more disk space. Security features, such as the SSL protocol, rely primarily on processors and physical memory, as opposed to the disks.

Security is an integral feature of the IIS services. You can protect your vital data without sacrificing the performance of your server by planning carefully.

Monitoring Web Applications

Web applications are one of the most exciting recent developments in Web technology. The power of Web applications has already led to their wide use on intranets and on the Internet.

If you run Web applications, or plan to, you need to know how to monitor their overhead. You must also build in sufficient excess capacity to accommodate their use. The following sections explain how to monitor Web applications, and how to use the Web Capacity Analysis Tool (WCAT) tool to help predict processor and memory requirements for ASP, ISAPI, and CGI applications. For a brief of overview of WCAT, see the section, "Using WCAT to Measure Security Overhead" earlier in this chapter.

Monitoring Client Requests to Web Applications

The most common indicator of the activity of a Web application is the rate of requests to the application. Web applications become active when they respond to requests, and are generally inactive between requests. The more requests the application responds to, the more active it is judged to be.

First, measure the activity level of an application. You can then compare the effect of different levels of activity of a single application on the computer. You can also compare the effect of the same activity levels of different applications.

Using Performance Monitor to Monitor Client Requests

Performance Monitor includes a set of counters that measure the rate of requests to Web applications. These counters are included in the Active Server Pages and Web Service objects.

The following table lists the counters that count ASP requests. Please note that with the exception of Active Server Pages: Requests/Sec these counters display the last observed value, not an average. It is important to log these counters over time and to display the results in a chart, as opposed to a report.

Table 4.17   Performance Monitor Counters for ASP Requests

Counter	Indicates
Active Server Pages: Requests Disconnected	Total number of disconnected requests
Active Server Pages: Requests Executing	Current number of requests in process
Active Server Pages: Requests Failed Total	Total number of requests that have failed
Active Server Pages: Requests Not Authorized	Total number of requests that were not authorized
Active Server Pages: Requests Not Found	Total number of requests for pages that weren't found
Active Server Pages: Requests Queued	Current size of the ASP queue
Active Server Pages: Requests Rejected	Total number of refused requests
Active Server Pages: Requests Succeeded	Total number of requests that were processed normally
Active Server Pages: Requests Timed Out	Total number of requests that timed out and were not processed
Active Server Pages: Requests Total	Grand total number: all requests
Active Server Pages: Requests/Sec	Current average

The following table lists the counters that count requests to ISAPI and CGI applications. Note that these counters display the last observed value, not an average. It is important to log these counters over time and to display the results in a chart, as opposed to a report.

Table 4.18   Performance Monitor Counters for ISAPI and CGI Requests

Counter	Indicates
Web Service: Current ISAPI Extension Requests	How many requests for pages generated by ISAPI DLLs are being processed simultaneously.
Web Service: Maximum ISAPI Extension Requests	The maximum number of requests for pages generated by ISAPI DLLs that were processed simultaneously since the service started.
Web Service: Total ISAPI Extension Requests	The total number of requests for pages generated by ISAPI DLLs since the service started. The value of this counter includes successful and failed requests.
Web Service: Current CGI Requests	How many requests for pages generated by CGI applications are being processed simultaneously.
Web Service: Maximum CGI Requests	The maximum number of requests for pages generated by CGI applications that were processed simultaneously since the service started.
Web Service: Total CGI Requests	The total number of requests for pages generated by CGI applications since the service started. The value of this counter includes successful and failed requests.

By themselves, these counters are indirect indicators of processor activity. When combined with information about server performance, however, these counters can help you judge the effects of different levels of activity on the performance and efficiency of your server.

Monitoring Servers Running Web Applications

This section suggests two approaches to monitoring the effects of Web applications on general server performance:

- Using Performance Monitor to monitor server performance while running Web applications on your server.

- Using the Web Capacity Analysis Tool (WCAT) to simulate the effects of ASP, CGI, and ISAPI applications on your server.

You can also use Performance Monitor to monitor your WCAT tests. The following sections explain these monitoring techniques in more detail.

Monitoring the Effect of Web Applications on Overall Server Performance

If you are running Web applications, you can use Performance Monitor to monitor the effect of these processes on your server. Use Performance Monitor counters to measure processor and memory use on the server during periods of very high or very low Web application activity. Log these counters while running one of the following tests:

- Monitor the effect of a Web application on overall server performance.

  Monitor the server while running with and then without the Web application. Log the counters for several days under similar conditions. Next, compare the rates of processor use, the average length of the processor queue, the number of available bytes, and the rate of page faults of the "with application" and "without application" tests. The difference between the values should be due to performance and memory overhead of the application.

- Compare the effect on your server of equivalent ASP, ISAPI, and CGI applications.

  If you have scripts that generate the same pages, you can use Performance Monitor to compare performance. Log server performance while the server is running each application, separately. Classify the data based on the average number of requests to the application during each period. Then, compare the values of the counters during periods when the rates of requests were similar.

Using WCAT to Simulate Web Applications

Even if you do not have any available ASP, ISAPI, or CGI applications, you can still test the effect of such applications on your server configuration by using WCAT. WCAT comes with several prepared tests designed for simulating the effects of ASP, ISAPI, and CGI applications on your server. The following table lists these tests and provides a brief explanation of each test.

Table 4.19 WCAT Tests of ASP, ISAPI, and CGI Applications

Test	Description
ASP25	25 percent of the workload consists of ASP requests; the remaining 75 percent represents requests for static files based on an average workload.
ASP50	50 percent of the workload consists of ASP requests; the remaining 50 percent represents requests for static files based on an average workload.
ASP75	75 percent of the workload consists of ASP requests; the remaining 25 percent represents requests for static files based on an average workload.
ISAPI25	25 percent of the workload consists of ISAPI requests; the remaining 75 percent represents requests for static files based on an average workload.
ISAPI50	50 percent of the workload consists of ISAPI requests; the remaining 50 percent represents requests for static files based on an average workload.
ISAPI75	75 percent of the workload consists of ISAPI requests; the remaining 25 percent represents requests for static files based on an average workload.
CGI25	25 percent of the workload consists of CGI requests; the remaining 75 percent represents requests for static files based on an average workload.
CGI50	50 percent of the workload consists of CGI requests; the remaining 50 percent represents requests for static files based on an average workload.
CGI75	75 percent of the workload consists of CGI requests; the remaining 25 percent represents requests for static files based on an average workload.

Using Performance Monitor to Monitor WCAT Tests

You also can use Performance Monitor to monitor server performance during WCAT tests. The method for activating Performance Monitor during a WCAT test is described in detail in the WCAT documentation, included on the IIS Resource Kit CD.

The WCAT **run** command includes a **-p** switch that activates Performance Monitor during a WCAT test. When you include the **-p** option in the WCAT **run** command, the WCAT controller samples and averages selected Performance Monitor counters during the WCAT test. You can specify the Performance Monitor counters that you want WCAT to sample by including them in a script file with a file name extension of .pfc. The name of your .pfc file is part of the syntax of the **-p** switch.

The following experiments involve running different WCAT tests in sequence and monitoring the effect of the test on your server, using Performance Monitor. When the tests are complete, you can compare the relative effect of each test on server performance.

Counters for monitoring the WCAT tests are included in Server.pmc, a Performance Monitor settings file on the IIS Resource Kit CD.

The suggestions for using WCAT and Performance Monitor to test server performance are:

- To determine the effect of an ASP application on your server, run the ASP25, ASP50, and ASP75 tests sequentially while logging the Performance Monitor counters in Server.pmc.

- To determine the effect of an ISAPI application on your server, run the ISAPI25, ISAPI50, and ISAPI75 tests sequentially while logging the Performance Monitor counters in Server.pmc.

- To determine the effect of a CGI application on your server, run the CGI25, CGI50, and CGI75 tests sequentially while logging the Performance Monitor counters in Server.pmc.

- To compare the effects of, say, CGI to those of ASP, run the CGI75 and ASP75 tests sequentially while logging the Performance Monitor counters in Server.pmc.

To analyze the data from these tests, note any change in processor and memory use as the proportion of requests for one or another Web application type increases, or between pairs of Web applications at the same request rate. The effect of the change in workload varies substantially among server configurations. You can use this data to determine whether your server is prepared to handle this workload efficiently. You can vary the workload or vary the server configuration by adding processors or memory between test trials.

The next section introduces another aspect of monitoring Web applications. In addition to monitoring general server performance, you can also monitor the processes in which the applications run.

Tracking Web Application Processes

The most common way to monitor the overhead of Web applications is to monitor general server performance under varying levels of application activity. This technique is described in the preceding sections.

In addition to monitoring changes in overall server performance, you can also monitor the processes in which the applications run. This section suggests some tools and methods for monitoring the processes in which Web applications run.

Monitoring ASP and ISAPI Applications

By default, ASP and ISAPI applications run within the IIS process, Inetinfo.exe. You can monitor the processor and memory use of the Inetinfo process, but it is difficult to distinguish the resource use attributable to Web applications from that of the rest of the services running under Inetinfo. It is also extremely difficult, though technically possible, to associate individual threads in Inetinfo with ISAPI requests. On the other hand, because ASP has its own counter object, it is much easier to distinguish its processor and memory use.

ASP and ISAPI applications that are marked to run within their own memory spaces are called *out-of-process* applications, because they run outside the Inetinfo process. Because these applications run within their own processes, they are easier to monitor than in-process applications. You can use most process-monitoring tools to view the processes in which these applications run.

Using Process Monitor and Task Manager to Monitor Processes

Process Monitor (Pmon.exe) and the Task Manager **Process** tab are both useful for monitoring processes. Although these tools do not log process-specific data over time and cannot export data for other uses, they are particularly effective for monitoring short-lived processes. Both tools display a list of all processes running on the computer, along with different measures of processor and memory use.

Task Manager is integrated into Windows NT. To start Task Manager, press CTRL+ALT+DEL. Click the **Processes** tab to see a list of processes running on the server. You can set the rate at which Task Manager is updated by clicking **Update Speed** on the **View** menu.

The Task Manager **Processes** tab displays a table listing the running processes along with performance information about each process. By default, Task Manager displays the **Process Identifier**, **CPU Usage**, **CPU Time**, and **Memory Usage** of each process. You can change the type of performance information listed about each process. To add or remove a Task performance measure, on the **View** menu, click **Select Columns**, then click a performance measure.

Note The Process Monitor and Task Manager **CPU Time** and **Page Faults** counts are cumulative. These performance measures show how much of a resource the process has used since the process started. A high value might indicate that a process has been running for a long time, not that the process is using the resource at a high rate.

Tuning the ASP Queue and Thread Pool

Under high-load conditions, ASP scripts can create a signficant ASP queue. This could occur if, for example, a script calls a component that receives more calls than it can handle. When this happens, incoming requests for the ASP page that calls the component are placed in a queue and processed on a first-in-first-out basis. If blocking conditions persist for only a few seconds, queueing smooths out the fluctuations in the load, and all incoming requests are serviced in a timely fashion, particularly if enough threads are available to handle other (non-ASP) requests as they come in. However, when the spikes last for a longer period of time (30 seconds, say) the queue grows. In the worst case, the queue builds up to the default maximum of 500 requests, or whatever the setting has been changed to.

When a request comes in and the number of queued requests exactly equals the value of **RequestQueueMax**, IIS returns a "Server Too Busy" error. This error accurately reflects the current condition, because incoming requests cannot be serviced in a timely fashion. If the number of queued requests is under 500 (say 498) the user with the 499th request will be kept waiting for all the other requests in the queue to be satisfied. This is an acceptable condition if the queue clears very rapidly (within 15 seconds), but the wait is typically closer to 60 seconds, which is intolerable to all but the most patient users. After about 15 seconds, most users click their browser's **Stop** button and then click the **Refresh** button. This only makes things worse, because the original request remains in the queue, still waiting to be serviced.

Relevant Registry Settings

The **ProcessorThreadMax** and **RequestQueueMax** registry settings for ASP can have a significant impact on the performance of your site. These settings are found in the registry at the following location:

HKEY_LOCAL_MACHINE\System
    \CurrentControlSet
        \Services
            \W3SVC
                \ASP
                    \Parameters

Tuning ProcessorThreadMax

The goal in tuning the **ProcessorThreadMax** value is to bring processor utilization above 50 percent under load, if possible. It is not possible to calculate what the appropriate number of threads should be, because live sites are too dynamic. You should gather statistics by using at least the following Performance Monitor counters:

- Processor: %Processor Time (for each processor)
- Active Server Pages: Requests/Sec
- Active Server Pages: Requests Rejected
- Active Server Pages: Total Queue Length
- Web Service: Connections/Sec

Watch these counters on one of your computers during peak load time, using a 1-second Chart interval. If you have a busy site with a variety of work going on and minimal blocking, you should see the Total Queue Length counter go up and down. If the Total Queue Length never goes up and you are running at low processor utilization, you probably have a smooth-running site with more capacity than you currently need.

If queue length is going up and down and your processors are running below 50 percent utilization, some requests are blocking and you can probably benefit by increasing the number of threads. Start by changing **ProcessorThreadMax** from 10 (thc default value) to 20. Restart the computer, or restart the Web service. You should expect to see some increase in processor utilization, and the queue length should tend to change more rapidly. Increasing the number of threads improves response time for non-blocking operations by putting the CPU to use satisfying requests.

The Next Step

If, after increasing **ProcessorThreadMax** to 20, you continue to see the queue lengthen and processor utilization actually go down, your server may have some serious blocking problems. This can occur if threads are waiting for response from an external resource such as a database. Similarly, if there are bugs in any of the components, they will tend to surface more quickly as you increase the number of threads. If your site has a single point of entry, make sure it doesn't cause blocking problems; if it does, redesign it. Likewise, if most users follow a single path through your site, and that path has several pages with blocking problems, you should redesign the entire path.

If the queue length stays down and processor utilization increases, you can continue increasing **ProcessorThreadMax** until you reach your target CPU utilization (stay under 70 percent, though, and try to keep **ProcessorThreadMax** below 100). You may find that the bottleneck is elsewhere; that you have more computers than you really need; or that your server is not blocking and that high CPU utilization cannot be achieved. IIS is extremely efficient for static HTML and non-blocking ASP, so it may require less processing capability than you expect.

The ASP Queue

Once the number of server threads is adjusted, you can focus attention on the ASP queue. The goal is to use the queue to handle short-term peaks, ensure consistent response time, and throttle the system to avoid overload from sustained unexpected spikes. You can calculate the response time by timing how long it takes for the queue length to return to zero after it goes up to the maximum value. On a smoothly running non-blocking site, the queue will typically stay near zero most of the time, because incoming requests are satisfied quickly.

Tuning RequestQueueMax

Determine your target response time (say, 10 seconds), and keep the queue at a size that will never hold more than that many seconds of work. (This size depends on your particular configuration, which you can determine by testing.) The ideal size for **RequestQueueMax** is below the limit determined by allowable response latency, but still above your typical peak load queue size.

A **RequestQueueMax** size that is too small will yield too many "Server Too Busy" errors during load spikes. A value that is too large can cause the site to appear to be unresponsive. Users will give up, because the site is not meeting *their* response time requirements. Watch the queue during routine periods of high activity; you should see it growing and shrinking normally. Make a note of the peaks and set **RequestQueueMax** just above the peak length, so long as that is under your Response time threshold. (If it isn't, you may need more memory or processing power.)

If you have no data, a good starting setting seems to be a 1-to-1 ratio of queue length to total threads. Example: If you have **ProcessorThreadMax** set at 25 and four processors (100 threads) then start with **RequestQueueMax** at 100 and tune from there.

Other Optimization Steps

To minimize queueing and improve response time:

- Use static HTML files rather than Web applications when you can.
- Use the **Server.CreateObject** method cautiously.
- Minimize external dependencies: anything that is not on the same computer as your site is a potential bottleneck.
- Maximize network performance and reliability, relative to external dependencies.
- Load-test and rate all custom components before deploying them on your site.
- Ensure that every component can execute faster than the highest rate at which it is called. If a component is called 20 times a second, it must complete each cycle in much less than 1/20 of a second or it will block. A single blocking component can ruin the performance of all ASP pages on your site.
- Use Performance Monitor to check your site every week. Keep a close eye on the results; a single blocking object can impact your entire site.

When Your Site Is Running Smoothly

On a smoothly running site you should see very little queueing, with all routine peaks staying well below the value of **RequestQueueMax** throughout the day, as all components are able to satisfy the load placed on them. Processor utilization stays close to your target rate during peak load periods.

Capacity Planning to Support Web Applications

Web applications have much higher overhead than static HTML pages. But the overhead of Web applications should not deter you from using them. By monitoring applications and estimating their overhead during periods of varying activity, you can make sure your server is prepared for the increased workload.

Here are some suggestions for optimizing your configuration for Web applications:

- *Upgrade processors.* Web applications benefit from faster processors.
- *Add processors.* Components called by ASP scripts can (and should) be multithreaded, which means they can run simultaneously on multiple processors. Adding a second processor to a single-processor system brings the most benefit.

- *Add memory.* Adding memory may help if application processes are running within their own processes. (By default, ASP and ISAPI applications run within the IIS process, but they can be set to run within their own memory spaces.)

- *Defragment your disks.* If your cache performance declines over time, defragment the disk. Your files might have become fragmented over time.

- *Redesign your static pages.* Running Web applications is slower than serving static pages. If you are generating pages dynamically to satisfy user preferences, consider substituting 10 or 20 different static variations for a single dynamically generated page. If you are generating pages dynamically to provide frequently updated data, consider redesigning your application so that it generates a single dynamic page on a fixed schedule and then stores that page for retrieval until the next update.

- *Convert CGI scripts to ASP or ISAPI scripts.* ASP and ISAPI applications are optimized to run on Windows NT. CGI applications are much less efficient. For more information on converting CGI scripts, see the "Migrating CGI Applications to IIS" section of Chapter 10, "Migrating Web Sites and Applications."

Web applications are continuing to increase in popularity. They constitute an ever-larger proportion of the average Web server file base. The challenge for administrators is to preserve speed and efficiency.

Resources

The following Web sites and books provide additional information relevant to Web server tuning and performance optimization.

Web Links

Web site information is current as of the date of publication, but is, of course, subject to change.

http://andrew2.andrew.cmu.edu/rfc/rfc1794.html
Text of RFC 1794, which deals with load balancing.

http://www.network-mag.com/9611/9611web.htm
"Revving up Your Web Server," an article on improving performance. Originally published in *LAN* Magazine.

http://www.network-mag.com/9711/11wan.htm
"Tuning Web Site Performance," an article originally published in *Network* Magazine.

http://www.nightflight.com/htdocs/web-performance.html
Links to several articles on performance.

http://www.starnine.com/webstar/overview.html
"A Model of Web Server Performance," an article by Louis Slothouber.

Books

Professional Web Site Optimization (Wrox Press Ltd., 1997).

WebMaster in a Nutshell (O'Reilly and Associates, 1997).

Web Server Technology: Advanced Guide for World-Wide Web Information Providers (Morgan Kaufman Publishers, 1996).

C H A P T E R   5

Developing Web Applications

5

Open Internet standards coupled with the immense popularity of the Web have changed the architecture of distributed computing forever. The multi-layered nature of the Web creates an ideal application environment for component-based development. Applications can be developed and customized quickly, with advanced system services such as database access and transaction processing. System resources can be managed and administered remotely. Moreover, new applications are available immediately, without requiring anything more than a browser on the user's system.

This chapter examines the effects that the Web has had on distributed application development as a whole, and demonstrates how to use Internet Information Server to develop the *n*-tier applications of the future. In the process, the chapter will introduce the technologies Microsoft has developed to implement this new breed of Web applications.

In this chapter:

- Building on Client/Server
- Client-Side Technologies
- The Middle Tier
- Design Patterns for Web Applications
- Summary
- Resources

Building on Client/Server

Market analysts predict rapid growth in distributed systems in the coming years. Some predict that by 2005, the familiar architecture of client/server applications will be replaced by "super-suites" of interconnected components, operating in frameworks of highly available distributed systems. In other words, systems with a single-user focus will no longer be sufficient. Rather, applications will be assembled from reusable building blocks, using a variety of cooperating subsystems.

Before delving into the implementation details of building Web applications, it may be helpful to take a quick look at the architecture of the Web from a historical perspective.

Client/Server Revisited

Cooperating and communicating applications are typically categorized as either a *client* or a *server*. The client application requests services and data from the server. The server application responds to client requests. Early client/server applications were generally data-centric and combined most, if not all, of the processing logic and user interface within the client application. The server's task was simply to process requests for data storage and retrieval.

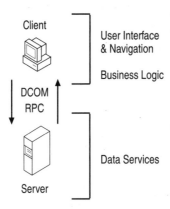

Figure 5.1   Functional diagram of a client/server application

Client/server (or, two-tier) applications perform many of the functions of stand-alone systems; they present a user interface, gather and process user input, perform the requested processing, and report the status of the request. Because servers only provide access to the data, the client uses its local resources to process it. Out of necessity, the client application is aware of where the data resides and how it is laid out in the database. Once the server transmits the data, the client is responsible for formatting and displaying it to the user.

The primary advantage of two-tier applications over monolithic, single-tier applications is that they give multiple users access to the same data simultaneously, thereby creating a kind of interprocess communication. Updates from one computer are instantly available to all computers that have access to the server.

However, the server must be willing to trust clients to modify data appropriately—unless data integrity rules are used, there is no protection against errors in client logic. Furthermore, client/server connections are hard to manage—the server is forced to open one connection per client. Finally, because much of the business logic is spread throughout a suite of client applications, changes in business processes usually lead to expensive and time-consuming alterations to source code.

Although two-tier design still continues to drive many small-scale business applications, an increasing need for faster and more reliable data access, coupled with decreasing development timelines, has persuaded systems developers to seek out a new distributed application design.

The New System Design

The new system design distributes computing tasks more evenly between the client and server. Viewed from a purely functional standpoint, most applications perform the following three main tasks: gathering user input, storing the input as data, and manipulating the data as dictated by established operational procedures. These tasks can be grouped into three or more tiers, which is why the new system design provides for three-tier, multi-tier, or *n*-tier applications. The application tiers are:

- **Client tier**   The user interface or presentation layer. Through this topmost layer, the user can input data, view the results of requests, and interact with the underlying system. On the Web, the browser performs these user-interface functions. In non-Web-based applications, the client tier is a stand-alone, compiled front-end application.

- **Middle tier** Components that encapsulate an organization's *business logic*. These processing rules closely mimic everyday business tasks, and can be single-task oriented, or part of a more elaborate series of tasks in a business workflow. In a Web application, the middle tier might consist of COM components registered as part of a Microsoft Transaction Server (MTS) package or instantiated by an Active Server Pages (ASP) script.

- **Third tier** A database management system (DBMS) such as a Microsoft SQL Server database; or an unstructured data store, such as Microsoft Exchange; or a transaction processing mechanism such as Microsoft Transaction Server, or Microsoft Message Queue Server. A single application can enlist the services of one or more of these data providers.

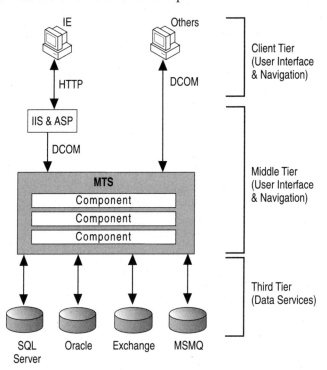

Figure 5.2   Three-tier architecture on the Web

Application tiers don't always correspond to physical locations on the network. For example, the middle and third tiers may coexist on the same server running both Internet Information Server and SQL Server, or they could be separate. The middle tier alone may tie together several computers, and sometimes the server becomes a client itself.

Separating the application into layers isolates each major area of functionality. The presentation is independent of the business logic, which is separate from the data. Designing applications in this way has its trade-offs—it requires a little more analysis and design at the start, but greatly reduces maintenance costs and increases functional flexibility in the end.

Although the *n*-tier system architecture is central to Web applications, it isn't solely for use on the Internet. One of the many benefits of building reusable middle-tier components is that they can be used outside of the Web model as well.

The explosive growth of the Internet is a strong motivation for organizations to adopt *n*-tier architectures in their products. However, organizations still face challenges. How can they take advantage of new technologies while preserving existing investments in people, applications, and data? How can they build modern, scalable computing solutions that are dynamic and flexible to change? How can they lower the overall cost of computing while making complex computing environments work? Microsoft's answer is Windows DNA.

Microsoft Windows DNA

The Windows Distributed interNet Applications Architecture (Windows DNA) is Microsoft's framework for building a new generation of *n*-tier computing solutions. Windows DNA defines a framework for delivering solutions that meet the requirements of corporate computing, the Internet and intranets, and global electronic commerce, while reducing overall costs of development.

The heart of Windows DNA is the Component Object Model (COM). Windows DNA architecture makes use of a common set of services, including HTML and Dynamic HTML, ActiveX Controls, COM components, client-side and server-side scripting, transactions, security and directory services, database and data access, systems management and HTML, and component authoring environments. These services are exposed in a unified way through COM, which enables applications to interoperate and share components easily.

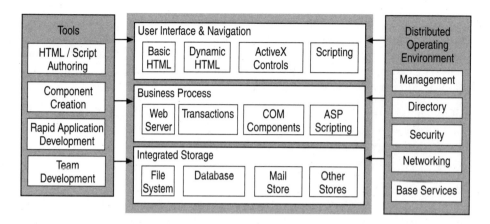

Figure 5.3   The Windows DNA family of technologies

Windows DNA builds on the client-side services of Windows and Microsoft
Internet Explorer, the distributed infrastructure of Windows NT Server and the
BackOffice family, and Microsoft's integrated tools such as the Visual Studio™
development system. Because Windows DNA architecture uses open protocols
and published interfaces, organizations can integrate third-party products and
solutions. In addition, because Windows DNA architecture embraces an open
approach to Web computing, it builds on the many important standards efforts
approved by bodies such as the World Wide Web Consortium (W3C) and the
Internet Engineering Task Force (IETF).

Although the technologies of Windows DNA are available today, the architecture
provides organizations with a road map for the future. Microsoft is enhancing
Windows DNA with Internet Explorer 4.0 (Dynamic HTML, Active Desktop™),
Internet Information Server 4.0 (Web, component, and transaction services), and
Microsoft Windows NT Server 5.0 (Active Directory, Zero Administration
services). COM+, the evolution of Microsoft's object model and component
services, will further extend the scope of Windows DNA applications.

For more information on Windows DNA, visit
http://www.microsoft.com/sitebuilder/dna/.

The Future of Applications on the Internet

The Internet promises dramatic new opportunities for savvy businesses. Businesses can create new computing solutions that improve the responsiveness of the organization, use the Internet and the Web to reach customers directly, and effectively connect people with information.

Customers have already started to demand global access to the information they need, both public and personal. Users increasingly want to use a single client application for their information access needs, and rely on the versatility of the server to provide content and services. Users will come to depend on these applications and want them to be universally available, even to *replace* local applications on their desktop systems. They are reluctant to invest time in installing new software, especially when a single powerful client—a browser—can deliver such a broad range of capabilities.

Consequently, there is likely to be an explosion of HTML-based server applications to feed the ubiquitous availability of the powerful Internet client. Applications will be factored into user-interface-only client components (with little software required beyond the standard Internet browser), and a middle tier of server components that have no user interface and provide services to the local desktop or across the Internet.

The following sections describe the roles that the client and middle-tier play in distributed Internet and intranet applications. The third tier is discussed in Chapter 6, "Data Access and Transactions."

Client-Side Technologies

This section presents a survey of the technologies that make up the client-tier of today's Web applications. Each technology is considered from the perspective of what it is, how it works as part of a Web application, and what the issues are regarding its use. This section does not address how to use these technologies.

Note Not all browsers support all client-side technologies. See "Browser Support," at the end of this section for advice on which client-side technologies to implement.

Text and HTML

Hypertext Markup Language, or HTML, is the basic formatting language of Web pages. Just like a printed page, text on a Web page can include a variety of font faces, colors, font weights and attributes, spacing, and columns. In addition, Web pages can include tables, frames, and HTML forms. Web applications make heavy use of tables and forms to display data, organize application elements, and collect user input.

HTML adheres to a set of standards that makes it useable over the entire Internet, and on intranets. For more information on HTML standards either visit the World Wide Web Consortium home page at http://www.w3c.org or consult your HTML reference materials. See the "Dynamic HTML" section later in this chapter for information on the newest extensions to HTML.

Graphics and Multimedia

Graphics and multimedia, if used effectively, can greatly enhance the look and feel of an application. They can instruct, as well as draw the eye to important areas of the screen.

Multimedia is an especially powerful tool on an intranet. Using streaming audio/video, like that available through Microsoft NetShow, you can broadcast special events as they happen, or use pre-recorded video to train employees in complex technical operations.

Because of the speed limitations of modems used for most Internet connections, heavy use of graphics and multimedia over the Internet should be restricted. Low-resolution graphics, if designed correctly, not only download more quickly but may actually look better than high-resolution graphics on most computer monitors.

Hyperlinks

Hyperlinks connect the parts of your application together, act as the application's "menu," and can perform both client-side and server-side actions. For example, clicking a hyperlink can cause a page to load in another frame, or can run a client-side script to change the layout of the page.

Hyperlinks are normally embedded directly on the page as text or graphics (such as an imagemap) where the user can view and click them. They can also be activated when a form is submitted. Or client-side script can dynamically create and trigger them.

There are lots of ways to present choices to the user. You can simplify the layout of a large number of hyperlinks by grouping similar choices together, using a similar style of presentation, or by hiding and displaying links as appropriate. For instance, you can choose to display links dynamically, based on the privilege level of your users. Only visitors with high-level access would be able to view links that perform advanced or administrative actions.

Client-Side Script

Client-side scripts run within the user's browser, using the processing power of the user's (client) computer. Client-side scripts can be written in any language supported by the browser; the most common is JavaScript. Some browsers, such as Internet Explorer, also support Visual Basic Scripting Edition (VBScript). Client-side scripting enhances Web pages with a variety of custom capabilities. For example, you can use scripts to perform field edits and calculations, manipulate the client window, or validate form input. Scripts normally appear directly on the page they affect, but they can be used to manipulate the content of pages in another frame or browser window as well.

Upgrading the Client's Scripting Engine

As a Web author, you will want to make sure your users are able to use the capabilities you've worked hard to provide for them. If your site requires the latest features of a client-side scripting engine, you should make sure your clients have the latest version installed. If your clients don't have the correct scripting engine, they may receive scripting errors that prevent your pages from loading or working properly.

Using a bit of client-side code, you can determine whether the client has the required version of the scripting engine. If the client doesn't have the required version, you can prompt the user to install the latest version of the scripting engine. Change the value of `requiredVersion` in the following script to specify the minimum version requirements for your application.

```
<SCRIPT LANGUAGE=JScript><!--
var version;
var requiredVersion = 2;

// Detect script engine version
if (typeof(ScriptEngineMajorVersion) + "" == "undefined")
   version = 1;
else
   version = ScriptEngineMajorVersion();

// Prompt client and navigate to download page.
if (version < requiredVersion) {
   if (confirm("This site requires a newer version of JScript. Would you
want to upgrade now?")) {
      location.href =
"http://www.microsoft.com/msdownload/scripting.htm";
   }
}
--></SCRIPT>
```

If the client doesn't download, or can't download, the latest scripting engine, you should handle that situation gracefully. For instance, you might want to provide alternate pages for clients without the latest scripting engine in the same way that pages in frames can be downgraded for browsers that are not frames-enabled. Or you can simply notify your client that the latest scripting engine is necessary to view your site.

Note   JavaScript 3.0 is now available and is included with all versions of Internet Explorer 4.0. JavaScript 3.0 complies fully with the ECMA (European Computer Manufacturers Association) scripting standard. To learn more about the ECMA scripting standard, see the ECMA-262 specification at http://www.ecma.ch/, and to learn about Microsoft's implementation of this standard, visit the Microsoft scripting site at http://www.microsoft.com/scripting/.

Java Applets

Java is a programming language designed especially for cross-platform applications, such as those that must operate on PC, Macintosh, and UNIX browsers. This cross-platform capability makes Java a natural companion to HTML for use on the Web and on intranets where users may use a variety of operating systems. Small, self-contained applications, called *applets*, can be written in Java to add fun and functionality. A Java applet can be anything from an ad banner that rotates between different ads to a complex animation for employee training.

Java applets are precompiled into "class" files consisting of *bytecodes*, Java instructions that are the same no matter which operating system the applet is running on. When the browser downloads the Java class file, the browser's built-in Java virtual machine reads the bytecodes and executes native instructions appropriate for the local operating system. That's how Java achieves operating-system independence.

Java applets are subject to strict security measures, and are usually limited to a secure processing area, dubbed the "sandbox." The sandbox prevents malicious applets from harming your computer, but it also prevents you from creating fully powerful, interactive Java applications. Internet Explorer 4.0 introduces a new security model for Java applications, in conjunction with "Security Zones," so that users can select the appropriate level of system interaction based on the origin of the applet. They can choose to lower the security requirements for trusted applets, enabling more powerful and interactive features.

ActiveX Controls

ActiveX Controls can be used either to customize the user interface, or as "plug-in" applications (such as the Macromedia Shockwave animation control and the RealNetworks streaming audio/video player). ActiveX Controls can perform a variety of tasks, from advanced user interface navigation to real-time interaction with stock quotes. ActiveX Controls can be written in any language that supports COM Automation, including Visual Basic, C++, Java, or even COBOL.

ActiveX Controls can be embedded into the HTML page by using the HTML <OBJECT> tag. If the control does not exist on the users system, it can be downloaded using the URL specified in the CODEBASE attribute. This tag also supports component versioning. Once the control is downloaded and installed, the browser continues to use the cached control until an updated version is available on the server. The following example demonstrates the CODEBASE parameter:

```
<OBJECT ID="BoomButton" WIDTH=225 HEIGHT=35
    CLASSID="clsid:56F1BF40-B2D0-11d0-A6D6-00AA00A70FC2"
    CODEBASE="http://example.microsoft.com/AControl.cab#Version=1,0,0,1">
</OBJECT>
```

A malicious ActiveX control could perform potentially destructive actions on the user's computer. To help users determine whether a control is safe to use, Microsoft has developed security guidelines for vendors to follow when releasing a control. A control should identify its creator with a "signature" issued by a well-known security authority, such as VeriSign. Authenticode, Microsoft's code-signing technology, assures accountability and authenticity for software components distributed on the Internet. Only the original owner can modify a signed control, which prevents tampering by third parties. (For more information on Authenticode and code-signing, visit http://www.microsoft.com/security/.)

As of this writing, only Internet Explorer 3.0 or later includes native support for ActiveX Controls. Because browser support for ActiveX Controls isn't universal, ActiveX Controls are probably most useful for intranet sites or sites created especially for Internet Explorer users.

Active Documents

Active Documents (also known as Doc Objects) are documents that can be embedded in any Active Document *container*. Microsoft Office Binder and Internet Explorer are two examples of Active Document containers. An Active Document exploits the native functionality of the *server* application used to create them. Microsoft Word, Excel, and PowerPoint® are all Active Document servers that can create Active Documents for use in Internet Explorer.

Users of Active Documents can create documents using the full power of their favorite applications, and treat the resulting project as a single entity. For example, if you have Microsoft Word (or Microsoft Word Viewer), you can open a Word document in Internet Explorer. The document is displayed just as it is in Word, except that it is contained inside Internet Explorer. In addition, Word adds all of its menus, toolbars, and status bars to create a familiar interface.

Like ActiveX Controls, Active Documents can also be signed with a security certificate, downloaded from the Web (by version), and executed inside any frame of the browser. Additionally, if Web server security allows, you can edit an Active Document within the browser and save your changes back to the server. For this reason, Active Documents are well suited for collaboration and workgroup applications.

For an example of an application that takes advantage of Active Document technology, see the sidebar "Case Study of a Web Application."

Cascading Style Sheets

The Cascading Style Sheet (CSS) standard gives authors more control over fonts, sizes, two-dimensional overlapping, and exact glyph positioning. CSS also separates formatting information from the Web page content, making it much easier to design and revise pages.

Style sheets control the appearance of HTML tags; they do not replace them. Style sheets give you the ability to attach style information to one or more HTML documents and to any of the tags therein, which greatly expands your control over the appearance and structure of a page. Formatting information can be applied to custom tags for a given browser as well as to standard HTML tags.

CSS information can be specified by linking, embedding, or as an inline style modifier. An HTML document can use any combination of these three methods. The most common method is linking, because it establishes a basis for embedded and inline style modifications. An example of a link to a style sheet is shown here:

```
<LINK REL=STYLESHEET TYPE="text/css" HREF="./myCustom.css">
```

Note Because of changes to the CSS standards recently adopted by the World Wide Web Consortium (W3C), the CSS support in Internet Explorer 3.0 is not fully compatible with that found in Internet Explorer 4.0, which supports the new standard. A detailed description of the latest CSS 2.0 standards is available at http://www.w3c.org/Style/.

Case Study of a Web Application

Microsoft recently introduced a new means of filing employee expense reports. The old system required employees to prepare expense report forms, attach receipts, and submit them to their managers, who would review the forms and submit them to the accounting department. Mistakes were common, and forms often had to be resubmitted. Once the paperwork was finished, the reports were painstakingly entered into a database.

To eliminate some of the problems with the existing system, the accounting department introduced a Web application to control and streamline the employee reimbursement process. The new application allows the employee to report expenses using a Microsoft Excel worksheet modeled after the paper version of the old form. The worksheet validates the data as it is submitted, catching most user errors up front. When the documents are ready, the electronic form can be routed to the employee's manager by e-mail. After the manager approves the form, a copy is returned to the accounts department and an approval notification is sent to the employee. The accounting department then performs all of its final work online, saving considerable effort.

The new expense-reporting system effectively:

- **Improved control**   Control was a recurrent theme throughout the design of the application. The worksheet and associated Web site were carefully designed to ensure that both employees and managers understood their responsibilities. Using an electronic form meant that reports could be tracked on their way through the system, making expense auditing on the back-end faster and more verifiable.

- **Reduced labor**   Because there was less paperwork to be processed, the company was able to improve control while reducing the labor required to process and audit expense reports.

- **Decreased resources**   Part of the goal was to reduce paper waste. The online system requires fewer forms, and hence, fewer resources.

- **Decreased payment cycle time**   The old process took 8 to 10 days from time of approval to employee reimbursement. Approval sometimes required weeks. The online solution enables a much faster turnaround time. In most cases, payment can be made within one or two days of approval.

Payoffs such as these are a recurrent theme in most Web applications. A well-designed application can improve the way you work, simply by being available wherever there's a browser.

Dynamic HTML

Dynamic HTML (DHTML), supported by Internet Explorer 4.0, is an emerging standard that is more than just an extension to standard HTML. With Dynamic HTML, you can easily add advanced functionality that was previously difficult to achieve without client-side controls. For example, you can:

- Hide text and images in your document and keep this content hidden until a given time elapses or the user wants to view it.

- Animate text and images in your document, independently moving each element from any point to any point in the document, following a path that you choose or that you let the user choose.

- Create a ticker that automatically refreshes its content with the latest news, stock quotes, or other data.

- Create a form, then instantly read, process, and respond to the data the user enters in the form.

Internet Explorer 4.0 does not require additional support from applets or embedded controls to achieve these effects. It automatically reformats and redisplays the DHTML page to reflect dynamic changes in content styles. It does not need to reload the document, load a new document or depend on the server to generate new content. Instead, it uses the power of the user's computer to calculate and carry out changes.

Dynamic HTML documents make heavy use of styles and script to process user input and directly manipulate the HTML tags, attributes, and text in the document. Through the Internet Explorer 4.0 object model, you can control every property of every HTML tag to precisely control the layout, appearance and function of your page.

For more information on Dynamic HTML, visit the Site Builder Dynamic HTML page at http://www.microsoft.com/workshop/author/dhtml/.

Data Binding

Using DHTML, the results of database queries can be "bound" to HTML elements, such as the rows of a table. (You can also use databinding ActiveX Controls, such as the Advanced Data Connector, included in earlier versions of Internet Explorer.) You can use data binding to remotely view and modify the results of database queries within the browser. Data binding is a function of the Remote Data Services (RDS), which is part of the ActiveX Data Objects (ADO) family of data access components. For more information on RDS and ADO, see Chapter 6, "Data Access and Transactions."

Active Desktop

The Active Desktop is a technology provided with Internet Explorer 4.0 that displays content from the Internet and intranet on the Microsoft Windows desktop. The Active Desktop combines:

- Static HTML pages.
- Graphic objects and animations.
- Dynamic HTML, Java, script, or ActiveX documents.
- Subscription content that downloads on a predetermined schedule.

Active Desktop can display any HTML-based page or graphic item. For example, users can customize their desktops to display stock market quotes or hyperlinks to Web pages.

The Active Desktop includes two layers: the transparent *Icon layer*, which exposes desktop shortcuts for the user and the background *HTML layer*, which hosts all desktop components.

The Icon Layer

The Icon Layer extends the features of hyperlinks on a standard Web page, such as single-click navigation and mouse-over highlighting. It also integrates a Web-like environment with features familiar to the Window 95 shell, such as drag-and-drop, file-type associations, double clicking, and so on.

The HTML Layer

The HTML layer is described by a single, local HTML file called Desktop.htm, which is created and edited automatically by Internet Explorer 4.0. This file contains:

- HTML tags that represent each desktop component.
- An ActiveX control that enables moving and resizing of the desktop components and helps to manage the list of desktop components.
- Any other static HTML that the user wants to display in the background. By default, Desktop.htm just contains a reference to the user's chosen wallpaper, which is displayed as the background image of the HTML page.

Users can customize their desktops by installing desktop components designed for Microsoft Internet Explorer 4.0, or by manually specifying a URL (Uniform Resource Locator) for an image or floating frame.

Channels

Channels are another Internet Explorer 4.0 technology with which content can be "pushed" onto a client's computer. You can set up a subscription channel, which the visitors to your site can use to subscribe to your content. When you update the content on that channel, the subscribers are automatically notified, and they can choose to load the data automatically at chosen times, or to load it manually at their convenience. Microsoft Internet Explorer 4.0 provides a standard method for users to schedule information delivery.

Multicast Webcasting

The Webcasting architecture in Internet Explorer 4.0 provides architectural hooks that allow third parties to provide value-added benefits to enrich the Webcasting experience. Microsoft provides an open, extensible information delivery architecture that makes it possible to integrate the market's existing "push" products with the Microsoft Internet Explorer 4.0 Webcasting client. Specifically, you can plug in third-party software that defines new transport protocols or that provides an alternative delivery mechanism for Active Channels.

By taking advantage of special network hardware, multicast protocols provide bandwidth-efficient broadcasting of content throughout a corporate network. Because of Microsoft's extensible Webcasting architecture, the NetShow networked multimedia software component in Internet Explorer 4.0 can receive Active Channel content broadcast with such a protocol.

Browser Support

In intranet scenarios where a single browser type can safely be assumed, you may design your sites around browser-specific technologies with impunity. (If you do so, you should alert your users to this fact with a "Best viewed with" graphic on the site's home page.)

On the Internet, however, you can't assume that everyone has an up-to-date browser. And, even among newer browsers, several different types are available; Microsoft, Netscape, and Sun Microsystems have all released browsers with varying degrees of support for ActiveX, Java, scripting, and HTML. The question of what functionality to perform on the client depends on the variety and capabilities of browsers you want to support.

With the lowest-common-denominator approach, pages contain no more functionality than the least capable browsers can process successfully. Content is guaranteed to be viewable in its entirety on any browser. Unfortunately, users may notice, and be disappointed by, the limited functionality this approach requires.

Some sites provide text-only versions of their pages, or frames-free areas for less capable browsers. This duplication ensures that all users can get the same information, but it requires you to develop, test, and maintain multiple versions of your site. Often the less functional version remains underdeveloped, as the focus of development tends toward "bells and whistles."

The best approach may be to develop pages using a medium level of technology, and to add specific features once you have determined the browser type. This is often a good middle ground, because all pages can be developed using one set of design elements and content. The advanced features of the site are made available only to browsers that support them.

The Browser Capabilities component included with Active Server Pages (ASP) provides a way to detect the browser type and tailor the returned document to exploit browser-specific capabilities. For more information on this component, see the "Scripter's Reference" section of the IIS online product documentation.

The following table summarizes browser support for different client technologies:

Table 5.1   Support for Client Technologies by Browser

Technology	Widely supported	Internet Explorer 3.0x	Internet Explorer 4.0 Only
HTML	X	X	X
Graphics and multimedia	X	X	X
JavaScript	X	X (version 2.0)	X (version 3.0)
VBScript		X	X
Java applets	X	X	X
ActiveX Controls		X	X
Active Documents		X	X
Cascading Style Sheets		X	X
Dynamic HTML			X
Active Channels			X
Active Desktop			X

Limitations of Client Technologies

Although it's possible to create applications that rely exclusively on client-side technologies, these systems effectively mimic client/server architecture, and are susceptible to identical shortcomings. There are several reasons why client/server architecture isn't suitable for full-scale enterprise applications on the Internet:

- A client application using client-side ActiveX Controls or client-side scripting is not supported by all browsers. A line-of-business application for the Internet must work with as many browsers as possible, including those that do not support HTML tables, frames, Java applets, client-side scripting or ActiveX Controls.

- Coding business logic as client-side script fails to protect your programming investment (because the source code is available to all). Java applets and ActiveX Controls are more secure, but whenever you combine business logic with user interface, your application becomes harder to support and debug. In addition, the resulting components are less likely to be reusable in other applications.

- Client-centric applications do not take full advantage of the three-tier programming model. Designs in which the client plays a more than supporting role typically take on tasks that are better suited for the server, such as resource management and data manipulation.

The Middle Tier

This section discusses what is perhaps the most important layer of Web programming, the middle tier. It is here that user input is combined with business logic to perform the work of your site.

The middle tier is not just a single layer of logic. It can consist of many interrelated technologies, seamlessly combined to create the illusion of a single multipurpose layer. For example, the client's request may be preprocessed by an ISAPI filter, then execute a script to run a custom-built component that manipulates a database with ActiveX Data Objects (ADO). Technology integrates with technology, layer upon layer: a demonstration of true *n*-tier architecture.

CGI Applications

In the past, Web server application programming would usually require developing Common Gateway Interface (CGI) programs or scripts.

Common Gateway Interface applications are most widely used on UNIX systems to create executable programs that run on the Web server. CGI programs are typically written in the C language, but can also be written in interpreted languages such as Perl. Remote users can launch CGI applications on the server simply by requesting a URL containing the name of the CGI application. Arguments following the question mark in the URL are passed to the CGI application as environment strings. The output of a CGI application isn't much different from a desktop application; HTTP headers and HTML are generated using the basic output functions of the language (for example, `printf` in C).

CGI applications are easy to write, but scale very poorly on Windows NT. Because a separate process is spawned for each client request, hundreds of clients create hundreds of instances of the CGI program, each requiring their own memory space and system resources. This isn't such a bad thing on UNIX, which is designed to handle multiple processes with very little overhead. Windows NT, which is optimized for thread management inside a process, expends more system resources when creating and destroying application instances.

ISAPI Extensions and Filters

The Internet Server API (ISAPI) was developed specifically for IIS as a high-performance Windows NT alternative to CGI. An ISAPI *extension* is a run time dynamic-link library (DLL) that is usually loaded in the same memory address space occupied by IIS. Since it is a DLL, only one instance of the ISAPI extension needs to be loaded at a time. Of course, the ISAPI extension must be thread-safe, so that multiple client requests can be received simultaneously. Although ISAPI extensions are more complex than CGI applications, ISAPI uses a relatively simple API. For each client request, the Web server invokes the **HttpExtensionProc** ISAPI call and passes a pointer to an ISAPI Extension Control Block (ECB), which contains information about the request. The ISAPI DLL can use server callback functions to access information such as server variables. The ISAPI ECB also provides the developer with access to some general-purpose support functions, such as URL redirection, session management, and response headers, which are not available to CGI applications.

Despite the obvious benefits over CGI, ISAPI extensions present some maintenance problems. For instance, if you want to make even a minor change to the HTML returned by an ISAPI extension, you have to recompile and link it. Also, despite its faster performance and smaller memory requirements, an ISAPI DLL can cause the Web server to crash if it isn't thoroughly tested and verified before being deployed and run in the Web server process.

Fortunately, with IIS 4.0 you can select which ISAPI extensions are loaded in-process with IIS and which extensions should be loaded in a separate process. ISAPI extensions in a separate process can be stopped and restarted independently of the server process, and can be restarted automatically after a crash. Although out-of-process extensions are slower than in-process ones, being able to isolate and reload applications under development is a distinct improvement over earlier versions of IIS. For more information on out-of-process extensions, refer to the section on "Process Isolation and Crash Recovery" in the next chapter.

ISAPI can also be used to create ISAPI *filters*. Filters are a fairly new concept in Web server extensibility—there is no CGI counterpart. ISAPI filters can intercept specific server events before the server itself handles them. The calling convention for filters is very similar to that of extensions. When a filter is loaded (usually as the Web service starts), it indicates what sort of event notifications it will handle. If these events occur, the filter has the option of processing the events, passing them on to other filters, or sending them to the server. In this way, you can use ISAPI filters to provide custom authentication techniques, or to automatically redirect requests based on HTTP headers sent by the client, such as **Accept-Language**.

Filters can be a drag on performance, if they are not written carefully. With IIS 4.0, ISAPI filters can be loaded for the Web server as a whole or for specific Web sites. They cannot, however, be run out-of-process.

Active Server Pages

Active Server Pages (ASP) was introduced as part of IIS 3.0, and has been greatly enhanced for the 4.0 release. ASP greatly simplifies server-side programming so that you easily create dynamic content and powerful Web-based applications.

ASP scripts can perform the same sorts of tasks as CGI and ISAPI applications, but are much easier to write and modify. ASP creates a higher level of interactivity by managing application and session state on the server, thereby reducing the amount of information that needs to be transmitted back and forth between the server and the client. ASP makes it easy to work with information entered into HTML forms, or in the URL as parameters. You can also control advanced HTTP features from script, such as client-side cookies and client security certificates.

At the heart of ASP is an ISAPI extension—Asp.dll— that compiles and caches .asp files in memory at run time using a script interpreter. The IIS *script-map* associates the .asp extension to Asp.dll. Because ASP must interpret and compile scripts before executing them, complex scripts can be about four times slower than plain HTML, and two to three times slower than ISAPI, *when they are first requested*. Afterward, the compiled version of the page is cached in server memory, making subsequent requests significantly faster and amortizing the initial cost of compilation over potentially thousands of page requests.

ASP is designed for usability and ease of development, giving you the opportunity to dramatically decrease the time spent in development. However, it will never outperform static content, or custom-written, task-focused C++ ISAPI extensions. Only carefully designed ASP applications, combined with server-side components, can approach the speed and performance of ISAPI applications.

ASP Server-Side Scripting

You can create highly interactive pages that are independent of the type of browser used to access those pages. Unlike client-side script, with ASP you can "hide" your scripting on the server so that you can protect your development ideas and intellectual property.

ASP script is "language agnostic," meaning that it isn't limited to a particular language. VBScript, JScript, or any language for which a third-party ActiveX Scripting Engine is available (such as PerlScript, REXX, or Python) can be used to create ASP scripts.

ASP scripting instructions appear side-by-side with HTML. (In fact, you can create an ASP page simply by changing the file extension of a plain HTML file to .asp.) To differentiate between HTML and script meant to run at the server, ASP uses special tags, called *server-side scripting delimiters*, to indicate server-side script: **<%** and **%>**. Script appearing inside these delimiters will be invoked on the server as the page is processed. A special form of these scripting delimiters, **<%=** *expression* **%>**, can be used as a shorthand for returning values from script.

The following line of server-side VBScript code returns the current date:

```
Today is <%= Date %>.
```

This instruction generates something like the following line (the exact text depends on the date):

```
Today is 7/4/98.
```

Note   You can also use the **Write** method of the ASP **Response** object to write the results an expressions to the page. For more information, see "Built-in Objects and Server-side Components," later in this chapter.

A slightly more complex example of ASP might use the conditional execution elements of the scripting language, intermixed with HTML, as follows:

```
<% If Hour(Now) < 12 Then %>
    <FONT COLOR=YELLOW>Good Morning!</FONT>
<% ElseIf Hour(Now) < 18 Then %>
    <FONT COLOR=LIME>Good Afternoon!</FONT>
<% Else %>
    <FONT COLOR=ORANGE>Good Evening!</FONT>
<% End If %>
```

You can use more than one scripting language on a single ASP page, though each page has a primary scripting language. You can use Internet Service Manager to set the primary scripting language for an application; you use *declaratives* (also known as *@-directives*) to define it for a page.

ASP subroutines and functions can be in any script language, although if you define them inline with the rest of the script, you're limited to the primary scripting language. To change the scripting language of the subroutine, you need to use HTML <SCRIPT> tags to define them. You will also need to add the RUNAT=SERVER attribute, to indicate that this script is intended for the server rather than the client.

The following example page demonstrates how to combine a variety of scripting languages and subroutine declaration styles into a single ASP file:

```
<%@ Language="VBScript" %>
<html>
<head>

<% Sub InlineSub %>
This text won't be displayed until this subroutine is called.<br>
<% End Sub %>

<script LANGUAGE="VBScript" RUNAT=Server>
   ' Immediate script (outside a function)
   Response.Write "This text is displayed last"
</script>

<script LANGUAGE="JavaScript" RUNAT=Server>
function TestJavaScript(str) {
   Response.Write(str);
}
</script>

<script LANGUAGE="PerlScript" RUNAT=Server>
sub TestPerlScript {
   $Response->Write($_[0]);
}
</script>
</head>

<body BGCOLOR=#FFFFFF>
<%
   Response.Write "This is VBScript<br>"
   TestJavaScript "This is JavaScript<br>"
   TestPerlScript "This is PerlScript<br>"
   InlineSub
%>
</body>
</html>
```

Note You can use <SCRIPT> tags to enclose immediate server-side script, but don't expect it to be run until the entire page has been processed. Earlier versions of ASP used <SCRIPT> tags before the introduction of the <% %> delimiters, but their use for immediate script is now discouraged. You should reserve server-side <SCRIPT> tags for defining functions and subroutines only.

Use the scripting language that best suits your needs. VBScript contains helpful string manipulation and financial functions not available in JavaScript. On the other hand, JavaScript includes support for Regular Expression pattern matching and an Internet-friendly URL class. You may want to combine the features of multiple scripting languages to get the greatest level of flexibility and performance for your application.

ASP Script Execution Behavior

When you write ASP applications, you're operating in the world of IIS and HTTP. Web developers who don't have a firm grasp of this architecture find themselves puzzled by strange errors in what seems to be straightforward code.

Consider the diagram shown in Figure 5.4.

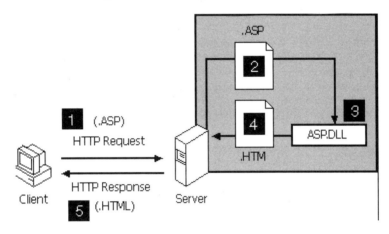

Figure 5.4   Requesting an ASP file from IIS

When a client browser requests an ASP page, a number of events occur in the following sequence:

1. The client requests an ASP page by sending an HTTP Request to the Web server.

2. Because the page has the .asp extension, the server (IIS) recognizes it as a script-mapped file, and sends the file to the appropriate ISAPI extension (in this case, Asp.dll) for processing. (This step does not occur when the client requests an HTML file.)

3. The ASP ISAPI processes any server-side include directives first, before any server-side script is compiled. Next, the script is executed, and dynamic text, if any, is incorporated into the page that will be returned to the client. (This step only happens when the page is first requested. Previously compiled pages are retrieved from a server-side cache for faster performance.)

4. The server sends the resulting HTML page back to the client in the form of an HTTP Response. The page output is sent incrementally as the page is generated, or all at once if the response is buffered.

5. Once the client receives the response, it loads any client-side objects and applets, executes any immediate client-side script code and displays the Web page according to the HTML specification.

While this process looks simple, keep in mind that the client and server could be hundreds, or even thousands, of miles apart. Therefore, when a problem arises, you must determine *where* the error is occurring: on the client or on the server? Equally important is understanding *when* each operation takes place. After ASP completes its processing in step 3 and sends the response in step 4, it moves on to other activities and other clients. The only way the client can recapture the server's attention is to request another page via the HTTP protocol. In other words, there is no real connection between the client and server. This is a very important concept.

Sometimes developers try to access server-side scripts or objects from the client, or conversely, client-side objects or scripts from the server. For example, consider client-side code that attempts to access one of ASP's built-in objects, such as the **Session** object. The attempt is destined for failure because the code running on the client has no way of accessing an object located on the server. A typical error message might appear as follows:

```
VBS Script Error: Object Required: Session
```

Now consider an example in which a server-side script attempts to manipulate a client-side object. Suppose the developer wants to use server-side script to populate a client-side control called Listbox1, using the following instruction:

```
<% ListBox1.AddItem Value1 %>
```

The problem is that the HTML page, including the list box, does not yet exist when the server-side code is executed. Therefore, this instruction generates an error.

On the other hand, you can use server-side code to generate client-side code to populate a list box. For example, you could create a **Window_OnLoad** event, which is executed by the browser as soon as the window and its child controls are created. The following code uses server-side script to provide the AddItem method with values stored in the variables Value1, Value2, and Value3.

```
<SCRIPT LANGUAGE="VBScript"><!--
Sub Window_OnLoad()
   ListBox1.AddItem "<%= Value1 %>"
   ListBox1.AddItem "<%= Value2 %>"
   ListBox1.AddItem "<%= Value3 %>"
End Sub
--></SCRIPT>
```

Note   If you use the HTML <SELECT> tag instead of an ActiveX control, the procedure is slightly more direct. Because a list box created with the <SELECT> tag is based on HTML code, you can use server-side scripting to generate the <OPTION> tags. Since the HTML is self-contained, you do not need to place any code inside a **Window_OnLoad** event.

Built-In Objects and Server-Side Components

If you have ever written client-side script, you have probably found yourself using built-in browser objects such as **document**, **form**, and **window**. These objects are provided as part of the browser's object model, and make interaction with the browser much more manageable. Likewise, ASP defines its own object model.

The **Response** object described earlier is one of ASP's built-in objects, of which there are currently six: **Server**, **Application**, **Session**, **Request**, **Response**, and **ObjectContext**. These objects greatly simplify the interaction between the server and the client. A description of each appears in the sidebar, "The Built-In ASP Objects."

In addition to the built-in ASP objects, you can create and manipulate a variety of custom server-side components. By combining Active Scripting with server-side COM components, also known as *server-side objects*, you extend the functionality of ASP with powerful, easy-to-use packages. You can instantiate server-side components by using the **CreateObject** method of the **Server** object and passing it the *ProgID* of the component you wish to create. Once the component is instantiated, you can access any of its properties or methods. For example, the following script instantiates a server-side object with **Server.CreateObject** and stores a reference to it in the variable objAdRotator:

```
<% Set objAdRotator = Server.CreateObject("MSWC.AdRotator") %>
```

The Built-In ASP Objects

Active Server Pages provides built-in objects that make it easier for you to gather information sent with a browser request, to respond to the browser, and to store information about a particular user.

Server Object

The **Server** object provides access to methods and properties on the server. The most frequently used method is the one that creates an instance of an COM component (**Server.CreateObject**). Other methods apply URL or HTML encoding to strings, map virtual paths to physical paths, and set the timeout period for a script.

Application Object

You use the **Application** object to store global application settings and share information among all users of a given ASP application.

Session Object

You use the **Session** object to store information needed for a particular user session. Variables stored in the **Session** object are not discarded when the user jumps between pages in the application; instead, these variables persist for the entire time the user is accessing pages in an application. You can also use **Session** methods to explicitly end a session and set the timeout period for an idle session.

Request Object

You use the **Request** object to gain access to any information that is passed with an HTTP request. This includes name/value pairs passed from an HTML form using either the POST method or the GET method, cookies, and client certificates. The **Request** object also gives you access to binary data sent to the server, such as file uploads.

Response Object

You use the **Response** object to control the information you send back to a user. This includes sending information to the browser, redirecting the browser to another URL, or setting cookie values.

ObjectContext Object

You use the **ObjectContext** object to either commit or abort a transaction initiated by an ASP script. For more information, see Chapter 6, "Data Access and Transactions." You can also use this object to access the other built-in ASP objects from within a component.

To get you started, the default ASP installation includes several task-oriented components, including the MyInfo, Ad Rotator, and Browser Capabilities components. When you install the Microsoft Data Access Components (MDAC), which is included in the Windows NT 4.0 Option Pack, you can also use the ActiveX Data Objects (ADO) to access information stored in a SQL Server, Oracle, or Microsoft Access database.

More components are available on the IIS Resource Kit CD, including the Content Rotator, Page Counter, and Permissions Checker components. You'll also find the Collaboration Data Objects (CDO), which you can use to send SMTP mail and access messages in a Microsoft Exchange Server message store. Of course, you aren't limited to these objects. You are strongly encouraged to create your own objects to enhance your Web site and implement your own style of business logic.

The following example demonstrates how to instantiate and use the Content Rotator component, a server-side object used to display different HTML content each time a Web page is loaded. In this case, it is used to display a "Tip of the Day" when the page is generated:

```
<% Set objTip = Server.CreateObject("MSWC.ContentRotator") %>
<%= objTip.ChooseContent("/tips/tiprot.txt") %>
```

The Content Rotator component works in conjunction with a Content Schedule File, a specially formatted text file that defines the content text. The schedule file also defines a weight value, which affects the percentage of time the content is displayed. This file must be available from the virtual directory root. For example, depending on the definitions contained in the Tiprot.txt file, the previous example might generate the following HTML, which is added to the response page's output:

```
Smile! Frowns put people off.
```

Why Components?

You could spend a lot of time writing ASP script that emulates component functionality, but there are several reasons not to do so:

- Script is much slower than a compiled object and will be less likely to scale to large numbers of users.

- Script doesn't separate presentation from functionality. Undifferentiated script scatters business logic throughout the application, making it hard to find bugs and increasing the cost of maintenance.

- Components are inherently reusable; scripts are not. Components may also be used by other applications, such as those built in Visual Basic or C++.

Therefore, your development motto should be: The less script, the better. If you are serious about performance and application scalability, you should use components to perform the bulk of your business logic.

So, what makes a good server-side object? Generally, anything that expands the functionality of the server and scripting language is a candidate for a server-side object. Some server-side objects generate HTML that cannot be easily generated by ASP itself. Others perform server functions, like accessing the registry, sending mail, or administering a resource.

A compact memory footprint, computational speed, and multi-user reentrancy are high priorities for server-side objects. Component stability is key too. Memory leaks affect other applications on the server, and badly behaved components can cause IIS to crash. (If a component is not fully debugged, you can isolate it in its own process. See "Process Isolation and Crash Recovery" in Chapter 6, "Data Access and Transactions.")

Because ASP component objects exist on the server, they should never rely on user-interface elements, like dialog boxes or pop-ups. When reporting errors, they should use the Windows NT Event Log, or return detailed error information in the **Err** object, so problems can be reported to the user with script.

Reuse, Buy, or Build

When it comes time to procure components for your application, reuse the objects you already have if possible. If none of your pre-built objects will do, consider buying third-party components from a reputable vendor.

If you can't locate a pre-built component, you will have to build it yourself. Server-side components can be built using any development tool that supports the creation of COM Automation servers, such as Visual Basic, Visual J++™, or Visual C++. As with scripts, choose the component language that suits your needs. Visual Basic 5.0 creates "Apartment" threaded components that can be used on a page-by-page basis. If computational speed and multiuser re-entrancy are important to your application, you should use Visual C or Visual C++ with ATL 2.0 to develop your component. Visual C and Visual C++ can create "Both" threaded components that are suitable for use in the Application and Session scope. (For more information on threading considerations, see "Selecting Object Scope" later in this chapter.)

For more information on creating a server-side component, see to the "ASP Tutorial" topics in the "Web Applications" section of the IIS online product documentation.

Using XRay to View Component Type Libraries

As you develop your scripts, the ability to view a component's methods and properties is extremely helpful. The XRay object browser, included on the IIS Resource Kit CD provides the ability to browse a variety of component type libraries.

Using XRay, you can view type libraries contained in executables, DLLs, and any OCX, TLB, or OLB file. Component methods and properties are initially displayed in the left-hand pane sorted by object, but can be "reverse sorted" into a unique list of members followed by the objects to which they belong. The right-hand pane can display method prototypes (which include the data types of all parameters) or Help information if it is available. Figure 5.5 shows how the **Request** and **Response** objects of Asp.dll appear when viewed with XRay.

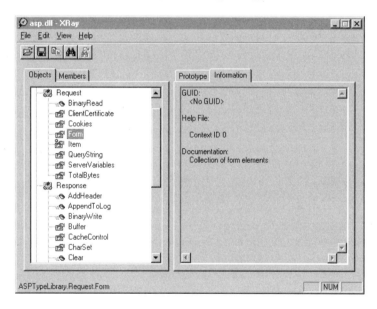

Figure 5.5   The ASP object library as viewed in Xray

ASP Applications

So far, this chapter has presented several examples of ASP scripts that create HTML on the fly. Stand-alone pages, however, are only the beginning of what you can do with ASP. This section discusses how to use the ASP **Session** and **Application** objects to create a coherent application out of an independent series of ASP files. It also walks you through the different elements of an ASP application, and discusses how to configure it using Internet Service Manager.

ASP Session Management

Since HTTP is a stateless protocol, the Web server retains no memory of past actions and treats each browser request as a one-time event. This statelessness makes it is difficult for Web developers to create the level of application interactivity that most users expect. Although persistent application state can be maintained in a database or stored in files, such solutions are often difficult to implement, and involve a hefty memory overhead and performance penalty. ASP surmounts these problems by providing its own session management.

Using the ASP **Session** object, one of the ASP built-in objects, developers can store any data they wish, including references to objects they have instantiated. The **Session** object is analogous to an associative array, into which values may be stored and retrieved by using a string (or keyword) as the index.

For example, the following instruction assigns "John Doe" to the MyName entry in the array:

```
<% Session("MyName") = "John Doe" %>
```

The value "John Doe" is retrieved from the **Session** object by using the MyName keyword, as shown here:

```
My name is:
```

The **Session** object exists in memory on the server and maintains its state for the duration of the user's Web session. The **Application** object is used in a similar fashion to store values that persist for the lifetime of the ASP application; it is also used to share values across user sessions. The values stored in the **Session** and **Application** objects persist between page requests, and can be retrieved at any point using the keyword to which they were assigned.

You can disable the **Session** object on a page-by-page basis using the declarative, `<%@ EnableSessionState=False %>`. Disabling the **Session** object does not affect values that have previously been stored in the **Session** object. However, it may speed up the processing of pages that don't use the **Session** object. Furthermore, multiple ASP pages in an HTML frameset may be serialized (run in sequential order) if they use session state. Disabling the **Session** object in child frames that don't require it will allow the frame requests to execute concurrently.

ASP Sessions Are Cookie-Based

ASP uses HTTP cookies to identify user sessions with unique session keys. Once an ASP session begins, ASP responds to a user's request with a Set-Cookie HTTP header. From that point on, each browser request is identified by the session ID cookie.

Web Farms and ASP Session State

ASP session information is stored in memory on the Web server, which creates a challenge for sites using ASP in a Web farm environment. Web farms balance the load of user requests among a number of Web servers. In order to use ASP **Session** management, the *same* Web server must handle all requests from a user for the life of the session, a prerequisite that most load-balancing schemes cannot guarantee.

Several options are available if you want to use ASP in a Web farm:

- Write your own session management logic to replace that provided by ASP. Keep your session state in a centralized place, such as a database.

- Use a third-party solution. For example, Cisco Systems' LocalDirector hardware load-balancer can ensure that the same client gets the same server for multiple connections.

- Load-balance *new* requests, but once a session begins, make sure that all subsequent requests return to the same server during the life of the session. This technique is called ASP session-aware load balancing.

ASP Session-Aware Load Balancing

In this scenario, all new requests continue to use the existing load-balancing mechanisms (such as round-robin DNS) to distribute requests to a site's published URL. Then, during the **Session_OnStart** event, the ASP script uses the **Response** object to **Redirect** the browser to the application's start page using the local computer's own IP address or unique name, as follows:

Finally, to ensure the browser will confine its requests to the same Web farm server, all application links must be *relative URLs*. Relative URLs only specify path information relative to the current location, for example:

```
<A HREF="MyAsp.Asp">...</A>
```

```
<FORM METHOD=POST ACTION="./SubDir/FormAction.asp">...</FORM>
```

When one of these links is selected, the browser will construct the full URL path using the current address (specified in the redirect) and the relative URL, thus enabling it to locate the computer hosting the user session.

This technique may not be appropriate for all Web applications. Also, if users save URLs using favorites or bookmarks, they will return to a specific computer which can defeat the purpose of proper load balancing.

Here's an example of an ASP session ID cookie:

```
Set-Cookie: ASPSESSIONIDGGGGGJZB=EFENHLNDIIEHJGJOAGICNPEK; path=/
```

This is different from earlier versions of ASP, which would set the cookie path to that of the ASP application's virtual directory. In IIS 4.0, only one cookie is sufficient for *all* applications on the server. Once the cookie is received, every browser request includes the same HTTP cookie header:

```
Cookie: ASPSESSIONIDGGGGGJZB=EFENHLNDIIEHJGJOAGICNPEK
```

ASP uses this value to retrieve the correct **Session** object for the client connection. All requests to the application directory include the session ID cookie, even those for static HTML content in subdirectories of the ASP application. In this example, the cookie does not specify an expiration time, so it is only valid as long as there is an open client session. The cookie expires when the user closes the browser.

Note If a user chooses not to accept the ASP cookie (or if the browser fails to return it in subsequent requests) the application will not be able to map the browser request to an existing **Session** object and will create a new one.

It is possible for several browser instances to share the same cookie, which means that more than one browser window can be accessing different sections of your application at the same time, but make modifications to the same **Session** object. This is especially bad news for applications that make heavy use of session state, and is another reason to use session state only when necessary.

ASP session IDs are mapped to the in-memory **Session** object on the server. This works well when only one server is managing the user session. When using ASP in a Web farm, however, more than one server may be handling the user's request. For more information on how to manage session IDs in a Web farm, see the sidebar, "Web Farms and ASP Session State."

ASP Session IDs Are Not Unique

Applications that require a unique user identifier should not use the ASP session ID. The ASP session ID is unique only for the life of the current application. If the application restarts, the server may conceivably reassign the same session ID to another user. In a multiple-server environment, like a Web farm, the likelihood of duplicate IDs increases. Consequently, it is not advisable to use an ASP-issued session ID as a unique key for tables, or any persistent user identity.

Instead of using the ASP session ID, you must use a separate mechanism designed to create unique numbers across multiple servers and sessions. Microsoft Transaction Server (MTS) includes the component TakeANumber, can be used to generate unique sequential numbers for user identification. (For more information on this component, see the sidebar "Take A Number: An MTS Example.")

Take A Number: An MTS Example

Microsoft Transaction Server (MTS) includes the TakeANumber component designed to produce sequential numbers. Because the number is incremented as part of a transaction, you are guaranteed a unique identifier that works across sessions and across servers.

The TakeANumber component is installed with MTS, but requires a little preparation to use. You first need to define a SQL Server table to store the current number. This table must be named "TakeANumber" and contain two columns named "NextNumber" (integer type) and "PropertyGroupName" (string type). The PropertyGroupName column identifies which counter you are using—more than a single counter can be stored in the table. Once your table is ready, you need to enter the first number of the series. The following SQL statement should do the trick:

```
INSERT INTO TakeANumber VALUES (1234, 'MyProp')
```

Finally, create a File DSN so that the component can connect to the table you just created. You can create a File DSN with the ODBC Administrator application in Control Panel. For step-by-step instructions, see "Data Source Names," in Chapter 6, "Data Access and Transactions."

Now you're ready to use the component. The following instructions retrieve the next number from the MyProp series:

```
<%@ Language=VBScript EnableSessionState=False %>
<HTML>
<HEAD><TITLE>Take A Number</TITLE></HEAD>
<BODY BGCOLOR=#FFFFFF>
<% Set tn = Server.CreateObject("MTS_TakeANumber.TakeANumber") %>
Next Number: <%= tn.GetANumber ("TakeANumber.dsn", "MyProp") %>
</BODY>
</HTML>
```

As long as each server in your site connects to the same TakeANumber database, you are guaranteed a unique identifier across servers.

ASP Session ID and Session Security

The cookie approach to session management could become a potential security problem. If a hacker were able to capture, or guess, the session ID cookie in use by an active session, he or she could submit valid HTTP requests that included this cookie. In this manner a hacker could hijack, or steal, a user's active session. For example, if a user had supplied valid credit card information, and an ASP script stored this information in the **Session** object, a hacker who managed to hijack the session could make purchases using the stolen session. For this reason, the following precautions are taken when generating ASP session cookies:

- Session ID values are 32-bit long integers.

- Each time the Web server is restarted, a random Session ID starting value is selected.

- For each new ASP session that is created, the Session ID value is incremented.

- The 32-bit Session ID is mixed with random data and encrypted to generate a 16-character cookie string. Later, when a cookie is received, the Session ID is decrypted from the 16-character cookie string.

- The encryption key is randomly selected each time the Web server is restarted.

ASP session ID values are selected from a huge range and are encrypted, making it difficult to capture a valid cookie. In addition, guessing a valid cookie once does not make it easy to guess another valid cookie.

If the complexity of the ASP cookie generation algorithm does not meet the security requirements of your site, user authentication and client certificates can be used in conjunction with session management to provide even more security to your Web applications. For more information, see Chapter 8, "Security."

Building an ASP Application

In its simplest form, an ASP application consists of all the HTML and script files stored within an application boundary. Before any sessions are created, the application initializes, instantiates application-scope components, and imports type-library declarations. From that point on, each connected user has a separate and distinct session, with its own values and component instances. The rest of this section explains how application and session management is accomplished.

Application Boundaries

An ASP-based application consists of all the files in its root virtual directory and in any subdirectories. An application defines a *namespace* (also called the *application root*), that begins at the root directory and includes all files, directories, virtual directories contained within—except those that are application roots themselves or ancestors of another application root. For example, if a virtual directory "Applications" and its subdirectory "Isolated Applications" are both application roots, then URLs that contain only "/Application" are part of one application, and URLs that contain "/Application/Isolated Application" are part of the other. Figure 5.6 illustrates how this looks in Internet Service Manager.

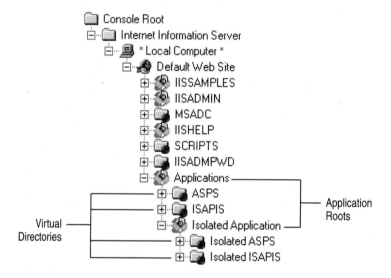

Figure 5.6   Application roots and virtual directories

In Figure 5.6, the virtual directories ASPS and ISAPIS are contained within the Applications namespace. The Isolated ASPS and Isolated ISAPIS virtual directories are part of the other application.

Application developers can enforce a logical division between applications with separate application roots. Any **Application** and **Session** variables created in an application's namespace are segregated from the **Application** and **Session** variables of other applications on the server. There is currently no way to view values from other applications.

If an ASP file appears in a directory for which no application root is defined, it runs within the context of the global application (the one defined for the Web server's root directory, WWWRoot). If the global application is removed, any stand-alone ASP files in the site will return an application error.

Global.asa

Global.asa is used to store information used globally by the application; it does not generate content that is displayed to users. Global.asa must be stored in the starting point (normally the root directory) of the application. An application can have only one Global.asa file.

Global.asa files contain only the following: **Application** events, **Session** events, object declarations, and type library declarations. If you include script that is not enclosed by <SCRIPT> tags, or define an object that does not have session or application scope, the server returns an error. The server ignores tagged script that the application or session events do not use, as well as any HTML in the file.

Application and Session Events

Every application has two events associated with it: **Application_OnStart** and **Application_OnEnd**. The script for these events is defined with server-side <SCRIPT> tags within Global.asa. Event script can be written in any language supported by the server. **Application_OnStart** is called once for each application when the first client makes a request for a page within the application boundaries. The **Application_OnStart** event procedure is a good place to set global state variables and create any objects that will be used by all users of the application.

After the **Application_OnStart** event and for each subsequent new session, the **Session_OnStart** event occurs. An ASP application should use the **Session_OnStart** event to perform any required session initialization tasks. At this point, a **Session** object and a **Request** object exist. The **Session** object includes a unique session ID; the **Request** object includes fully parsed collections of values passed by the browser, as well as the server environment variables.

The **Session_OnStart** event procedure is a good place to redirect to the start page of your application. If you don't redirect, the application begins execution with the document requested in the URL, or it will begin with one of the default documents configured in Internet Service Manager for the application's virtual root. Redirection allows you to control where your application will go first.

Since the **Response.Write** method is not available during the processing of event procedures, you won't immediately be able to report errors if they occur. However, if you want to notify the user of any problems, you can save the error text in the **Session** or **Application** object (depending on which event handler caused the error) and report it on the first page that is loaded thereafter.

A session ends either when it times out or when the **Session.Abandon** method is called. When this happens, the **Session_OnEnd** event procedure is called, giving you the chance to destroy any object references, and perform any other session clean up. Of the server built-in objects, only the **Application**, **Session** and **Server** objects are available to the **OnEnd** event handlers. Additionally, you can't use the **MapPath** or **CreateObject** methods of the **Server** object during the **Session_OnEnd** event.

Ending the ASP Session

Unless you have provided a means for explicitly logging off, there is no way to determine if the user is still actively connected to your application. HTTP is a stateless protocol, and doesn't keep track of user connections. The user could be off on a Web surfing holiday, and may never return.

For this reason, ASP provides a mechanism to close a session when a specified timeout period expires. If a user begins a session but stops making requests to the Web application, ASP automatically triggers the **Session_OnEnd** event. The timeout period defaults to 20 minutes, but can be adjusted by setting the **Timeout** property of the **Session** object. You can also change the default value by right-clicking the application's virtual directory in Internet Service Manager, clicking **Properties**, clicking the **Configuration** button, selecting the **App Options** tab, and typing a value in the ASP Script timeout box.

For applications that cache a database connection or consume a lot of server resources, the session timeout period may represent a time that other users cannot access server resources. If your application falls into this category, you should consider letting the user end the session when finished. You can do this by simply providing a Log Out button. When the button is clicked, the application calls the **Session.Abandon** method, which immediately triggers the **Session_OnEnd** event.

This session-timeout characteristic of Web applications is equally troublesome to applications that rely on resources that require user authentication. If the user ignores a running application for too long, the application will end the session and log off any connections it has established. If the user makes another request, the application may not function as expected.

You can avoid this timeout problem with a little planning. One popular method of detecting session timeouts is by storing the **Session** object's **SessionID** property as a **Session** variable. Then, each time the user tries to navigate to a page requiring a valid connection, you check the current **SessionID** against the ID stored in the **Session** object. If they did not match (or if the **Session** variable is empty), you have detected a session timeout, and you can take appropriate action.

Importing Type Library Constants with Global.asa

A COM component typically includes a list of named constants as part of its type library, along with other information about the component that enables it to be automated by other applications.

If your Web application uses a COM component that has declared enumerated data types in its type library, you can import them into your application space in Global.asa. Doing so makes it possible to refer to the data types declared in the type library by name from any script within the application boundary. The syntax for importing a type library is as follows:

```
<!--METADATA TYPE="TypeLib"
NAME="typelibraryname"
FILE="file"
UUID="typelibraryuuid"
VERSION="majorversionnumber.minorversionnumber"
-->
```

You're required to specify either the FILE or the UUID parameter, but your application will be more portable if you specify both. The NAME parameter may come in handy if you have to disambiguate enumerated constants that have the same name but are from from different type libraries. The following example imports the constants declared in the ActiveX Data Objects (ADO) type library:

```
<!--METADATA TYPE="TypeLib" NAME="ADO"
FILE="C:\Program Files\Common Files\System\ado\msado15.dll"
UUID="00000200-0000-0010-8000-00AA006D2EA4" VERSION="2.0"
-->
```

Declaring Objects in Global.asa

You can declare objects in Global.asa with session or application scope by using the extended <OBJECT> tag. This tag is placed outside of any <SCRIPT> tags. In addition to setting ID and CLASSID parameters, you must set SCOPE (either "Session" or "Application") and RUNAT=SERVER. This example creates an instance of the Page Counter component:

```
<OBJECT ID=GlobalPageCounter SCOPE=Application RUNAT=Server
    CLASSID="clsid:4B0BAE86-567A-11D0-9607-444553540000">
</OBJECT>
```

Having defined the **GlobalPageCounter** object in Global.asa, you can use it from any ASP file in your application without first retrieving it from the **Application** or **Session** object, or specifically calling **Server.CreateObject** first.

```
There have been <%= GlobalPageCounter.Hits("default") %> hits.
```

Note The objects declared in Global.asa with <OBJECT> tags are not fully instantiated until the server processes a script that references that object. This saves resources by creating objects only as necessary.

Selecting Object Scope

Components can exist and operate within the scope of an application or session, or they can be created and destroyed on a page by page basis.

Objects stored in the **Application** are available to all users of the application. The **Application** object is a suitable place to store objects, such as a page counter, that have no user affinity. Normally, values and objects with application scope are created when the application begins, and are accessed in a read-only fashion by users of the application. When you make changes to **Application** object values, you should use the **Lock** and **Unlock** methods to prevent users from accessing data while it is changing.

In general, very few components should be given application scope. Application scope components should support the "Both" threading model, as "Apartment" threaded components force the **Application** object into a single thread of execution, and free-threaded components tend to be slower overall. MTS components should never be given application scope.

The **Session** object is designed to store information about the current user's session. Components stored in this object can exist as long as the user's session is active. Since each value and object stored in the **Session** increases the server's memory requirements for each user of the application, you should store values for only as long as they are necessary, and free them when they are no longer needed.

Page-scope components are created each time the page is requested. Page-scope components can use any threading model, but only the "Apartment" and "Both" models are recommended for scalability purposes.

A Note about Application Testing

Performance testing, especially using multiuser scenarios, is a critical part of Web application design and development, and needs to be considered as a part of the overall planning of the application. Performance testing is much more critical for server applications than for desktop applications, because managing simultaneous users places higher demands on the application.

Using the **Session** object to store values increases the memory requirements of your application, and therefore decreases the number of concurrent users an application can support. When you build your application, the following three factors determine how much server memory your application will consume:

- **Concurrent sessions** The number of sessions that exist at any given moment is cumulative over the lifetime of the **Session** object. So, if you have a **Session.Timeout** value of 20 minutes, your concurrent sessions will be equal to the number of connections you expect to service over a 20 minute period.

- **Variables and objects per session** How many objects or variables are you storing? A few session settings are fine. Long lists of session-scope variables (especially if they are components) should be avoided. As the number of variables increases, the time it takes to retrieve them also increases.

- **Size of each variable or object stored** Are you storing lengthy strings, or large component objects? Store them for as long as necessary, and then free them—replace long strings with empty string and objects with **Nothing** (or **Null**).

For more tips on application optimization and tuning, see Appendix C, "Debugging Applications and Components."

Design Patterns for Web Applications

Web application developers may find that the model used by applications on the Web conflicts with the conceptual model they have developed for other platforms. For instance, unless you use client-side ActiveX Controls or Java applets, your user interface is limited to an HTML description of the form inputs or a list of links to other areas of your site. Despite Dynamic HTML and ASP, most Web-based applications will never consist of more than an interconnected series of dynamically generated static states. Click a button, something happens. Click a link, a new page appears.

This final section of the chapter explores effective Web-application design, and covers a variety of techniques that you can use to enhance your applications. It also introduces two sample Web applications, which are available on the IIS Resource Kit CD.

Factoring Your Application

A Web application is a hierarchy of interdependent pages, each one representing a distinct stage of the application. Web applications map an ordered sequence of input events to a corresponding sequence of output events, using a finite number of elements.

It's helpful to name the elements used to build Web applications. Most applications make use of (or should make use of) the following elements: content, hyperlinks, forms, components, server-side actions, redirection, and loops.

- **Content** Content—data presented in the form of text, graphics, or even music or video files—is the most common element in most Web applications. Content can be presented on static HTML pages or be dynamically generated by an ASP page. Content elements usually have one well-defined entry point with links to other pages.

- **Hyperlink** The primary purpose of hyperlinks is to facilitate movement to other pages or parts of the same page. Site maps, toolbars, hrefs, anchors, form buttons, and navigational controls are all examples of hyperlinks. These elements often appear in their own browser frame and control the navigation throughout the site. They can also appear as a separate index page or table of contents, which is replaced once a link is selected. Hyperlinks represent a user choice, very much like a menu option does in a stand-alone application.

- **Form** Forms are used to collect information from the user. Depending on how a form is designed, what happens when it is submitted may be fixed, or may change as a condition of the user input. Forms can be chained together consecutively to create "Web wizards," and are usually followed by client-side or server-side actions to process them.

- **Component** A component is any code-level unit that provides a relatively independent piece of logic that can be used either separately or in combination with other components throughout the application. Their level of granularity and scope of responsibility distinguishes components from other application elements. Components can generate content or provide server-side logic.

- **Action** Action in this case means an action taken by the application in response to user action. When the user submits a form, for example, the application takes action (it processes the form). Action pages perform business logic, such as data entry, calculations, or administrative functions. Action (processing) can occur both on the server and on the client, and can be used to generate content such as confirmations or error messages.

- **Redirection**   Redirection is usually more adaptable and flexible if implemented as a separate ASP page. A redirection page or script can perform logic to branch the flow of the application. Although it doesn't actually perform a redirect, a page containing a frameset can also be considered a redirection page, since it causes other pages to load.

- **Loop**   Loop pages are ASP pages that refer to themselves to present different content, depending on user input.

You can create a huge variety of complex applications using just the elements described in this list.

The Survey Sample Application

The Survey application presents a survey for users to fill out. After a period of time has passed, users can return to the same Web page to view a compilation of the results. If a user returns to the survey page after having filled out the survey, but before the publication date of the compilation, the user is presented with a notice indicating that each user is allowed to fill out the survey only once. The Survey application is an example of how a single Web address can present different content, according to the logic of an application.

Figure 5.7 displays a flowchart of the Survey application:

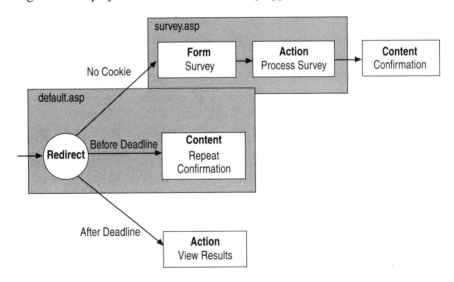

Figure 5.7   Flowchart of the Survey application

The application's home page, Default.asp, uses redirection to display one of the following: the survey (Survey.asp), if the user has not already filled it out; the results of the survey on or after the publication date; or a repeat-visit notice before the survey-results publication date, if the visitor has already filled out the survey.

The Survey application uses a cookie to determine whether a user has visited: only if there is no cookie does the application present the survey (users are not allowed to fill out the survey more than once).

Web applications can be easier to manage if application elements are kept on separate pages. In the Survey application, some elements are on separate pages; others are not. For example, the redirection element is separate from the survey form, but the form's processing logic is contained on the same page as the survey (Survey.asp). If the survey were larger, it might make sense to remove the form processing logic to a separate page—to separate, in effect, data and presentation from application logic.

Of all the application elements, forms and the redirection are perhaps the most powerful if used correctly. The next sections describe these in more detail.

Using Forms for Input

The standard method of interacting with Web pages is the HTML form. Forms can contain any number of inputs, including text entry, command buttons, "radio" selection controls, and check boxes. Forms can be as simple as a single button, or they can contain a complex layout of client-side controls. A Web page may contain several distinct form structures, each with its own processing logic to be performed when the form is submitted.

Suppose you want your users to log on to your Web application by providing a user name and password. To accomplish this task, you create a simple HTML page with two text fields and a Submit button in an HTML form.

The HTML for the form might look like the following example:

```
<FORM ACTION="./Logon.asp" METHOD="GET">
Your name:     <INPUT TYPE="TEXT"     NAME="User">
Your password: <INPUT TYPE="PASSWORD" NAME="Pwd">
<INPUT TYPE="SUBMIT" VALUE="Log On">
</FORM>
```

When this form is submitted, the values entered by the user are collected and sent to the server as a request. These values are passed as name/value pairs to the page referenced in the ACTION attribute of the <FORM> tag, and are appended to the requested URL after a question mark (?), and separated by ampersands (&). If the user had entered "John Doe" as the user name, and "Amnesia" as the password, the following URL would be requested when the Submit button was clicked.

```
http://myServer/test/Logon.asp?User=John+Doe&Pwd=Amnesia
```

Any information appended to the URL like this is said to be *URL encoded*. URL encoding replaces reserved characters, like spaces and ampersands, with URL-neutral characters. The space in "John Doe" is replaced by a plus character (+). Pluses, equal signs, commas, percent symbols, and question marks also need to be encoded. These and other special characters can be represented in the format *%hh*, where *hh* is the hexadecimal value of the ASCII code for that character.

ASP provides a server-side method to perform encoding (and decoding) for your parameterized URLs, **Server.UrlEncode**. Whenever you create hyperlinks that contain name/value pairs, you should always encode them to avoid invalid URL syntax. Unfortunately, you cannot use this ASP method on the client, since it is a method of a server-side object. You could write a client-side script function to do this, but it's easier to let the form processing logic of the browser do it for you.

The Difference between GET and POST

When the user enters information in a form and clicks Submit, there are two ways the information can be sent from the browser to the server: in the URL, or within the body of the HTTP request.

The GET method, which was used above, appends name/value pairs to the URL. Unfortunately, the length of a URL is limited, so this method only works if there are only a few parameters. The URL could be truncated if the form uses a large number of parameters, or if the parameters contain large amounts of data. Also, parameters passed on the URL are visible in the Address field of the browser—not the best place for a password to be displayed.

The alternative to GET is the POST method. This method packages the name/value pairs inside the body of the HTTP request, which makes for a cleaner URL and imposes no size limitations on the form's output.

ASP makes it simple to retrieve name/value pairs. If the form's output is passed after the question mark (?) on the URL, as occurs when using the GET request method, the parameters can be retrieved using the **Request.QueryString** collection. Likewise, if the form is sent using the POST method, the form's output is be parsed into the **Request.Form** collection. These collections let you address the form and URL parameters by name. For example, the value of the form variable User can be passed into a VBScript variable with one line of script:

```
<% UserName = Request.Form("User") %>
```

You don't need to specify the collection (**Form** or **QueryString**) in which you expect to find the User parameter. The following is an equally valid method of searching for the User parameter:

```
<% UserName = Request("User") %>
```

In the absence of a specific collection, the **Request** object will search *all* of its collections for a matching parameter. This is meant to be a programming convenience. However, the ASP **Request** object also contains collections for **ServerVariables** and **ClientCertificates**, which contain sensitive server and user authentication information. To avoid the possibility of "spoofed" values, values entered by the user in the URL, it is highly recommended that you explicitly use the collection name when searching for parameters from these collections.

The following script combines a form and an action (the script that processes the form) into a single page. By posting the form data back to the same ASP page that displays the form, server-side script can process the output of the form. This is perfectly valid, and for simple script is often more convenient than posting to a second ASP page.

```
<%@ Language="VBScript" %>
<!-- FILE: logon.asp -->
<HTML>
<HEAD><TITLE>Authentication Form</TITLE>
</HEAD>

<BODY BGCOLOR=#FFFFFF>
<% If Request.Form("User") = "" Then %>
    <P>Please enter your Name:
    <FORM ACTION="./logon.asp" METHOD="POST">
    Your name:     <INPUT TYPE="TEXT"     NAME="User">
    Your password: <INPUT TYPE="PASSWORD" NAME="Pwd">
    <INPUT TYPE="SUBMIT" VALUE="Log On">
    </FORM>
<% Else    'User verification and logon code goes here %>
    Welcome <%= Request.Form("User") %>!
<% End If %>

</BODY>
</HTML>
```

Note If you use a separate ASP file to handle the processing of a form, the **Request.Form** collection will be emptied when you redirect to the new page. In order to retain the form values, you must copy them to the **Session** object from which they can be accessed on subsequent pages.

Although the sample Authentication Form shown here works, there's a good reason why you would not want to use it in practice. Logon information is sensitive and should be subject to rigorous protection from prying eyes. Although you can use the POST method to contain the user's password within the body of the HTTP response, it is still possible to intercept and read it.

For mission-critical applications, IIS provides both secure authentication (Windows NT Challenge/Response and Client Certificates), and data encryption (Secure Sockets Layer). For more information on authentication and encryption, see Chapter 8, "Security."

Client-Side Form Validation

Forms require some sort of input. If the user hasn't entered any information or has entered a bad combination of information, it makes little sense to go to the trouble of sending the information back to the server. Forms that are submitted without preliminary data validation increase the server's load (and the user's frustration) unnecessarily. Validate information as much as possible when the form is submitted.

In fact, don't stop with the client tier. Just in case the client doesn't support client-side scripting, validate again as data is passed to the middle tier. Most importantly, use the data integrity and validation rules of your database to protect yourself against inadvertent mistakes in your own business logic. This defensive approach to data validation can save you frustration in the long run; you'll know that data is protected at all levels of your application.

To validate form input with client-side script, you need to declare an event-handler for the submit event of the form. If your form uses a SUBMIT input type, create an event handler using name of the form followed by "**_OnSubmit**." To submit the form, return **True** from the validation routine. Return **False** to abort the submission and return to the form.

If you prefer to use the BUTTON input type on your form, you'll need to define an event handler using the name of the button followed by "**_OnClick**." Instead of returning **True** to submit the form, however, you will need to call the **Submit** method of the **Form** object explicitly. This method may not be available on some browsers.

The following client-side script verifies that the form's user name and e-mail address fields (both required by the form) have been filled in, and submits the form by returning **True** from the **OnSubmit** event-handler:

```
<script language="VBScript"><!--
Function FeedbackForm_OnSubmit()
    '--- Disallow submit until the form fields have been validated
    FeedbackForm_OnSubmit = False

    '--- Get a reference to the form
    Set theForm = Document.FeedbackForm

    '--- First, check that UserName has been filled in
    If Trim(theForm.UserName.Value) = "" Then
        MsgBox "Enter your name.", vbCritical, "Need Input"
        theForm.UserName.Focus
    Else
        '--- Next, check for the e-mail name
        If Trim(theForm.UserEmail.Value) = "" Then
            MsgBox "Enter your e-mail address.", vbCritical, "Need Input"
            theForm.UserEmail.Focus
        Else
            '--- Continue with submission
            FeedbackForm_OnSubmit = True
        End If
    End If
End Function
--></script>
```

```
<form name=FeedbackForm action=TeeFeedback.asp method=POST>

<b>Tell us how to get in touch with you:</b></p>
<pre>
     Name      <input type=TEXT name="UserName"> (Required)
     E-mail    <input type=TEXT name="UserEmail"> (Required)
     Tel       <input type=TEXT name="UserTel">
</pre>

<input type=SUBMIT value="Submit Comments"> 
<input type=RESET  value="Clear Form">
</form>
```

Figure 5.8 shows the form-validation routine at work:

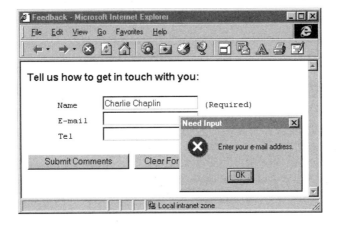

Figure 5.8   Client-side form input validation

Hidden Form Fields

When you chain forms together to create a "Form wizard," the information entered on each form needs to be stored until the last form has been filled in. There are three ways to pass values between ASP files:

- Accumulate information in the **Session** object.

- Append information to the end of the URL, and use **QueryString** to pass it.

- Use hidden HTML form variables.

Sometimes the requirements of your application don't permit you to store form data in the **Session** object, even temporarily. This might be the case for a large-scale site with thousands of concurrent users, where memory is at a premium.

Passing values on the URL works for small amounts of information, but will be insufficient when the quantity of data is large.

So, although the amount of information passed between the client tier and the middle tier increases, hidden form fields make it possible to include previously entered or application-specific information as part of the current form submission. A hidden form field isn't displayed to the user, but is sent as a name/value pair when the form is submitted.

Note   You should avoid using hidden form fields to send back information that you are using for security or authentication purposes. Since they are available as text in the form body, these values can easily be "spoofed" by anyone who can view the HTML source. Even an unsophisticated hacker could develop a small routine to try many possible values in an attempt to crash (or otherwise break) whatever server code is using the hidden value.

Redirection

Sometimes, the page being requested by the browser isn't the one you'd like to send. For example, suppose a user requests Oldpage.htm, which has been replaced by NewPage.asp. Standard HTML syntax provides a means whereby you can redirect (or divert) a request to another location. The syntax looks something like this:

```
<HEAD><META HTTP-EQUIV="REFRESH" CONTENT="0;URL=NewPage.asp"></HEAD>
```

The REFRESH form of the <META> tag was originally included in the HTML specification to allow a page to repeatedly reload itself after a specified time lapse. With a small adjustment to its syntax, it becomes an effective method of redirecting a standard HTML request.

You can also use ASP to redirect a request to another page based on the logic of your application. The syntax is simple:

```
Response.Redirect "./NewPage.asp"
```

The **Redirect** method of the **Response** object operates by sending the "302 Object Moved" response header, plus the new location of the file, to the client. When it receives this response, the user's browser automatically requests the new page.

In the Survey application, described earlier, the entry point of the application started with a redirection; the final destination of the request is determined programmatically. If the user hasn't responded to the survey, the browser is sent to the survey form. Before the response deadline, return visitors see a repeat-visit notification. Otherwise, if the response deadline has passed, the results of the survey appear. One way to accomplish this sleight of hand is to create an ASP file containing the following script:

```
<%@ Language=VBScript EnableSessionState=False %>
<%
   '--- If survey deadline has passed, redirect to results
   If Date > #November 13, 1998# Then
      Response.Redirect "./ViewResults.asp"
   Else
      '--- Look for cookie sent to respondents of the survey
      nResponseID = 0
      For Each cookie in Request.Cookies
         If cookie = "MySurvey" Then
            nResponseID = CInt(Request.Cookies(cookie))
         End If
      Next

      '--- If no cookie is found, then redirect to survey
      If nResponseID = 0 Then
         Response.Redirect "./Survey.htm"
      Else
         '--- Survey already completed
         Response.Redirect "./ConfirmRepeat.asp?ID=" & nResponseID
      End If
   End If
%>
```

Because redirection depends on HTTP headers, which come at the beginning of the document, you can't redirect once text has been sent to the client. If you redirect in a server-side script after data has been sent to the client, the following error occurs:

```
Header Error
The HTTP headers are already written to the client browser. Any HTTP
header modifications must be made before writing page content.
```

If you can't know at the beginning of the page whether you need to redirect, you can use the buffering capabilities of the **Response** object. If **Response.Buffer** is **True**, HTML output is collected in a buffer and sent all at once to the client. If at some point you need to redirect to another page, ASP automatically discards any existing output in the buffer when you call **Response.Redirect**. You may also use **Response.Clear** at any time to clear the buffer and start again.

The following example demonstrates this concept:

```
<% '--- Begin buffering the HTML
    Response.Buffer = True %>
<html>
<body>
HTML text before potential redirect.

<%
   On Error Resume Next

   '--- Script generates an error here

   If Err.Number > 0 Then
      Response.Clear
      Response.Redirect "./error.asp"
   End If
%>
```

Once you call **Response.Redirect**, the script ends and the redirection headers are sent immediately. Any code following the redirect will not be executed, although it is required for syntactical correctness.

You can use **Response.End** to end a response from the server immediately and send the current output to the browser. Since the response ends at that point, any HTML that follows is not sent. The following script detects that the user has connected anonymously (the LOGON_USER server variable is empty) and forces a logon by returning a "401 Access Denied" message.

```
<%
   strLogon = Request.ServerVariables("LOGON_USER")
   If IsEmpty(strLogon) Or strLogon = "" Then
      ' Up to this point, no HTML has actually been sent.
      Response.Status = "401 Access Denied"
      Response.End
   End If
%>
<html>
You are logged on as: <%= strLogon %>
</html>
```

A well-behaved browser will try this page a second time, with logon credentials. If you don't use **Response.End**, the ASP script will execute twice, leading possibly to unexpected side-effects (such as adding duplicate records to a database).

Client-Side Redirection

Redirection can also occur in client-side script. A client-side redirect shifts focus from the current page to another. Client-side redirection can occur as the page is loaded, or be deferred until the user performs an action, such as clicking a button.

The browser's object model includes a **Location** object, which represents the URL of the content currently displayed in the browser window. The following example uses this object to reload a frame-dependent page inside its parent frame. The script (which appears at the top of each frame page) detects that the page has been loaded as the top frame and changes the browser window location to the parent frame. (Note that this script can be placed in an include file, to avoid duplicating it on all your pages.)

```
<script LANGUAGE=JavaScript><!--
if(top == self) {
    var currURL = unescape(window.location.pathname);
    var newURL  = "parentFrame.asp?" + currURL;
    var appVer  = navigator.appVersion;
    var NScp = (navigator.appName == 'Netscape') &&
               ((appVer.indexOf('3') != -1) ||
                (appVer.indexOf('4') != -1));
    var MSIE = (appVer.indexOf('MSIE 4') != -1);
    if (NScp || MSIE)
        location.replace(newURL);
    else
        location.href = newURL;
}
//--></script>
```

This method requires that parentFrame.asp accept the child frame location as a URL parameter, and deal with it appropriately if it is set. The following script manages the last part of this redirection:

```
<%@ Language=VBScript EnableSessionState=False %>
<%
    frmSrc = Request.QueryString  '--- Get entire URL parameter
    If frmSrc = "" Then frmSrc = "homepage.htm"
%>

<frameset rows="60,*" frameborder=0 framespacing=0>
    <frame name="nav_fr"  src="navbar.htm"  scrolling=auto noresize>
    <frame name="page_fr" src="<%=frmSrc%>" scrolling=auto>
</frameset>
```

Redirecting during Session_OnStart

Redirection during the **Session_OnStart** event is possible, and sometimes required by your application (see the sidebar "Web Farms and ASP Session State," earlier in this chapter). Here is an example:

```
Sub Session_OnStart
    Response.Redirect "MyStartPage.asp"
End Sub
```

Not all of the **Response** object's methods are available during the **Session_OnStart** event. Most notably, you cannot use the **Write** method to display messages since the client would never see them. You can however, redirect to an error message if your application cannot successfully initialize a new user session.

The Feedback Sample Application

The Feedback application is a form with which Web site users can submit comments. Users choose whether to send comments as e-mail to the site administrator or to post them to a forum for viewing by other users. Once users have written their comments, they have the opportunity to "preview" them before submitting them. When comments are previewed, the application can also perform a spelling check. A confirmation page lets the user know that everything worked.

Figure 5.9 displays a flowchart of the application.

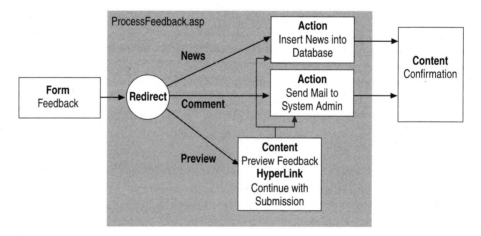

Figure 5.9   Flowchart of Feedback application

Sending Mail with CDO

Microsoft Collaboration Data Objects (CDO) exposes messaging objects that provide the ability to send and receive mail quickly and easily from within an application. CDO for NTS interfaces with the SMTP service included with IIS 4.0. When you install the SMTP service, CDO for NTS components are installed as well. Microsoft Exchange does not have to be installed on the computer on which CDO for NTS is used.

CDO for NTS supports a number of objects that can be used to access messages and attachments, and to send mail. Of these, the **CDONTS.NewMail** object provides the quickest and easiest way to send an e-mail message. With the **NewMail** object, you can create and send a message in one step, as shown in the following example:

```
<%
    ' Construct FROM address--tack on domain part, if missing
    strFrom = Request("UserEmail")
    If InStr(strFrom,"@") = 0 Then
        strFrom = strFrom & Application("FeedbackDomain")
    End If
    strFrom = Request("UserName") & "<" & strFrom & ">"

    ' Create a Newmail object, and send it off!
    Set oMail = Server.CreateObject("CDONTS.NewMail")
    oMail.Send strFrom, Application("FeedbackAdministrator"),_
            Request("Subject"), Request("Comments")
%>
```

Note If you plan to install Microsoft Exchange Server on the Web server, the CDO for NTS objects (except for **NewMail**, unfortunately) can be configured to use the SMTP services that Exchange provides. You must run the Internet Mail Service (IMS) Setup Wizard to configure CDO for NTS correctly. If the IMS Wizard is not run, CDO for NTS continues to use the SMTP services installed by IIS 4.0. For more information, see the Exchange Server documentation.

Checking Spelling with Microsoft Word

The Feedback application provides a spelling check when users preview comments they want to submit as news items. The Feedback application enlists the services of Microsoft Word to check spelling. Using the **Word.Application** object, you can do almost anything Word does, including using the proofing tools to check spelling.

Important Microsoft Word is an Active Document server, which runs as a out-of-process component. Before you can use this application you must set the **AspAllowOutOfProcComponents** value in the IIS metabase. For more information, see the next section, "Out-Of-Process Components."

Not all methods of the Word Object Library are suitable for Web applications, but the **CheckSpelling** method accepts a string as an argument, and returns False if the string cannot pass the spelling check. Because it has no user interface, and uses standard data types, it is suitable for automation from a Web page. Here's the declaration of **CheckSpelling** method of the **Word.Application** component, as shown by XRay.

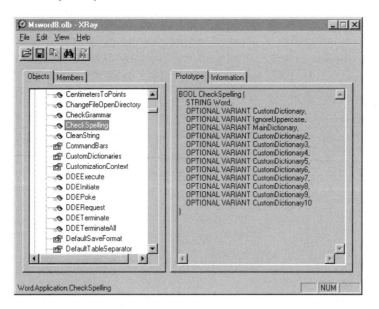

Figure 5.10   Using XRay to view an component type library

Although the **CheckSpelling** method correctly parses strings as complete sentences, you cannot tell which words are misspelled without further investigation. To avoid duplicating effort, the script breaks the text into individual words before passing them to **CheckSpelling**. The following functions are contained in a server-side include file, Spelling.inc (the complete file is included on the IIS Resource Kit CD):

```
<script LANGUAGE=VBScript RUNAT=Server>
Dim cReportedErrors

'--- Checks spelling, and report "bad" words to the user
Sub CheckWord(ByVal strWord)
   If Not GlobalWordApp.CheckSpelling(strWord) Then
      If cReportedErrors = 0 Then Response.Write "Errors detected:<BR>"
      Response.Write strWord & "<BR>"
      cReportedErrors = cReportedErrors + 1
   End If
End Sub

Sub CheckSpelling(ByVal strText)
   '--- Reset the global count of errors reported
   cReportedErrors = 0

   '--- Create list of delimiters for parsing words from text
   strDelim = Chr(9) & Chr(13) & Chr(10) & " ,.!?:;()/-" & Chr(34)

   '--- Return tokens from strText, using delimiters in strDelim
   '--- NOTE: GetToken is defined in the complete source on the CD
   x = GetToken(strText, strDelim, strToken)
   Do While (x > 0)
      CheckWord(strToken)
      strText = Mid(strText, x)    '--- Remove token from strText
      x = GetToken(strText, strDelim, strToken)
   Loop
   CheckWord(strToken) '--- Check last token

   If cReportedErrors = 0 Then
      Response.Write "<I>No errors detected.</I>"
   Else
      Response.Write "Total Errors: " & cReportedErrors
   End If
End Sub
</script>
```

On the Preview page, you simply include the spelling library functions and pass the entire body of text you want to validate (in this case, both Subject and Comments):

```
<html>
<head>
<title>Spelling Check</title>
<!-- #include virtual="./spelling.inc" -->
</head>
<body BGCOLOR=#FFFFFF>
<h1>Spelling Check</h1>
<% '--- Concatenate multiple fields, and pass all at once
    CheckSpelling( Request("Subject") & " " & Request("Comments") )
%>
</body>
</html>
```

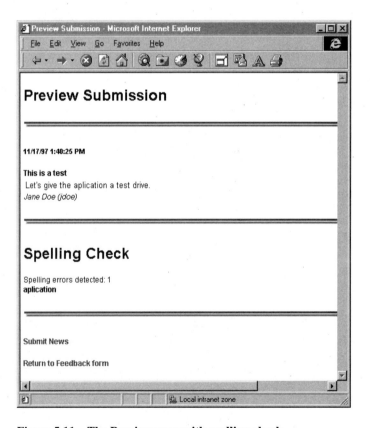

Figure 5.11   The Preview page with spelling check

The Global.asa file for the Feedback application instantiates the
Word.Application object, and destroys it when the application ends. The
important sections of Global.asa are shown here:

```
<object ID=GlobalWordApp SCOPE=Application RUNAT=Server
   PROGID="Word.Application.8">
</object>

<script LANGUAGE=VBScript RUNAT=Server>
Sub Application_OnEnd
   GlobalWordApp.Quit
End Sub
</script>
```

Out-Of-Process Components

When the **Word.Application** object is created, it is launched as an Active
Document server application on the Web server. The client browser can still take
advantage of the application without needing to install it on the local computer.
Since it is an executable rather than a DLL, however, it is run outside the IIS
process as an *out-of-process component*.

Out-of-process components are different from out-of-process applications (or,
isolated processes). Out-of-process components are COM components that run in
separate processes on the same computer as the client. Out-of-process components
are also called "LocalServers."

Running Out-Of-Process Components

When **Server.CreateObject** is used to run an out-of-process component, the
following error can occur:

```
Server object error 'ASP 0196'
Cannot launch out of process component
```

This error is the result of a safety mechanism in ASP that prevents executables
from being launched directly from ASP. Not all executables are safe to use on the
server, and may pose security risks as well. Because in-process components are
faster, more secure, and can be hosted by MTS, they are much better suited for
server-side use.

Because out-of-process components do not scale as well as component DLLs, the
use of LocalServer components is *strongly discouraged* if scalability is a top
priority of your site. For many intranet applications, however, it is possible to use
an out-of-process component without adversely affecting your performance.

Before you can use the **Word.Application** object in your Web application, you must first set the IIS metabase property **AspAllowOutOfProcComponents** to **True**. This metabase setting is accessible on both the **IIsWebService** and **IIsWebVirtualDir** Admin objects.

- If you set the **AspAllowOutOfProcComponents** property to **True** on the **IIsWebService** object, all in-process applications will be able to run executables from script. An "in-process application" is a virtual root which has been marked as an application, but which has not been designated to run in a separate memory space.

- If you set the **AspAllowOutOfProcComponents** property to **True** on the **IIsWebVirtualDir** object, and the application is designated to run out-of-process, only the affected application can run executables from script. If the application is set to run in-process, the setting will have no effect.

You must have adequate permission to modify the metabase. If you attempt to modify the metabase from an ASP script as an anonymous user, or a user without sufficient privileges, you may encounter an "Invalid Syntax" error.

The following example demonstrates the steps required when setting the **AspAllowOutOfProcComponents** parameter on the **IIsWebService** Admin object:

```
<%
    ' Get the IIsWebService Admin object
    Set oWebService = GetObject("IIS://LocalHost/W3svc")

    ' Enable AspAllowOutOfProcComponents
    oWebService.Put "AspAllowOutOfProcComponents", True

    ' Save the changed value to the metabase
    oWebService.SetInfo
%>
```

Important You must restart the Web service after making this change. You can restart the service by using the Services application in Control Panel, or from a command line by typing **net stop IISADMIN /y** followed by **net start W3SVC**.

A working version of this script example, Oopcomp.asp, is available on the IIS Resource Kit CD as part of the Feedback sample application. Before you can run Word from within the Feedback application, you must use this file to set the **AspAllowOutOfProcComponents** metabase setting for the Feedback application. Then you'll need to make sure the Feedback application is running in a separate process, and restart the Web Server service.

Summary

The *n*-tier paradigm is the culmination of years of technological advancement and the logical outgrowth of today's interconnected applications. It extends the client/server model of by promoting reuse, encouraging good development style, and simplifying the task of the developer.

The different ways that client-tier and middle-tier technologies work together may be obscure at first, but should become clear once you've designed one or two distributed Web applications. There may come a time when you can honestly say that you wouldn't think of building applications any other way.

Resources

The following books and Web sites provide additional information relevant to developing Web applications.

Web Links

http://www.15seconds.com/
A free resource for developers working with Microsoft Internet solutions. There are four main resources: the *15 Seconds* newsletter, Stephen Genusa's Frequently Asked Questions, List Servers, and the Consultant Program. There are also book reviews, how-to articles, and job opportunities that deal with ASP and Microsoft Internet solutions.

http://www.activeserverpages.com
Contains ASP-related articles, ASP FAQs, tutorials, tools, development discussion, and free ASP component downloads.

http://www.activestate.com
ActiveState Tool Corporation distributes a free PerlScript engine for Active Scripting platforms, such as ASP and Win32; and an ISAPI implementation of Perl. The Perl samples in this chapter were tested with ActiveState's PerlScript.

http://www.chilisoft.net/
Chilisoft's Chili!ASP brings the power of ASP to servers other than IIS. Chili!ASP can host ASP pages and components on a variety of web servers without any changes to code. Includes support for Windows NT–based Netscape Web servers.

http://www.genusa.com/asp/
The premier "unauthorized" support site for ASP. Provides an excellent collection of ASP resources.

http://support.microsoft.com/support/
The Microsoft Knowledge Base (KB) contains many useful articles on Active Server Pages.

http://www.microsoft.com/intranet/
Microsoft and Hewlett Packard have created the Intranet Solutions Center—a comprehensive Web site that has everything you need to plan and build an intranet site. Explore white papers, FAQs, and case studies, or download free intranet solutions written by top Microsoft Solution Providers.

http://www.microsoft.com/iis/
The official Microsoft site for Internet Information Server 4.0. Provides news, discussion, and downloads.

http://www.microsoft.com/workshop/server/
This is the Active Server Pages workshop area of Microsoft's Site Builder Network, a must-see resource.

Books

Official Microsoft Intranet Solutions (Microsoft Press, 1997).
A tools-based approach to intranet site development using Microsoft Office 97 applications and Microsoft FrontPage 97.

Corning, *Working with Active Server Pages* (Que Corporation, 1997).
Covers design, development, and implementation of ASP pages. Includes examples of database-driven customer scenarios using ASP and ADO.

Hettihewa, *Windows NT 4 Web Development* (Sams.net Publishing, 1996).
Complete Web site design from client to server.

Homer, *Professional Active Server Pages* (Wrox Press Ltd., 1997).
A highly recommended and comprehensive tutorial of ASP and ADO. Includes practical techniques for creating *n*-tier Web applications.

C H A P T E R 6

Data Access and Transactions

6

Information is the lifeblood of the Web, yet more information is not always better. To be useful, information must be accurate and accessible, and it must conform to the needs of users. Users should be able to react to, and act upon, the information presented to them. The tool that makes this flexibility possible is, of course, the database, an essential element in many Web applications.

The previous chapter introduced the *n*-tier application model, and described how to use a combination of client-side scripts and components with Active Server Pages (ASP) to create dynamic Web-based applications. This chapter builds on those concepts, introduces essential components of data access, and discusses how to harness the power of a data driven approach for content publishing and information management on the Web.

In this chapter:

- Web Database Access
- Client-side Data Access
- Accessing Data from ASP Pages and Components
- Transaction Processing on the Web
- Resources

Web Database Access

The Internet is changing the world's expectations about the availability of information. What we expect from the Internet and from the Web is changing as well. Once you've visited a site that lets you browse a product catalogue and initiate a sales transaction online, nothing is more frustrating than visiting another site that talks about products but doesn't let you purchase them immediately.

As online commerce and electronic publishing become increasingly common, sites that provide a higher level of interactivity will replace those that simply present information. Interactivity and complexity call for information to be stored in a way that makes it easy to manipulate and modify—thus the central role of the database in today's Web applications.

Why a Web Database?

What makes the Web such a good mechanism for accessing a database? When you use a data management solution as part of your site, you reap the following benefits:

- **Ease of deployment**   It's no secret that the World Wide Web is a cheap and practical alternative to traditional client/server application deployment, and that it provides immediate cross-platform support on the client side. Implementing a dynamic Web database solution can be done relatively quickly and doesn't require a large team of developers.

- **Database Standards**   The components that enable Web database access are built on proven standards. Web pages can access data from a variety of locations, such as Microsoft Access, SQL Server, or any OLE DB or ODBC-compliant data source.

- **Data Security**   By using IIS, you benefit from the security model of Windows NT. By using Microsoft Transaction Server (MTS), you automatically gain the data protection and operational integrity provided by a distributed transaction coordinator. You have a lot invested in your content— protect it! (For more information about MTS and transactions, see "Transaction Processing on the Web" later in this chapter.)

- **Dynamic content**   Applying modifications to HTML from a database is easier than making manual changes to individual pages. By automating the creation of HTML from content stored in a database, you save time and make site management easier. In the end, you can focus on updating your content, not your HTML.

Data Publishing Considerations

Before you start hooking databases and HTML together, there are some important issues to consider:

- **Tool Support**   The tools used to develop Web-based applications sometimes aren't being updated as fast as the technology is changing. Research and choose your tools carefully before you implement a large-scale database project.

- **Server load**   Be sure you have sufficient server resources to handle the increased load of database access. Consider memory, CPU speed, Internet connection speed, disk subsystems and other critical hardware factors. If you are expecting heavy database traffic, separate your Web server and database management system (DBMS) onto two (or more) computers. Also, use existing database management tools and performance management tools to help balance your server load.

- **Database scalability and reliability**   Determine how much the database is likely to grow. On average, how often will users access it? What kinds of tasks will they perform? What is your Web site's overall growth estimate—in both content and readership?

- **Client presentation**   How will users access the data on your site? Will they be able to add to it, or modify it? Will the users have their own copies of the data, or will they only have access to the information while online? Using Microsoft Data Access Components (MDAC), information can either be manipulated on the server as part of a server-side query, or be bundled as a package and transmitted to the client in a process known as "remoting." Choosing how the information will be presented to the user is perhaps the hardest decision you'll have to make—often a hybrid approach is best.

- **Static versus Dynamic**   How much of your site really needs data access? How often does the content change? Dynamic solutions, especially if they access a database, are slower than plain HTML pages. If you display data that doesn't change frequently, you can improve performance (for your server and your client) by converting dynamic pages to HTML. (Use the ASP2HTM conversion utility, found on the IIS Resource Kit CD.)

Industrial-strength Information

Database-centric publishing is not just a convenience—it's a form of commerce applied to the commodity of information. You should consider the content of your site as you would your company's product. In addition to providing the latest information, a good Web administrator makes sure the information suits the needs of the customer.

Database-centric Publishing

Database-centric Web publishing is a technique in use today by many successful Internet sites. Instead of authoring in HTML, many sites initially store their content in a database and combine it with HTML layout tags only when deploying the content for publication. Combining raw information with a layout template or HTML boilerplate imbues the content with the same look and feel as other pages on the site. The end result is a site that has a uniform appearance from page to page, although the information may have been created by dozens of people.

For instance, Sidewalk.com, Microsoft's city and entertainment guide site, uses a custom-built application based on HTML forms and Microsoft SQL Server to collect content from its contributors. Once the information is entered, it can be managed separately from the visual representation of the site. Sidewalk.com employs a large number of freelance correspondents to keep the content flowing, and a much smaller team of Web administrators to keep their site going.

Intranet and Extranets

If information is your commodity, you certainly don't want to lose it. Here and there throughout your organization, someone is daily producing a good idea. If that idea does not find a home in your process, or in your products, you have lost an opportunity. The corporate intranet is not only a reliable way to disseminate information, it is quickly becoming an effective way to present and capture it. It's also becoming a means of interacting with companies that contribute to your business. You can extend your private information and applications onto the Web and to other companies through a tightly controlled firewall.

You can replace paper forms with online data entry, which can save you money. Groups can improve their communication and productivity by sharing common resources, data, and knowledge. The next time you consider writing a document, consider publishing it—on your company's intranet.

Content Search and Personalization

Site content in a database can be sorted, filtered, and queried for relevance. It is surprising how much raw data a site contains. Not every piece of information in the site is of interest to everyone. Users don't want to spend time searching through data, and will be less likely to visit sites with poor search tools. To attract visitors, many sites provide a list of current headlines, or compilations of topics that appeal to people with common interests. Others allow the user to select which items will be displayed on the site's home page. Without a data-driven solution, it would be impossible to develop a site that could be tailored to display the latest items of interest each time a visitor returned.

A Word of Caution

Just because you can access a database doesn't mean you should. Before you start building an application, determine whether it is worth the time, effort, and server resources that will be needed to create and use it.

Suppose you're creating a site that publishes bus schedules for a hundred routes. The "static" solution might be an index page—perhaps with an HTML form—that allows the user to select and view any of a hundred static, route-specific pages. The "dynamic" solution might use a query page to look up each bus schedule as it is requested, and return it on a custom, dynamic page.

Both approaches offer the same solution, but the "static" one offers better performance, for two reasons:

- Delivering a static page demands far less processing than creating the same page on the fly.

- The static page solution creates each page once; the dynamic page solution may create a new page for each request (depending on how the server's cache is utilized) for information that generally doesn't change much.

Don't infer from the example that the data always determines the approach: that the static approach is best for static data (such as bus schedules), and the dynamic one is always best for dynamic data. If people need infrequent access to huge amounts of data, the best solution may be the dynamic approach: a query page.

The best solution is to provide a controlled mix of static and dynamic pages as your users require and as your site can support. If you use data access frivolously, you will be plagued with excessive delays and bottlenecks as pages are generated over and over again for each request. Judicious use of dynamic data, however, will enhance and complement the static elements of your site.

The Microsoft Data Access Components

The Universal Data Access initiative is Microsoft's platform, application, and tools strategy that defines and delivers standards and technologies essential for application development. A subset of the Microsoft Windows Distributed interNet Applications (Windows DNA) architecture, Universal Data Access is designed to provide high-performance access to a variety of data and information sources on multiple platforms using a unified programming interface that works with practically any tool or language.

The Microsoft Data Access Components (MDAC) are the primary technologies that enable Universal Data Access. MDAC 1.5, which ships with the Windows NT 4.0 Option Pack, includes the latest versions of ActiveX Data Objects (ADO), Remote Data Services (RDS), the OLE DB Provider for ODBC, the ODBC Driver Manager, and updated Microsoft ODBC drivers for Microsoft SQL Server, Oracle and Microsoft Access. Figure 6.1 shows how these components interact.

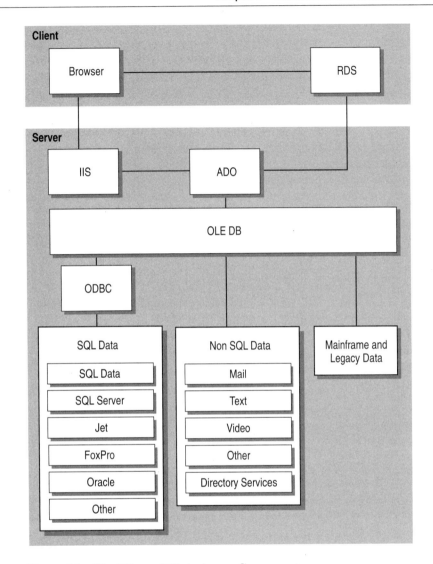

Figure 6.1   The Microsoft Data Access Components.

The next few sections describe each of the MDAC technologies. If you already have a working knowledge of these technologies, you may want to skip ahead and return to this section later. Most of your applications will use ADO, which is described in detail later, so ignoring this section now will not prevent you from understanding the examples later.

ODBC and OLE DB

The *Open DataBase Connectivity (ODBC)* standard is a widely recognized method of accessing data in a variety of relational databases. It is fast, lightweight, and provides a common method that is not optimized for any specific data source. Components written in Visual Basic, Java, C, or C++ can call ODBC.

OLE DB is an open specification designed to build on the success of ODBC by providing an open standard for accessing all kinds of data throughout the enterprise. OLE DB is a low-level set of interfaces designed for driver vendors who want to expose a data source, and for C++ developers wanting to develop custom data components. Visual Basic, which does not support OLE Automation, cannot use OLE DB directly.

Applications that use OLE DB fall into two categories: *consumers* and *providers*. A consumer application uses (or consumes) data through the OLE DB interfaces or components. A provider is any component or data source that allows consumers to access data in a uniform way through the OLE DB interfaces. In a sense, an OLE DB Provider is similar to an ODBC driver that provides a uniform mechanism for accessing relational data.

Whereas ODBC was created to access relational databases, OLE DB interfaces are designed to communicate with any data source including relational and non-relational data, such as Microsoft Excel spreadsheets, e-mail, and text files. There is no restriction on the type of data you can access with OLE DB—relational databases, ISAM, text, or hierarchical data sources.

Several OLE DB Providers are currently available, including the Microsoft ODBC Provider, which exposes any ODBC-compliant database through OLE DB. Developers can implement an OLE DB Provider for whatever data access they require, if one does not already exist.

ADO and RDS

ActiveX Data Objects (ADO) and Remote Data Service (RDS) use OLE DB to communicate with data sources. Any application that uses the ADO objects indirectly consumes from OLE DB. You can use ADO to write both server-side and client-side applications that can access and manipulate data.

ADO was designed to provide a universal high-level data access method, and is a collection of OLE Automation objects that can retrieve, update, and create records using any OLE DB service component. If there is an OLE DB Provider for it, the data is accessible through the unified object model of ADO.

ADO exposes a set of "core" functions that all data sources are expected to implement. Using these core functions, ADO can access the unique features of specific data sources through OLE DB. Additionally, unlike earlier data access methods, you no longer need to navigate through a hierarchy to create objects. You can create most ADO objects independently and reuse objects in different contexts. The result is fewer ADO object calls and a smaller working set.

There's a downside to all this flexibility, however. Because ADO is an OLE DB consumer, the peculiarities of the OLE DB Provider that you are using directly influence the behavior of ADO. Just because you can write it in ADO, doesn't mean that the provider will support it. Often, ADO errors are a direct result of performing operations not supported by the OLE DB Provider, or the underlying ODBC data source. As you develop database access components and applications, keep in mind that there are sometimes several different ways to perform any given action.

The Remote Data Service (RDS) is a feature of ADO that facilitates client-side programming by optimizing the transfer of data between the client and the ADO components in the middle tier. RDS uses ADO as a programming interface between the code and the data exposed by the underlying OLE DB Provider.

The client-side components of RDS are ActiveX controls that use DCOM or HTTP to communicate with the server components. Internet Explorer 4.0 includes the newest RDS client-side components.

Special Note for Internet Explorer 3.x Users MDAC 1.5 provides server components that are compatible with both the RDS version 1.5 and version 1.1 client-side components. Version 1.5 client-side components are included with Internet Explorer, and require Internet Explorer 4.0 or higher. For mixed network environments that may include clients running Internet Explorer 3.x and 4.0, RDS version 1.1 client-side components are required.

A detailed look at RDS and ADO is included in the section "Client-side Data Access" later in this chapter

Older Data Access Methods

It's usually not a good idea to throw away older technology just to adopt the latest software craze. The developer's existing expertise is one consideration. Legacy applications are another. Fortunately, all of the older data-access technologies listed in this section are still supported in IIS. But unless you have good business reasons to use these access methods, use ADO and RDS instead. ADO and RDS are designed to balance maximum flexibility with programmatic simplicity. For the majority of cases, no additional means of accessing your data is needed.

ADC

The Advanced Data Connector (ADC) can be thought of as the parent of RDS, which replaces it. The RDS data remoting technology is inherited directly from ADC. Because early versions of ADC didn't support the ADO programming model, ADC was integrated with ADO to provide a uniform means of accessing remote data. ADC itself is now considered obsolete; RDS and ADO, which use the same objects for both the client and middle tiers, have replaced ADC programming.

ADO invokes RDS when needed in order to provide a common programming model for accessing either local or remote data. RDS objects are installed with Internet Explorer 4.0 on your client, or you can download them at run time by referring to the .cab files shipped with MDAC 1.5 components.

Jet and DAO

The Joint Engine Technology (Jet) database engine is a workstation-based storage system. Jet databases can be accessed using Data Access Objects (DAO). You can also access Jet databases with the ODBC drivers provided with Microsoft Access, but only limited functionality is exposed using these drivers. The Jet engine has its own query and result-set processors and is capable of executing queries against homogeneous or heterogeneous data sources. Developers who are familiar with DAO can use ODBCDirect to bypass the Jet engine when connecting to back-end data sources.

You don't need to change programming models depending on whether your data is stored in a Jet Database or some other data store. ADO provides a common programming model for accessing Jet data or any other OLE DB data source.

RDO

Remote Data Objects (RDO) were specifically designed to access remote ODBC relational data sources, and add a thin object layer to the ODBC API. RDO performance is, in most cases, close to that of the ODBC API.

RDO was specifically designed to deal with remote intelligent data sources as opposed to ISAM databases—so it does not support some of the DAO table-based interfaces or Dynamic Data Exchange (DDE). RDO can execute ordinary table-based queries, but it is especially adept at building and executing queries against stored procedures. It also handles all types of result sets including those generated by multiple result set procedures, those returning output arguments, and those requiring complex input parameters.

RDO 2.0 provides a high level of control over remote data sources, so it is not necessary to expose ODBC handles except in the most unusual cases. It also can create Client Cursors to manage "disconnected" result sets.

ADO provides equivalent functionality and performance to RDO, with an easier-to-use object model, and can access a larger variety of data stores.

IDC/IDQ and HTX

The Internet Database Connector (IDC) was a precursor to ASP and ADO. An IDC file contains information used to connect to a specific ODBC data source and execute a SQL statement to query a database. The query results are automatically integrated with special tags in a separate HTML template (HTX file). The Index Database Query (IDQ) format extends the IDC format with specialized query parameters for Microsoft Index Server searches. Although IIS 4.0 still supports both of these formats, ADO and the Index Server server-side objects can be combined with ASP to produce similar results.

Overall, ADO provides a more dynamic and flexible programming model for accessing data that integrates with the rest of your ASP application.

Client-Side Data Access

Microsoft Data Access Components are designed for distributed applications that take advantage of the processing power on client, middle-tier, and database server computers. These components are part of a simple yet rich programming model for manipulating data and building applications that are easy to configure and maintain. ADO, with RDS, enables the Web-application developer to:

- Invoke OLE automation objects on the Web server over both the HTTP and DCOM protocols.

- Bind ADO **Recordset** objects to intrinsic Dynamic HTML controls (and other data-aware controls) hosted in the browser using the Dynamic HTML "databinding" model.

- Create and manage remote ADO **Recordset** objects.

ADO is suitable for applications that need a high degree of database accessibility. ADO normally maintains a persistent connection to the database, but it can invoke RDS to work with cached, or disconnected, data. ADO uses RDS for applications in which the client needs to browse records or connect to and modify data.

When you create an ADO application, you can partition it into two or three logical tiers. You can implement your application on an intranet without using HTTP; if the client and middle tier components are on computers within a local-area network (LAN), you can use DCOM to marshal the interfaces and method arguments across the network. However, it is much less complicated to take advantage of IIS and Internet Explorer when building data-centric applications.

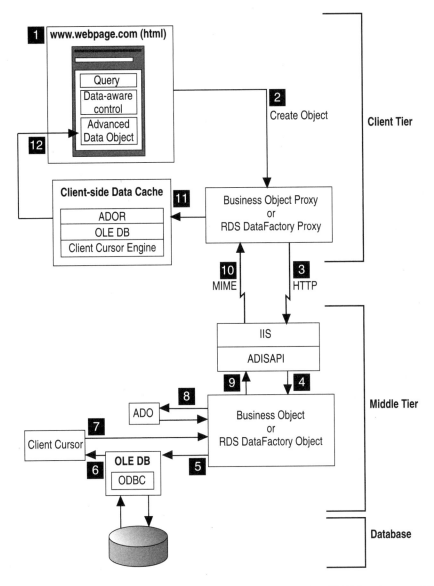

Figure 6.2   Process diagram of an ADO application using RDS for data partitioning

The illustration on the previous page shows how the client-side and server-side components of a Web-based ADO application work together to process a user's query and display information from a database.

1. The user enters the query text, chooses a preformatted request, or navigates to a page containing an embedded query.

2. When an event fires on the Web page, such as the **Window_OnLoad** routine or **OnClick** event of a Search button, ADO creates an RDS Data Factory proxy (or business object proxy) on the client.

3. The proxy translates the user request into an HTTP request by formatting the parameters of the business object method as URL parameters, and then sends the request to the Web server specified in the RDS Data Control's **Server** property. IIS forwards the HTTP request to an ISAPI extension, normally the Advanced Data ISAPI (ADISAPI).

4. ADISAPI interprets the URL parameters, creates an instance of the requested business object, and makes the method call. (By default, it calls the **Query** method of the server-side RDS Data Factory object.)

5. The RDS Data Factory object executes the user's query via OLE DB (and ODBC). It sets the **CursorLocation** property of the **Recordset** so that a Client Cursor Engine is used as its buffering component.

6. OLE DB passes the complete results of the query to the Client Cursor Engine. The Client Cursor Engine populates its buffers with the data, including all of the metadata for tables that are part of the result set.

7. The Client Cursor Engine passes a reference to the result set back to the RDS Data Factory object.

8. The RDS Data Factory object creates an instance of an ADO **Recordset** and initializes it with the result set. The ADO **Recordset** is then passed back as the return value of the original **Query** call from Step 4.

9. The RDS Data Factory passes the **Recordset** back to ADISAPI, which packages the return value of the call into MIME format.

10. ADISAPI sends the **Recordset** over HTTP as multi-part MIME packets to the business object proxy on the client side.

11. The client-side proxy unpacks the results of the method call, and re-creates the **Recordset** in the client-side Data Cache.

12. Finally, the embedded RDS Data Control object binds the data in the client-side Data Cache to the visual controls.

The Client Cursor Engine of RDS caches the set of records returned by the query on the client computer. The only client actions that require another trip to the server are updates to the data or requests for new data.

The RDS client-side and server-side components are described in detail in the following sections.

Client-Tier Elements

As described in the previous chapter, the client tier provides the visual interface for presenting and gathering data. In a Web-based RDS application, the Web page represents the Remote Data Service front end. The RDS client tier usually contains the following components:

- A Web page containing an **RDS.DataControl** object and one or more data-aware controls.
- An RDS Data Factory proxy or a custom business-object proxy.
- A client-side cursor engine and data cache.

Data-Aware Controls

You can bind data-aware controls to data from remote servers, and view, edit, and update data from the Web page.

The data-binding mechanism for displaying query results on a Web page in Internet Explorer is the **RDS.DataControl** object. Each **RDS.DataControl** binds one ADO **Recordset** object, which represents the results of a query, to one or more data-aware controls (for example, a text box, combo box, grid control, and so on). It is possible to have more than one **RDS.DataControl** object on the page. Each **RDS.DataControl** object can be connected to a different data source and contain the results of a separate query. The following script establishes a connection to a database using a client-side **Recordset**:

```
rs.Open "SELECT * FROM Authors", "Provider=MS Remote;" &_
        "Remote Server=http://mysite;DSN=Pubs;UID=sa;PWD=;"
```

When this code is executed, ADO invokes RDS to send a request to the query method on the **RDS.DataFactory** object on the server. The server-side object creates an ADO **Recordset** by executing the query against the specified data source. The results are then transmitted to the client where the **RDS.DataControl** reconstructs the **Recordset** for the client application. Once the data has been retrieved, the client can disconnect from the data source, which helps to eliminate the contention for database connections that sometimes occurs as multiple clients simultaneously access the same data source.

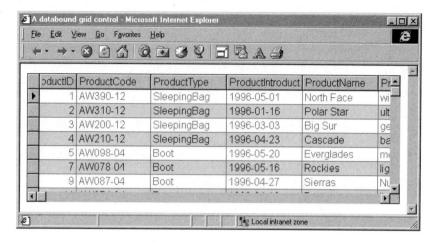

Figure 6.3   A data-bound grid control in Internet Explorer

Figure 6.3 shows a data-bound grid control in Internet Explorer. When the page loads, the grid control is automatically filled with records from the Adventure Works database. The following listing shows the ASP script used to create this page. Note that very little of the script actually executes on the server; most of it operates using objects created on the client.

```
<!-- #include file="./adcvbs.inc" -->
<HTML>
<HEAD>
<TITLE>A databound grid control</TITLE>
</HEAD>

<BODY BGCOLOR=#FFFFFF>
<!-- RDS.DataControl -->
<OBJECT ID="DATA" WIDTH=1 HEIGHT=1
  CLASSID="clsid:BD96C556-65A3-11D0-983A-00C04FC29E33">
</OBJECT>

<!-- Data-aware grid control (note Datasrc parameter) -->
<OBJECT ID="GRID" WIDTH=600 HEIGHT=200 Datasrc="#DATA"
  CLASSID="clsid:AC05DC80-7DF1-11d0-839E-00A024A94B3A">
</OBJECT>
```

```
<SCRIPT Language=VBScript><!--
Sub Window_OnLoad
  If DATA.ReadyState <> <%=adcReadyStateComplete%> Then
    MsgBox "Query results still arriving, Please wait"
  Else
    DATA.Server  = "http://<%=Request.ServerVariables("SERVER_NAME")%>"
    DATA.Connect = "DSN=AdvWorks"
    DATA.SQL     = "Select * from Products"
    DATA.Refresh
    GRID.Rebind
  End if
END SUB
--></SCRIPT>
</BODY>
</HTML>
```

When you use the **RDS.DataControl** object to send a query to a database, the RDS server-side components return an **ADODB.Recordset** object to the client. On the client, the Advance Data Connector proxy creates a client-side cursor and an **ADOR.Recordset** object to manipulate the returned records. You don't necessarily have to write any ADO-specific code to make this happen—RDS handles this for you when you use the **RDS.DataControl** object.

ADOR and ADODB Recordset Objects

A **Recordset** on either the client or the middle tier behaves in much the same way. (A **Recordset** object stores the results of a database query.) **ADODB.Recordset** objects on the middle tier have information associated with them that would not be desirable to download to remote HTML pages. Unless ADO has been installed on the client, only a lightweight **ADOR.Recordset** object is provided.

ADOR and **ADODB** are component identifiers (ProgIDs) that indicate how and where the **Recordset** object will be manipulated.

The type of marshaling protocol in use determines which **Recordset** type is made available to the client program. Internet applications and a majority of intranet applications use HTTP to transmit remote recordsets to the client, and require the use of the **ADOR.Recordset**. DCOM and RPC support both types of **Recordset** objects, so a client-side object proxy must choose which one to use based on the available registered types.

For the most part, if the **Recordset** exists on the client, use the **ADOR** ProgID. When writing code, use the **ADODB** ProgID if the **Recordset** exists on the middle tier.

Business Object Proxies and the RDS.DataSpace Object

RDS uses proxies for business objects to enable client-side components to communicate with business objects located on the middle tier. Proxies facilitate the packaging, unpackaging, and transport (marshaling) of the application's data across process or computer boundaries. For more information on business objects, see "Business Objects," later in this chapter.

The **RDS.DataSpace** object creates client-side proxies for custom business objects located on the middle tier. For example, the following client-side script instantiates a custom Customer component using the **RDS.DataSpace** object:

```
<!-- RDS.DataSpace object -->
<object ID=RDSDS WIDTH=1 HEIGHT=1
  CLSID="clsid:BD96C556-65A3-11D0-983A-00C04FC29E36">
</object>
<script LANGUAGE=VBScript>
  Set objProxyCust = RDSDS.CreateObject("Customer.Cls", "http://mysite")
  Set rs = objProxyCust.GetCustomers
</script>
```

When you use ADO to open a remote **Recordset** by specifying "Provider=MS Remote," or use the **RDS.DataControl** to obtain a disconnected **Recordset**, RDS calls the **RDSServer.DataFactory** object on the middle tier for you. You don't need to call **RDSServer.DataFactory** or **RDS.DataSpace** explicitly.

Data Cache

One of the most important features of the Remote Data Service is its in-memory data caching on both the client and middle tiers. The data cache:

- Reduces the number of requests for data between client-side application components and the database server. The performance improvement is especially noticeable for data access across the Internet.

- Makes data immediately available to client-side application logic, without the application having to wait for data to travel across the network.

Because the data is cached on the client workstation, a user can quickly scroll through the data. By using RDS, users also avoid having to know details about the data source.

Client Cursor Engine

The Client Cursor Engine is invisible to the user—Remote Data Service calls the Client Cursor Engine to perform tasks for you automatically. It caches, in memory (or temporarily on disk, for large sets of data), the set of query results retrieved from a data source, as well as client updates to those results. It also contains layout information about the data such as table layouts, row counts, primary and secondary keys, column names, and timestamps, as well as the actual table data itself. To manage the cache, the Client Cursor Engine can:

- Create and delete temporary tables.

- Populate tables.

- Manage updates to the data values.

- Provide schema information (such as base tables, key columns, read-write columns, and computed columns).

- Provide the mechanism to send updates as a batch to the server with minimum network traffic, by sending only the modified records.

Middle-Tier Elements of Client-Side Data Access

The middle tier is the "bridge" between client computers and database servers. The components on the middle tier respond to requests from the user (or business services) in order to execute a business task.

In an RDS application, business objects on the middle tier handle the data request from the client sent through a transport protocol such as HTTP. Data, in the form of **Recordset** objects, is made available as an update to client-side controls through the OLE DB Provider.

The middle tier usually consists of the following components:

- Internet Information Server (IIS) and ADISAPI

- RDSServer.DataFactory and Business objects

- Server-side data cache

Internet Information Server

The underlying Remote Data Service code uses an ISAPI extension to help create server-side stubs to communicate with client-side business object proxies. The Advanced Data ISAPI (ADISAPI) breaks up the MIME packets that pass through IIS and invokes methods on the server-side Advanced Data Factory object.

The ADISAPI component communicates with business objects for you, and provides parsing, automation control, and **Recordset** object marshaling; it also provides tabular data packaging, streaming, and unpackaging. This ISAPI extension performs the necessary work to instantiate business objects, invoke their services through automation interfaces, and process the return parameters for transport back to the calling client through the tabular data streaming protocol.

The RDSServer.DataFactory Object

The Advanced Data Factory object (**RDSServer.DataFactory**) resides on the Web server and is instantiated by the ADISAPI component. It provides read/write access to specified data sources, but doesn't contain any data constraint validation or business rules logic.

The **RDSServer.DataFactory** object is a SQL query and update control used in coordination with the ADO remoting components on the client to retrieve and post data to OLE DB data sources. When you use the **RDS.DataControl** object's methods and properties, the Remote Data Service is calling **RDSServer.DataFactory** behind the scenes.

Business Objects

The main application components on the middle tier are business objects that contain information such as application logic, business rules, and specialized data-access code to retrieve information from underlying databases.

Business objects can be generic OLE Automation objects created with Visual Basic, Visual C++, or Java. Your business objects can also use ADO to query and update the underlying databases. For more information on working with business objects, see "Transactional Components," later in this chapter.

In RDS, the lifespan of a business object is as long as the execution of a method call invoked by the client. Instances of the business objects are created with each method call, and no interim state is maintained.

The RDS Data Factory and Custom Business Objects

There are two ways to pass a **Recordset** object back from your server to the client with the Remote Data Service. You can:

- Use the **RDSServer.DataFactory** object.
- Create a custom business object that exposes data access methods.

RDS includes a default business object, the **RDSServer.DataFactory** object, that provides read and write access to data sources, but contains no business rules or application logic. The **RDSServer.DataFactory** is a server-side business object (an ActiveX DLL, specifically) that uses ADO to dispatch SQL statements to a DBMS through the OLE DB Provider, and packages the results for transfer across the Internet or an intranet.

You can create your own custom ActiveX DLLs to replace the default **RDSServer.DataFactory** implementation. Your custom DLL would need to pass **Recordset** objects back to the client and could contain methods that aren't provided by **RDSServer.DataFactory**, such as those that encompass a business rule. For more information on using the Advanced Data Factory object, or writing your own custom business object, refer to the RDS documentation.

Accessing Data from ASP Pages and Components

You can use either RDS or ADO, or a combination of both technologies, in the same application. For example, your application can create a custom business object that uses ADO to manage server-side data, and uses RDS to transfer remote data to the client tier where the user can interact with it.

Because ADO can be accessed from server-side ASP pages or components, it doesn't require any controls on the Web client—a serious consideration for mixed-browser environments like the Internet. Unlike RDS, a server-side ADO solution is browser independent. When you create an application, decide which technology is most appropriate for you.

This section discusses the issues involved in creating a server-side ADO application, using Active Server Pages (ASP) and components.

Preparing the Database

Before you can connect to a database using ADO, you must take a few preliminary steps to properly configure your data source.

Connection Strings

ADO uses OLE DB connection strings to define the specifics of the data source. The connection string consists of a series of keyword/value pairs separated by semicolons, which specify information used for establishing a connection to the data source. Such a string might look like this:

```
"DSN=AdvWorks;UID=sa;PWD=;SERVER=MyServer;DATABASE=pubs;APP=MyApp"
```

When using the OLE DB Provider for ODBC to connect to an ODBC driver through ADO, elements of the OLE DB connection string are passed down to the ODBC Driver for the data source. Refer to your driver's documentation for a complete list of recognized connection string values.

Data Source Names

When designing a Web database application, it is often easier to initially prototype with a desktop database like Microsoft Access and then scale up to an enterprise-level database like Microsoft SQL Server once the design work has been finished. With a connection string, you can confine the effects of such a change to one or two lines of code within your application. This is an easy alteration to make if you are using script, but it would require you to recompile your business object DLLs.

You can use an ODBC Data Source Name (DSN) entry to store the connection string values externally, and greatly simplify the information you need to provide in the connection string itself. This makes such changes to the data source completely transparent to the code itself. To create a new DSN:

1. Click the **Start** menu button, point to **Settings,** and click **Control Panel.**
2. Double-click the ODBC icon, and select the **System DSN** tab.
3. Click **Add** to create a new DSN entry, and then select the appropriate OLE DB Provider for your database from the list of installed providers. Click **Finish** to configure your provider.
4. Enter the Data Source Name and other parameters. Don't forget to select the server or file name of your database. Click **OK**.

Note Make sure you create either a File or System DSN. User (or local) DSNs aren't recognized by ADO.

"DSN-less" Connections

You can open a connection to a database without creating or specifying a named data source. Connections made in this way are called "DSN-less," because they don't require the system administrator to create an ODBC DSN. Rather than relying on information stored in a file or in the system registry, DSN-less connections specify the driver name, and all driver-specific information in the connection string.

Whether or not to use a DSN is a matter of flexibility. Because connection parameters are readily visible to system administrators no matter which connection style you use, there are no extra security benefits. Probably the most common reason for using a DSN-less connection is to connect to a database on a system that is not under your direct control. This makes DSN-less connections good for testing, and for applications under development.

The following DSN-less connection strings contain the minimum parameters required by the OLE DB drivers of Microsoft Access and Microsoft SQL 6.5:

```
strConAccess = "Driver={Microsoft Access Driver (*.mdb)};DBQ=C:\db.mdb"
strConSQL65  = "Driver={SQL Server};Server=(local);UID=sa;PWD="
```

Essentially, a DSN-less connection is "hard-coded" to use a certain driver, user identity, and network location, which makes it bothersome and difficult to update when the database parameters change. Because the variety of connection parameters can differ greatly from one ODBC data source drive to another, it is recommended that you use a DSN whenever possible.

Data Source Permissions

Setting up a DSN is the first step toward connecting to a database. You also need the right permissions before you can access data from the Web. For instance, if you don't have the correct permissions and you try to open a Microsoft Access database stored on an NTFS system, you may get the following error:

```
Microsoft OLE DB Provider for ODBC Drivers error '80004005'
[Microsoft][ODBC Microsoft Access 97 Driver] The Microsoft Jet database
engine cannot open the file '(unknown)'. It is already opened
exclusively by another user, or you need permission to view its data.
```

This problem occurs when the anonymous (IUSR_*computername*) account doesn't have the necessary permissions for the directory containing the Microsoft Access database (.mdb) file. In order to make modifications to the data, the Jet database engine (on which Microsoft Access is built) needs to create a temporary working file in the same directory as the database. If the anonymous user can't write this lock file, an error will occur. Make sure that you grant sufficient permission on the database and its directory for the anonymous user account and that exclusive access and record locking are turned off.

Security and Microsoft SQL Server

For SQL Server, permissions issues multiply, especially if SQL Server and IIS are running on different computers. By default, connections to a Microsoft SQL Server use a service of the Windows NT operating system known as a "named pipe." In order for a SQL server client to gain access to a Windows NT named pipe, the client needs to be validated by the server. This is normally accomplished either by means of a Workgroups-style validation (identical user names and passwords are created on the client and the server) or by using the domain method (both the client and server are domain members).

The SQL Server connection uses the identity of the user associated with the Web connection. If the connection is anonymous, you need to create a guest account that corresponds to the IUSR_*computername* account. If this guest account already exists, then make sure it has rights to log onto the SQL Server computer.

Support for the Anonymous user account can be configured by any of the following means:

- Add the IUSR_*computername* account to the local user account database on the server that hosts SQL Server.
- Make the account a member of the domain that SQL Server resides in.
- Enable the Windows NT Guest user account on the remote SQL Server computer.

If you have configured IIS to use Windows NT Challenge/Response authentication (by either disabling Anonymous access, or forcing a logon by returning a "401 Access Denied" response), IIS tries to connect to the SQL Server by using the user's security context. If SQL Server resides on a separate computer from IIS, Windows NT detects the attempt to use a network named pipe handle that had been opened in a different user context and forces the pipe closed, according to its security rules.

The following OLE DB error is an indication of this problem:

```
Microsoft OLE DB Provider for ODBC Drivers error '80004005'
[Microsoft][ODBC SQL Server Driver][DBNMPNTW]ConnectionWrite
(GetOverLappedResult()).
```

If SQL Server is running on the *same* server as IIS, use a local named pipe connection instead of a network named pipe connection. In the SQL Server connection string or in the DSN configuration, change "SERVER=*computername*" to "SERVER=(local)." The name "(local)" (with parentheses) is a special keyword to the SQL Server ODBC driver, and indicates a local connection should be used.

If SQL Server is running on a *different* server than IIS, you can use a non-authenticated protocol between IIS and SQL Server, such as TCP/IP sockets. To use TCP/IP sockets, you must configure both the SQL Server and the SQL Server client on the IIS server, as follows:

▶ **To set up a TCP/IP connection on the server hosting SQL Server**

1. Run SQL Server Setup.

2. In the **Options** dialog box, click **Change Network Support,** and click **Continue**.

3. Select the entry for TCP/IP Sockets (leave Named Pipes also selected) and click **OK**. Accept the default Named Pipe name and TCP/IP Socket number.

4. Exit SQL Server Setup. Stop and restart the SQL Server.

▶ **To set up a TCP/IP connection on the server hosting IIS**

1. Open the ODBC Data Source Administrator application in Control Panel. Select a SQL Server data source, and click **Configure** to start the SQL Server configuration Wizard. Click **Next**, then click **Client Configuration**.

2. Select the **Net Library** tab, and select TCP/IP Sockets as the default network protocol. Click **Done**. IIS will now use TCP/IP sockets when connecting to the SQL Server specified in this DSN. (You can also use the Microsoft SQL Server Client Configuration utility to configure the client connection protocol. See your SQL Server documentation details.)

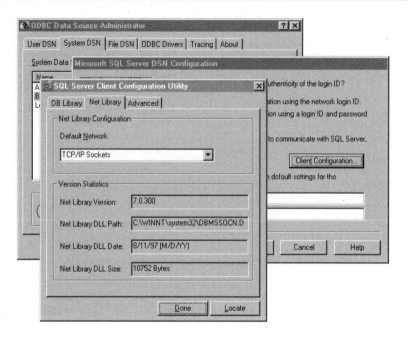

Figure 6.4   Configuring the SQL Server client connection

The Database Connection

There are several ways to establish a database connection. One way is to create an ADO **Connection** object explicitly, and use its **Open** method to connect to the database using a DSN, user name, and password. The following example shows you how this would look in an ASP script:

```
<%
   '--- Open the database
   Set cn = Server.CreateObject("ADODB.Connection")
   cn.Open strDSN, strUserName, strPassword
%>
```

If your application needs to perform more than one database operation, this approach makes a good choice, because it creates the **Connection** object as a stand-alone object. The object can be reused as necessary and closed when all operations have been performed.

You can also create a connection without using the **Connection** object. Instead, you create a **Recordset** or **Command** object and use a connection string to define the connection. When called, the object creates a database connection on its own. The following example uses a **Recordset** object in conjunction with a DSN to create a new database connection:

```
'--- Open the database and retrieve the records
Set rs = Server.CreateObject("ADODB.Recordset")
rs.Open strSQL, strDSN
```

When you bypass the **Connection** object in this way, you run the risk of inadvertently using extra server resources and slowing down the processing of your queries if you aren't careful, particularly if ODBC Connection Pooling is disabled. If you have already created a **Connection** object, it is always more efficient to reuse the connection.

Selecting an OLE DB Provider

Before you establish a connection to your database from ADO, you can choose which OLE DB Provider to use. A provider is a component that manages access to a data source. In most cases, you don't have to specify an OLE DB Provider; you can just use the ODBC driver.

But the OLE DB Provider is not limited to ODBC; you can select other providers for your connection. The following ASP example uses an sample provider ("sampprov") to create a **Recordset** object from a Comma Separated Values (CSV) file using the **Connection** object's **Provider** method:

```
Set cn = Server.CreateObject("ADODB.Connection")
cn.Provider = "sampprov"
cn.Open "Data Source=C:\oledbsdk\samples\sampclnt"
Set rs = cn.Execute("customer.csv")
```

Note The "sampprov" provider is shipped with the OLE DB SDK, which is available for free download from http://www.microsoft.com/oledb/download.htm.

ODBC Connection Pooling

Database applications that frequently open and close connections can reduce database server performance. Fortunately, ODBC 3.5 implements *connection pooling*, which enables applications to share connections across user requests, and thereby improves performance by reducing the number of idle connections.

Before making a new connection to an ODBC data source, the ODBC driver searches the connection pool for any idle connections that may satisfy the connection request. For the connection to be reused, the connection string of the pooled connection must exactly match that of the request. If a matching idle connection is found, it is returned to the calling application.

When an ODBC connection is released, the connection returns to the pool, rather than being closed. The **Connection Pool Timeout** (**CPTimeout**) setting of your ODBC driver determines the length of time that a connection remains in the connection pool. If the connection is not reused during this time, the connection is closed and removed from the pool. The default CPTimeout value is 60 seconds.

You can modify the CPTimeout value of each ODBC database driver by changing the following Windows NT registry key:

HKEY_LOCAL_MACHINE\SOFTWARE
  \ODBC
    \ODBCINST.INI
      driver-name
        \CPTimeout = timeout (REG_SZ, units are in seconds)

For example, the following setting configures the ODBC driver for SQL Server connection pool timeout to 180 seconds (3 minutes):

HKEY_LOCAL_MACHINE\SOFTWARE
  \ODBC
    \ODBCINST.INI
      \SQL Server
        \CPTimeout = "180"

A severed connection to the database could prevent applications that use a connection pool from connecting successfully. Client applications would continue to make new connection requests even though the connection is broken. It takes time for each request to determine that the server is unavailable, and new connection requests must wait for others to timeout. Eventually, the server will be unable to accept any more requests.

The ODBC Connection Manager can be configured to retry dead connections on a preset interval. If the connection attempt fails, the connection is marked as "bad" and placed back in the pool. Once a bad server has been identified, subsequent connection requests for that server *immediately* return an error. Periodically, the Connection Manager attempts to reestablish the connection. If the attempt succeeds, the connection returns to a valid state and normal processing resumes.

You can configure the Retry Wait property for a specific ODBC driver by creating a registry key with the following settings:

```
HKEY_LOCAL_MACHINE\SOFTWARE
   \ODBC
      \ODBCINST.INI
         \driver-name
            \Retry Wait = timeout (REG_SZ, units are in seconds)
```

The following setting instructs the ODBC driver for SQL Server Connection Manager to retry a dead connection after a 60-second wait:

```
HKEY_LOCAL_MACHINE\SOFTWARE
   \ODBC
      \ODBCINST.INI
         \SQL Server
            \Retry Wait = "60"
```

Note Every process uses its own connection pool. If you are using an out-of-process component (or, LocalServer application), you cannot take full advantage of ODBC connection pooling. Because each application process uses a separate pool, your application can only share connections with itself. In order to share connections with other components, you must write your business logic as a DLL.

Tips for Optimizing Database Connections

One of the main challenges of designing a sophisticated Web database application, is a properly managed database connection. Opening and maintaining connections, even when no information is transmitted, can deplete a database server's resources and result in connectivity problems. Well-designed Web database applications manage connections wisely and compensate for delays due to network traffic.

Here are six tips to help you optimize your use of database connections.

Tip 1: Enhance Performance on SQL Server Systems

If you intend to access only Microsoft SQL Server from ASP, you can enhance your application's performance by changing the threading model for the main ADO components from "Apartment" to "Both" in the registry.

By default, the ADO objects are assigned the Apartment threading model in the registry. This model guarantees that each object is allocated a single thread for the life of the object, and all calls to the object execute on the same thread. Although this model provides significant improvements over the single-threading model, and works with providers that are not free-threaded (like Microsoft Access), it also has its performance drawbacks. For instance, if you store ADO components, such as the **Connection** object, in the ASP **Session** object, IIS will enforce a limit of one thread per user session.

To switch ADO to a Both threading model, open Windows Explorer and double-click Makefre15.bat in the ADO installation folder (C:\Program Files\Common Files\System\Ado, by default). To reverse the process, (that is, to return the threading model to the Apartment model) double-click Makeapt15.bat in the ADO installation folder.

Tip 2: Set the Connection Timeout

Limit the amount of time your application waits before abandoning a connection attempt and issuing an error message.

A database server experiencing a sudden increase in activity can become backlogged, which greatly increases the time required to establish a database connection. Excessive connection delays increase the time that users wait to find out that requests cannot be processed.

By changing the Connection object's ConnectionTimeout property, you can reduce the time it takes for a connection to timeout. Not all providers support this property, but it can dramatically increase the perceived responsiveness of those that do. The default for the ConnectionTimeout property is 30 seconds.

The following script sets the ConnectionTimeout property to wait 20 seconds before canceling the connection attempt:

```
Set cn = Server.CreateObject("ADODB.Connection")
cn.ConnectionTimeout = 20
cn.Open "FILEDSN=MyDatabase.dsn"
```

Tip 3: Close Your Connections

Close your connections when you are finished with them.

By proactively closing connections when they are no longer needed, you reduce demand on the database server and make resources available to other users. Connections are closed when they go out of scope, but you can use the **Close** method to close a connection at any time.

The following code creates a **Command** object, implicitly creates a new connection, and calls a stored procedure.

```
<%
    Set cmd = Server.CreateObject("ADODB.Command")
    cmd.ActiveConnection = "dsn=sqlsrvr"
    cmd.CommandText = "{call mysproc}"
    cmd.Execute
%>
```

The **Command** object opens a connection automatically and releases it when the **Command** object goes out of scope at the end of the page. To release it before that time, you can either set the **Command** object reference to **Nothing**, as in:

```
Set cmd = Nothing
```

or, you could close the connection by closing the active connection:

```
cmd.ActiveConnection.Close
```

Remember that storing **Connection** objects in the ASP **Session** object is not a good idea, because active connections hold open database resources and would defeat the purpose of the ODBC connection pool.

Tip 4: Share Active Connections

Don't use more database connections than you need; share them if possible.

Whenever you specify a connection string, rather than a connection variable, you are requesting a new connection to the server. Instead of a connection string, create a single connection variable, and use it with the **ActiveConnection** property of the **Command** and **Recordset** objects. By using a connection variable, you can share an existing connection among several database queries.

For example, the following script stores a reference to an open database connection in a global variable, and uses it to perform a variety of queries against information stored in a database:

```
<%@ Language=VBScript EnableSessionState=False %>
<html>
<head>
<title>Items and Neighbors</title>
</head>
<body BGCOLOR=#FFFFFF>
<h2>Items</h?>
<%
    Set cn = Server.CreateObject("ADODB.Connection")
    cn.ConnectionTimeout = 20
    cn.Open "DSN=Dagwood"

    Set rs = Server.CreateObject("ADODB.Recordset")
    rs.Open "Items", cn, adOpenStatic, adLockReadOnly, adCmdTable
    Do Until rs.EOF
        Response.Write rs("i_name") & "<BR>"
        rs.MoveNext
    Loop
    rs.Close
%>
<h2>Neighbors</h2>
<%
    rs.Open "Neighbor", cn, adOpenStatic, adLockReadOnly, adCmdTable
    Do Until rs.EOF
        Response.Write rs("name") & "<BR>"
        rs.MoveNext
    Loop

    rs.Close
    cn.Close
%>
</body>
</html>
```

Tip 5: Restrict Connections Across Pages

If your provider doesn't support automatic connection pooling, find a balance between the greatest number of connections on the one hand, and the hidden costs of creating and destroying connections on the other.

Storing **Connection** objects (or any of the database access components, for that matter) in the ASP **Application** object is not recommended. Unless your OLE DB Provider supports the Both threading model (Microsoft Access does not, though SQL Server does; see "Tip 1: Enhance Performance on SQL Server Systems," earlier in this section), you will cause the Web server to serialize all user requests for the application—not exactly the best way to improve performance. Even if your OLE DB Provider supports free threading, you must be cautious when storing any components in the **Application** object.

If you must hold connections open, it is better to create them as individual users require, and store them in the user's **Session** object. Like the **Application** object, Apartment threaded providers such as Microsoft Access lock the session to a single thread for all requests. Because sessions must time out before the server resources are finally released, applications that store connections in the **Session** object should also provide a means for terminating the session to allow other clients to use the connection. For example, you could provide a Log Off button to explicitly end the user's session and release the active connection. (See "Ending the ASP Session," in the previous chapter.)

The following example opens a connection at the start of the user's session. The connection is automatically closed when the session ends.

```
<OBJECT ID=cnSession RUNAT=Server SCOPE=Session
   CLASSID="clsid:00000514-0000-0010-8000-00AA006D2EA4">
</OBJECT>

Sub Session_OnStart
   '--- Open ADO connection to "UsersDB1" database
   cnSession.Open "UsersDB1", "userdblogin","userdbpassword"
End Sub
```

Remember, although you can utilize a single connection across more than one page, doing so holds the connection open and defeats the advantages of connection pooling.

Tip 6: Increase the Record Cache

Increase connection throughput by requesting multiple records at once.

By default, the **CacheSize** property of the **Recordset** object is set to 1 for all cursor types. By increasing **CacheSize**, you can increase the number of records the provider will retrieve at one time into local memory. For example, if **CacheSize** is 10, the provider will retrieve the first 10 records when first opening the **Recordset** object. As you move through the **Recordset** object, the provider uses the data from the local memory buffer. When you move past the last record in the cache, the provider retrieves the next 10 records from the data source.

```
rs.CacheSize = 10
rs.Open strSQL
```

Recordset caching doesn't work well for binary data, like images and text streams, because only the data from the last record in the cache will be available. When using binary data types, you must retrieve one row at a time. Also, records retrieved from the cache don't reflect changes other users may have made since the records were retrieved. To force an update of all the cached data, use **Resync**.

Recordsets and Cursors

A **Recordset**, in its simplest form, is a collection of rows returned from an ADO database query. You can create a **Recordset** with just a few lines of VBScript:

```
<%
    Set rs = Server.CreateObject("ADODB.Recordset")
    rs.Open "SELECT * FROM Authors", "DSN=Pubs;UID=sa;PWD="

    '--- Loop through the recordset with MoveNext
    Do Until rs.EOF
        '--- Access record fields here
        rs.MoveNext
    Loop
    rs.Close
%>
```

When a **Recordset** is opened, the current record is marked by a cursor position, which points to the first record that matched the query. As you move the cursor forward, with **Recordset.MoveNext**, it will eventually run out of records and set its **EOF** (End Of File) property to **True**. In addition to checking for **EOF** when a **Recordset** is opened, you should check its **State** property for the **adStateClosed** value.

The table on the next page lists the four types of cursors available for ADO **Recordset** objects. Since most applications typically access the **Recordset** sequentially from the first record, the default cursor type is optimized for forward-only traversal. (In the case of Microsoft SQL Server, it is read-only as well. See "Forward-only Cursors," later in this chapter.)

Table 6.1   ADO Cursor Types

Cursor Type	Description
adOpenForwardOnly	Forward-only cursor. You can only scroll forward through records. This is the default cursor type.
adOpenStatic	Static cursor. A static copy of a set of records that you can use to find data or generate reports. Additions, changes, or deletions by other users are not visible. The **Recordset** is fully navigable, forward and backward.
adOpenKeyset	Keyset cursor. Like a dynamic cursor, except that you can't see records that other users add (although records that other users delete are inaccessible from your **Recordset**). Data changes by other users are still visible.
adOpenDynamic	Dynamic cursor. Additions, changes, and deletions by other users are visible, and all types of movement through the **Recordset** are allowed (except for bookmarks if the provider doesn't support them).

If you use the **Execute** method of the **Connection** (and **Command**) object, you will always get a forward-only, read-only cursor. (This is also the default behavior of **Recordset.Open** if no extra parameters are specified.) When you use the **Recordset.Open** method, however, you have the opportunity to configure your **Recordset** exactly as you'd like it (cursor type, record locking method, number of records to cache, and so on). The following examples demonstrate how to create **Recordset** objects with varying degrees of cursor functionality:

```
Sub SimpleCursor()
   Set cn = Server.CreateObject("ADODB.Connection")
   con.Open "pubs", "sa", ""
   ' creates a forward-only, read-only cursor
   Set rs = cn.Execute("select * from authors")
End Sub

Sub MoreFunctionalCursor()
   Set cn = Server.CreateObject("ADODB.connection")
   con.Open "pubs", "sa", ""
   Set rs = Server.CreateObject("ADODB.Recordset")
   ' requests dynamic keyset cursor and optimistic concurrency
   rs.Open "select * from authors", cn, adOpenKeyset, adLockOptimistic
End Sub
```

All of the cursor types will let you insert and update records in a **Recordset**, unless you have specified **adLockReadOnly** as the lock type. Different cursor types give you varying degrees of visibility for database actions performed by other users. The following table lists the cursor types based on their level of functionality:

Table 6.2   Recordset Functionality by Cursor Type

Cursor Type	Insert, Update Records	View Updates, Deletions	View Inserts
Forward-only, read-only	False	False	False
Static	True	False	False
Keyset	True	True	False
Dynamic	True	True	True

The following sections further describe the differences in these cursor types.

Forward-Only Cursors

The first type of cursor is optimized for the most common type of database access, in-order traversal of records. This is the default cursor type for **Recordset** objects created when you use the **Execute** method of the **Command** and **Connection** objects. Although you can still add, delete, and update records with a forward-only cursor, you cannot use bookmarks. Also, you cannot use the **Resync** method to refresh the records in the **Recordset**.

Some providers (like Microsoft SQL Server) implement the default forward-only, read-only cursor using a "firehose" mode, meaning that the connection is held open as long as there is data to retrieve. Once the cursor has been opened in this mode, the server does not wait for the client to request the next record and then provide it. Instead, the server sends the records as a continuous stream of data. Firehose cursoring is very fast, as overhead is only incurred as the data is read. Firehose cursors do not allow updates to the data.

Forward-only Restrictions on Binary Large Objects

The Binary Large Object (BLOB) is a type of data field that contains large blocks of text, or binary data such as graphics, sound, or compiled code. BLOBs can be fetched with a forward-only or "firehose" cursor, but there are some access restrictions on the resulting **Recordset**.

- The **CacheSize** property of the **Recordset** must be set to 1. You can't cache BLOBs, and you can't go back, so if you cache more than a single row, only the BLOB on the last row is available.

- The BLOBs must be to the right of any scalar (non-BLOB) fields fetched in the query and you must access them in a left-to-right order.

These restrictions have nothing to do with the underlying table layout—the rules apply only to **Recordset** objects. For instance, you could have a BLOB column in the middle of your table definition (with scalar columns to the left and right), but when you execute your SELECT statement, you must select the BLOB column after the scalar columns. The storage engine on SQL Server doesn't impose limitations on where a BLOB column lies, but it is significant to the ODBC driver for SQL Server where the BLOB column is placed in the result list.

Static versus Dynamic Cursors

When you request a static cursor, you are requesting a snapshot of the data at the time the **Recordset** is created. Once the client has received all the rows, the cursor can scroll through all data without any further interaction with the server. The cursor position can be changed using both *relative positioning* (offsets from the current, top or bottom row) and *absolute positioning* (using the row number). The static cursor's only shortcoming is that changes made to the database aren't made available to a client using a static cursor.

A dynamic cursor, on the other hand, makes database changes available as they happen. Because the dynamic cursor requires the database provider to reorder data in the **Recordset** as it changes on the server, it is much more expensive than the static cursor in terms of the processing it requires. Also, because the order of the underlying records may change, only relative positioning is available to dynamic cursors.

Keyset Cursors

A keyset cursor combines the functionality of the static and dynamic cursor types. It can view all database updates made by other users and it can seek to both absolute and relative positions. A *keyset* is a set of values used to access specific rows or records in a database. The "key" is actually an index into the cursor. When the database needs to update the cursor's value, it does so based on the row's key. Therefore, a "keyset recordset" must include enough columns to ensure unique records in an updatable **Recordset**.

There is a cost for using a keyset cursor, as opposed to a static or dynamic cursor. You will invariably incur a performance hit as you increase cursor functionality.

There is no single cursor type that you should always use. Your choice of cursor type depends on the functionality you require. If there are a lot of rows in the table, opening a keyset cursor may take a long time building the key information; opening a dynamic cursor is much faster. You can, however, configure a data provider (such as SQL Server) to populate the key information asynchronously. Dynamic cursors don't support bookmarks. If you need bookmark support, use a keyset or static cursor.

Cursor Concurrency

The server-side **Recordset** supports four types of record locking (also called *concurrency*):

- **adLockReadOnly** The database doesn't lock records since you are only accessing them in read-only state. This is the default concurrency.
- **adLockPessimistic** The database locks the records being changed as soon as editing begins. The records are unlocked when all changes are complete. No two users can access the same records at the same time.
- **adLockOptimistic** The database locks the records being changed only when the changes are committed. Two users can access the same record at the same time, and the database must be able to reconcile (or simply reject) changed records that have been edited by multiple users prior to commit.
- **adLockBatchOptimistic** This mode is required for batch updates using client cursors, and is very similar to optimistic concurrency.

Implementing a record cache implies optimistic concurrency. The server does not have to hold locks on the database, thus freeing resources.

However, if there is high contention for the resource, pessimistic concurrency may be preferred. It is easier to reject a request to access a database and have the server try again than it is to reconcile data that is rapidly becoming out-of-date in a record cache.

Client Cursors

All **Recordset** objects use cursors. You can use the Client Cursor Engine of RDS to open and populate a disconnected **Recordset.** Because RDS is integrated with ADO, it is possible to create and use client-side cursors on the server as well.

Before you open a Recordset, you can change its level of cursor support by setting the **CursorLocation** property, like this:

```
rs.CursorLocation = adUseClient
```

Selecting **adUseClient** as the **CursorLocation** creates a disconnected RDS **Recordset**, such as you would find on the client tier.

Client-side cursors can be used to extend the functionality of the existing driver-supplied OLE DB cursor support. The Client Cursor Engine will support functionality that is unavailable from the DBMS driver itself, as is the case with the Microsoft Oracle 1.0 ODBC driver. The RDS client-side cursor may also allow features that your server-side cursors do not. For example, you can't open a cursor on a stored procedure that has anything other than a single SELECT statement in it, unless you have set the **CursorLocation** property of the **Command** object to **adUseClient**. Likewise, you can only use absolute page positioning against an ODBC data source using a client-side cursor. (See the Visual Basic example "Paging through a Recordset," later in this chapter.)

Two additional **CursorLocation** values are available, **adUseClientBatch** (for use with **adLockBatchOptimistic** concurrency setting) and **adUseNone**. The **adUseNone** value instructs ADO to forgo its normal *rowset helper* support, which provides extra cursor functionality beyond that which the OLE DB Provider may support. When you specify **adUseNone**, you are effectively telling ADO not to include this additional service provider, and as a result, limiting **Recordset** cursor functionality to that which your OLE DB driver supports.

Note Because updates to a disconnected **Recordset** aren't immediately communicated to the server, you won't be notified of **Recordset** concurrency errors immediately, as you are with server-side cursors.

Advantages of Using Server-Side Cursors

Before you decide to write everything with client-side cursors, be aware of the advantages to using server-side cursors.

- **Performance** If you only intend to access a small fraction of the data in a **Recordset** (typical of many browsing applications), server-side cursors boost your performance, because only the required data (and not the entire result set) is loaded into memory.

- **Additional cursor types** Client cursors are either forward-only with read-only concurrency, or static with read-only and optimistic concurrency. Server-side cursors support the full range of concurrency values and a variety of different cursor types. For instance, keyset and dynamic cursor types are available only if you use server-side cursors.

- **Memory usage** When using server-side cursors, the client does not need to cache large amounts of data or maintain information about the cursor position; the server provides that functionality.

Managing Records in a Recordset

This section describes a few techniques to help you through the more troublesome aspects of ADO **Recordset** management.

Keeping Track of New Records

When you add a new record, several factors determine where in the **Recordset** it will be inserted. If you need to move the cursor after you've added a new record, keeping track of where the record was inserted can be a little tricky.

If your cursor type supports bookmarks, you could save a bookmark to the current row if you need to come back to the record later. However, if you insert records into a table without an index, you will not be able to get back to the newly inserted row until after you use the **Requery** method to request a new **Recordset**.

Identity fields, which are updated automatically when you insert a record, can be useful for tracking new records. However, you must use the **Resync** method to refresh the **Recordset** with the new value after you insert the new row. The following example opens a table, creates a record, and displays the new row's identity value:

```
<%
   '--- Open a static cursor on the Survey table, and add record
   Set rs = Server.CreateObject("ADODB.Recordset")
   rs.Open "Survey", Application("ConnectionString"),_
         adOpenStatic, adLockOptimistic, adCmdTable
   rs.AddNew

   '--- Add form fields to Recordset, using field names as columns
   For Each Item In Request.Form
      strItem = Trim(Request.Form(Item))
      If strItem <> "" Then
         rs(Item) = Server.HTMLEncode(strItem)
      End If
   Next

   '--- Set time of update, and update new record with form values
   rs("Date") = Now()
   rs.Update

   '--- Force an update of the Recordset with the identity information
   rs.Resync
   Response.Write "You are response number: " & rs("ID").Value & "<BR>"
   rs.Close
%>
```

Avoiding Query Timeouts

It's not uncommon to find databases tables of 10 to 50 million records. On these systems, even stored procedures can sometimes take longer than a few minutes to run. When a user runs a report, he or she knows that the query may take several minutes and this is acceptable. However, a Web page doesn't normally wait that long.

To solve this problem, you first need to set the **CommandTimeout** property of the **Connection** object. This property indicates how long to wait for a query to execute and applies to the **Connection.Execute** and **Recordset.Open** methods when the **Source** property is not a **Command** object. If the **Recordset.Open** call is using a genuine **Command** object, you'll need to set the **CommandTimeout** property of the **Command** object instead. This property establishes the length of time the application should wait for a **Command** object to execute.

You will also need to increase the values of the **ScriptTimeout** property of the ASP **Server** object. If this property isn't set, it doesn't matter how long the ADO query takes, the script will have stopped executing in the meantime. Both the **CommandTimeout** and **ScriptTimeout** properties accept values indicating the number of seconds to wait before canceling the operation.

Purging Deleted Records

After you delete a record, the **RecordCount** property still includes the deleted record.

If you refresh (or requery) the **Recordset**, it will not include the deleted record and **RecordCount** is accurate. If you set **CacheSize** to 1 (so that you are caching only a single record at a time) **RecordCount** will accurately exclude deleted rows. You should avoid increasing **CacheSize** with a keyset cursor type in circumstances when you are expecting to be able to use **RecordCount** after you delete records.

References to Field Values

One of the more surprising consequences of using a loosely typed VBScript variable is that you sometimes don't know exactly what you are referencing. In the following ASP example, the **Session** variable `strAuthor` apparently loses its value once the **Recordset** is closed.

```
Set Session("strAuthor") = rstPublishers.Fields("Author")
rstPublishers.Close
```

And then later in the script:

```
Response.Write Session("strAuthor") ' Where'd it go?
```

The problem is that strAuthor is a Variant data type containing a reference to a **Field** object, not a string, as it appears to be. When the **Recordset** is closed, the **Field** object is no longer valid, and the variable appears empty. You can avoid the problem by qualifying the code with the **Value** property:

```
Session("strAuthor") = rstPublishers.Fields("Author").Value
```

Why would you want to store a reference to a **Field** object? Rather than performing a lookup from the **Recordset** collection each time you need a field (which is what happens when you use the column name), you can use a reference to a **Field** object to keep track of the current value of a field.

```
<%
    Set rs = Server.CreateObject("ADODB.Recordset")

    rs.Open "Products", "DSN=AdvWorks",_
            adOpenForwardOnly, adLockReadOnly, adCmdTable

    '--- Select fields now, using single lookups
    Set fldProdId   = rs("ProductID")
    Set fldProdName = rs("ProductName")
    Set fldProdDesc = rs("ProductDescription")

    '--- Loop through records using field references
    Do Until rs.EOF
        Response.Write fldProdId & ": <b>" & fldProdName &_
                    "</b>: " & fldProdDesc & "<BR>"
        rs.MoveNext
    Loop

    rs.Close
%>
```

With this technique, it is possible to perform a query even without specifying a SQL command.

VBScript Example: Filling a List Box

When using a server-side script to fill a list box for use on the client's HTML page, keep in mind that the list box doesn't exist yet when your server-side code is executed. For this reason, you need to generate client-side code using server-side scripting. You can use either the standard HTML SELECT tag (which creates a drop-down list box), or a custom ActiveX Listbox control. Using the SELECT tag, you simply use server-side HTML to fill in the VALUEs. The following example demonstrates how you could fill in a SELECT control from an ADO **Recordset**:

```
<SELECT>
<% Do While NOT rs.EOF %>
      <OPTION VALUE="<%= rs("Name") %>"><%= rs("Name") %></OPTION>
      <% rs.MoveNext
   Loop %>
</SELECT>
```

When you are working with client-side ActiveX objects like the Listbox control, it's a good idea to use server-side scripting to programmatically pass values to **ListBox.AddItem** calls during the **Window_OnLoad** event. Here is an example (the groups of double quotation marks are used to keep the Name data together as a string):

```
<SCRIPT LANGUAGE="VBScript"><!--
Sub Window_OnLoad()
   <% Do While NOT rs.EOF
      Response.Write "ListBox.AddItem """ & rs("Name") & """" & vbCr
      rs.MoveNext
   Loop %>
End Sub
--></SCRIPT>
```

PerlScript Example: Filling a Table

Filling a table is nearly identical to filling a SELECT tag. Here's an example that uses PerlScript to fill the rows of a table:

```
<%@ Language=PerlScript %>
<% #--- Open the connection and query
   $Conn = $Server->CreateObject("ADODB.Connection");
   $Conn->Open( "AdvWorks" );
   $RS = $Conn->Execute( "SELECT * FROM Products" );
%>

<TABLE BORDER=1>
<TR>
<% #--- Create a row of column headings
   $count = $RS->Fields->Count;
   for ( $i = 0; $i < $count; $i++ ) {
      %><TH><%= $RS->Fields($i)->Name %></TH><%
   };
%>
</TR>
```

```
<% #--- Fill in the rows of the table with data
   while ( ! $RS->EOF ) {
      %><TR><%
      for ( $i = 0; $i < $count; $i++ ) {
         %><TD VALIGN=TOP>
         <%= $RS->Fields($i)->Value %></TD><%
      };
      %></TR><%
      $RS->MoveNext;
   };

   #--- Close connection
   $RS->Close;
   $Conn->Close;
%>
</TABLE>
```

Limiting the Number of Records

If you know you'll require only the first few records, it makes sense to limit the number of records retrieved from the database. You can do this with the **MaxRecords** property of the **Recordset** object. The default setting for this property is zero, which means that the provider normally returns all requested records. Setting it to some other value will limit the size of the rowset returned from the query. The effect is the same as if you had used the Microsoft SQL Rowcount directive as part of your query.

The **MaxRecords** property is often used together with a SQL "ORDER BY" clause to produce a "Top Ten" list based on some attribute of the data. The next example returns a **Recordset** containing the 10 most expensive publications in the Titles table.

```
<%
   '--- NOTE: DSN-less connection
   strCnn = "driver={SQL Server};server=(local);" &_
           "uid=sa;pwd=;database=pubs"

   Set rs = Server.CreateObject("ADODB.Recordset")
   rs.MaxRecords = 10
   rs.Open "SELECT Title, Price FROM Titles ORDER BY Price DESC",_
      strCnn, adOpenForwardOnly, adLockReadOnly, adCmdText
%>
```

Note You must set the **MaxRecords** property before the **Recordset** is opened. After that time, the property is read-only.

Visual Basic Example: Paging through a Recordset

After browsing the top ten results, users may want to view the remaining records. In this case, you don't necessarily want to limit the records, you just want to stop after the first page is filled, and wait for the signal to continue. It's easy enough to stop after a certain number of records, but what's the best way to pick up where you left off?

The **Recordset** object exposes three properties to assist you in your task: **PageSize**, **PageCount** and **AbsolutePage**. Once you have set the page size, your database provider can calculate how many pages of data it will return to you, and let you jump to locations at the beginning of each page. (If you set the **CacheSize** equal to **PageSize,** only the records you display will be cached in the **RecordSet**.) Note that you must use a client-side cursor to enable absolute positioning in ODBC data sources.

The following Visual Basic example uses the **AbsolutePage**, **PageCount**, and **PageSize** properties to display names and hire dates from the Employee table (of the Pubs database) five records at a time in a message box:

```
Public Sub AbsolutePageExample()

    Dim rstEmployees As New ADODB.Recordset
    Dim strCnn As String
    Dim strMessage As String
    Dim intPage As Integer
    Dim intPageCount As Integer
    Dim intRecord As Integer

    strCnn = "driver={SQL Server};server=(local);" & _
        "uid=sa;pwd=;database=pubs"

    '--- Use client cursor to enable AbsolutePage property.
    rstEmployees.CursorLocation = adUseClient
    rstEmployees.CacheSize = 5
    rstEmployees.Open "employee", strCnn
    rstEmployees.MoveFirst
```

```
'--- Display names and hire dates, five records at a time.
rstEmployees.PageSize = 5
intPageCount = rstEmployees.PageCount
For intPage = 1 To intPageCount
   rstEmployees.AbsolutePage = intPage
   strMessage = ""
   For intRecord = 1 To rstEmployees.PageSize
      strMessage = strMessage & _
         rstEmployees!fname & " " & _
         rstEmployees!lname & " " & _
         rstEmployees!hire_date & vbCr
      rstEmployees.MoveNext
      If rstEmployees.EOF Then Exit For
   Next intRecord
   MsgBox strMessage
Next intPage
rstEmployees.Close

End Sub
```

Recordset paging gets a little more complex when you are using an ASP page. Because you can return only a single page of data at a time, you'll have to decide what to do with the open **Recordset** object while waiting for the next client request. You have two options—throw away the results and keep just the current page number, or stow the **Recordset** object in the user's **Session** object for later retrieval. Which approach you choose will be based on the needs of your user and your application—whether you want to save time by caching the results, or would rather release the memory for another application to use.

Note An example of **Recordset** paging is included on the IIS Resource Kit CD, as part of the Feedback application.

Retrieving Image Data

Images (as with long bodies of text) are stored in a database as Binary Large Object (BLOB) fields. Because of the added overhead for the DBMS, retrieving images from a database is slower than referencing an image URL on disk, so whether or not you store images in a database depends on the requirements of your application. You can retrieve image data with ADO using the **GetChunk** method of the **Field** object. This method requires that you specify the number of bytes or characters that you wish to retrieve.

It takes two files working together to retrieve multiple images on the same page. The main file, which contains HTML formatting and IMG tags, requires the use of a separate ASP file to perform the actual image query. The secondary ASP file, Image.asp, retrieves the requested image, and returns it as a binary object in the HTTP response using a MIME content type of "image/gif". The following is the source for Image.asp:

```
<%@ Language=JScript EnableSessionState=False %>
<%
    var ID, rs, fld, cBytes

    ID = Request.QueryString("ID");
    if (ID + "" != "undefined") {
        rs = Server.CreateObject("ADODB.Recordset");
        rs.Filter = "ImageID=" + ID;  //--- Search criteria

        rs.Open ("Images", Application("ConnectionString"),
                    adOpenForwardOnly, adLockReadOnly, adCmdTable);

        if (!rs.EOF) {
            fld = rs("ImageData");     //--- Get field reference
            cBytes = fld.ActualSize;   //--- Determine size

            //--- Return raw binary image data as "image/jpeg" MIME type
            Response.ContentType = "image/jpeg";
            Response.BinaryWrite(fld.GetChunk(cBytes));
        }
        else {
            Response.Write("Image '" + ID + "' not found.");
        }

        rs.Close();
    }
    else {
        Response.Write("No ID");
    }
%>
```

In the main file, images stored in the database can now be retrieved using the image ID as a URL parameter to Image.asp, like this:

```
<IMG SRC="./image.asp?ID=<%=ImageID%>">
```

When you use a firehose cursor, there isn't a good way to discover the size of a BLOB field before you read it. If you must use a firehose cursor, consider maintaining a separate column in the database table that stores the image's size in bytes. Otherwise, you could call the **GetChunk** method repeatedly until it returns nothing, or, if you think that the image will fit into available memory, simply use the **Value** property to retrieve the data all at once.

Stored Procedures

If you find yourself performing complex data manipulation, consider organizing database dependencies and rules into stored procedures.

Stored procedures are precompiled queries stored on the database server. They can simplify development and significantly speed up complex queries. When a stored procedure is called, it controls which operations are performed and which database fields are accessed. A single stored procedure can even execute multiple queries.

Stored procedures have explicitly defined parameters, each with a specific data type, direction, and size. Before calling a stored procedure, the **Parameters** collection of the **Command** object must be prepared to precisely match the number and type of parameters defined for the procedure on the server. Although you can request the complete **Parameter** collection by calling the **Refresh** method, building the collection parameter by parameter is preferred because it results in faster execution and avoids a network round-trip to the server. (Also, some providers do not support populating the **Parameter** collection with the **Refresh** method.) The code, however, ends up looking a bit more complex, as shown here:

```
<%
Set cm = Server.CreateObject("ADODB.Command")
cm.CommandText = "AddCustomer"
cm.CommandType = adCmdStoredProc
Set p = cm.Parameters
p.Append cm.CreateParameter("@Name", adChar, adParamInput, 40)
p.Append cm.CreateParameter("@Address", adChar, adParamInput, 80)
p.Append cm.CreateParameter("@City", adChar, adParamInput, 20)
p.Append cm.CreateParameter("@State", adChar, adParamInput, 2)
p.Append cm.CreateParameter("@Zip", adChar, adParamInput, 11)
cm("@Name") = Trim(Request.Form("Name"))
cm("@Address") = Trim(Request.Form("Address"))
cm("@City") = Trim(Request.Form("City"))
cm("@State") = Trim(Request.Form("State"))
cm("@Zip") = Trim(Request.Form("Zip"))
cm.Execute
%>
```

Returning Values from Stored Procedures

The following lines of ISQL define two stored procedures—one that returns the value 10 directly, and one that returns a value by reference in its output parameter:

```
Create procedure sp_retvalparam as return 10
Go
Create procedure sp_inoutparam(@in char(200),@out char(200) out) as
select @out = @in
Go
```

The following examples use two different but equally valid means of invoking these stored procedures. Here's the first method:

```
cmd.CommandText = "sp_retvalparam"
cmd.CommandType = adCmdStoredProc
' Quietly retrieve parameter info from server
cmd(0).Direction = adParamReturnValue
cmd.Execute
Response.Write cmd(0)
```

The collection lookup, `cmd(0).Direction = adParamReturnValue`, causes an implicit **Refresh** to retrieve parameter descriptions automatically, which causes an extra trip to the server. You can avoid this extra trip by creating your own parameter collection with the **CreateParameter** method, as follows:

```
cmd.CommandText = "{ call sp_inoutparam(?,?) }"
cmd.CommandType = adCmdText
' Specify parameter info
p.Append cmd.CreateParameter("in", adChar, adParamInput, 200, "foo")
p.Append cmd.CreateParameter("out", adChar, adParamOutput, 200)
cmd.Execute
Response.Write cmd(1)
```

Prepared Queries

If a SQL statement will be used multiple times, you can potentially improve the performance of your application with prepared queries. When a SQL statement is prepared, a temporary stored procedure is created and compiled. The temporary stored procedure is executed when the prepared statement is called, which saves the overhead of parsing the command each time it is used.

The following example demonstrates the use of a prepared query:

```
<%
    Set cmd = Server.CreateObject("ADODB.Command")
    cmd.ActiveConnection = Application("ConnectionString")
    cmd.Prepared = True

    cmd.CommandText = "Select * From Catalogue Where Id=?"

    Set p = cmd.Parameters
    p.Append cmd.CreateParameter("prodId",adInteger,adParamInput)

    cmd("prodId") = Request("Id1")
    Set rs = cmd.Execute

    cmd("prodId") = Request("Id2")
    Set rs = cmd.Execute
%>
```

Usually, prepared queries are dropped when the connection is released. When connection pooling is enabled, however, you risk running out of space in your temporary database if your connections are recycled often enough. If you use prepared queries, you can configure the SQL Server driver to drop queries "as appropriate" when connection pooling is enabled. You can select this option in the ODBC Administrator application of Control Panel. (See the "Data Source Names" section earlier in the chapter.)

Tips to Optimize Query Performance

Here are some more pointers to help speed up the processing of **Recordset** queries.

- Avoid SELECT * FROM Table. Request only the fields that your application will use. You waste time and resources if you request more fields than the application needs.

- Use SQL Server or another relational database, rather than Microsoft Access. Access is a desktop-oriented application, and does not handle threading and multi-user reentrancy as effectively as SQL Server, which is a highly optimized, business-oriented DBMS.

- If the SQL Server system has sufficient memory available, you can improve query performance by increasing the SQL Server default memory allocation. In the Microsoft SQL Enterprise Manager, select the server you want to configure and click **Configure SQL Server**. Select the **Configuration** tab and double or quadruple the value of the "memory" parameter. Click **OK** to save your changes, and restart SQL Server.

- Optimize your queries to use indexed fields. Design your database layout around the types of queries you perform against the data.

- Turn on the Microsoft SQL Server Show Query Plan query option (SET SHOWPLAN ON) and learn how to interpret its output. You can use this flag to better understand how SQL Server optimizes its queries and determine if the optimizer is actually considering table indexes when performing queries.

- Let SQL Server perform table joins, grouping, and sorting for you. There's no reason to burden your own components with complex table logic; SQL Server can manage records much more efficiently.

- Use the objects, methods, and parameters of ADO wherever possible. If you can, avoid writing queries as text-based SQL commands.

Transaction Processing on the Web

People have been talking about client/server applications and middleware for years. But the truth is that, even with supposedly simple facilities like RPC and named pipes, writing server-based applications that readily and efficiently interact with desktop-based applications has remained just out of reach for most developers. Part of the reason for the huge success of Transact-SQL triggers, despite its limitations, is that it makes writing server-based code relatively easy. Now, for the first time, Microsoft Transaction Server (MTS) makes it possible to easily write true *n*-tier applications.

MTS extends the functionality of applications running on Windows NT Server and Internet Information Server 4.0. The integration of IIS and MTS makes it easy to manage transactions, even transactions that that would otherwise require specialized software to manage. Yet, important as transactions are, Microsoft Transaction Server provides other benefits that are perhaps even more important:

- **Simplified programming**   Component programming in the MTS environment is as non-invasive as possible. In most cases, fewer than five lines of code are required to make an object transaction-aware. In fact, most COM objects can participate in MTS transactions without modification.

- **Distributed applications framework**   In the MTS run-time environment, distributed applications are the norm, not the exception. MTS seamlessly integrates the MTS Executive, server processes, resource managers, and resource dispensers with the Microsoft Distributed Transaction Coordinator (DTC) to create an environment that can run on the same system or be scattered across multiple systems.

- **Components**   Application components can be built in any language that supports the creation of Component Object Model (COM) objects.

- **Security** MTS automatically enforces user roles and Windows NT security for you.

- **Recovery and Restart** When failures occur, MTS applications are automatically restarted, and data consistency is maintained.

- **Scalability** Context and thread management, automatic resource recycling, and Just-In-Time activation help MTS applications perform extremely well in high-usage scenarios.

- **Transactions** MTS applications inherit the power and reliability of automatic distributed transactions. Not only MTS applications, but any DTC-compliant OLE DB or ODBC data source, such the Microsoft Message Queue Server (MSMQ), can participate in those transactions.

Transactions Defined

A transaction, simply put, is an "all or nothing" sequence of database transformations. No modifications are committed to the database until all steps of the transaction have completed successfully. If any of the actions cannot be completed, the entire transaction is automatically "rolled back," or undone. Transactions are a technique applied to guarantee the "correctness" of database operations.

The properties of transactions are collectively known by the acronym *ACID:*

- **Atomicity** Transactions are either committed or rolled back as a whole. Unless all database transformations are successful, none of them will be committed to the database.

- **Consistency** A transaction never leaves the system in a state that cannot be recovered if the transaction fails.

- **Isolation** Until the transaction has completed successfully, its modifications are not visible to other users.

- **Durability** Committed transactions persist beyond any subsequent software or hardware failures. Transactions that have not committed are rolled back when the system is restarted.

At the most basic level, transactions ensure that data is protected from accidental modifications that would invalidate it. If an event occurs that upsets the intended sequence of changes, all the previous changes can be undone to restore the database to its original form. What happens if the second (or third) update fails? What if the application making changes crashes? What if the computer is accidentally turned off? Transactions that are stopped short are guaranteed to have no lasting effect on your data.

A transaction defines a boundary that encapsulates several database interactions and makes them appear as a single atomic interaction. Once a transaction has begun, an application can make changes to multiple records, and the effect of these changes is isolated from the rest of the database and from other users. When the transaction is committed, all the changes appear to happen simultaneously, in such a way as to guarantee that no data is lost or compromised.

Although transactions are important in commerce, transactions aren't just about money. They arbitrate the contention that occurs with demand for any "hard" resource that cannot be created or destroyed.

Extending the Limits of Transactions

Although you can perform transactions using the ADO **Connection** object, the transaction is limited to a single server. In fact, most transaction processing systems allow only one server to participate in a transaction at a time.

But what if, for example, you are transferring money from checking accounts on two separate systems, and the systems use different database management systems? In this case, transaction protection limited to a single connection isn't enough. To manage both database operations as a single transaction, you need a distributed transaction coordinator like MTS.

With MTS, applications can easily use transactions that access multiple databases with true two-phase commit. The two-phase commit protocol ensures that transactions that apply to more than one server are completed on all servers or none at all. Two-phase commit is coordinated by the transaction manager and supported by resource managers.

MTS supports a component-based programming model and run-time environment for developing and deploying enterprise Web server applications. You can configure components to run in the MTS environment by adding them to an MTS package. The packaged components run together in the same server process. Packages also define declarative security constructs that define how access to components is controlled at run time. With packages, developers and administrators can configure applications at deployment time to match the topology and security requirements of their target environment.

Transactional ASP

IIS 4.0 makes it possible for the first time to easily write scalable, reliable, and transactional Web applications. The features of MTS are available to all ASP and ISAPI applications. IIS frees developers to focus on what is really important in an application—the business logic.

For all ASP transactions, the "unit of work" is the ASP page. Transactions are limited to a single page; they cannot span multiple pages.

To perform a transaction, the ASP file containing the application script simply needs to include a command at the beginning of the script to declare that a transaction is needed: `<%@ transaction=required %>`. For these pages, a new ASP built-in object, **ObjectContext**, is defined which is used to commit or abort the transaction.

You indicate when the transaction is over by using the **ObjectContext** object. If all is well, you commit the transaction using the **SetComplete** method. If the operation has failed, use **SetAbort**. Unless one of these methods is called explicitly, the transaction will commit automatically when the page has completed processing. Two event-handlers are available on transactional pages, **OnTransactionCommit** and **OnTransactionAbort**.

The following example demonstrates each of these transaction elements by randomly aborting a transaction. Although it doesn't do any real database processing, it illustrates how easy it is to add the power of transactions to Web-based applications. Click the browser's Refresh button repeatedly to see the event-handlers at work.

```
<%@ Language=VBScript Transaction=Required EnableSessionState=False %>
<HTML>
<HEAD>
<TITLE>Transactional ASP</TITLE>

<SCRIPT Language=VBScript Runat=Server>
Sub OnTransactionCommit()
    '--- Code used when transaction succeeds
    Response.Write "<FONT color=green>committed</FONT>"
End Sub

Sub OnTransactionAbort()
    '--- Code used when transaction fails
    Response.Write "<FONT color=red>aborted</FONT>"
End Sub
</SCRIPT>
</HEAD>

<BODY BGCOLOR=#FFFFFF>
The transaction was:
<% '--- Randomly abort the transaction
    Randomize
    If Rnd > 0.5 Then
        ObjectContext.SetAbort
    End If
%>
</BODY>
</HTML>
```

Because the transactional event-handlers aren't called until the page has completely finished processing, the final messages in the example appear after the closing HTML tag. A better implementation would consist of pure ASP script, whose event-handlers redirect to a separate page containing the appropriate HTML response. For a discussion of redirection, see "Redirection" in Chapter 5, "Developing Web Applications."

Any components used on the transactional ASP page indirectly affect the outcome of the transaction, even if they themselves are not transactional.

Business Objects versus ASP Script

It is a common mistake to code business logic using ASP script alone. ASP is interpreted at run time, so pure script implementations are much slower than those that use precompiled objects. Also, because the business logic is exposed as script, it can be viewed by anyone with access to the server, and is vulnerable to tampering. Lastly, scripted business logic is not easily and cleanly reusable. As the application grows, so does its complexity. Objects become enmeshed with other objects, the system becomes hard to manage, and the bugs multiply.

For all these reasons, ASP should only be used as the "glue" that holds components together. If you're serious about scalability, you must implement your business logic as components.

Transactional Components

Applications that access databases can be built two ways: Business logic can reside in a particular database, or it can be packaged into components. The advantage of using components is that business rules can be generalized to work with any database, and can be reused in multiple applications.

When business logic is segregated into components that work in multiple scenarios, the components become building blocks for applications. The same components can be used for both network and Web-based applications. Reusing components speeds development time and lowers costs.

Business Logic in Components

A component doesn't have to access a database to be considered a business object. In fact, some business objects simply perform complex calculations and automate common business tasks. This section presents some guidelines for designing effective MTS components.

Component Granularity

The number of tasks a component performs determines its granularity.

A *fine-grained* component consumes and releases resources quickly after completing a task. Components such as these isolate individual tasks in well-defined modules, which are easily reused in other packages. For example, you might design a component to facilitate adding and removing customer records in a database. Because its task is simple, it can be written efficiently and is easy to debug and maintain. It is also more likely to be reused in other applications that maintain customer data.

A *coarse-grained* component performs multiple tasks that are often unrelated to each other. For example, a component called PlaceOrder might not only create a new order, but modify inventory and update customer data too. Coarse-grained components are somewhat harder to debug, and are less likely to be reused.

Component State

Objects that discard information between uses are considered *stateless*. Business objects usually don't need to maintain state to correctly process new requests; nor do they need to maintain database connections between calls. Stateless objects use fewer system resources, so they can scale better and perform more quickly.

Stateful objects, on the other hand, accumulate information over several method calls. Because MTS cannot commit transactions until **SetComplete** is called, stateful objects effectively prevent MTS from completing its work. Frequent network roundtrips and slower connections extend the lifetime of the object. The extra delay may cause server resources, such as database connections, to be held longer, and decrease the system resources available for other clients. A decision to hold state information in an object should be considered carefully.

As the number of concurrent transactions increases, stateless objects begin to outperform stateful ones significantly. In other words, stateless components scale better. Despite the limitations of stateful objects, it sometimes makes sense to maintain some state information, especially if it is the result of a complex or time-consuming query. Stateful objects might be used when reconstructing the object state is potentially more costly than the resources held open while it remains active.

Note Objects that need to retain state across multiple calls from a client can protect themselves from having their work committed prematurely by the client. By calling the **DisableCommit** method of the **ObjectContext** object before returning control to the client, the object can guarantee that its transaction cannot be committed until the object has called **EnableCommit**.

Participating in Transactions

You can create a transactional component that takes advantage of the benefits of MTS with only a few extra lines of code.

1. Call **GetObjectContext** to get a reference to the **ObjectContext** object, which enables your component to "vote" on the success or failure of the transaction in progress.

2. Create other components by using the **ObjectContext** object's **CreateInstance** method. When a base client instantiates an object by using the **CreateInstance** method, the new object and its descendants will participate in the transaction unless the new object's transaction attribute is set to **Requires a new transaction** or **Does not support transactions**.

Just-In-Time Activation

All this talk about component state really only makes sense within the scope of a transaction. So what happens to the object once the transaction has been completed?

The answer: MTS deactivates it.

Whenever an application calls **SetComplete**, whether from ASP or from within an MTS component, all the objects involved in the transaction—even stateful ones—are recycled by the system. In the process of deactivation, the object's member variables are reinitialized to their initial values.

This process is part of *Just-In-Time activation*, which allows the MTS run-time environment to free up object resources, including any database connections it holds, without requiring the application to release its references to component objects. Components are activated only as needed for executing requests from clients, allowing otherwise idle server resources to be used more productively. Just-In-Time activation allows your application to conserve system resources as it scales up to multiple users.

This is yet another reason to be careful about maintaining state in objects. Clients of a stateful MTS component object must be aware of how it uses **SetComplete** to ensure that any state the object maintains won't be needed after the object undergoes Just-In-Time activation.

---

3. Call either **SetComplete** when the object has completed successfully, or **SetAbort** to cancel the transaction.

The following Visual Basic code template demonstrates how to incorporate these elements into a component:

```
Sub DoMTSTransaction()
    Dim objCtx As ObjectContext
    Dim objNew As NewObject

    On Error Goto ErrHandler

    Set objCtx = GetObjectContext()
    Set objNew = objCtx.CreateInstance("MyObject.NewObject")


    '-------------------------------
    '--- More component logic here ---
    '-------------------------------

    objCtx.SetComplete
    Exit Sub

ErrHandler:
    objCtx.SetAbort

End Sub
```

Be sure not to use **CreateObject** or **GetObject** when creating objects in an MTS component. MTS role-based security works only if you use **Server.CreateObject** from ASP or **ObjectContext.CreateInstance** from within your MTS component. When you use **CreateObject** or **GetObject**, the component identity is inherited from the application process. Conversely, when you use **Server.CreateObject**, the identity is that of the impersonated user. In order for MTS role-based security to work properly, the correct caller identity must be determined.

For more information on MTS security and roles, see Chapter 8, "Security." For more examples of how to create transactional components, refer to the Exploration Air (ExAir) sample site included with Internet Information Server.

Using Database Access Interfaces with MTS

Because the ODBC Driver Manager is an MTS resource dispenser, data accessed via ODBC is automatically protected by your object's transaction. For object transactions, an ODBC-compliant database must support the following features:

- The database's ODBC driver must be thread-safe. MTS must be able to connect to the database, utilize the connection, and disconnect using different threads. (The Microsoft Access driver cannot participate in MTS transactions, because it is not completely thread-safe.)

- If ODBC is used from within a transactional component, the ODBC driver must also support the ODBC SQL_ATTR_ENLIST_IN_DTC connection attribute. It's through the use of this attribute that the ODBC Driver Manager can allow the ODBC driver to enlist a connection on a transaction. If you are using a database without a resource dispenser that can recognize MTS transactions, contact your database vendor to obtain the required support.

The following table summarizes database requirements for full MTS support.

Table 6.3   ODBC Driver Requirements for MTS-Compliance

Requirements	Description
Support for the OLE transactions specification, or support for XA protocol	Enables direct interaction with the Distributed Transaction Coordinator (DTC). Use the XA Mapper to interact with DTC.
ODBC driver	Platform requirement for MTS server components.
Support for ODBC version 3.0's SQL_ATTR_ENLIST_IN_DTC attribute	MTS uses this call to pass the transaction identifier to the ODBC driver. The ODBC driver then passes the transaction identifier to the database engine.
Fully thread-safe ODBC driver	ODBC driver must be able to handle concurrent calls from any thread at any time.

Because ADO is an indirect consumer of ODBC data sources, it makes a good candidate for data access from MTS components. In fact, there is very little semantic difference between using ADO inside an MTS component, and using it from a Web page.

Distribution and Scaling Issues

Hosting a large volume of business transactions from clients around the world introduces a demanding set of programming and administrative requirements. Distributed applications very often rely on diverse resources beyond the application's scope of control. Web applications must be prepared to host a large volume of connections without suffering a significant loss in performance.

The key factors that influence a component's ability to service a large volume of users are:

- Resources allocated per user (memory, data connections)
- Amount of information retrieved from and sent to the browser

- Location of processing (client, server, or both)
- Impact of component distribution topology on response time
- Time to process common requests

Components should be located as close as possible to the data source. If you are building a distributed application with a number of MTS component packages running on local and remote servers, try to group your components according to the location of your data. For example, the Accounting server should host both the Accounting MTS package and the Accounting database.

Pool your resources by server process. Note that MTS runs each hosted package in a separate server process. The fewer pools are running on a server, the more efficiently resources are pooled. Try to group components so that they share "expensive" resources, such as connections to a specific database. If you reuse these resources within your package, you will improve the performance and scaling of your application. For example, if a database lookup and a database update component are running in a customer maintenance application, package those components together so that they can share database connections.

Introducing Microsoft Message Queue

For components that are not directly connected, diminished network throughput can be a severe impairment to the scalability of an application. This section discusses the use of Microsoft Message Queue Server (MSMQ) to increase the reliability of transactions that use disconnected components.

MSMQ is a fast store-and-forward service that enables applications to communicate across heterogeneous networks and systems. Applications send messages to MSMQ, and MSMQ ensures that the messages eventually reach their destination. MSMQ provides guaranteed message delivery, efficient routing, security, and priority-based messaging.

Most importantly, MSMQ also supports MTS transactions. Because MSMQ is a resource manager under the control of the Microsoft Distributed Transaction Coordinator (DTC), you can use MSMQ to safely implement transaction-compliant applications that ensure that message operations either succeed or fail in conjunction with other transactions. A transactional application can send an MSMQ message and update a database as part of the same transaction. The transaction coordinator ensures that both actions succeed or fail together.

For instance, a single online purchase might consist of a credit card validation, an adjustment to inventory on hand, and a notification to an external supplier. Of course, the external supplier's system may be temporarily offline, which prevents the system from notifying the external supplier. In the context of a transaction, failures such as this dictate that the entire process be aborted, whether or not the inventory was available and in spite of a successful credit card debit.

A better solution is to use MSMQ. MSMQ guarantees that the vendor will be notified eventually. In this way, MSMQ enables systems to respond more flexibly to factors that can cause transaction failures, effectively eliminating errors caused by server outages and long pauses caused by network latency. This makes MSMQ ideal for "time independent" transactions.

Time Independent Transaction Processing with MSMQ

Complex transactions may have several smaller sub-transactions, each with differing levels of importance. Determining which operations are required to complete the transaction, and which may be eligible for deferral, is a crucial first step in designing a robust system with MSMQ. You should only consider using messages for operations that are not essential to the overall stability of the system.

MSMQ operations always commit, and return control to your application quickly. When you use MSMQ to process part of your transaction, MSMQ saves a "message" to an on-disk queue, instead of performing a database operation. The message should contain enough information to describe the operation that would have been performed on the remote system, had it been connected.

Some time later (or, at a time you choose) MSMQ establishes a connection with MSMQ running on the remote system and transmits the message. As soon as the remote system has successfully received it, the message is dequeued and processed as part of a new database transaction. If all goes well, a confirmation message is sent back to the MSMQ system that initiated the transaction. This message path is shown in the following diagram:

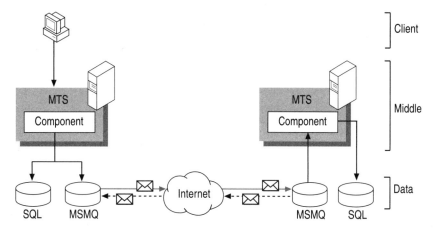

Figure 6.5   Diagram of an MSMQ transaction

MSMQ messages are system specific. You are responsible for collecting the information your system will need to complete the transaction. MSMQ merely guarantees that your message will be delivered to the appropriate queue on the remote system. The following example demonstrates how you might add support for MSMQ to an MTS component within a system that processes orders for a vendor's products:

```
Sub OrderProduct(
    OrderID As Int,
    ProductID As Int,
    Quantity As Int)
Dim objCtx   As ObjectContext
Dim query    As New MSMQQuery
Dim msg      As New MSMQMessage
Dim infoSend As New MSMQQueueInfo
Dim infoResp As MSMQQueueInfo
Dim queue    As MSMQQueue

    On Error Goto ErrHandler
    Set objCtx = GetObjectContext()

    '--- Open destination queue
    infoSend.PathName = "Contractor\ProductOrderQueue"
    Set queue = infoSend.Open(MQ_SEND_ACCESS,MQ_DENY_NONE)

    '--- Construct application specific message
    msg.Label = "Product Order"
    msg.Body  = Str(OrderID) & ";" & Str(ProductID) & ";" & Str(Quantity)
    msg.PrivLevel = MQMSG_PRIV_LEVEL_BODY

    '--- Lookup response queue
    Set infoResp = query.LookupQueue(Label:="ContractorResponse")
    infoResp.Reset

    '--- Set application specific response queue
    Set msg.ResponseQueueInfo = infoResp.Next

    '--- Send message to remote queue
    msg.Send queue, MQ_MTS_TRANSACTION

    queue.Close
    objCtx.SetComplete
    Exit Sub

ErrHandler:
    objCtx.SetAbort

End Sub
```

An MSMQ transaction merely sends a message, so the application must assume that the work can be performed. In this case, no effort has been made to determine if the contractor can supply the requested number of products. This inability to determine in advance if the transaction will be honored is a problem known as "deferred integrity."

Once the decision has been made to allow portions of a transaction to take place asynchronously, a business policy needs to be implemented to determine what happens if the transaction cannot be satisfied. In certain cases, transaction failures may require an application-level rollback of prior committed transactions. Or, it may require special treatment in the form of correspondence with the customer to decide the best course of action. A good example of deferred integrity in the real world might be that of a bank handling the case of insufficient funds for a check that has already been cashed.

Process Isolation and Crash Recovery

Besides adding the power of transactions to ordinary Web pages, the marriage of IIS and MTS produced another powerful result: *process isolation.*

Applications and Processes

Extending a Web server has always involved trade-offs between performance and safety. In earlier versions of IIS, all ISAPI applications (including ASP) shared the resources and memory of the server process. Although this design increased performance, unstable components could cause the server to crash—not an acceptable behavior for mission-critical applications like IIS. To make matters worse, in-process components couldn't be unloaded unless the server was restarted—which meant that reloading existing components required all sites that shared the same server to restart, whether they were directly affected by the upgrade or not.

IIS 4.0 introduces a new paradigm for hosting Web application processes. By creating an isolated process, IIS maintains the performance of the ISAPI/ASP model, while providing the safety of CGI. Segregating applications into their own process space protects the entire Web server from unexpected application failures. This is the main idea behind process isolation.

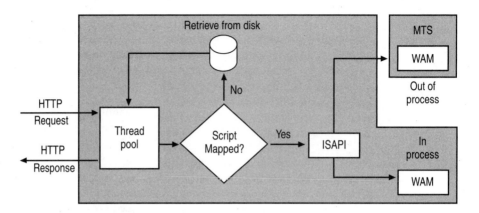

Figure 6.6   Process flow for IIS applications running in and out of process

Out-of-process applications run within their own processes, separate from the rest of IIS. When a ASP file is requested by the browser, the Web server first assigns a thread from the pool to handle the request. Then, IIS determines how to handle the requested file according to its internal MIME and script mappings. For an ASP file, the ISAPI filter for ASP is invoked.

Next, the Web Application Manager (WAM) determines whether the file is part of an application marked to run in a separate memory space. If so, the request will be handled by an external MTS process. Otherwise, the request is completed in-process with IIS. WAM hosts all Web applications, whether they're in-process or not, and controls loading and interfacing with ISAPI DLLs. WAM itself is a COM component, and can be run in the IIS process or isolated in a separate process. MTS, which is a run-time environment for COM components, hosts a WAM proxy object for each isolated process.

There are three main reasons for running an application as an isolated process: component development, fault isolation, and Web site safety.

Component Development   Rather than taking down the entire server to update a single component, process isolation makes it possible to stop and restart just a single application. You can use Internet Service Manager to add an updated component to an application. Right-click the application root directory, click **Properties**, and select the **Virtual Directory** tab; click **Unload**. Once the old component has been replaced, IIS will restart the application when it receives the first request.

Fault Isolation   Process isolation limits the effects of a crash to the single application that caused it. In addition to protecting your server from the crash, the application can be configured to restart automatically. In the case of a fatal error, the application's process is automatically terminated. Because the application is running in the MTS system process, all transactions in progress are aborted. The system event log stores a record of the event, and MTS restarts the application.

The only ones affected by the failure are clients with outstanding requests to that specific application.

Safer Web Sites   The process isolation provided by MTS makes it possible to host untested or unstable applications without risking the stability of the entire server. Now the Web server can gracefully tolerate failures with minimal disruption to clients of other applications. By separating unstable applications into their own memory space, you prevent a single application error from bringing down the rest of your site.

Configuring an Isolated Process

By default, an IIS application runs in the IIS process. If you decide to run your application as a separate process, you can use Internet Service Manager to make the setting. Right-click the application root directory, click **Properties**, and select the **Virtual Directory** tab; select the **Run in separate memory space** check box. (You must first create an application for your virtual root, if you haven't already done so. See "Building ASP Applications," in Chapter 5, "Developing Web Applications.")

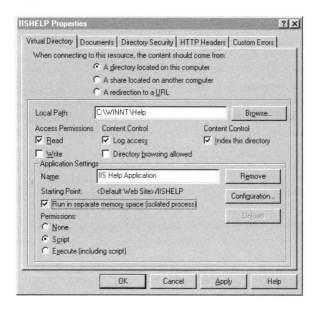

Figure 6.7   Virtual directory property configuration in Internet Server Manager

Internet Service Manager automatically creates an MTS package for your application. For example, if you were to configure the IISHelp application to run in an isolated process, a new MTS package would be created, named IIS-{Default Web Site//Root/IISHELP/}. Transactional components to be run within the context of this new process can be installed into this MTS package by using Internet Service Manager.

Security Considerations

Out-of-process applications and components, including ISAPI extensions, are not able to access IIS metabase properties using the built-in administration objects of IIS. This restriction is designed to prevent changes to the metabase from unauthorized sources. If you want to allow out-of-process applications to access the metabase, you must do one of the following:

- Give the IWAM_*computername* account access to the metabase (this is probably a bad idea from a system security standpoint, since all out-of-process applications run in this user context.)

- Change the identity of the out-of-process MTS package from the interactive user to a specific user account, and give that account access to the metabase (this is also somewhat risky, but the risk is limited to a single application package).

References

The following books and Web sites provide additional information relevant to Web server data access and transactions.

Web Links

http://www.apexsc.com/

The definitive source for information on a variety of data-bound grid controls. As a service to DBGrid users everywhere, Apex Software Corporation provides free online help, samples, and downloads.

http://www.microsoft.com/data/

Provides a central location for information on Universal Data Access and the technologies that make it possible. Here you will find information and the latest news on ADO, OLE DB, ODBC, and much more.

http://www.microsoft.com/transaction/

The latest Microsoft Transaction Server news, white papers, and development guides. Find out about the latest news, trends, events, and product information.

Books

Fleet, Warren, Chen, and Stojanovic. *Teach Yourself Active Web Database Programming in 21 Days* (Sams.net Publishing, 1997). A step-by-step tutorial of ADO, and data-centric business object development fundamentals.

C H A P T E R   7

ISP Administration

7

Microsoft Internet Information Server 4.0 (IIS), along with the other products in the Windows NT 4.0 Option Pack, provide a powerful and versatile platform for Internet service providers (ISPs). IIS provides a comprehensive environment complete with tools for automation, customization, and administration.

In this chapter:

- Robustness Features
- Site Management
- Customization
- Resources on the IIS Resource Kit CD
- Applying Other Microsoft Technologies Within an ISP
- Resources

Robustness Features

This section discusses process isolation and crash recovery. These features help ensure the robustness of Web sites and Web applications.

Process Isolation

Process isolation allows multiple Web applications to run on one server with a high level of reliability. Each application on the Web server can be run in a separate memory space (out-of-process). This means that the failure of one application will not affect others running on the server. Common Gateway Interface (CGI) applications are run out-of-process, but they offer poor scalability. Every instance of a CGI application requires the creation of a new process with its associated overhead, and application parameters are passed through environment variables.

Internet Server Application Programming Interface (ISAPI) applications can also be run out-of-process. This provides the same level of application integrity as CGI, but with faster performance. Performance can be further improved by running ISAPI applications in the same process as the server (in-process). However, in-process applications don't provide as much application integrity as those run out-of-process.

Each individual server can host a mix of in-process (isolated) and out-of-process applications. This means that you can run well-tested applications in-process for performance reasons, and run others out-of-process during development or beta stages for "fail-safety" reasons.

Only dynamic content is generated in a separate process. Static content (such as JPEG and HTML) is generated by the IIS Web service.

Both ISAPI and ASP process isolation in IIS relies on Microsoft Transaction Server (MTS) architecture. However, process isolation in IIS is managed in the IIS MMC.

Some ISAPI DLLs can't be isolated. For example, those that rely on locking resources—open files, shared memory, and so on—can't run in a separate memory space. In such cases, it is better to rewrite the application to remove the dependencies.

Hosting Applications

ISPs often establish pre-production sites to test customer applications before they are hosted on the production site. During this test phase, you can save resources by using one server to host multiple customer test sites.

ISPs hosting Web-based applications should consider the following recommendations:

- Discourage the writing of applications that can be run *only* as in-process. Those that can be run as isolated processes are safer.
- Establish guidelines for your customers to use when writing Web-based applications.

Crash Recovery

When the MTS environment hosts applications, it is possible to automatically recover from application crashes. In the case of a fatal application error, the process is terminated automatically. If a transactional application crashes, all transactions in progress are aborted and any changes to the data are rolled back. The system event log stores a record of the error that occurred and the run-time MTS environment automatically restarts the application process.

Site Management

This section discusses ways that you can manage and administer multiple Web sites using IIS, Windows NT Server, and the Internet Service Manager administration tool.

Bandwidth Throttling

With IIS you can control the bandwidth of each Web site on a server, and ensure that it is fairly distributed. By using bandwidth throttling, an ISP can also offer Web hosting solutions that are tailored to the bandwidth needs of individual customers.

You can manipulate the threshold values, and enable or disable bandwidth throttling, without stopping and restarting the service. The metabase is used to store the configuration options for the bandwidth throttler, and IIS is notified as changes are made.

In the current version of IIS, you can throttle bandwidth for static content, including HTML, JPEG, and GIF. Because the average Web site consists of 70 percent static content and only 30 percent dynamic content, throttling static HTML controls the bandwidth distribution on your server effectively.

As the bandwidth utilization approaches the limit that has been set by the administrator, the Web site will begin to exhibit slower response times. If requests are received faster than the site can respond (meaning that the queue is full), the server will return an error message (500: Server Busy) to the client.

Multihosting Using a Single IP Address

Previous versions of IIS provided multihosting with multiple IP addresses. IIS 4.0 not only provides support for hosting multiple Web sites on a single computer running Windows NT Server, but also for hosting them on a single IP address. IIS provides this capability through the use of a host header that most new browsers (Internet Explorer 4.0 and Netscape 4.0, for example), and some older ones, support. Host headers are part of HTTP 1.1. For more information about HTTP 1.1, see Chapter 1, "Overview."

The following examples illustrate how host headers are used.

In the first example, two Web sites, www.example1.com and www.example2.com, are hosted on a single computer with two different IP addresses (www.example1.com = 172.21.13.45 and www.example2.com = 192.168.114.201). The host header field is visible in the HTTP log, but note that the distinction between the Web sites is made using the network IP address, not the Host Header field.

```
CLIENT REQUEST FOR www.example1.com
IP: Destination Address = 172.21.13.45
HTTP: Request Method = GET
HTTP: Uniform Resource Identifier = /
HTTP: Protocol Version = HTTP/1.1
HTTP: Accept = image/gif, image/x-xbitmap, image/jpeg, image/pjpeg,
application/vnd.
HTTP: Accept-Language = en-us
HTTP: Accept-Encoding = gzip, deflate
HTTP: User-Agent = Mozilla/4.0 (compatible; MSIE 4.0; Windows NT)
HTTP: Host = www.example1.com
HTTP: Connection = Keep-Alive
```

```
CLIENT REQUEST FOR www.example2.com
IP: Destination Address = 192.168.114.201
HTTP: Request Method = GET
HTTP: Uniform Resource Identifier = /
HTTP: Protocol Version = HTTP/1.1
HTTP: Accept = image/gif, image/x-xbitmap, image/jpeg, image/pjpeg,
application/vnd.
HTTP: Accept-Language = en-us
HTTP: Accept-Encoding = gzip, deflate
HTTP: User-Agent = Mozilla/4.0 (compatible; MSIE 4.0; Windows NT)
HTTP: Host = www.example2.com
HTTP: Connection = Keep-Alive
```

In the second example, two Web sites (www.example1.com and www.example2.com) are hosted on one computer with the same IP address (172.21.13.45). In this case, the sites are distinguished by the host header names.

```
CLIENT REQUEST FOR www.example1.com
IP: Destination Address = 172.21.13.45
HTTP: Request Method = GET
HTTP: Uniform Resource Identifier = /
HTTP: Protocol Version = HTTP/1.1
HTTP: Accept = image/gif, image/x-xbitmap, image/jpeg, image/pjpeg,
application/vnd.
HTTP: Accept-Language = en-us
HTTP: Accept-Encoding = gzip, deflate
HTTP: User-Agent = Mozilla/4.0 (compatible; MSIE 4.0; Windows NT)
HTTP: Host = www.example1.com
HTTP: Connection = Keep-Alive

CLIENT REQUEST FOR www.example2.com
IP: Destination Address = 172.21.13.45
HTTP: Request Method = GET
HTTP: Uniform Resource Identifier = /
HTTP: Protocol Version = HTTP/1.1
HTTP: Accept = image/gif, image/x-xbitmap, image/jpeg, image/pjpeg,
application/vnd.
HTTP: Accept-Language = en-us
HTTP: Accept-Encoding = gzip, deflate
HTTP: User-Agent = Mozilla/4.0 (compatible; MSIE 4.0; Windows NT)
HTTP: Host = www.example2.com
HTTP: Connection = Keep-Alive
```

For more information about how to set up host header names, see the Windows NT 4.0 Option Pack online documentation.

Support for Non–HTTP 1.1 Compliant Browsers

Many non-HTTP 1.1 compliant browsers support host headers. To make your site available to those that don't, you can use cookies or URL-munging.

Cookie Mechanism for Downlevel Browser Support

This method requires a browser that can accept cookies. Cookies are objects that are sent to a Web server along with client requests. They can be "attached" to hosts on the client side, and will be sent with a request whenever a client accesses the Web site in question. A downlevel browser that supports cookies can use a cookie as a pseudo host header. In order to do this, the administrator must set up several components, including registry settings, and add .asp files to the Scripts directory of the instance.

When a downlevel client first accesses a multihosted site, there is no way for the server to detect which site the user wants to visit. With IIS, you can deliver a custom menu to these users, listing the Web sites available. This menu can be any document—an .html file or an .asp file. There are two possible host menu documents that can be set by the administrator. One is directed toward clients that support HTTP cookies; the other is sent to clients that do not. The menu documents must exist in the virtual space of one of the instances on the Web server. The administrator must specify the document names, and also the host name, of the instance where these documents can be found. For example, if a downlevel client attempts to access http://www.example1.com, the following will be observed on the client side:

- Client accesses http://www.example1.com.
- Since there is no host header with the request, the server does not know which instance is desired.
- IIS presents the client with an HTML menu prepared by the administrator that lists the available instances on this IP address.
- The client selects the desired site, and is redirected to that server instance. All subsequent requests for http://www.example1.com will directly access the appropriate documents without being presented a menu again.

In the following example, a request was made for the www.example1.com and www.example2.com sites. Notice the HTTP 1.0 GET requests and the host lines below. While initiating an HTTP 1.0 request, Internet Explorer 3.02 is able to communicate with IIS 4.0 through a host header.

```
CLIENT REQUEST FOR http://www.example1.com (from an HTTP/1.0 browser)
GET / HTTP/1.0
Accept: application/vnd.ms-excel, application/msword,
application/vnd.ms-powerpoint, image/gif, image/x-xbitmap, image/jpeg,
image/pjpeg, */*
Accept-Language: en
UA-pixels: 800x600
UA-color: color16
UA-OS: Windows NT
UA-CPU: x86
User-Agent: Mozilla/2.0 (compatible; MSIE 3.02; Windows NT)
Host: www.example1.com
Connection: Keep-Alive

CLIENT REQUEST FOR http://www.example2.com (from an HTTP/1.0 browser)
GET / HTTP/1.0
Accept: application/vnd.ms-excel, application/msword,
application/vnd.ms-powerpoint, image/gif, image/x-xbitmap, image/jpeg,
image/pjpeg, */*
Accept-Language: en
UA-pixels: 800x600
UA-color: color16
UA-OS: Windows NT
UA-CPU: x86
User-Agent: Mozilla/2.0 (compatible; MSIE 3.02; Windows NT)
Host: www.example2.com
Connection: Keep-Alive
```

In the example below, notice that the GET request does not have a host header. Clients that do not support host headers, such as Internet Explorer 2.0, will return the error message "404 Object Not Found."

```
CLIENT REQUEST FOR http://www.example1.com (from Internet Explorer 2.0)
GET / HTTP/1.0
Accept: image/gif, image/x-xbitmap, image/jpeg, */*
Accept-Language: en
User-Agent: Mozilla/1.22 (compatible; MSIE 2.0d; Windows NT)
Connection: Keep-Alive

SERVER RESPONSE
HTTP/1.1 404 Object Not Found
Server: Microsoft-IIS/4.0
Date: Wed, 15 Oct 1997 17:05:55 GMT
Content-Type: text/html
Content-Length: 102
```

Components for Administration (Sample Setup)

The following registry configuration is necessary to make this example work. All of the host menu documents have been placed on the http://www.example1.com instance. Registry values have been added to Hkey_Local_Machine/System/CurrentControlSet/Services/W3SVC/Parameters.

Warning

To add or modify a registry value entry, use administrative tools such as Control Panel or System Policy Editor whenever possible. Using a registry editor (Regedit or Regedt32) to change a value can have unforeseen effects, including changes that can prevent you from starting your system.

The registry values include:

DLCMenuString = /HostMenu (Data Type is REG_SZ)
> This parameter specifies the special prefix of URLs that apply to the host menu. The server will check this string on all downlevel client requests (in other words, requests without a real host header) against.

DLCHostNameString = www.example1.com
> This parameter supplies the host name of the instance that contains the menu documents.

DLCMungeMenuDocumentString = /scripts/munge.asp
> This is the name of the host menu document that will be sent to downlevel clients that don't support cookies.

DLCCookieMenuDocumentString = /scripts/cookie.asp
> This is the name of the host menu document that will be sent to downlevel clients that support cookies.

DLCCookieNameString = PseudoHost
> This parameter specifies the name of the special cookie that will be interpreted by the server as representing a pseudo host header. This can be used with clients that support cookies.

DLCSupport = 1 (Data Type is REG_DWORD)
> Set this parameter to ensure that downlevel client support is enabled.

The host menu documents include three files (Munge.asp, Cookie.asp, and Redirect.asp):

Contents of www.example1.com/scripts/munge.asp

Copy this sample code into a text file and name it Munge.asp. Then copy the file into the Scripts directory of the instance you are using. In this example, it is www.example1.com.

```
<html>
<head><title>Server Selection Page</title></head>
<body>

<a href="http://www.example1.com/*www.example1.com/<%=
Request.QueryString() %>">Try this Site www.example1.com</a><br>
<a href="http://www.example1.com/*www.example2.com/<%=
Request.QueryString() %>">Try this Site www.example2.com</a><br>

</body>
</html>
```

Contents of www.example1.com/scripts/cookie.asp

Copy this sample code into a text file and name it Cookie.asp. Then copy the file into the Scripts directory of the instance you are using. In this example, it is www.example1.com.

```
<html>
<head><title>Server Selection Page</title></head>
<body>

<a
href="/HostMenu/Scripts/Redirect.asp?Host=www.example1.com&NewLocation=<
%= Request.QueryString() %>">Try this Site www.example1.com</a><br>
<a
href="/HostMenu/Scripts/Redirect.asp?Host=www.example2.com&NewLocation=<
%= Request.QueryString() %>">Try this Site www.example2.com</a><br>

</body>
</html>
```

Contents of www.example1.com/scripts/redirect.asp

Copy this sample code into a text file and name it Redirect.asp. Then copy the file into the Scripts directory of the instance you are using. In this example, it is www.example1.com.

```
<%

Option Explicit

Dim DLCCookieNameString

DLCCookieNameString = "PseudoHost"

Response.Cookies(DLCCookieNameString) = Request.QueryString("Host")
Response.Cookies(DLCCookieNameString).Domain =
Request.QueryString("Host")
Response.Cookies(DLCCookieNameString).Path = "/"

Response.Redirect "http://" & Request.QueryString("Host") &
Request.QueryString("NewLocation")

%>
```

URL-Munging Approach for Downlevel Browser Support

Another way to support down level browsers involves embedding the host header name in the URLs being sent to the Web server. On the server side, these embedded hosts are recognized and stripped out of the URL and used as a pseudo host header prior to regular URL processing. For URL-munging to work, each request from the browser must have a host header embedded. If it does not (as is the case with an initial request), the downlevel support will send a host menu to the client. For an example of URL-munging, see the Cookie Munger ISAPI filter provided on the IIS Resource Kit CD.

Resource Logging (Per–Web–Site Logging)

With IIS you can generate detailed log files to help you analyze the activity on your server.

Historically, Web servers collected all information about activity on a server and put it into a single file (sometimes several hundred megabytes in size). ISPs were then forced to filter out information about specific Web sites from this file, a time-consuming task.

With IIS 4.0, this task is simplified. Administrators can now set logging at various levels of granularity. Log files can include or exclude information about requests for individual Web sites, individual directories, and individual files.

For example, in the following log file, requests for files in the images directory are included. If this page were to be requested several thousand times, the GET request for the image would be logged several thousand times as well.

```
#Software: Microsoft Internet Information Server 4.0
#Version: 1.0
#Date: 1997-10-16 22:20:57
#Fields: time c-ip cs-method cs-uri-stem sc-status
22:20:57 172.16.1.1 GET /samplecorp/ 404
22:21:03 172.16.1.1 GET /Default.htm 304
22:21:37 172.16.1.1 GET /images/undercon.gif 304
```

The following example shows a log file that doesn't log the images directory. Note that it doesn't include the GET request for /images/undercon.gif.

```
CLIENT REQUEST
#Software: Microsoft Internet Information Server 4.0
#Version: 1.0
#Date: 1997-10-16 22:23:32
#Fields: time c-ip cs-method cs-uri-stem sc-status
22:23:32 172.16.1.1 GET /samplecorp/ 404
22:24:14 172.16.1.1 GET /Default.htm 304
```

To further customize logging, you can create your own custom logging modules with Visual C++ or Visual Basic. To create such a module, consult the documentation in the Microsoft IIS SDK.

The W3C Extended Log Format allows administrators to gather details about important fields. The following extended log options are available:

Field	Appears As	Description
Date	date	The date on which the activity occurred.
Time	time	The time at which the activity occurred.
Client IP Address	c-ip	The IP address of the client that accessed your server.
User Name	c-username	The name of the user who accessed your server.
Service Name	s-sitename	The Internet service that was running on the client computer.

continued

Field	Appears As	Description
Server Name	s-computername	The name of the server on which the log entry was generated.
Server IP	s-ip	The IP address of the server on which the log entry was generated.
Method	cs-method	The action the client was trying to perform. For example, a GET command.
URI Stem	cs-uri-stem	The resource accessed. For example, an HTML page, a CGI program, or a script.
URI Query	cs-uri-query	The query, if any, that the client was trying to perform.
Http Status	sc-status	The status of the action, in HTTP terms.
Win32 Status	sc-win32-status	The status of the action, in terms used by Windows NT.
Bytes Sent	cs-bytes	The number of bytes sent by the server.
Bytes Received	sc-bytes	The number of bytes received by the server.
Server Port	s-port	The port number the client is connected to.
Time Taken	time-taken	The length of time the action took.
Protocol Version	cs-protocol	The protocol (HTTP, FTP) version used by the client. For HTTP this will be either HTTP 1.0 or HTTP 1.1.
User Agent	cs(User-Agent)	The browser used on the client.
Cookie	cs(Cookie)	The content of the cookie sent or received, if any.
Referrer	cs(Referrer)	The site the user came from.

Access Privileges

IIS provides several new access levels. You can set the type of access allowed to specific directories to the following values:

Read

Enables Web clients to read or download files stored in a home directory or a virtual directory. If a client sends a request for a file that is in a directory without read permission, the Web server will return an error.

Write

Enables Web clients to upload files to the enabled directory on your server, or to change content in a write-enabled file.

Script

Enables trusted applications to run in this directory without having execute permissions set. Use the script permission for ASP scripts, Internet Database Connector (IDC) scripts, and others. Script permission is safer than execute permission because you can limit the applications that can be run in the directory.

Execute

Enables Web clients to run programs and scripts stored in a home directory or a virtual directory. If a client sends a request to run a program or a script in a directory that does not have execute permission, the Web server returns an error message.

Log Access

Enables the recording of visits to a site to system's log file. You must enable logging for the Web site to establish a log file.

Directory Browsing Allowed

Enable a hypertext listing of the files and subdirectories in this virtual directory. A hypertext directory listing is generated automatically and sent to the user when a browser request does not include a specific HTML file name and when no default document is provided for in the specified directory.

If the directory is on a Windows NT File System (NTFS) drive, the NTFS access settings for the directory must match the settings on IIS. If this is not the case, the most restrictive settings take effect. For security purposes, do not give a directory both read and execute permissions, as this can allow a user to read your script or program files. Also, do not give a directory both write and execute permissions, as this can allow a user to load and run destructive programs on your server.

Remote Administration

You can administer your Web site over an intranet or the Internet with the HTML version of Internet Service Manager. For example, you can change access privileges, create Web sites, read log files, check or change properties, and start, stop, or pause servers from any computer on the network that is running Internet Explorer 4.0. Figure 7.1 shows the browser-based version of Internet Service Manager.

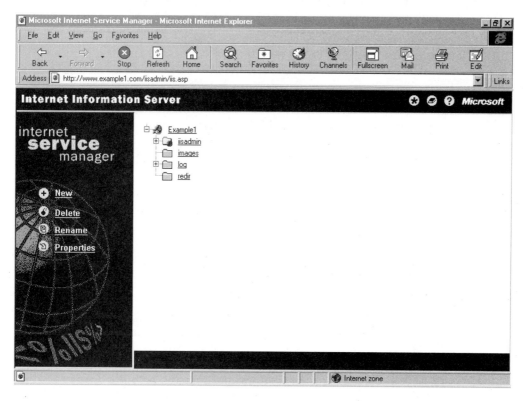

Figure 7.1   The Web browser version of Internet Service Manager

Web Site Operators

Delegating administrative rights to customers of ISPs is challenging in light of security considerations. An administrator needs to ensure that each customer can only administer his or her own site. The Web site Operators feature of IIS gives ISPs who are hosting multiple sites on a single server the ability to provide the individual site administrators with complete control over the properties, applications, and security of their site—without jeopardizing the security or configuration of other sites running on the same server. A Web site Operator is not permitted to change bindings or port numbers, configure the anonymous user name and passwords, change the identification of the Web site, throttle bandwidth, change accounts on the server, add virtual directories, configure process isolation or ISAPI filters, or stop, pause, or restart a site.

Remote Administration of Previous Versions of IIS-Based Web Servers by Using the MMC

Downlevel Web Server Support

With Microsoft Management Console (MMC) you can also administer previous versions of IIS. For example, if you have 5 Web servers running IIS 3.0 and you initially upgrade 1 of them to IIS 4.0, you can administer all of them from MMC.

To do this, perform the following steps:

1. Create a temporary folder.
2. From the Windows NT 4.0 CD, copy Fscfg.dll, W3scfg.dll, and Gscfg.dll from the \I386\inetsrv\ directory and Fscfg.hlp, W3scfg.hlp, and Gscfg.hlp from the \I386\inetsrv\help\ directory into the temporary folder you have created.
3. Rename the files in the temporary folder. For example:

Old Name	New Name
Fscfg.dll	Fscfg3.dll
W3scfg.dll	W3scfg3.dll
Gscfg.dll	Gscfg3.dll
Fscfg.hlp	Fscfg3.hlp
W3scfg.hlp	W3scfg3.hlp
Gscfg.hlp	Gscfg3.hlp

The Gopher dll (gscfg.dll) does not have to be renamed, but this has been done for consistency.

5. Copy the renamed files into your C:\WINNT\system32\inetsrv directory.

6. You need to indicate that the current files have been superseded. To do this, append "::SUPCFG:<newer dll>" to the existing DLL file name.

7. Add the following registry values (with data type REG_SZ) to (HKEY_LOCAL_MACHINE\SOFTWARE\Microsoft\InetMgr\Parameters\AddOnServices):

WWW3 = C:\WINNT\System32\inetsrv\w3scfg3.dll::SUPCFG:C:\WINNT\system32\inetsrv\w3scfg.dll

FTP3 = C:\WINNT\System32\inetsrv\fscfg3.dll::SUPCFG:C:\WINNT\system32\inetsrv\fscfg.dll

GOPHER3 = C:\WINNT\System32\inetsrv\gscfg3.dll

Warning Using the registry editor incorrectly can cause problems, including the failure of a Web site or FTP site. If you make mistakes, your Web site or FTP site's configuration could be damaged. You should edit registry entries only for settings that you cannot adjust in the user interface, and be very careful whenever you edit the registry directly.

8. Connect to a server running IIS 3.0 from MMC. To do this, open MMC, select **Internet Information Server**, click **Action**, then click **Connect**. Enter the name of the Web server to which you want to connect.

At this point, the Web server can be viewed from MMC.

The Properties toolbar button in MMC is not available for downlevel sites. Instead, you must right-click on the name of the site and select **Properties**. You can also select **Properties** on the **Action** menu.

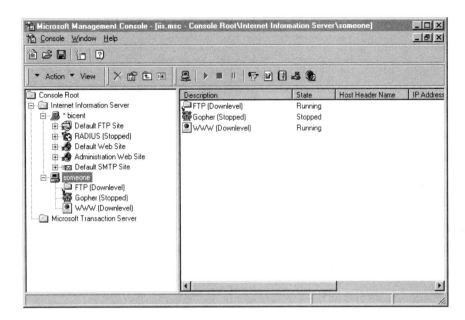

Figure 7.2   Viewing and running the services on a remote computer running Windows NT Server

Customization

This section discusses customization options in IIS 4.0.

Redirect

Redirection is used by administrators to redirect requests for one Web page to another. In an intranet environment, for example, many sites could point to a common resource such as a Human Resources Web site. If the location of that site was changed for some reason, all of the sites pointing to that page would have to change as well to reflect the new URL. By using redirection, a Web administrator can point the old URL to the new location. The pages pointing to the old URL will continue to work while the administrators update the links.

See the IIS online product documentation for information about how to configure redirection.

Custom Error Messages

You can create custom error messages with IIS. For example, instead of displaying the "HTTP Error 404 Object Not Found" message, you could provide one that explains the error in more detail. This message could include the e-mail address of the site administrator, or any other information that might be helpful.

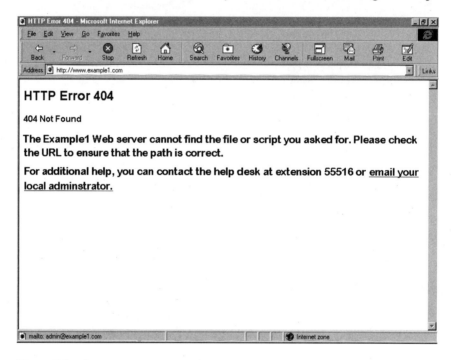

Figure 7.3   A custom error example

Custom HTTP Headers

With custom HTTP headers, an administrator can control the lifetime of the content in the browser's cache. In the example below, the client has made a request to a computer named http://bicent/samplecorp. Without a custom HTTP header, the request would look as follows:

```
CLIENT REQUEST
GET /samplecorp/images/undercon.gif HTTP/1.1
Accept: */*
Referer: http://bicent/samplecorp/
Accept-Language: en-us
Accept-Encoding: gzip, deflate
User-Agent: Mozilla/4.0 (compatible; MSIE 4.0; Windows NT)
Host: bicent
Connection: Keep-Alive
Cookie: ASPSESSIONIDGQQGQGBE=OGIFFNMBNOHDMKLFECBOKFPM

SERVER RESPONSE
HTTP/1.1 200 OK
Server: Microsoft-IIS/4.0
Date: Tue, 14 Oct 1997 17:49:38 GMT
Content-Type: image/gif
Accept-Ranges: bytes
Last-Modified: Tue, 14 Oct 1997 15:53:27 GMT
ETag: "0d1974fb9d8bc1:eca"
Content-Length: 293
```

The next example was created with a custom header that causes content to expire within 30 minutes:

```
CLIENT REQUEST
GET /samplecorp/images/undercon.gif HTTP/1.1
Accept: */*
Referer: http://bicent/samplecorp/
Accept-Language: en-us
Accept-Encoding: gzip, deflate
User-Agent: Mozilla/4.0 (compatible; MSIE 4.0; Windows NT)
Host: bicent
Connection: Keep-Alive
Cookie: ASPSESSIONIDGQQGQGBE=PGIFFNMBCAOPEHGGKOGJODID

SERVER RESPONSE
HTTP/1.1 200 OK
Server: Microsoft-IIS/4.0
Cache-Control: max-age=1800
Expires: Tue, 14 Oct 1997 18:24:21 GMT
Date: Tue, 14 Oct 1997 17:54:21 GMT
Content-Type: image/gif
Accept-Ranges: bytes
Last-Modified: Tue, 14 Oct 1997 15:53:27 GMT
ETag: "0d1974fb9d8bc1:ecb"
Content-Length: 293
```

Notice that the two lines enabling content expiration have changed in the second example. The difference between Cache-Control and Expires is that the former affects the Proxy cache and the latter affects the browser cache.

You can set custom HTTP headers and Content Expiration globally or apply these settings to a specific directory.

Custom HTML Footers

Many corporations place a standard footer on each page within a Web site. This can be difficult to maintain because each individual page must be updated when a change is made to the footer. With IIS, you can include custom footer information in an HTML file that can be appended to the bottom of specified pages. When the footer is changed, all pages are updated automatically.

Custom HTML footers currently work only with static HTML pages and cause performance degradation. Use them with care.

The footer file should contain only the HTML tags necessary for formatting the appearance and function of the footer content. For example, to create a custom footer that contains copyright information, write an HTML document that contains only the following tag: <B> Example1 Copyright 1997–1998 </B>.

PICS Ratings

Ratings were designed to help parents and teachers control what children could gain access to on the Internet. With IIS, you can apply PICS (Platform for Internet Content Selection) ratings to your site. This is a method for associating labels (metadata) with Internet content by applying a custom HTTP header to the requested documents. By default, the assigned rating will apply for one year. It can be customized to apply for any length of time.

The following example illustrates the HTTP custom header information, including a PICS rating. Note that IIS will append this information to all of the designated documents requested from the site.

```
CLIENT REQUEST
GET / HTTP/1.1
Accept: */*
Accept-Language: en-us
Accept-Encoding: gzip, deflate
User-Agent: Mozilla/4.0 (compatible; MSIE 4.0; Windows NT)
Host: www.example1.com
Connection: Keep-Alive
Cookie: HTMLA=FONTSIZE=SMALL;
ASPSESSIONIDQGQGQGPQ=ADHNMFMDOCNECFKLJGGNMBBL
```

```
SERVER RESPONSE
HTTP/1.1 200 OK
Server: Microsoft-IIS/4.0
PICS-Label: (PICS-1.0 "http://www.rsac.org/ratingsv01.html" l by
"someone@example1.com" on "1997.10.17T12:35-0400" exp "1998.10.17T12:00-
0400" r (v 0 s 0 n 0 l 1))
Content-Location: http://www.example1.com/Default.htm
Date: Fri, 17 Oct 1997 16:36:16 GMT
Content-Type: text/html
Accept-Ranges: bytes
Last-Modified: Tue, 14 Oct 1997 22:55:26 GMT
ETag: "50f59e42f4d8bc1:cd7"
Content-Length: 288
```

Resources on the IIS Resource Kit CD

The IIS Resource Kit CD includes several items of particular interest to ISPs.
They are:

- Scripts for automating administration
- HTTPMon tool
- ISP Sign-up Server

Sample Scripts on the IIS Resource Kit CD

The IIS Resource Kit CD includes several sample scripts for automating
administrative tasks.

These scripts are provided for educational purposes only. They have not been
tested in a production environment, and Microsoft will not provide technical
support for them.

The list provided here is intended for reference. There are more than 40 sample
scripts written in VBScript. They are divided into the following categories:
display, group/user administration, server creation, server state operation,
communication, file and directory administration, logging services, virtual
directory administration, and metabase backups and restore. There are also several
sample scripts written in JScript. To view the source files for the scripts, and to
run them, see the CD that accompanies the *IIS Resource Kit*.

Executing Scripts from the Command Line

To use Cscript.exe, open a command prompt and type a Cscript command line with this syntax: **cscript** //[*WSH options...*] [*script name*] /[*script options*]

where:

WSH options enable or disable various Windows Scripting Host (WSH) features, which are described below. Always indicate WSH options by preceding them with two slashes (//).

Script name is the name of the script file; for example, Mkw3site.vbs. You must supply a script name, and may need to specify the path to the name, depending on how you have set up your system.

Script options are options passed to the script. These are the options that are written into the script itself, and that it expects to be passed in. Always indicate script parameters by preceding them with only one slash (/).

Windows Scripting Host Parameters

//T:nn   Enables timeout: the maximum number of seconds the script can run. The default is no limit. This parameter prevents excessive execution of scripts to protect your system from runaway processes and infinite loops that might exist in untested scripts.

//logo   Displays a banner (default; opposite of //noLogo).

//nologo   Prevents display of an execution banner at run time.

//S   Saves the current command-line options for this user.

For more information, see the Windows Scripting Host documentation in the Windows NT 4.0 Option Pack online documentation.

Display Scripts

These scripts display locations and file names in nodes and directory trees.

Script Name	Description
DisplayNode	Displays the relevant fields for a particular administrative node in the tree.
DisplayProperty	Displays any property of an arbitrary administration object.
DisplayTree	Displays the tree of administration objects starting from the specified root node root or at IIS://LocalHost/ if no root node is specified. For each node, it displays the node's name, class, and if it is a Web site (virtual server), the ServerComment. By default, the script recurses through the tree, displaying all the deeper nodes as well. This behavior is disabled by the NoRecurse argument.
Find	Traverses the tree of administration nodes searching for a node that matches the parameters specified at the command line. Displays the full ADSI path of all matching nodes.

Group/User Administration Scripts

These scripts perform user administration tasks—adding or deleting users, assigning users to groups, changing passwords and properties, and so on.

Script Name	Description
AddUserToGroup	Adds the specified user to the specified group.
ChangeUserPassword	Changes the password for the specified user.
ChangeUserProperty	Changes the specified properties to their new specified values for each user passed in.
CreateUser	Creates a new user in the specified domain. It adds the user to all the specified groups (if they exist) and inserts the full name and description into the Windows NT user database.
DeleteUser	Deletes one or more users from the specified domain.
DeleteUserFromGroup	Deletes the specified user to the specified group.
UserGroups	Adds and removes the specified users to and from the specified Windows NT user groups.

Server Creation Scripts

These scripts create virtual FTP servers and Web servers. As noted, some are full-featured scripts that you can use to set up a Web or FTP site for a new customer.

Script Name	Description
CreateVirtualFTPServer	Creates a new virtual FTP server (FTP site) for an ISP's new customer. A full-featured script.
CreateVirtualWebServer	Creates a new Web site (virtual server) for an ISP's new customer. A full-featured script.
CreateVirtualWebServerPool	Creates a "pool" or group of virtual Web servers.
CreateWebSite	Creates a new Web site for an ISP's new customer.
MkWebSrv	Creates a Web site.

Server State Operation Scripts

These scripts start, stop, pause, and resume Web servers and FTP servers.

Script Name	Description
PauseServers	Pauses a group of servers specified on a list.
PauseWebServers	Pauses the specified Web servers.
StartServers	Starts a group of servers specified on a list.
StartWebServers	Starts the specified Web servers.
StopServers	Stops a group of servers specified on a list.
StopWebServers	Stops the specified servers.
StopFtpServers	Stops the specified FTP servers.
StartFtpServers	Starts the specified FTP servers.
PauseFtpServers	Pauses the specified FTP servers.
UnPauseWebServers	Resumes the specified paused Web servers.
UnPauseServers	Resumes a group of servers.
UnPauseFtpServers	Resumes the specified paused FTP servers.

Communication Scripts

These scripts send e-mail messages enabling you to automate notification services for creating or servicing Web sites, users, and groups.

Script Name	Description
SendMail	Sends an e-mail message to the specified user.
SendText	Packages and sends a text file in an e-mail message to the specified user.

File and Directory Administration Scripts

These scripts enable you to set root directories, perform searches, perform file copies, and so on.

Script Name	Description
AppCreate	Designates a Web directory as an application root.
ChangeProperty	Modifies the access restrictions on a site or virtual directory (ModifyAccessRestrictions)
Clone	Copies an object including its parent object.
DeleteNode	Delete an arbitrary node in the administrative tree.
DFoot	Configures document footers.
MatchProperty	Searches the administration tree from a given node for an object property value.
SearchTree	Searches the administration tree from a given node for an object name.

Logging Services Script

This script configures logging services.

Script Name	Description
LogEnum	Configures logging services for IIS.

Virtual Directory Administration Scripts

These scripts create or delete virtual directories for FTP or Web servers. In the case of similar scripts such as CreateFtpVirtualDir and CreateVirtualFTPDir, the available options vary.

Script Name	Description
CreateFTPVirtualDir	Creates a new virtual directory for an FTP server.
CreateVirtualFTPDir	Creates a new virtual directory for an FTP server.
CreateWebVirtualDir	Creates a new virtual directory for a Web server.
CreateVirtualWebDir	Creates a virtual Web directory on the specified Web server, with the specified path.
DeleteFTPVirtualDir	Deletes an FTP virtual directory.
DeleteWebVirtualDir	Deletes a Web virtual directory.

Metabase Backup and Restore Scripts

These scripts administer metabase backup files.

Script Name	Description
MetaBack	Creates a backup of your metabase.
MetaBackDel	Deletes a metabase backup.
MetaBackEnum	Lists the current versions of metabase backups.
MetaBackRest	Restores the specified backup of your metabase.
RegFilt	Installs a new ISAPI filter on the server or service.

JScript Sample Scripts

Script Name	Description
AppCreate.js	Designates a Web directory as an application root.
Dfoot.js	Configures document footers.
LogEnum.js	Configures logging services for IIS.
MakeWebServers.js	Creates a Web site (virtual server).
MetaBack.js	Creates a backup of your metabase
MetaBackDel.js	Deletes a metabase backup.
MetaBackRestore.js	Restores the specified backup of your metabase.
RegFilters.js	Installs a new ISAPI filter on the server or service.

The HTTPMon Web Farm Performance Monitor Tool

HTTPMon is a browser-based tool that monitors the performance of Web sites in a Web farm.

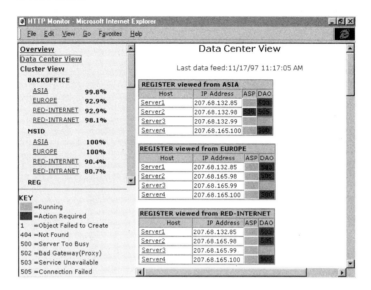

Figure 7.4   HTTPMon's real-time display in Internet Explorer 4.0

Installation

To install HTTPMon, run the setup program provided on the IIS Resource Kit CD. In order to use HTTPMon, you must install Microsoft SQL Server 6.5 on a computer that can be accessed by the computers running this utility.

Using HTTPMon

You can run HTTPMon on several servers simultaneously to test connectivity and display the connectivity statistics of the sites in your Web farm. The database for these Windows NT-based servers is centralized on a single SQL Server.

HTTPMon emulates the way that users attempt to connect to Web sites. HTTPMon is a multithreaded process that operates according to the parameters and values set in its associated HTTPMon.ini file. These parameters specify the Web sites to be tested, as well as the number of times and frequency to retry a failed connection before moving on to the next specified site. You can set other parameters that optimize HTTPMon to your installation, including a maximum thread pool count, an output file and directory, a working directory, and so on.

ISP Sign-Up Server

Included on the IIS Resource Kit CD is the Small Business Server ISP Resource Guide, which includes an ISP Sign-up server. This is a comprehensive Web-based tool that allows small business customers to sign up for your services. You can find the Resource Guide in the \Utility directory on the CD.

The Small Business Server ISP Resource Guide is designed for network administrators and business analysts who are involved in providing Internet access for customers running Small Business Server. The Resource Guide includes the following components and services:

- The ISP Sign-Up Server. This is a personalized Web site that provides forms that potential customers can use to sign up for your services.
- Directions for setting up an Access System. This is a set of services that provide Internet access for customers running Small Business Server.
- Web hosting.
- E-mail delivery.

The Sign-up Server includes all of the scripts (written in VBScript) necessary to automate Web site provisioning for a small business customer.

Applying Other Microsoft Technologies Within an ISP

Windows NT Server Enterprise Edition and Microsoft Site Server Enterprise Edition provide useful technologies for ISPs.

Windows NT Server Enterprise Edition

With the Internet becoming one of the most popular means of communication, there is clearly a demand for "mission critical" Web servers. To meet this level of functionality, server clustering and failover capabilities are becoming increasingly important. A cluster is a group of independent servers managed as a single system for higher availability, easier manageability, and greater scalability. A cluster provides services such as failure detection, recovery, and the ability to manage several Web servers as a single system.

Windows NT Server Enterprise Edition includes support for clustering. It can automatically detect the failure of an application or Web server, and quickly restart it on a surviving Web server. With clustering, users experience only a momentary pause in service if a server fails.

Site Server Enterprise Edition

Although the Windows NT 4.0 Option Pack includes Microsoft Site Server Express, ISPs should consider purchasing Microsoft Site Server Enterprise Edition.

Site Server Enterprise Edition provides a comprehensive set of server components and management tools that you can use to rapidly develop and deploy a new commerce site, deliver personalized content to customers, manage the consistency and integrity of your Web site, and analyze usage patterns. The Enterprise Edition also includes Microsoft Membership System, which you can use to unify your billing, personalization, and customer groups into one relational database. You can find current information on Site Server by visiting http://www.microsoft.com/siteserver/.

Resources

The following books and Web sites provide additional information relevant to ISP Administration.

Web Links

http://www.microsoft.com/products/prodref/458_ov.htm
This site provides information about Windows NT Enterprise Edition.

http://www.microsoft.com/products/prodref/435_ov.htm
This site provides information about Microsoft Site Server Enterprise Edition.

http://www.microsoft.com/isn/
Here you can review an online version of the Small Business Server ISP Resource Guide.

Books

Windows NT Server 4.0 Resource Kit (Microsoft Press, 1996–1997).

Windows NT Server 4.0 Resource Kit Supplement One (Microsoft Press, 1997).

Gunter, David., et. al. *Windows NT and UNIX Integration Guide* (Osborne McGraw-Hill, 1997).

C H A P T E R   8

Security

8

This chapter addresses how to configure a secure Web server running
Windows NT Server 4.0 and Internet Information Server 4.0 (IIS) for use on the
Internet or an intranet. It is assumed that the reader has a basic understanding of
Internet security principles and has read the material on IIS security in the
Windows NT 4.0 Option Pack online product documentation.

In this chapter:

- Guidelines for Creating a Security Policy
- Using the Built-In Security Features of Windows NT Server 4.0
- Configuring IIS for Security
- Security for Web Applications
- Defending Against Malicious Attacks
- Auditing Access with IIS Logs
- IIS Security Checklist
- Resources

Guidelines for Creating a Security Policy

No system is truly secure unless there is a security policy in place. A security policy establishes who can do what with the computer system, and under what circumstances. Your security policy must be documented, disseminated throughout your company, revised regularly, and enforced.

The following lists provide questions to consider when writing a security policy for your organization.

Physical Policy

- Have you described and documented your hardware assets?
- How does your organization physically lock computers to reduce the theft of portable equipment inside the corporation?
- Do you allow floppy disk drives?
- Can computers be left logged on for long periods of inactivity?
- Who has access to the servers?
- How do they gain access?
- Must they sign a logbook?
- Is there a smoke detector in the server room?
- Is there a disaster recovery plan?

Backup Policy

- Who is allowed to make backups?
- When are backups made?
- What type of backup is made?
- Where are the backup media stored, and for how long?

Auditing and Logging Policy

- What events do you log in the Windows NT Event Log?
- What events do you log in the Internet Information Server 4.0 logs?
- Who can view the logs?
- How often are the logs analyzed?

Password Policy

- How long can passwords last before they expire?
- How do you prevent users from choosing bad passwords?
- How many characters long must a password be?
- Do you support alternate devices such as smart cards?

Try to discourage using easy-to-guess passwords such as the name of your spouse or your pet, birthdays, or common words. One way to derive an effective password is to use the first letter of each word in a memorable phrase. For example, the phrase "Hobbits are small with hairy feet" yields the password "haswhf." To make this password even more difficult to guess, you can make the last two letters uppercase, and add an exclamation point: "haswHF!" Another common method of creating effective passwords is to require that they contain both uppercase and lowercase characters, or both letters and numbers.

Privilege Policy

- Many operating systems, including Windows NT, support privileges. A privilege is a special "ability" such as the ability to back up and restore files, debug an application, or log on locally to the computer. How do you determine which privileges are applicable to your users?

Virus Policy

- How do you detect a virus? What software do you run and how often?
- Do you scan software from the Internet for viruses?
- Do you scan commercial software for viruses?
- What happens in the event of a virus outbreak?

Internet Access Policy

- Who has access to the Internet?

- Are computers with Internet access allowed on your corporate network?

- What browser do you use?

- Do you allow active content such as Java applets and ActiveX Controls to be downloaded?

- What sort of proxy or firewall do you use?

Tip Security is designed to "get in the way." As you make a system more secure, you may also make it harder to use or administer. Every time you enable or disable a feature to make a system more secure, you must determine which is more important: the increased security, or the reduced ease-of-use and functionality.

Using the Built-In Security Features of Windows NT Server 4.0

The following section focuses on Windows NT security, but is written with Internet security in mind. This information will help you secure an IIS installation successfully.

You should have answers to the following questions before starting any server configuration changes, because they affect file-level security, IIS virtual directories, user accounts, user profiles, TCP/IP port connections, and more.

- Will the Web server be accessed from the Internet?

- Will the Web server be accessed from the corporate intranet?

- Will the Web server permit anonymous or authenticated user access?

- Will you support Secure Sockets Layer (SSL) connections?

- Will the server be used only for Web access via HTTP?

- Will developers and users need to access the server to copy, open, delete, and write files?

- Will the server be administered remotely?

- Will the server be placed behind a proxy or firewall?

- Will you run proxy software on the server running IIS?

For most of the configurations, it is necessary to work from either the Administrator account or an account which is a member of the Administrators group on the server running IIS. It is recommended that you use an account in the Administrators group rather than the actual Administrator account. This is discussed in more detail later in the chapter.

A Quick Overview of Windows NT Security Principles

The following discussion provides a brief overview of how security is managed with Windows NT.

Authenticated Logon

Windows NT supports authenticated logons, meaning that users must present their credentials (a combination of user name and password) for identification. Once the user is authenticated by the operating system, a security token is attached to all applications that the user runs. All processes (applications), must have a token associated with them. The token identifies the user and the Windows NT groups to which that user belongs. It also contains the user's Security Identifier (SID) and the SIDs of all the groups to which the user belongs. A SID uniquely identifies all users and groups (of users) in Windows NT.

What Does a SID Look Like?

Fortunately, most administrators will never have to deal with SIDs directly. Here is a sample one:

```
S-1-5-21-2127521184-1604012920-1887927527-46029
```

The first part, S-1-5-21, identifies Windows NT; the next three blocks of numbers identify the Windows NT *domain* or *workgroup*; and the last number identifies this user or group.

Services

Windows NT can run special applications called *services*, which are similar to UNIX daemons. Services generally start along with the operating system and run in the background, without any user interface. Examples include Microsoft SQL Server, the Spooler, IIS Web Server, and the Event Log. Because they are applications, services must run in the context of a user account. The LocalSystem account is set aside for this purpose.

The LocalSystem Account

The LocalSystem account has no password, and no one can log on as this account. Locally, this account can perform many tasks required of administrators. It has very few privileges beyond the boundries of the server on which it is being used, thus helping to prevent attacks if an attempt is made to compromise a service.

Privileges and Attack Prevention

When a process runs, it does so in the context of a user account. If the process is running as a highly privileged account (such as the Administrator), and is compromised, any malicious attack will be in the context of the Administrator account. Because of this, it is recommended that you always run in a low-privilege account. This is known as the *principle of least privilege*.

Warning Changing the **Log On As** option from the LocalSystem account to another user account can cause the service to fail on startup.

Access Control Lists

To determine whether the user of an application is allowed to gain access to a resource such as a file or a printer, Windows NT takes the user information in the token associated with the application, attempts to access the resource, and compares this information with the access control lists (ACLs) associated with that resource. An ACL is a list of access control entries (ACEs) that contain a user name or group, and which permission that user or group has on each resource.

To use and set ACLs on files you must be using the Windows NT File System (NTFS).

The comparison of ACLs and user information is what determines who can gain access to a resource in Windows NT. If the ACL and the user information in the token are not the same, the user is denied access to that resource.

Impersonation

Windows NT also supports the ability to impersonate another user. Impersonation is useful in a distributed environment when servers must pass client requests to other servers or the operating system. This way, the operating system can perform the request as if it had been made by the original client. You don't have to maintain a set of user accounts and passwords on the remote server, nor do you have to ask the user to log on again to access the remote resource.

Why Is Impersonation Important?

Impersonation is important because it reduces the number of times a user is required to enter a password.

Most services run as LocalSystem. A user's attempt to delete the file is successful because the process doing the deleting is actually running as LocalSystem, and LocalSystem has full access.

To safeguard against this, all server processes must impersonate the requesting user before accessing the resource. In this case the server will impersonate the user and attempt to delete the file, but this will fail because the user does not have delete permission.

The Ramifications of NTFS Security on IIS

Regardless of what access you provide to a resource, Windows NT (and most visibly NTFS), is the final bastion of security. Use NTFS to restrict the access of a series of files to only a few people. This way you can set the access policy at the file level and use IIS to filter out users before they gain access to files.

Securing Windows NT

Before you can secure an IIS installation, you must secure your Windows NT Server environment by doing the following:

- Choose the server type while installing Windows NT.
- Physically lock access to the server.
- Disable unnecessary services.
- Configure network settings.
- Protect the registry.
- Add users and groups to the computer.
- Set Security Auditing.

Each of these tasks will be discussed individually.

Choosing the Server-Type

Windows NT Server supports the following server types:

- **Primary Domain Controller (PDC)**   In a Windows NT Server domain, this is the computer running Windows NT Server that authenticates domain logons and maintains the directory database for a domain. The PDC tracks changes made to accounts of all of the computers on a domain, but it is the only computer to receive these changes directly. A domain has only one PDC.

   Note The PDC is where password changes are made and user accounts are created and deleted. In many large installations a PDC is a dedicated computer.

- **Backup Domain Controller (BDC)**   In a Windows NT Server domain, a BDC is a computer running Windows NT Server that receives a copy of the domain's directory database. This directory database contains all account and security policy information for the domain. This copy is synchronized periodically and automatically with the master copy on the primary domain controller (PDC). BDCs also authenticate user logons, and can be easily upgraded to function as PDCs as needed. Multiple BDCs can exist on a domain.

- **Member Server**   This is a computer that runs Windows NT Server but is not a primary domain controller (PDC) or backup domain controller (BDC) of a Windows NT domain. Member servers do not receive copies of the directory database; they have their own local accounts. A member server is sometimes called a stand-alone server.

If your computer will be running on the Internet or will be running as an intranet server in a *non*-Windows NT environment, make it a member server. If it will be running as an intranet server in a Windows NT environment, then make it a BDC or a member server.

Physically Locking Access to the Server

Protect your server as you would any valuable piece of equipment:

- Lock the room in which the server is located.
- Use a locked cable to attach the server to the wall.
- Establish a procedure for moving or repairing the server so that it cannot be taken under false pretenses.

Setting Windows NT Security Options With the C2 Configuration Manager

The C2 Configuration Manager is a software utility available in the Windows NT 4.0 Resource Kit. You can use it to modify your system security to comply with the U.S. Department of Defense Trusted Computer System Evaluation Criteria (TCSEC) C2 criteria.

Use the following recommendations when you set up the Configuration Manager:

File Systems   Set all system volumes to the NTFS file system.

OS Configuration   Set to **C2 compliant**. With this setting you won't be able to start from the MS-DOS operating system.

OS/2 Subsystem   Remove.

POSIX Subsystem   Remove.

Security Log   Set to overwrite events older than 30 days.

Display Logon Message   Set to a suitable message. For example: "Exploration Air. Programs and data held on this system are private property."

AUTHORIZED USERS ONLY
Last User Name Display   Hide the name of the last user to log on.

Shutdown Button   Don't show the shutdown button in the Logon dialog box.

Password Length   Set to **C2 compliant** (must contain at least six characters).

Guest Account   Disable.

Drive Letters and Printers   Set up so that only administrators can assign drive letters and assign printers.

Registry Security   Set to **C2 compliant**.

File System Security   Set to **C2 compliant**.

Disabling Unnecessary Services

The more services you have running on a computer, the more entry points you make available to malicious users. A service is a potential entry point because it processes client requests. To help reduce this risk, you should disable unnecessary system services.

The following list outlines the services you'll need to successfully run Internet Information Server version 4.0, those that *may* be required, and those that usually are not. Your particular configuration can change some of the parameters. For example, some intranets require WINS and DHCP.

Required:

- Event Log
- License Logging Service
- Windows NTLM Security Support Provider
- Remote Procedure Call (RPC) Service
- Windows NT Server or Windows NT Workstation
- IIS Admin Service
- MSDTC
- World Wide Web Publishing Service
- Protected Storage
- Server
- Workstation

May Be Required:

- FTP Publishing Service (required if using FTP service)
- NNTP Service (required if using NNTP Service)
- SMTP Service (required if using SMTP Service)
- Content Index (required if using Index Server)
- Certificate Authority (required if you plan on issuing certificates)
- Plug and Play (recommended, but not required)
- RPC Locator (required if doing remote administration)
- Server Service (can be stopped, but you'll need to start it if you want to run User Manager)

- Telephony Service (required if access is via dialup)
- Remote Access Services (required if you use dialup access)
- Workstation (optional; important if you have UNC virtual roots)
- Uninterruptible power supply (UPS) (optional; it is recommended that you use a UPS)

Not Required by Most Installations:

- Alerter
- ClipBook Server
- Computer Browser
- DHCP Client
- Messenger
- Net Logon
- Network DDE & Network DDE DSDM
- Network Monitor Agent
- Simple TCP/IP Services
- Spooler
- NetBIOS Interface
- TCP/IP NetBIOS Helper
- WINS Client (TCP/IP)
- NWLink NetBIOS
- NWLink IPX/SPX Compatible Transport (not required unless you don't have TCP/IP or another transport)

Tip Don't install application software or development tools on your server.

Configuring Network Settings

Use the **Bindings** feature in the Network application in Control Panel to unbind any unnecessary services from any network adapter cards connected to the Internet. For example, you can use the Server service to copy new images and documents from computers in your internal network. If you use the Windows NT Server service over the Internet, you should fully understand the security implications of doing so, and comply with Windows NT Server Licensing requirements.

Disable the NetBIOS binding for the WINS Client (TCP/IP). The network binding of the NetBIOS Interface to the WINS Client (TCP/IP) supports the use of NetBIOS over TCP/IP. This allows the mapping of NetBIOS computer names to IP addresses to support remote administration of Windows NT.

Warning Disabling the NetBIOS Interface binding affects the Messenger Service and the Alerter Service.

Advanced TCP/IP Settings

To make an environment highly secure, you can selectively enable TCP, UDP ports, and IP protocols and disable all others on each network card.

Figure 8.1 shows a server configured to accept only TCP traffic (IP protocol 6) on ports 80 and 443. All UDP traffic is disabled.

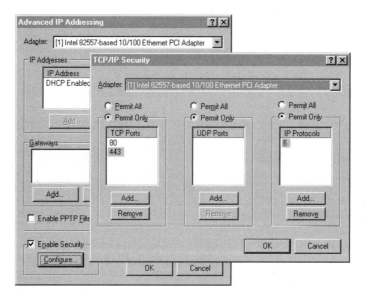

Figure 8.1   Setting Advanced TCP/IP Protocol Security on the first network adapter card

Warning Use the **TCP/IP Security** dialog box with caution. Setting invalid port numbers or IP protocols may render your server inaccessible by other network users.

Disable IP Routing

You should disable routing when you configure the TCP/IP protocol. If routing is enabled, you run the risk of passing data from your intranet to the Internet. To do this, open the **Network** icon in Control Panel, click the **Protocols** tab, select **TCP/IP Protocol**, and then click **Properties**. On the **Routing** tab, clear the **Enable IP Forwarding** check box if it is selected.

Protecting the Registry

The system registry is a critical location for storing all sensitive information regarding the machine and user accounts.

Warning

To add or modify a registry value entry, use administrative tools such as Control Panel or System Policy Editor whenever possible. Using a registry editor (Regedit or Regedt32) to change a value can have unforeseen effects, including changes that can prevent you from starting your system.

To restrict network access to the registry, set the security permissions on the HKEY_LOCAL_MACHINE key. These permissions define which users or groups can connect to the system for remote registry access. The default Windows NT Workstation installation does not define this key and does not restrict remote access to the registry. Windows NT Server permits only Administrator remote access to the registry.

Adding Users and Groups to the Computer

The following users are added by the Windows NT Option Pack:

Table 8.1 Default Windows NT Server User and Group Accounts After a Complete IIS Installation

Name	Description	Comment
Administrator	Built-in account for administering the computer or domain.	Rename to something other than Administrator.
Guest	Built-in account for guest access to the computer or domain.	Disable.
IUSR_*computername*	Internet Server Anonymous Access.	This is the account used by IIS when the user connecting to the server has been authenticated using Anonymous Authentication.

Continued

Name	Description	Comment
IWAM_*computername*	Internet Server Web Application Manager identity.	This account is used to start out-of-process Web applications in IIS.
Administrators	Members can fully administer the computer or domain.	
Backup Operators	Members can bypass file security to back up files.	
Cert Requesters	Members can request certificates.	Added by Microsoft Certificate Server.
Cert Server Admins	Certificate Authority Administrators.	Added by Microsoft Certificate Server.
Guests	Users granted guest access to the computer/domain.	
MTS Trusted Impersonators	Microsoft Transaction Server trusted process identities.	By default, the only member is IWAM_*computername*.
Power Users	Members can share directories and printers.	
Replicators	Supports file replication in a domain.	
Users	Ordinary users.	

In general, keep the number of accounts to a minimum on the IIS computer. If you are running your server as a BDC, you will automatically receive a synchronized list of user accounts from the PDC.

Administrative Accounts Versus User Accounts

Each individual who performs administrative tasks on the computer should have two user accounts on the system: one for administrative tasks, and another for general activity. To avoid accidental changes to protected resources, try to use the account with the lower level of privileges whenever possible. For example, the damage done by a virus can be more severe if activated from an account with Administrator privileges.

It is recommended that you change the built-in Administrator account to a name that is less obvious. This is a powerful account. Because it can't be locked out due to repeated failed logon attempts, it is attractive to hackers who can try to break in by repeatedly guessing passwords. If you rename the account, hackers will need to guess not only the password, but the account name as well.

Using Strong Passwords in Windows NT

Windows NT 4.0 Service Pack 3 includes a new DLL file (Passfilt.dll) that lets you enforce stronger password requirements for users. Passfilt.dll provides enhanced security against "password guessing" or "dictionary attacks" by outside intruders. Passfilt.dll implements the following password policy:

- Passwords must be at least six characters long.

- Passwords must contain characters from at least three of the following four classes: English upper case letters such as A, B, C, . . . Z; English lowercase letters such as a, b, c, . . . z; Westernized Arabic numerals such as 0, 1, 2, . . . 9; Non-alphanumeric ("special characters") such as punctuation symbols.

- Passwords cannot contain your user name or any part of your full name.

These requirements are hard-coded in the Passfilt.dll file and cannot be changed through the user interface or registry.

How to Install Strong Password Filtering

Make the following changes on all of your servers:

- Use Registry Editor (Regedt32.exe) and open
  HKEY_LOCAL_MACHINE\SYSTEM\CurrentControlSet\Control\Lsa
- If it does not already exist, add the value "Notification Packages," of type
  REG_MULTI_SZ, under the LSA key.
- Double-click the "Notification Packages" key and add the following value:
  PASSFILT.

If the value FPNWCLNT is already present, place the PASSFILT entry beneath
the FPNWCLNT entry.

- Click **OK** and then exit Registry Editor.
- Restart the computer.

Two Other Recommended Security Steps

- **Use SYSKEY**   Windows NT version 4.0 Service Pack 3 includes a utility
  called SYSKEY which will further protect the Windows NT Accounts
  Database (often referred to as the Security Account Manager or SAM). This
  utility uses strong encryption and thus reduces the potential for compromise.
- **Set the Blank Screen Screensaver**   Use the Blank Screen screensaver
  because it consumes no CPU time once it is in effect. Set it to be Password
  Protected and set the Wait time to a short duration such as 15 minutes.

Auditing

Auditing refers to tracking security events at the Windows NT level. Don't
confuse it with IIS Logging, in which IIS-specific events related primarily to
HTTP traffic in and out of the server are tracked.

When you set up security auditing, you need to strike a balance between recording
any and all events that may be security violations, versus spending too much
processor time writing to the disk and creating enormous log files of little value.

You can create a system-level Audit Policy by using Windows NT User Manager
in combination with the file-level audit events that are set in Windows NT
Explorer. The audit log is currently set to write events for up to 30 days. After
this, it overwrites the events in the log.

Important   Check your audit logs often for suspicious activity, such as multiple
invalid logon attempts.

Configuring IIS for Security

The following topics will be discussed in this section:

- IIS authentication models
- The IUSR_*computername* account
- File and directory security
- Virtual directory security
- Using Secure Sockets Layer (SSL)
- A brief overview of certificates and Microsoft Certificate Server
- Mapping client certificates to Windows NT accounts
- How access is controlled
- Securing Internet Service Manager (HTML)

IIS Authentication Models

All users must be authenticated before they can gain access to resources in IIS. Each HTTP request from a browser runs on IIS in the security context of a user account on the Windows NT operating system. IIS executes the request in a thread of execution that impersonates the user's security context. The operations that are performed during the execution of that HTTP request are limited by the capabilities granted to that user account in Windows NT Server. The user account needs to be defined either on the IIS server or in a domain of which the server running IIS is a member. The latter is more common in intranet applications.

IIS supports four Web authentication models: Anonymous, Basic, Windows NT Challenge/Response, and Client Certificate Mapping. There are also two FTP authentication models: Anonymous and Do Not Allow Anonymous.

Anonymous (Web) Authentication

Windows NT is configured to accept only valid users, not anonymous ones. Because the Internet is extremely anonymous—in that very few Web sites prompt visitors for a user name and password—IIS creates the IUSR_*computername* account to deal with this dichotomy. This account, which is granted the Log on Locally user right, generates a random password on the local computer, and is used for anonymous users. Anonymous User access can be reset to use any valid Windows NT account.

Note With IIS you can set up different anonymous accounts for different Web sites, virtual directories, directories, and files.

If the computer running Windows NT Server is a stand-alone server, the IUSR_*computername* account is on the local server. If the server is a Primary Domain Controller, the IUSR_*computername* account is defined for the domain.

Windows NT uses IUSR_*computername* when a user is authenticated by IIS using Anonymous Authentication. In other words, a real Windows NT user account is being used for all non-trusted anonymous access.

Figure 8.2 shows that the Audit Log will show Logon/Logoff entries for the IUSR_ *computername* account when Anonymous Authentication is used.

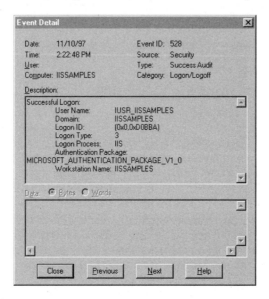

Figure 8.2 An Audit Log example: IIS is logging on the IUSR_IISSAMPLES account

Basic Authentication

Basic Authentication is the method supported by most Web servers. Basic Authentication requires you to enter credentials (in other words, it's not anonymous), and therefore you can determine who has access to what based on the user ID. You can use this method to restrict access to some parts of the Web server when:

- You cannot guarantee that the user's browser supports Windows NT Challenge/Response Authentication (Microsoft Internet Explorer 2.0 or later supports Windows NT Challenge/Response Authentication).

- You need to authenticate through a firewall via a proxy server.

To use Basic Authentication, grant each user account the Log on Locally user right on the IIS server. These accounts should have file access controlled by placing them in a user group which has access only to the required files on the server.

When using Basic Authentication, the browser prompts the user for a user name and password. This information is then transmitted across HTTP (lightly scrambled using UUEncoding or Base64 encoding). IIS uses this user name and password and to authenticate the user as the corresponding Windows NT user.

With Basic Authentication, you can restrict access to files on the server running IIS by using NTFS security.

Keep the following in mind when using Basic Authentication:

- Basic Authentication will not succeed if the user doesn't have local logon rights.
- If a user can obtain physical access to the host running the Web server that user will be permitted to start an interactive session at the computer because they have local logon rights. This can be controlled by setting the appropriate NTFS file protections.

Basic Authentication is inherently insecure. Passwords are encoded but not securely encrypted. Because of this, a simple network sniffer can watch for the HTTP authentication headers and UUDecode this data to obtain the real password.

```
⊕FRAME: Base frame properties
⊕ETHERNET: ETYPE = 0x0800 : Protocol = IP:  DOD Internet Protocol
⊕IP: ID = 0x4DBF; Proto = TCP; Len: 587
⊕TCP: .AP..., len:  547, seq: 112796675-112797221, ack:   2283384, win: 8760
⇒HTTP: GET Request (from client using port 1556)
  HTTP: Request Method = GET
  HTTP: Uniform Resource Identifier = /iissamples/
  HTTP: Protocol Version = HTTP/1.1
  HTTP: Accept = application/vnd.ms-excel, application/msword
  HTTP: User-Agent = Mozilla/4.0 (compatible; MSIE 4.01; Windows NT; ITG)
  HTTP: Host = iissamples
  HTTP: Connection = Keep-Alive
  HTTP: Accept-Language = en-us
  HTTP: Accept-Encoding = gzip, deflate
  HTTP: Authorization = Basic am9objpaZXNOK0Zyb2Rv
```

Figure 8.3   A sample network trace using Microsoft Network Monitor. Note the Authorization header at the bottom.

To get around this, you can use the Secure Sockets Layer (SSL) support to establish a secure session. This way, the password will still be encoded but the HTTP session carrying the data will be encrypted using cryptographically secure mechanisms. However, the use of SSL does affect performance dramatically.

Note By default, Internet Information Server caches security tokens for locally logged on accounts such as IUSR_*computername*. You may not see multiple logon entries in the audit logs because the token is already accessible to IIS. The default cache time is 15 minutes.

Windows NT Challenge/Response Authentication

Windows NT Challenge/Response Authentication is more secure than Basic Authentication. It can be used to restrict access to some parts of the Web server, especially in an intranet environment where users have Windows NT domain accounts.

In Windows NT Challenge/Response Authentication, the browser attempts to use the current user's cryptographic credentials from a domain logon. If those credentials are rejected, Windows NT Challenge/Response Authentication will prompt the user for a user name and password by means of a dialog box. When Challenge/Response Authentication is used, the user's password is not passed from the client to the server. If a user has logged on as a domain user on a local computer, the user won't have to be authenticated again when accessing a remote computer in that domain.

The user is not prompted for a user name and password for each HTTP request; rather, this will happen only when the cached credentials do not have sufficient permissions to access a specific page or file.

Challenge/Response Authentication has the following limitations:

- It cannot be performed through a firewall via a proxy.
- Currently, it is only supported by Microsoft Internet Explorer 2.0 and later.
- It does not support delegation to other servers. In other words, the user's credentials cannot be passed onto another process. For example when a request comes in to IIS, the user account credentials cannot be passed to Microsoft SQL Server.

Client Certificate Mapping

You can use your Web server's Secure Sockets Layer (SSL) 3.0 security features to authenticate users by checking the contents of an encrypted digital identification submitted by the user's Web browser during the logon process. A user obtains these digital identifications, called *client certificates,* from a mutually trusted third-party organization. Client certificates usually contain identifying information about the user and the organization that issued the certificate.

Note If you have installed Microsoft Certificate Server, your site can issue its own certificates to users on the intranet or to business partners. Certificates scale better than password-based systems.

IIS has a client-certificate *mapping* feature that authenticates users who log on with client certificates, without requiring the use of Basic or Windows NT Challenge/Response Authentication. A mapping relates the contents of a user's client certificate to a corresponding Windows NT account which defines the rights and access policies of the user. Once you create and enable a mapping, your Web server automatically connects, or maps, that user to an appropriate Windows NT account each time a user logs on with a client certificate.

FTP Authentication

FTP uses user-level security. This means that the user must log on to gain access to the FTP server. The IIS FTP services can use the Windows NT account database to authenticate users logging on. However, all FTP transmissions are in clear text, thus exposing user names and passwords.

```
FRAME: Base frame properties
ETHERNET: ETYPE = 0x0800 : Protocol = IP:  DOD Internet Protocol
IP: ID = 0x2259; Proto = TCP; Len: 50
TCP: .AP..., len:   10, seq:  82091653-82091662, ack:  83518918, win: 8707
FTP: Req. from Port 1507, 'USER joe'

FRAME: Base frame properties
ETHERNET: ETYPE = 0x0800 : Protocol = IP:  DOD Internet Protocol
IP: ID = 0x2459; Proto = TCP; Len: 57
TCP: .AP..., len:   17, seq:  82091663-82091679, ack:  83518950, win: 8675
FTP: Req. from Port 1507, 'PASS zest+frodo'
```

Figure 8.4   Two packets of FTP data, showing the user name and password in cleartext

To eliminate exposed passwords, you can configure your FTP server to permit anonymous logons. Anonymous logons require the user to type **anonymous** as the user name and the user's Internet e-mail address as the password. Anonymous users can gain access to files under the IUSR_*computername* account.

You can also allow anonymous-only logons to the FTP service. Anonymous-only logons are useful because they prevent real passwords from being revealed on a public network. In IIS, the FTP service is configured for anonymous access by default.

Create a drop box in which your Internet customers can leave files. In Windows NT Explorer, right-click the folder that will contain the drop box and set the permissions to **Everyone**. Allow only administrators or trusted personnel Read access. This drop box must be on a drive formatted with NTFS.

The IUSR_*computername* Account

The IUSR_*computername* account is created by IIS and given a randomly generated password when the product is installed. Because access to any resource must be in the context of a Windows NT user account, the IUSR_computername account is used by IIS when a user is authenticated by the Anonymous Authentication method.

The IUSR_*computername* account is a member of the Guests group, but it has one additional privilege: it can log on to the system locally. The account will fail to log on if you remove this privilege.

Windows NT always logs on a user either locally (when the user enters their credentials while seated at the computer), or remotely (when the user attempts to access a resource over the network).

IUSR_*computername* requires the Log on Locally privilege by default because when users connect across the Internet, they are authenticated with Anonymous Authentication. IIS logs them on to the computer by logging on to the IUSR_*computername* account locally. Technically, the logon is not being attempted across the network.

Tip By default, the Anonymous account, and any account used with Basic Authentication, must have the Log on Locally privilege. It is possible to programmatically change this by configuring the IIS Configuration Store using COM or the ADSI interfaces. For more information, see the IIS online product documentation.

When you create a new anonymous account, you must make sure that your Web site and Windows NT password settings are identical. Select the **Enable Automatic Password Synchronization** option to automatically synchronize your anonymous password settings with those set in Windows NT. Password synchronization should only be used with anonymous user accounts defined on the local computer, not with anonymous accounts on remote computers.

File and Directory Security

It is recommended that you place your data files on an NTFS partition because NTFS provides security and access control for your data files.

Access control lists (ACLs) grant or deny access to the associated file or folder by specific Windows NT user accounts, or groups of users. When an Internet service attempts to read or execute a file on behalf of a client request, the user account offered by the service must have permission.

You can use IIS virtual directory access control combined with Windows NT accounts and NTFS file ACLs to configure access to specific files within a Web site. After a user is authenticated for the IIS virtual directory, IIS uses the context of the requesting user (Anonymous or specific) to gain access to the NTFS file based on the user account, user rights policy, and file permissions.

It is possible to use the Windows NT Interactive user and Network user accounts to provide broad access control for files available to IIS.

- If the Interactive user is given Read (RX) permission for a file, the Anonymous user or *any* client authenticated by Basic Authentication will be able to access the file. This is because these accounts are being logged on locally (in other words, they are interactive).

- If the Network user is given Read (RX) permission for a file, *any* client authenticated by Windows NT Challenge/Response authentication will be able to gain access to the file.

In general, set the following NTFS file permissions (ACLs) for files on a server running IIS:

Directories containing DLLs needed by the system

Set directories and files to Read (RX) access for the IUSR_*computername* account and all accounts that have specific authentication for the directories:

- \Winnt\System32 (and all subdirectories)
- \Program Files\Common Files (and all subdirectories)

Directories corresponding to Web virtual directories

- **Special (R)**   If the directory contains only static HTML.
- **Special (X)**   If the directory contains only executable files (for example, .dll).
- **Read (RX)**   If the directory is a mix of readable and executable files.
- **Special (RW)**   If the directory contains a file database (for example, .mdb).
- **Change (RWXD)**   If developers need to be able to modify or delete the files (this is not recommended).

Recommended file and directory permissions for the following user accounts:

- **IUSR_*computername***   If Anonymous access is being used.
- **Interactive**   If you are allowing access to *all* users authenticated by Basic Authentication and if the default logon method is Log on Locally.
- **Network**   If you are allowing access to *all* users authenticated by Challenge/Response authentication.
- **Specific users and groups**   Ensure that they have the correct user rights profiles.

Tip If you are not using the server for any other file access, restrict access to all files to only Administrators, System, and, in less secure environments, Power Users.

Virtual Directory Security

Virtual directories have a small number of options for controlling access and content control. They are:

- Read
- Write
- Log Access
- Directory Browsing
- Indexing
- FrontPage Web (Web site only)

The default settings are Read, Log Access, Index this Directory, and FrontPage Web (for a Web site only).

If a virtual directory is on an NTFS drive, the settings for the directory must match the following settings. If they don't, the most restrictive settings take effect. For example, if you give a directory Write permission but give a particular user group only Read access permissions in NTFS, those users cannot write files to the directory because the Read permission is more restrictive.

Note   Write access can be performed only with a browser that supports the PUT feature of the HTTP 1.1 protocol standard.

IIS also supports Application Settings that determine how executable content such as Active Server Pages operate. The three permissions are:

- **None**   Doesn't allow any programs or scripts to run in this directory.

- **Script**   Enables applications mapped to a script engine to run in this directory without having the Execute permission set. Use Script permission for directories that contain ASP scripts, Internet Database Connector (IDC) scripts, or other scripts. Script permission is safer than Execute permission because you can limit the applications that can be run in the directory.

- **Execute**   Allows any application to run in this directory, including applications mapped to script engines and Windows NT binaries (.dll and .exe files). It is suggested that you use this option with care.

Using Secure Sockets Layer

The Secure Sockets Layer (SSL) protocol provides communications privacy, authentication, and message integrity by using a combination of public-key and symmetric encryption. By using this protocol, clients and servers can communicate in a way that prevents eavesdropping, tampering, or message forgery.

Public and Symmetric Key Cryptography

Cryptography provides a set of techniques for encoding data and messages so that the data and messages can be stored and transmitted securely. The following section introduces the basic terminology of cryptography and explains some of the common methods used.

- You can use cryptography to achieve secure communications, even when the transmission medium (for example, the Internet) is untrustworthy. You can also use it to encrypt your sensitive files so that an intruder cannot understand them.

- Cryptography can be used to ensure data integrity as well as maintain secrecy.

- Using cryptography, it becomes possible to verify the origin of data and messages. This can be done using digital signatures and certificates.

- When using cryptographic methods, the only part that must remain secret is the cryptographic keys. The algorithms, key sizes, and file formats can be made public without compromising security.

The two fundamental operations are encryption and decryption. *Encryption* involves scrambling the data in such a way that it is infeasible to deduce the original information unless you know the key used. *Decryption* is the reverse process—scrambled data is turned into the original text using a key.

To encrypt and decrypt you need an encryption algorithm and a key. Many encryption algorithms exist, including DES, RSA, RC2, and RC5. A key is used in conjunction with the algorithm to convert the plaintext (human readable) into ciphertext (scrambled, non-human readable).

DES, RC2, and RC5 are known as symmetric key technology because the key used to encrypt the data is the same key used to decrypt the data. Hence the key must be a shared secret between the party encrypting the data and the party decrypting the data. You can use public key technology to pass the key securely to the other party.

RSA is known as public key, or asymmetric, technology, because two keys are used: a public key and a private key. The keys are mathematically related but it is infeasible to deduce one without knowing the other. The private key is kept private—only the party generating the key pair should have access to it. The public key can be freely shared over an insecure medium such as the Internet.

With public key systems there is no shared secret between the two parties. If the public key is used to encrypt the data, then only the private key can decrypt it. If the private key is used to encrypt the data, then only the public key can decrypt it. See the following scenario for an example.

A Public Key Scenario

In this scenario, Alice wants to send Bob a message, but she wants to make sure only Bob can read it. To do this, the following steps are performed:

- Alice gets a copy of Bob's public key, possibly from the directory, a Web site or an e-mail message.

- She uses this key to encrypt the data.

- She sends the encrypted data to Bob. Because the data was encrypted using his public key, only his private key can be used to decrypt it.

- Bob uses his private key to decrypt the data, and reads Alice's message.

Enabling SSL

To use SSL on IIS you need to perform the following steps:

- Request and install a server certificate.
- Enable the appropriate settings in the **Secure Communications** dialog box.

The **Secure Communications** dialog box will not appear unless you have a server certificate installed.

SSL in Action

SSL is most effectively used by encrypting only communications that contain private data, such as credit card numbers, phone numbers, or company records. Because SSL uses complex encryption, and because encryption requires considerable processor resources, it takes much longer to retrieve and send data from SSL-enabled directories. Because of this, you should place only those pages that will contain or receive sensitive information in your SSL-enabled directory. Also, keep the pages free of elements that can be resource-consuming, such as images.

A Brief Overview of Certificates and Microsoft Certificate Server

Digital certificates, also known simply as certificates, are documents that provide authentication of persons and entities on a network. Proper use of certificates makes it impossible for malicious users to intercept a message or falsify their identity.

In the public key scenario presented earlier, one issue was not resolved—how do we know that Bob's public key is *really* being used, and not that of an imposter? This issue can be resolved by using certificates.

It's All a Matter of Trust

To verify that Alice is using Bob's public key, and not one which is fraudulent, the following steps are performed:

- Bob uses Key Manager to create his public/private key pair.
- Bob sends his public key to a trusted certifying authority such as a certificate authority on his intranet, or an Internet company such as Verisign.
- The certifying authority verifies that it is indeed Bob who made the request. They might request that he fax a copy of a photograph of himself, or a copy of his driver's license.

- Once satisfied that Bob is who he claims to be, the certificate authority (CA) uses its own private key to encrypt Bob's public key along with some other data such as an expiration date, serial number, name, and so on. This is used as a certificate. The current industry standard is a X.509 v3 certificate.

- The CA passes the certificate back to Bob.

- Bob can make his certificate available to Alice.

- Alice acquires Bob's certificate.

- To verify that the certificate is indeed Bob's, Alice must use the certificate of the CA that issued Bob's certificate to decrypt his certificate information. Additionally, Alice must *trust* the CA.

- Most browsers, including Microsoft Internet Explorer and Netscape Navigator, include the root certificates for a number of common, trusted certifying authorities.

How Can I Add New Root Certificates to IIS?

There is no user interface to add new root certificates to IIS. Instead you must use Microsoft Internet Explorer 4.0 or later and a tool called Iisca.exe.

To do this, perform the following steps:

- Start Internet Explorer

- Add any new root certificates by copying them from the certifying authority's home page. In the case of Microsoft Certificate Server, you could use http://*server*/CertSrv/CertEnroll/CACerts.htm.

- Type the following at a command prompt:

```
%SystemRoot%\system32\inetsrv\iisca
Net Stop IISAdmin /y
Net Start W3Svc
```

Microsoft Certificate Server

Microsoft Certificate Server provides customizable services for issuing and managing certificates used in software security systems that employ public key cryptography. Certificate Server generates certificates in standard X.509 format. This format is commonly used to authenticate servers and clients performing secure communications using the Secure Sockets Layer (SSL) protocol.

Mapping Client Certificates to Windows NT User Accounts

The SSL protocol supports server certificates, and optionally, client certificates that can be used to verify the identity of a client. You can also use IIS to map client certificates onto Windows NT user accounts.

For example, let's say that a travel site called Exploration Air has decided to offer access to highly confidential parts of their Web site to all users in Washington State who hold certificates signed by the site. By mapping these users onto an account called BusinessPartnersWA, Exploration Air can set permissions (ACLs) on individual files or directories to which only the BusinessPartnersWA users have access. The following steps would be required:

- Select **Require Client Certificates**.

- Enable **Client Certificate Mapping**.

- Click the **Edit** button.

- Select the **Advanced** tab.

- Click the **Add** button.

- In the rule description, type **Washington Partners**.

- Enable **Match** on selected certificate issuers, and click the **Select** button.

- Choose a valid certificate issuer by clicking the **Toggle** button.

- Click **OK**, then click **Next**.

- If you want more control based on the contents of the client certificate, click **New** and add certificate field criteria.

- Enter the Windows NT account and password you wish to map onto.

How Access Is Controlled

When a user attempts to access a resource through IIS, a number of technologies come into play. Figure 8.5 provides an overview of this process:

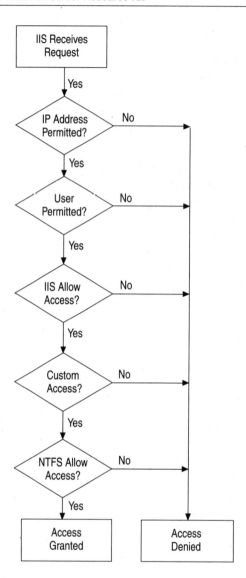

Figure 8.5   Internet Information Server access logic

Note In the interest of simplicity, the diagram above shows many paths leading to Access Denied. In fact, some paths yield a 401 or 403 HTTP error. A real Access Denied message can prompt the user to re-enter the user name and password; a 401 or 403 cannot.

IP Address Access Control

IIS can be configured to grant or deny access to specific IP addresses. For example, you can prevent a company or individual from accessing your site by listing the appropriate IP address, IP address range, or DNS name (IIS checks the IP address first, then the DNS name). You can even prevent entire networks from gaining access to your server. Conversely, you can choose to allow only specific sites or IP addresses to have access to your service.

Note IIS 4.0 is more flexible than earlier versions. It allows you to restrict or allow access to Web sites, virtual directories, directories, and files.

If IIS is configured to allow access by all IP addresses except those listed as exceptions to that rule, then access is denied to any computer with an IP address included in that list. Conversely, if IIS is configured to deny all IP addresses, access is denied to all remote users except those whose IP addresses have been specifically granted access. IP address access restrictions are available for each of the IIS services.

When controlling access by IP address, be aware that many Web users will be passing through a proxy server or a firewall. The incoming connection to your Web server will appear to have originated from the proxy server or firewall itself (in other words, the IP address of the originator will be that of the proxy server or firewall). This may be useful in a corporate network as an added security measure to prevent access by anyone from outside your IP address domain.

User Permitted

In the "User Permitted" step, there are five criteria for a successful logon. These are:

- Valid user name and password supplied.
- Windows NT account restrictions such as time of day, allow logon.
- Account is not disabled or locked out.
- Account password has not expired.
- The applicable logon policy (for example, Log on Locally or Access this computer from the Network) for the logon protocol used permits logon.

By default, on a server running Windows NT, ordinary users (in other words, those who don't belong to the Administrator group) do not have the Log on Locally user right. If FTP or WWW Basic Authentication is used, IIS, by default, attempts to log on the user as a local user.

Internet Information Server Permissions

Once a user has been granted access, the server examines the URL and type of request and checks the permissions and SSL Client Authentication Certificate.

Permissions

For WWW service, the request can indicate a Read, Write, Execute, or script action. The applicable WWW virtual directory must have the appropriate permission enabled. Otherwise, the WWW service returns a "403,x: Access Forbidden" error; where "x" represents the type of access attempted.

Secure Sockets Layer (SSL) Client Authentication Certificate Required

IIS may require a valid client authentication certificate before access to a resource is permitted. If such a certificate is not passed to the server, IIS will return a "403,7: Forbidden—client certificate required" error.

Custom Authentication

Custom Authentication means that you must create your own authentication mechanisms. Implementation examples include:

- ISAPI Authentication Filters
- Active Server Pages
- CGI applications

These implementation technologies could perform tasks such as:

- Perform a database lookup of user name and password.
- Look inside a client authentication certificate and make decisions based on its contents.
- Analyze a cookie.
- Identify a browser type.
- Provide the time and date.

NTFS File System Permissions

IIS currently attempts to gain access to the specified resource (based on the URL) using the security context of the authenticated user. For anonymous access, this is typically the IUSR_*computername* account. If authentication has been performed, it will be a valid Windows NT user account.

Using UNC Names

With IIS you can have the starting point of a virtual directory on another computer. To do this, use the Universal Naming Convention (UNC) to access the other computer. UNC names are of the form *computername**share**directory*. With UNC, IIS uses the credentials you supply rather than those of the connecting user.

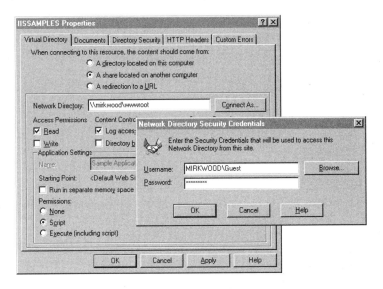

Figure 8.6   Using a network share and setting the security credentials

Securing the HTML Administration Tool

By default, the browser-hosted Internet Service Manager (HTML) will run only on the local computer for security reasons—it is quite simple to capture administration data using a network sniffer.

If you want to use the tool beyond the realm of the local computer, there a few options available:

- **Use SSL**   When you install IIS, a random port is chosen for use by the Administration Web site, but not for SSL. Select an SSL port that does not conflict with other Web sites on the computer (443 is the standard SSL port). Once you have done this, you can safely access the administration site using SSL.

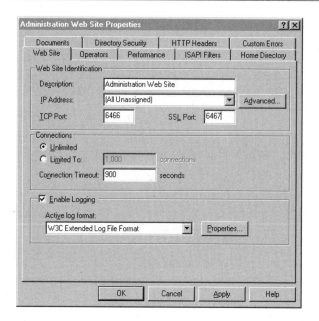

Figure 8.7   Choosing an SSL port for the Administration Web site

- **Add the IP addresses of those you trust** To do this, you need to reduce the IP address restrictions. To do this, right click the Administration Web site, select **Properties**, then **Directory Security**, then **IP Address and Domain Name Restrictions**. You can now add the IP addresses of computers you trust.

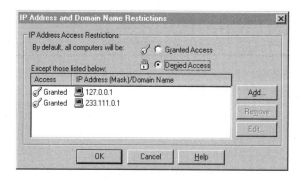

Figure 8.8   Adding another IP Address to the list of trusted computers

Security for Web Applications

Web applications running on state-of-the-art servers such as IIS use many technologies including Active Server Pages (ASP), COM components, transactions, message queuing, NNTP, and others.

The following section covers security issues and best practices from a Web application perspective:

- DCOM security
- Microsoft Transaction Server security
- Scripting security
- Server-based executable content security
- Microsoft Index Server security
- Use of FrontPage Extensions
- Uploading content to IIS
- Accessing Microsoft SQL Server from ASP
- An end-to-end example

DCOM Security

Active Server Pages makes considerable use of Distributed COM (DCOM) components. You can use a tool called Dcomcnfg.exe to configure DCOM security settings. The following can be set as defaults for all components, although you can override these on a component-by-component basis:

- **General Default Properties**   Such as enabling DCOM on a computer or setting default authentication levels and impersonation levels.

The authentication levels are the same as the Microsoft Remote Procedure Calls (RPC) authentication levels. *None*: No Authentication; *Connect*: Authentication is performed on first connection; *Call*: Authentication is performed on each call; *Packet*: Authenticates each packet of data; *Packet Integrity*: Authenticates each packet of data and validates that it has not been tampered with; *Packet Privacy*: Authenticates each packet of data, validates it has not been tampered with and encrypts the data.

- **Default Access Security**   Determines who can access a COM interface on the running object.
- **Default Launch Security**   Determines who can cause a non-running executable to start running.
- **Default Configuration Security**   Determines who can change the settings.

Security details for a remote DCOM component fall into the following categories:

- **Access Security**   Determines who can access a COM interface on the running object.
- **Launch Security**   Determines who can launch the server. In other words, who can cause a non-running executable to start running.
- **Configuration Security**   Determines who can change the settings.

These levels of functionality can also be configured using COM APIs.

Note   When you call a DCOM component from an ASP page, it will be called in the security context of the user account that IIS is using.

Important   It is recommended that you execute in-process components or components in MTS packages rather than out-of-process components. Most COM .exe files are out-of-process, for performance reasons.

Microsoft Transaction Server Security

Microsoft Transaction Server (MTS) defines an application programming model for developing distributed COM-based applications. It also provides a run-time infrastructure for deploying and managing these applications.

Roles and Packages are two key parts of Microsoft Transaction Server:

- *Roles* define logical groups of users. They also determine who can invoke interfaces in a component.
- *Packages* are a set of components (such as COM components written in C++, Visual Basic, Java, or COBOL) that perform related functions. All components in a package run together in the same process controlled by MTS. A package is also a trust boundary that defines when security information is verified.

Note   When you call a DCOM component residing in a Microsoft Transaction Server package from an ASP page, it will be called in the security context of the user account that IIS is using

MTS security consists of declarative security and programmatic security.

Declarative Security

Declarative security can be performed by administrators using MTS Explorer. It allows control of access to packages, components, and interfaces by using roles. To enable declarative security you must first define the roles and then enable authorization checking for the package.

Programmatic Security

With programmatic security, you can control access to a business function through program calls and selectively allow access to programmatic logic based on a user's role membership.

Note   IIS uses the IWAM_*computername* account to start an out-of-process Web application. If the application contains an ASP document that calls a component in an MTS-controlled package, all role-based security is performed in the context of the IIS-authenticated user, such as IUSR_*computername*.

Warning   COM servers can call **CoImpersonateClient()** which allows them to impersonate the client of the current function call. If this is called from a component in an out-of-process Web application, it will not impersonate the IIS-authenticated client. Rather, it will impersonate IWAM_*computername*.

Scripting Security

The scripting engines that ship with IIS are Visual Basic Scripting Edition (VBScript) and JScript. Both have a number of features disabled to make them more secure:

- **Ability to execute programs**   Shell-like commands are not supported.
- **Dynamic Data Exchange (DDE)**   Commands such as **LinkExecute**, **LinkPoke**, **LinkRequest**, **LinkSend** are not supported.
- **All traditional file I/O**   To read or write files you must use the **FileSystemObject** component.
- **Clipboard**   Access to the clipboard is not supported.

Accessing Files

You can read from and write to files using VBScript and JScript. However, access to the files is determined by the context of the account making the request. For example, the user context might be IUSR_*computername.* You can place ACLs on the file or the directory containing the file and let Windows NT enforce permission checking. You can also verify this by using the Windows NT audit log.

Server-Based Executable Content Security

Because executables can call system functions (within the confines of the permissions and privileges of the requesting user), any content that executes at the server should be tested thoroughly.

Executable content includes:

- COM objects invoked by Active Server Pages.
- CGI applications and scripts written in any programming language including Tcl, Perl, C++, C, Visual Basic, and Java.
- ISAPI Applications.
- ISAPI Filters.

Microsoft Index Server Security

Index Server utilizes the security system built into Windows NT to check whether users have permission to view query results. Index Server will also check these file and directory ACLs before returning a query result file by file.

> **Warning** If you index directories containing ASP scripts, users may be able to view your server source code. Disable indexing in Internet Service Manager. Right-click the directory, select **Properties**, and clear the **Index this directory** check box.

Using FrontPage Extensions

In Microsoft FrontPage, there are three kinds of users defined for every Web site: administrators, authors, and browsers (end-users). All permissions are cumulative in that all authors also have browsing permission and all administrators also have authoring and browsing permissions.

In FrontPage, the list of administrators, authors, and browsers is defined on a per–Web site basis. All content in a Web site created with FrontPage will be accessible to the same set of users and groups. It isn't possible to control permissions on a per-file or per-directory basis. All FrontPage sub-webs either inherit the permissions (list of administrators, authors, and browsers) of the FrontPage root Web site, or use their own unique permissions.

Each FrontPage Web site (including each sub-web), contains copies of three ISAPI DLLs that make up the FrontPage Server Extensions. These DLLs are created in directories below the top-level directory:

- _vti_bin/_vti_adm/admin.dll   For administrative tasks.
- _vti_bin/_vti_aut/author.dll   For authoring FrontPage Web sites.
- _vti_bin/shtml.dll   For browse-time FrontPage components such as form handlers.

FrontPage performs all authoring and administrative tasks by sending HTTP POST requests to these DLLs. The FrontPage Server Extensions are stored in separate directories in the document root:

```
/document root
   /_vti_bin
      shtml.dll
   /_vti_adm
      admin.dll
   /_vti_aut
      author.dll
```

FrontPage Access Control List Settings

FrontPage implements Web security on IIS by changing the access control lists (ACLs) for all files and directories in each Web site created with FrontPage.

FrontPage controls who can administer a Web site by setting the ACL on Admin.dll, the administrative DLL. Similarly, FrontPage sets authoring permissions by setting the ACLs on Author.dll. The default ACL sets browsing permission on Web content and lets all users execute the run-time DLL, Shtml.dll.

You can set the ACLs for a FrontPage Web by using FrontPage Explorer's **Permissions** command, on the **Tools** menu. To add new users and groups, this command makes the Windows NT computer account list available. In FrontPage 98, you can set up a restricted list of users and groups that does not expose the entire contents of the Windows NT computer and domain account lists. This lets you protect the confidentiality of your user community.

FrontPage sub-webs can have unique permissions that maintain separate access-control lists on their own copies of the Admin.dll, Author.dll, and Shtml.dll. Alternatively, a FrontPage sub-web can inherit the permissions of the root Web by keeping the access-control lists on its Admin.dll, Author.dll, and Shtml.dll the same as the root Web's lists.

The set of ACLs for a Web site created with FrontPage is illustrated in Figure 8.9, which shows the ACLs for the content of a Web site created with FrontPage and the ACLs for the FrontPage directories. All directories begin with the vti prefix.

Note that two sets of permissions are given. The first set applies to the directory; the second to the files in the directory. For example, the permissions (rx) (r) specify read and execute permissions on the directory but only Read permissions on the files in the directory.

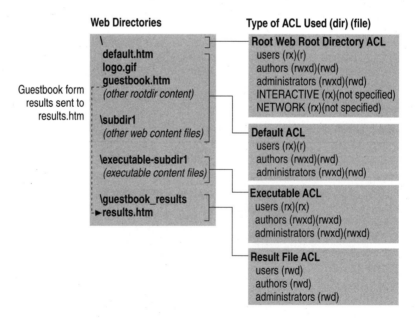

Figure 8.9   Web directories and the types of ACLs used

For information about Microsoft FrontPage Server Extensions, see http://www.microsoft.com/frontpage/wpp/serk.

Uploading Content to IIS

The following list provides best practices to minimize the risk involved in uploading content onto your server.

- Disable all support for file upload if you do not need any file upload ability. This includes the Posting Acceptor and FrontPage Server Extensions. Also disable support for HTTP PUT.
- Place all upload areas on a separate hard disk. This prevents users from uploading massive files, or thousands of files, to fill up your system hard disk.
- Authenticate the user who wants to perform the upload.
- Consider using SSL if uploading sensitive data.
- Log all attempts to upload.
- Do not put execute permission on the directory and do not leave any executable content in the upload area.
- Make the upload area write-only.

Accessing Microsoft SQL Server from ASP

SQL Server can use multiple authorization methods:

- **Standard**   In standard mode, SQL Server manages its own logon validation process for all connections. As a consequence, connections must supply a logon ID and password.
- **Integrated**   In this mode, SQL Server uses Windows NT authentication mechanisms for all connections. Only trusted connections are allowed into SQL Server. Any user name passed to SQL Server is ignored, and the client's Windows NT credentials are used instead. The integrated method only works when SQL Server is configured to use Named Pipes or Multiprotocol drivers.
- **Mixed**   In this case, SQL Server allows both trusted (in other words, Integrated) and non-trusted (in other words, Standard) connections. SQL Server tries the Integrated method first. If this fails, it uses the Standard method.

When accessing SQL Server with integrated security from ASP there are some Web-site design limitations. Microsoft SQL Server Integrated Security requires Windows NT Challenge/Response authentication in order to map user accounts to SQL Server accounts. This process requires that a token be created during the authentication process, and that the token require a user password to create a private encryption key. Because of this, the token can only be created on a domain controller or the logged-on user's computer. Also note that Windows NT 4.0 does not allow such tokens to be forwarded.

After a Web browser is authenticated by IIS, an authenticated connection to the SQL Server is not possible. At this point, when IIS attempts to connect to SQL Server using Windows NT Challenge/Response authentication, IIS will not have the necessary information to complete the authentication process.

You can work around this limitation by doing the following:

- **Use SQL Server Standard Security**   This involves passing the user ID and password across the Internet or intranet. This is not secure unless it is performed over an SSL connection.

- **Host IIS and SQL Server on the same machine**   Eliminate the need for IIS to create an authenticated connection to SQL Server. Instead of using a DSN that looks to the network for the SQL Server, use one that looks directly to the local machine.This can be done by using the "(local)" setting in a System DSN.

- **Use Basic authentication instead of Windows NT Challenge/Response in IIS**   By using Basic authentication, the password is UUEncoded and sent to IIS during the authentication process. With the password, IIS can now complete the Windows NT Challenge/Response Authentication process when connect to SQL Server. This method is not secure because Basic Authentication does not encrypt the password, rather the password is UUEncoded. UUEncoded passwords can be decrypted by anyone about to sniff network packets over the Internet or intranet.

- **Map the Anonymous user account from IIS to a guest account in SQL Server**   This method assumes that all users will have the same level of privileges to the SQL Server resources. This method is most often the *least* acceptable option.

An End-to-End Example

In the following scenario, a travel site called Exploration Air has developed a Web-based employee benefits application using IIS. The application can be accessed from the Internet and corporate intranet. Because the application is open to the Internet, security must be high.

All employees are validated before gaining access to the server, and all data is encrypted to prevent people from "sniffing" the data as it moves across the Internet. The benefits application in this scenario deals with medical, dental, legal assistance, stock options, stock purchase plans, investment, and relocation benefits.

To access these resources, the Web application requires data from several sources:

- A SQL Server database that contains all the corporate online benefits data. This is a complex database schema including 96 tables, 27 stored procedures, and 12 triggers. The database is approximately 270 MB in size and grows about 10 MB per month.

- A legacy Oracle database on UNIX that contains the original Human Resources information including payroll. For the purposes of this application, it is read-only and is used to verify the user.

- The IIS Configuration Store that is used to gather some configuration details about the server and display them on the benefits homepage.

- A "hit count" file that keeps a list of the number of times the home page has been accessed.

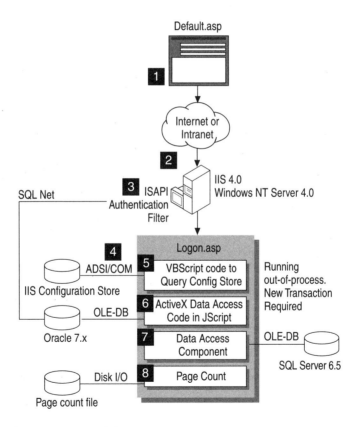

Figure 8.10   Anatomy of the benefits Web Application at Exploration Air

This scenario involves eight main steps:

- Step 1: User logon.
- Step 2: An ISAPI authentication filter.
- Step 3: IIS attempts to authenticate the user.
- Step 4: IIS loads the Logon page, Logon.asp.
- Step 5: Logon.asp attempts to read data from the configuration store.
- Step 6: ADO performs a lookup on the Human Resources page.
- Step 7: A data access component written in Visual Basic 5.0 performs a complex update.
- Step 8: The page count is updated using a Page Count component.

In each step, issues that could prevent you from proceeding to the next are outlined.

Step 1: User logon.

The user is prompted to enter some sort of user-authentication information on a page called Default.htm. The information is collected in an HTML form and posted to the server using an SSL session. Security problems at this stage are unlikely.

Issues to consider:

- With SSL, use the HTTPS protocol rather than HTTP. Failure to do so will yield a 403;4 error (SSL required).
- Make sure that the server certificate is not out of date, or it could be rejected by the browser.
- Problems can occur if the administrator has set up .asp files so that they won't process HTTP POST methods. Although this is unlikely, with IIS you can restrict HTTP method types if necessary.

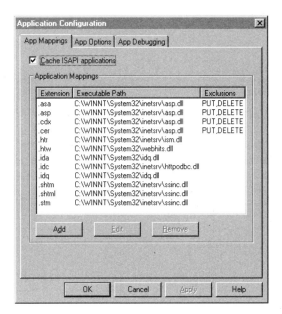

Figure 8.11   Setting HTTP method exclusion

Step 2: An ISAPI authentication filter.

ISAPI filters are quite common for custom logging and authentication, although with the advent of ASP the latter is becoming less popular. ISAPI filters are implemented as dynamic link libraries (DLLs).

You can use an ISAPI filter to receive notification of various events during the processing of HTTP requests. Filters are loaded when you start IIS, and are kept in memory until you shut IIS down. Once a filter is loaded, it indicates the events that IIS should send notification about. Subsequently, IIS will notify the filter each time one of the registered events occurs.

One type of notification is the Authentication notification. The ISAPI filter is notified when an initial request is made by the client, and can then make decisions about whether to allow or deny access to the server. In the case of Exploration Air, this filter takes the user name and password entered in step 1 and uses this to perform a database query. If the name and password combination is correct, the user is allowed access to the Benefits Web application. ISAPI filters are commonly used for custom logging and authentication.

Problems can occur if:

- The ISAPI filter rejects the user for some reason, probably based on some data in the Human Resources database.
- The user types in a name or password incorrectly, or the database is out of synch.
- The UNIX server has crashed or the SQL*Net connection is failing. Check the Oracle database logs for any further clues, and use Oracle Trace for low-level information.

Step 3: IIS attempts to authenticate the user.

There are a number of steps that take place here, including IP and domain name restrictions.

Issues to consider:

- At this point the user will be logged on as either an anonymous user or a normal Windows NT account. You can verify this by looking in the Windows NT audit log.

Step 4: IIS Loads the Logon page, Logon.asp.

Logon.asp is loaded by IIS in a separate memory space. This is done for robustness reasons. Eventually, this option will be turned off once the code is more trustworthy.

Also, Logon. asp includes the following at the top of the page:

```
<%@ Transaction = Requires_New %>
```

This tells IIS that it must start a new transaction for any component or data access which supports transactions. In the case of Logon.asp this includes the Visual Basic 5.0 data access component and the ADO code performing the Oracle query. MTS is used to control the transaction.

Issues to consider:

- Any Web application that is marked to run in a separate memory space (out-of-process) runs in the security context of a special user account called IWAM_*computername*. However, the process will impersonate the calling user (for example IUSR_*computername*) before accessing any resource. You can verify this in the Windows NT Audit Log.

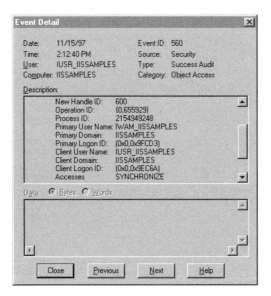

Figure 8.12   Audit log entry showing primary user and client user access to a file in an out-of-process Web application. The Primary User Name identifies the account under which the process is running (the out-of-process Web application), and the Client Account Name identifies the account that is being impersonated while accessing the resource.

Note   Out-of-process applications run as a special account, IWAM_*computername*, not the one with which you logged on to the server. Access to a resource is achieved by impersonating the caller first.

- While not a security limitation per se, you need to keep in mind the transaction semantics that are now in place. If a transactional component fails or explicitly rolls back its part of the transaction, other transactional components will lose their changes.

Step 5: Logon.asp attempts to read data from configuration store.

Using Active Directory Services Interfaces (ADSI), the page tries to read data from the configuration store. The code looks like this:

```
<%
Dim oADSI
Dim strAppName
Set oRoot=GetObject("IIS://LocalHost/W3SVC/1/Benefits")
strAppName=oRoot.AppFriendlyName
Set oRoot=Nothing
%>
```

This code has the friendly name "Benefits application." If an administrator decides to change a comment about the application using the IIS administration tools, it will be reflected automatically in the Logon. asp page. Once again, you can verify this in the Windows NT Audit Log.

This can fail because:

- Accessing the configuration store requires Administration privileges on the Web site in question.

Step 6: ADO performs a lookup on the Human Resources page.

This is a straightforward database lookup, similar to that performed by the ISAPI filter in step 2.

Issues to consider:

- Problems can occur if the user does not have access to the database being queried.

- If the database connection is being performed with ODBC, use the ODBC Trace tool to check for any access problems. Check the Oracle database logs for further clues. Use Oracle Trace for low-level information.

Step 7: Data access component written in Visual Basic 5.0 performs a complex update.

This section assumes knowledge of an RDBMS such as Microsoft SQL Server.

The Visual Basic 5.0 component is an ActiveX DLL that understands transactions. The component contains data-access code written using ADO to access a Microsoft SQL Server 6.5 stored procedure.

The stored procedure performs a SELECT from two tables and then an INSERT into another. The last table also has an insert trigger.

Issues to consider:

- If you are attempting to access SQL Server using Integrated security from an ASP application, you can have security problems because the account used to log you on to IIS may not be valid on SQL Server.

- The user account might not have access to the appropriate SQL Server objects (tables, stored procedures, and so on). Check the **Object Permissions** dialog box in SQL Enterprise Manager.

- Enable Auditing in the SQL Enterprise Manager for successful and failed SQL Server logon.

- If the database connection is being performed with ODBC, then use the ODBC Trace tool to check for any access problems.
- Check the SQL Server Error Log.
- Use the SQL Trace tool to check low-level traffic.

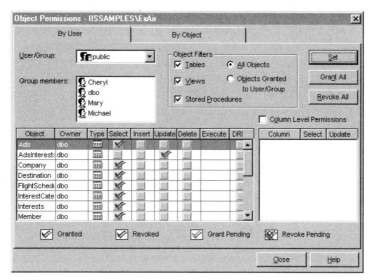

Figure 8.13   Object Permissions in SQL Server. Note that public users do not have *Select* permission on the *AdsInterests* table. This means that most users won't be able to view the data in the table.

- The INSERT trigger could be failing. For example, it may be performing some business-rule check which is failing so the insert is rolled back. Check the trigger by selecting **Manager Triggers** on the table in question.

Step 8: Page count is updated using a Page Count component.

Web pages are often counted. Normally when a user accesses a page, some server code is executed to open a file, increment a count in that file, and then resave it.

Issues to consider:

- This can be a cause of failure because the user account performing the request might not have access to the file on the server where the page hit information is stored. Remedy this by allowing Everyone (Read and Write) access. You can verify this by auditing for file/object access:

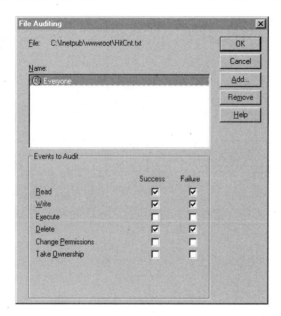

Figure 8.14   Auditing access to the Hitcnt.txt file

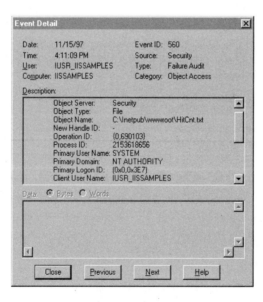

Figure 8.15   Access denied. IUSR_IISSAMPLES doesn't have access to the file.

Defending Against Malicious Attacks

Malicious attacks take many forms including:

- Attempts to access restricted resources.
- Attempts to make a computer system unusable by consuming system resources. These are often called denial-of-service attacks.

Note To keep up-to-date with security issues, check the Microsoft Knowledge Base at http://www.support.microsoft.com/support/ regularly.

Accessing Restricted Resources

This includes attempts to gain access to restricted directories, files, and printers. Attempted file access is by far the most common.

Denial-of-Service Attacks

A denial-of-service attack occurs when a user consumes so much of the shared resources—such as CPU consumption, modems, telephone lines, disk space, printer paper, memory utilization, and so on—that none is left for others to use. A common way to launch such an attack is to set up a tool to automate access to a shared resource, quickly consuming CPU resources on the server.

TCP/IP SYN Attack

A SYN attack (sometimes called SYN flooding), targets computers running TCP/IP. It is a protocol-level attack that can render a computer's network services unavailable. You may be subject to a SYN attack if some or all network services are rendered unavailable and error messages such as the following appear on the network client screen: "The connection has been reset by the remote host."

How SYN Flooding Works

SYN flooding works as follows:

- A TCP connection request (SYN) is sent to the target computer. The source IP address in the packet is "spoofed," or replaced with an address that is either not in use on the Internet, or one that belongs to another computer. An attacker will send many of these TCP SYNs in order to tie up as many resources as possible on the target computer.

- Upon receiving the connection request, the target computer allocates resources to handle and track the new connection. It then responds with a "SYN-ACK." In this case, the response is sent to the nonexistent IP address.

- There is no response to the SYN-ACK. A computer running default-configured Windows NT 3.5x or 4.0 will retransmit the SYN-ACK five times, doubling the time out value after each retransmission. The initial time out value is three seconds, so retries are attempted at 3, 6, 12, 24, and 48 seconds. After the last retransmission, 96 seconds are allowed to pass before the computer gives up on receiving a response, and deallocates the resources that were set aside earlier for the connection. The total elapsed time that resources are in use is 189 seconds.

For more information see CERT Advisory CA-96.21 at ftp://info.cert.org/pub/cert_advisories/.

How to Verify Your Computer is Under a SYN Attack

If you suspect that your computer is the target of a SYN attack, you can type the following command at a command prompt to view connections in the "SYN_RECEIVED" state: **netstat -n -p tcp**

If a large number of connections are in the SYN_RECEIVED state, as in the example below, it is possible that the system is under attack. A network analyzer can be used to track down the problem further, and it might be necessary to contact your ISP for assistance in attempting to trace the source.

```
Active Connections

Proto       Local Address         Foreign Address       State

TCP         127.0.0.1:1030        127.0.0.1:1032        ESTABLISHED

TCP         127.0.0.1:1032        127.0.0.1:1030        ESTABLISHED

TCP         10.57.8.190:21        10.57.14.154:1256     SYN_RECEIVED

TCP         10.57.8.190:21        10.57.14.154:1257     SYN_RECEIVED

TCP         10.57.8.190:21        10.57.14.154:1258     SYN_RECEIVED

TCP         10.57.8.190:21        10.57.14.154:1259     SYN_RECEIVED

TCP         10.57.8.190:21        10.57.14.154:1260     SYN_RECEIVED

TCP         10.57.8.190:21        10.57.14.154:1261     SYN_RECEIVED

TCP         10.57.8.190:21        10.57.14.154:1262     SYN_RECEIVED

TCP         10.57.8.190:21        10.57.14.154:1263     SYN_RECEIVED

TCP         10.57.8.190:21        10.57.14.154:1264     SYN_RECEIVED

TCP         10.57.8.190:21        10.57.14.154:1265     SYN_RECEIVED

TCP         10.57.8.190:21        10.57.14.154:1266     SYN_RECEIVED

TCP         10.57.8.190:4801      10.57.14.221:139      TIME_WAIT
```

Figure 8.16   A sample trace from netstat -n -p tcp showing a computer that is possibly being attacked by a SYN flood.

The effect of tying up connection resources varies depending upon the TCP/IP stack and applications listening on the TCP port. For most stacks, there is a limit on the number of connections that can be in the half-open (SYN_RECEIVED) state. Once the limit is reached for a given TCP port, the target computer responds with a reset to all further connection requests until resources are freed.

Resolution

Windows NT 4.0 Service Pack 3 (required to run IIS 4.0) includes several fixes.

Tcpip.sys Times Out "Half-Open" Connections Faster

With the current version of Tcpip.sys you can control the number of times a response to a TCP connection request (SYN-ACK) is retransmitted. Control is handled through the following registry parameter:

```
HKEY_LOCAL_MACHINE
  \SYSTEM
    \CurrentControlSet
      \Services
        \NetBt
          \Parameters
            \TcpMaxConnectResponseRetransmissions
```

Value Type: REG_DWORD
Valid Range: 0-0xFFFFFFFF
Default: 3

The default value for this parameter is 3. The following table shows Windows NT 4.0 TCP/IP behavior for various values of this parameter:

Table 8.2   TcpMaxConnectResponseRetransmissions values

Value	Retransmission Times	Elapsed	Comments
3	3, 6, and 12 seconds	45 seconds	Cleanup 24 secs after last retx
2	3 and 6 seconds	21 seconds	Cleanup 12 secs after last retx
1	3 seconds	9 seconds	Cleanup 6 secs after last retx

This parameter changes the default time that it takes to clean up a half-open TCP connection from 189 seconds to 45 seconds. A site that is under heavy attack might set the value as low as 1. You can also set the value of this parameter to 0, but doing so would cause the SYN-ACKs not to be retransmitted at all, and they would time-out in 3 seconds. Also, with the value this low, legitimate connection attempts from distant clients could fail.

NetBT Has a Higher, Configurable Backlog

NetBT (NetBIOS over TCP/IP) uses TCP port 139, and is used by Microsoft Network Services such as file and print sharing. Version 3.51 and 4.0 NetBT has a "backlog" of available connections that is based on the number of NetBT clients (such as the redirector, server and any NetBIOS applications running). On a typical server, this number will be between 7 and 11. The current version of NetBT automatically allocates more connection blocks as needed, in a configurable manner. On a connection event, it checks to see if the number of free blocks is less than 2 and, if so, adds an "increment" number of blocks, where "increment" is configurable in the registry as shown below:

```
HKEY_LOCAL_MACHINE
    \SYSTEM
        \CurrentControlSet
            \Services
                \NetBt
                    \Parameters
                        \BacklogIncrement
```

Value Type: REG_DWORD
Valid Range: 1–0x14 (1–20 decimal)
Default: 3

Each connection block consumes 78 bytes of memory. The total number of connection blocks that can be allocated by NetBT is also registry configurable:

```
HKEY_LOCAL_MACHINE
    \SYSTEM
        \CurrentControlSet
            \Services
                \NetBt
                    \Parameters
                        \MaxConnBackLog
```

Value Type: REG_DWORD
Valid Range: 1–0x9c40 (1–40,000 decimal)
Default: 1000

MaxConnBackLog defaults to 1000, but can be set as high as 40,000. Connection blocks are "scavenged," or recycled, when the SYN-ACK retransmission timer expires and TCP fails the connection attempt.

Afd.sys Has Been Modified to Withstand Large Numbers of "Half-Open" Connections Efficiently

Windows Sockets applications such as FTP and Web servers have their connection attempts handled by Afd.sys. Afd.sys has been modified to support large numbers of connections in the "half-open" state without denying access to legitimate clients. It does so by allowing the administrator to configure a dynamic backlog. The current version of Afd.sys supports four new registry parameters that can be used to control the dynamic backlog behavior.

EnableDynamicBacklog is a global switch to enable or disable dynamic backlog. It defaults to 0 (off). This setting provides no change from the existing versions. Setting it to 1 enables the new dynamic backlog feature.

```
HKEY_LOCAL_MACHINE
  \SYSTEM
    \CurrentControlSet
      \Services
        \AFD
          \Parameters
            \EnableDynamicBacklog
```

Value Type: REG_DWORD
Valid Range: 0,1
Default: 0
Suggested value for a system under heavy attack: 1

MinimumDynamicBacklog controls the minimum number of free connections allowed on a listening endpoint. If the number of free connections drops below this value, then a thread is queued to create additional free connections. This value should not be made too large, because the dynamic backlog code engages whenever the number of free connections falls below this value. Too large a value can cause a performance reduction.

```
HKEY_LOCAL_MACHINE
  \SYSTEM
    \CurrentControlSet
      \Services
        \AFD
          \Parameters
            \MinimumDynamicBacklog
```

Value Type: REG_DWORD
Valid Range: 0–0xFFFFFFFF
Default: 0
Suggested value for a system under heavy attack: 20

MaximumDynamicBacklog controls the maximum number of "quasi-free" connections allowed on a listening endpoint. "Quasi-free" connections include the number of free connections plus those connections in a half-connected (SYN_RECEIVED) state. No attempt is made to create additional free connections if doing so would exceed this value.

HKEY_LOCAL_MACHINE
  \SYSTEM
    \CurrentControlSet
     \Services
      \AFD
       \Parameters
        \MaximumDynamicBacklog

Value Type: REG_DWORD
Valid Range: 0–0xFFFFFFFF
Default: 0

Suggested value for a system under heavy attack: This is memory dependent. The value should not exceed 5,000 for each 32 MB of RAM installed in the server, in order to prevent exhaustion of the non-paged pool when under attack.

DynamicBacklogGrowthDelta controls the number of free connections to create when additional connections are necessary. Use this value with caution, because a large value could lead to explosive free connection allocations.

HKEY_LOCAL_MACHINE
  \SYSTEM
    \CurrentControlSet
     \Services
      \AFD
       \Parameters
        \DynamicBacklogGrowthDelta

Value Type: REG_DWORD
Valid Range: 0–0xFFFFFFFF
Default: 0
Suggested value for a system under heavy attack: 10 (0xa)

To take advantage of the changes to Afd.sys, Windows Sockets applications must specifically request a backlog greater than the value configured for **MinimumDynamicBacklog** when they issue their **listen()** call. Microsoft applications, such as IIS (which has a default backlog of 25), are configurable. Application-specific details are available from the Microsoft Knowledge Base at http://www.support.microsoft.com/support/.

Auditing Access with IIS Logs

You can use Internet Information Server logs to track access to your server. Logging is very flexible, and it can be used in conjunction with the Site Server Express or a database analysis tool to detect suspicious activity such as:

- Multiple failed commands, especially to the /Scripts directory or another directory configured for executable files.
- Attempts to upload files to the /Script directory or another directory configured for executable files.
- Attempts to access .bat or .cmd files and subvert their purpose.
- Attempts to send .bat or .cmd commands to the /Scripts directory or another directory configured for executable files.
- Excessive requests from a single IP address, attempting to overload or cause a denial-of-service attack.

IIS Security Checklist

You can use this list when configuring a computer running IIS to make sure that you include all of the recommended steps. This checklist is also available on the IIS Resource Kit CD.

General Information

Server Name	_____	Manufacturer	_____
Asset #	_____	Location	_____
Setup Date	_____	Set up by	_____

Windows NT Security Checklist

☐	Latest Service Pack and Hot-fixes applied	☐ Hard disk(s) formatted to NTFS
☐	Install/Enable Power Conditioner/UPS	☐ Domain controller type set to:
☐	OS/2 Subsystem removed	☐ POSIX Subsystem removed
☐	Audit log set to overwrite after ___days	☐ System boot time set to zero seconds
☐	Hide last logon user name	☐ Logon message changed
☐	Set password length to ___characters	☐ Remove **Shutdown** button from logon dialog
☐	Only admins can assign printers/drive letters	☐ Disable Guest account

☐ Unbind unnecessary network protocols

☐ Restrict TCP/UDP ports and IP protocols

☐ Protect registry from remote admin

☐ Rename Administrator account

☐ Use SYSKEY to protect account database

☐ Enable security auditing

☐ Remove all application and development software

☐ Physically secure computer

☐ Disable unnecessary services

☐ Unbind NetBIOS Interface from WINS Client (TCP/IP)

☐ Disable IP Routing

☐ Minimal user accounts and groups

☐ Install Passprop.dll and strengthen the administrator's password

☐ Set blank screen saver with short delay

☐ Update Emergency Repair Disk

Internet Information Server Checklist

☐ Install *minimal* Internet services required

☐ Set appropriate virtual directory permissions

☐ Migrate new Root Certificates by using Iisca.exe

☐ Set IP Address/DNS Address restrictions

☐ Logging enabled

☐ Index Server *only* indexing documentation

☐ Set appropriate authentication methods

☐ Set up Secure Sockets Layer

☐ Map Client Auth Certificates to Windows NT Accounts

☐ Placed executable content in (X) only location

☐ Executable content validated for trustworthiness

Resources

The following Web links and books provide additional information relevant to security issues.

Web Links

http://www.microsoft.com/security/
The Microsoft Security Advisor Web site.

http://www.microsoft.com/msdn/
The Microsoft Developer Network Web site.

Books

Amoroso, E. *Fundamentals of Computer Security Technology* (Prentice Hall, 1994).

Amoroso, E, and R. Sharp. *PCWeek Intranet & Internet Firewall Strategies* (ZD Press, 1996).

Anonymous. *Maximum Security: A Hacker's Guide to Protecting your Internet Site and Network* (Sams, 1997).

Castano, S., M. Fugini, Martella G., ct al. *Database Security* (Addison Wesley, 1994).

Cheswick W.R., and S.M. Bellovin. *Firewalls & Internet Security: Repelling the Wily Hacker* (Addison Wesley, 1994).

Davis, P.T., ed. *Securing Client/Server Networks* (McGraw-Hill, 1996).

Ford, W., and M.S. Baum. *Secure Electronic Commerce* (Prentice Hall, 1997).

Ford, W. *Computer Communications Security* (Prentice Hall, 1994).

Garfinkel, S. and G. Spafford. *Practical Unix & Internet Security* (O'Reilly & Assoc., 1996).

———. *Web Security & Commerce* (O'Reilly & Assoc., 1997).

———. *Practical Unix Security* (O'Reilly & Assoc., 1996).

Grimes, Richard. *Professional DCOM Programming* (WROX Press, 1997).

Hughes, L. *Actually Useful Internet Security Techniques* (New Riders, 1995).

Jackson, K.M., and J. Hruska. *Computer Security Reference Book* (CRC, 1992).

Kyas, O. *Internet Security—Risk Analysis, Strategies & Firewalls* (Thomson, 1996).

Lynch, D.C., and L. Lundquist. *Digital Money* (Wiley, 1995).

McGraw, G., and E. Felten. *Java Security, Hostile Applets, Holes & Antidotes* (Wiley, 1996).

Neumann, P. *Computer Related Risks* (Addison Wesley, 1995).

Rubin A.D., D. Geer, and M.J. Ranum. *Web Security Sourcebook* (Wiley, 1997).

Russell, D., and G.T. Gangemi. *Computer Security Basics* (O'Reilly & Assoc., 1991).

Schneier, B. *Applied Cryptography*. 2nd Edition (Wiley, 1996).

Stallings, W. *Protect Your Privacy* (Prentice Hall, 1995).

Stoll, C. *The Cuckoo's Egg* (Pan, 1995).

Web Security—A Matter of Trust (World Wide Web Journal, Vol. No. 3 Summer) (O'Reilly & Assoc., 1997).

Windows NT 4.0 Server Resource Kit, Windows NT Server Internet Guide (Microsoft Press, 1996). Chapter 3, "Server Security on the Internet."

Windows NT 4.0 Server Resource Kit: Supplement 1 (Microsoft Press, 1997). Chapter 1, "Securing Your Web Site."

C H A P T E R   9

Accessing Legacy Applications and Data

9

This chapter describes how you can use Microsoft development tools and production software packages to make legacy applications and data available to Web applications based on Internet Information Server 4.0 (IIS).

In this chapter:

- Identifying Strategies
- Integrating IIS and Legacy Applications
- Gaining Access to Legacy File Data
- Replicating Legacy Databases
- Migrating Transaction Processes
- Resources

Identifying Strategies

To employ Web technology to best advantage, an enterprise must make its business applications and data easily accessible—over the Internet or a company intranet—to its employees, key business partners, and the public. This goal is often difficult to achieve because mission-critical data is stored in host-based file systems and relational databases on IBM mainframes or AS/400 computers (estimates run as high as 80 percent for many large corporations and government agencies).

Delivering large amounts of legacy data to a wide audience has always been problematic because:

- Hardware and system software is expensive.
- Standards are proprietary and not widely supported outside the legacy environment.
- Development costs are high.

This chapter outlines four strategies for accessing applications and data in MVS (mainframe) and OS/400 (AS/400 minicomputer) systems running within SNA (Systems Network Architecture) environments. You can:

- Integrate host applications running in legacy environments with IIS by connecting host transaction processors to Windows NT Server 4.0 by using Microsoft SNA Server 4.0 and Microsoft COM Transaction Integrator for CICS and IMS (COM TI). COM TI is included on the IIS Resource Kit CD.
- Use Microsoft SNA Server 4.0 and Microsoft OLE DB Provider for AS/400 and VSAM (Data Provider) to access legacy files at the record level and send the data to the Windows NT environment.
- Use Microsoft Host Data Replicator (HDR) to acquire host database structures and replicate them for Microsoft SQL Server and IIS 4.0.
- Move the automated processes from the restrictive and expensive legacy environment to the open, more cost-effective Windows NT environment with IIS 4.0 and Microsoft Transaction Server (MTS).

Connecting to SNA

Each of the legacy access strategies discussed in this chapter requires connections to IBM host computers through SNA. To understand how each strategy is implemented, you need a basic understanding of how the SNA environment is constructed, how to connect to SNA resources, and how to exploit these resources.

The SNA Environment

SNA is IBM's architecture for designing and implementing computer networks. To communicate user data over SNA, a session must be established between two Logical Units (LUs), one on the host system and the other on the client system. Because LU 6.2 is a peer-to-peer protocol, either the mainframe host or the client can initiate a session. By using this protocol, computers running Windows NT Server 4.0 can participate in the SNA environment and gain access to legacy host environments including transaction processing (TP) monitors, VSAM and AS/400 files (both flat and unstructured), and database data structures, such as DB/2 data tables.

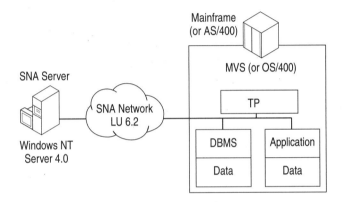

Figure 9.1   The SNA environment

Connecting with Microsoft SNA Server

You can use SNA Server 4.0 to connect to the SNA environment from Windows NT 4.0 and IIS. SNA Server translates Windows NT Server 4.0 communications to LU 6.2.

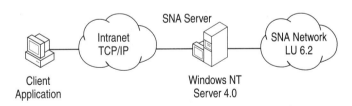

Figure 9.2   SNA Server Connects Windows NT to SNA

Developing and Deploying under Windows NT and IIS

With SNA Server LU 6.2 capabilities, you can develop and deploy applications that access the legacy environment from the Windows NT side of the connection.

- Software tools used to gain access to SNA applications and data reside on Windows NT platforms and take advantage of the unified administrative tools and lower-cost resources in the Windows NT environment.

- Application development and modification is accomplished in the Windows NT environment as well. This means that you can avoid the high overhead associated with development and modification of legacy host-side resources.

Integrating IIS and Legacy Applications

For years, IBM has encouraged its customers to code their business logic into programs that are separate from their terminal access logic. Many Information Services (IS) organizations have responded by coding their business rules into TP programs that execute under CICS or IMS. Gaining access to these programs on the host side from the Windows NT environment can open up the business rules for an entire application, such as inventory control or budgeting, creating new opportunities for distributed applications.

Using tools and techniques to access business logic offers significant advantages over methods such as "screen-scraping" data from terminal emulation programs because:

- All the data and processes that the business logic allows are accessible, rather than the limited data and processes accessible to individual terminal access program logic.

- There is no requirement for a terminal emulator on the Windows NT Server platform because the processing involves no terminal access software.

- The integration of legacy processes with IIS-based processes is easier to accomplish and less costly to develop.

The COM Transaction Integrator

The Microsoft COM Transaction Integrator for CICS and IMS (COM TI) is a technology for integrating legacy TPs running on mainframes with Web application and transaction processes running in the Windows NT environment.

COM TI reduces the effort required to develop applications integrating COBOL (COmmon Business Oriented Language) programs running on mainframes with Automation clients running Windows NT Server, Windows NT Workstation, Windows 95, or any other computer that supports Automation. Specifically:

- COM TI can automatically create a recordset of the data returned from a mainframe TP program. The recordset data, formatted in a tabular array, can then be accessed by ASP.

- COM TI coordinates legacy TPs on the mainframe with transaction processes managed by Microsoft Transaction Server (MTS), thus extending the MTS transaction environment to include transactions managed by CICS or IMS on an IBM mainframe computer.

- COM TI development tools map COBOL data declarations to Automation data types.

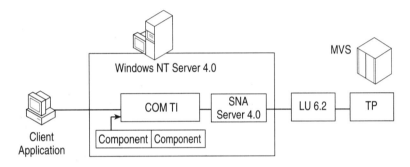

Figure 9.3   COM TI is a proxy for the mainframe.

Functional Overview of the COM Transaction Integrator

The following list summarizes how COM TI gains access to CICS applications and integrates data returned from CICS TPs with Internet Information Server through ActiveX Data Objects (ADO) and MTS.

- **Gain access to CICS TPs**   COM TI directly supports any TP that executes in CICS or IMS. Because COM TI can access CICS programs, developers can issue application calls to the legacy environment by using CICS to gain access to any program under its control. This includes DB2 databases, VSAM files, or IMS databases.

- **Redirect method calls**   COM TI is a generic proxy for the mainframe. It intercepts method calls from the client application and redirects those calls to TPs running on the mainframe. For example, when an Internet browser sends data that ASP interprets as requiring COM TI, IIS forwards the data to COM TI.

- **Reformat method calls**   When COM TI intercepts the method call, it converts and formats the method's parameters from Automation data types into IBM System 390 mainframe data types.

- **Handle return values**   COM TI handles the return of all output parameters and values from the mainframe and converts and reformats them for IIS as needed.

COM TI runs under Windows NT, not on the SNA host. Its processing takes place on a computer running Windows NT Server, and does not require any new executable code to be installed on the mainframe, or on the desktop computer that is running the Internet browser. COM TI communicates through SNA Server and uses standard communication protocols (for example, LU 6.2 provided by Microsoft SNA Server version 4.0) to communicate between the computer running Windows NT Server and the mainframe TP.

COM TI Development Scenarios

The following two scenarios illustrate how the COM TI environment can be used to develop applications that integrate TPs with ASP.

Scenario One: Integrating Legacy TP Data Using COM Transaction Integrator

This scenario illustrates how to connect a Windows NT–based Web site to an existing COBOL TP. Suppose you want to dynamically add content from a legacy database running under CICS on an IBM mainframe computer to a Web application running under IIS. You can begin by using ASP to interpret user requests and format the data returned by the mainframe application. Next, you can use COM TI to develop a component that will process the method calls from the IIS environment and the mainframe environment.

This scenario involves six main steps:

- Step 1 (setup time): Configuring COM TI.

- Step 2 (design time): Defining required methods and parameters.

- Step 3 (design time): Writing the application.

- Step 4 (design time): Testing the application.

- Step 5 (deployment): Deploying the application components.

- Step 6 (post-deployment): Maintaining the application.

Step 1: Configuring COM TI

To develop a COM TI component, you must meet the following system requirements:

- Microsoft Windows NT Server 4.0 or Windows NT Workstation 4.0 updated with Service Pack 3.
- Microsoft IIS 4.0 with Microsoft Transaction Server 2.0.
- Microsoft Windows NT Client for SNA Server 4.0.
- Microsoft Data Access Components 1.5.

Additionally, the following COM TI components must be installed:

- The administration component, which collects information about the user's SNA environment.
- The run-time component, which intercepts the method calls to the mainframe and uses the COM TI–created component library to perform the actual conversion and formatting of the method parameters. In addition, the run-time component interacts with SNA Server and builds LU 6.2 packets, which are sent to the mainframe.
- Development tool components, featuring the component builder, a GUI used to create component libraries from mainframe COBOL programs.

The component builder is installed as an add-in to Microsoft Visual Basic 5.0, and does not need to be installed on the same system as the other components. Developers who are not using Visual Basic 5.0 can use the component builder as a stand-alone tool.

Step 2: Defining Required Methods and Parameters

To accomplish this step:

- Acquire the COBOL source code from the mainframe using a file transfer mechanism, such as the FTP/AFTP gateway that is delivered with SNA Server.
- Use the COBOL Import Wizard to:
  1. Select the COBOL source code.
  2. Specify the methods and mainframe TP names.
  3. Select input, output, and return value parameters.
- When necessary, change the mappings between the COBOL and Automation data types.
- Use the component builder to make a COM TI component library (.tlb), a standard library that can be used by client software and MTS.

If you have changed the data type mapping in the COBOL code, there are two more actions required in this step:

- Use the component builder to generate new COBOL declarations.
- Update the mainframe program with the new COBOL data declarations. This is the only instance requiring modifications to the mainframe environment.

Step 3: Writing the Application

To accomplish this step:

- Write the client in a language that supports referencing of Automation objects, such as Microsoft Visual Basic, Visual C++, or Visual J++.
- Add the appropriate COM TI component library to the references list in the project and add the references of the component in the program.
- Invoke methods as appropriate throughout the application.

If the existing mainframe TP is to be modified, do one of the following:

- Perform the modification on the mainframe.
- Use a Windows-based COBOL development environment, such as Microfocus COBOL, then move the code to the mainframe.

Step 4: Testing the Application

If the mainframe TP is unchanged, the TP does not require testing. If the TP has been modified, then the COBOL program should be tested independently to ensure that it runs correctly in its own environment.

Test the new application as follows:

- Ensure that the COM TI component library is registered in MTS.
- Test the mainframe TP independently if it has been modified in any way.
- Test the newly developed COM TI component independently to ensure that it is working correctly.
- Test the application, running the mainframe TP.

Step 5: Deploying Application Components

To deploy the client-side of the application, the following software components must be installed on each production computer:

- Microsoft Windows NT Server 4.0 or Windows NT Workstation 4.0 (or later) updated with Service Pack 3.
- Microsoft Windows NT Client for SNA Server 4.0.
- Microsoft Transaction Server 2.0.
- COM TI administration and run-time components.
- COM TI component libraries registered in MTS.
- Client applications accessing COM TI components.

Step 6: Maintaining the Application

As changes are made to the mainframe TP program, do one or more of the following, as appropriate:

- Acquire the COBOL source code from the mainframe.
- Use the COBOL Import Wizard to re-specify the method names and host TP names, and to re-select the input, output, and return parameter values.

What if the Required Mainframe TP does not Exist?

In this case, you must modify steps 2 and 3 of the scenario by developing a TP to run under CICS on the mainframe host.

In step 2, use the COM TI component builder to:

- Enter the methods and parameters for the application.
- Add information about the name and location of the new TP.
- Change the default mappings produced by the component builder, if necessary.
- Create the COM TI component library.

In step 3:

- Write the mainframe TP, either on the mainframe or in the Windows environment using a product such as Microfocus COBOL, then move the program to the mainframe for testing.

Scenario Two: Extending Transactions with COM TI

When deployed in the Windows NT Server environment, COM TI can extend MTS transactions to include mainframe TPs running under CICS and IMS.

A developer can use each of the following steps to connect a Windows NT–based Web site to an existing COBOL TP program for the purpose of making legacy data available to ASP. In this scenario, additional tasks are needed in order to extend MTS transactions to the mainframe-based transactions under the control of CICS.

Step 1: Configuring COM TI

To develop the COM TI object, you must meet the following system requirements:

- Microsoft Windows NT Server 4.0 or Windows NT Workstation 4.0 (or later) updated with Service Pack 3.
- Microsoft IIS 4.0.
- Microsoft Windows NT Client for SNA Server 4.0.
- Microsoft Transaction Server 2.0.

Additionally, the following COM TI components must be installed (for descriptions of each of the components, see Scenario One):

- The administration component.
- The run-time component.
- The component builder.

Step 2: Defining Required Methods and Parameters

To make the mainframe TP data available to IIS, perform the following tasks:

- Acquire the COBOL source code from the mainframe using a file transfer mechanism such as the FTP/AFTP gateway that is delivered with SNA Server.
- Use the COBOL Import Wizard to:
    1. Select the COBOL source code.
    2. Specify the methods and mainframe TP names.
    3. Select input, output, and return value parameters.
- When necessary, change the mappings between the COBOL and Automation data types.
- Use the component builder to make a COM TI component library (.tlb). This is a standard library that can be used by client software and MTS.

If you have changed the data type mapping in the COBOL code, there are two more actions required in this step:

- Use the component builder to generate new COBOL declarations.

- Update the mainframe program with the new COBOL data declarations. This is the only instance requiring modifications to the mainframe environment.

Step 3: Writing the Application

To accomplish this step:

- Write the client in a language that supports referencing of Automation objects, such as Microsoft Visual Basic, Visual C++, or Visual J++.

- Add the appropriate COM TI component library to the references list in the project and add the references of the component in the program.

- Invoke methods as appropriate throughout the application.

- Define any transaction-related attributes in the COM TI component. The attributes will handle transactions in a manner transparent to the client application (for example, an IIS application using Active Server Pages). The COM TI component will call both MTS/DTC (distributed transaction coordinator) and the TP running under CICS.

Step 4: Testing the Application

If the mainframe TP is unchanged, it does not require testing. If the TP has been modified, then the COBOL program should be tested independently to ensure that it runs correctly in its own environment.

Test the new application as follows:

- Test the mainframe TP independently if it has been modified in any way.

- Test the newly developed COM TI component independently to ensure that it is working correctly.

- Test the application completely, driving the COM TI object with the client application and running the mainframe TP.

- Carry out a transaction test—test the COM TI object with the transactions made available to check operation between COM TI and MTS in conjunction with COM TI and the TP running under CICS.

Step 5: Deploying Application Components

Each of the following applications must be installed on the production computer before you deploy the client side of the application:

- Microsoft Windows NT Server 4.0 or Windows NT Workstation 4.0 updated with Service Pack 3.
- Microsoft Windows NT Client for SNA Server 4.0.
- Microsoft Transaction Server 2.0.
- COM TI administration and run-time components.
- COM TI component library.
- Client application accessing COM TI components.

Step 6: Maintaining the Application

If you change the mainframe TP application, you must do at least one of the following:

- Acquire the COBOL source from the mainframe.
- Use the COBOL Import Wizard to re-specify the method names and host TP names, and re-select the input, output, and return parameter values.

Using COM TI with IMS

Current versions of COM TI do not support transactional semantics (also known as a two-phase commit) under the IMS subsystem. However, you can access an IMS/DB database transaction through a CICS subsystem front-end TP program. That is, if the mainframe environment supports CICS transaction processing against IMS/DB, you can extend MTS transactional semantics to the IMS/DB database. In this case COM TI provides the same services as any other TP running under CICS. If you do not require transactional semantics, and just want to gain access to your data, you can access IMS directly.

Gaining Access to Legacy File Data

The following section describes how you can incorporate legacy file systems into your Web applications by employing a data provider to files at the record level and move the data to the IIS environment.

Legacy File Data and IIS

To develop Web applications that deliver data stored in VSAM and AS/400 files, you need to be able to gain access to VSAM and AS/400 files from the Windows NT environment. You can do this by making the data available to data consumer applications running under ASP:

- Access legacy file systems running under MVS and OS/400 to retrieve the business data stored in them.

- Integrate legacy data with applications and data in the IIS environment using the OLE DB Provider for AS/400 and VSAM.

Gaining Access to VSAM and AS/400 files with OLE DB and ADO

The OLE DB Provider for AS/400 and VSAM (Data Provider) is the first application to make record-level mainframe VSAM and AS/400 files systems available to ASP applications. The Data Provider makes it possible for consumer ASP applications to gain access to the mission-critical data available in those file systems. The Data Provider ships with Microsoft SNA Server 4.0, Windows NT Client for SNA Server 4.0, and the SNA Server SDK 4.0.

For more information about developing ASP applications, see Chapter 5, "Developing Web Applications."

The Data Provider and the Demand for Legacy File Data

Microsoft released a beta-test version of the OLE DB Provider for AS/400 and VSAM in the summer of 1997, and the Microsoft SNA site received over 600 registrations and download requests during the first four weeks that the beta test kits were available.

This response is not surprising. There are over 400,000 AS/400 computers and about 30,000 mainframe computers deployed world-wide. Some run database management systems, but virtually every one of them stores information in VSAM data sets, and nearly every AS/400 hundred site stores data in conventional file structures—all accessible with the Data Provider.

Functional Overview of the Data Provider

The OLE DB Provider for AS/400 and VSAM (Data Provider) comprises two core components:

- An OLE DB–compatible data provider that insulates the complexities of APPC (LU 6.2) programming from the OLE DB or ADO programmer
- An SNA Distributed Data Management (DDM) transaction management program that runs as a Windows NT service under Windows NT 4.0, or as an application under Windows 95.

The following list summarizes the uses of the Data Provider:

- From Windows NT, you can gain access to VSAM and AS/400 file systems through the IBM DDM protocol server components installed on many IBM host systems. There is no need to install Microsoft software on the host system.
- You can use customizable applications to read and write to VSAM and AS/400 files that are in place on IBM host computers. There is no need to migrate the files to the Windows NT environment.
- You can gain access to fixed and variable logical record-length classes and file and record locking, while preserving file and record attributes.
- You can gain access to most AS/400 file types (both physical and logical) and most popular mainframe dataset types: sequential (SAM); VSAM key-sequenced (KSDS), VSAM entry-sequenced (ESDS), VSAM relative record (RRDS), and partitioned (PDS/PDSE).

Capitalize on Development with the OLE DB/DDM Driver

The Data Provider makes it possible to integrate unstructured legacy file data with data in the Windows NT environment.

- The DDM protocol provides program-to-program communications through SNA Server (version 4.0 or later), and native host protocols (such as LU 6.2). No custom development is required on the host for SNA communications.
- IBM DDM servers are available on host systems supporting record-level access to files. For example, Distribute File Manager, a component of IBM DFSMS (Data Facility Storage Management Subsystem) (V1R2 or later), is one target DDM server installed on many mainframes running under MVS or OS/390. On AS/400 computers, OS/400 (V2R2 or later) runs as a DDM server. The Data Provider communicates with Data File Manager and OS/400 through Advanced Program-to-Program Communications (APPC).

- The Data Provider makes it easy for developers to gain access to high-level component interfaces such as OLE DB or ADO. It supports development in Visual Basic, Visual C++, VBScript, and JScript. Web developers don't need to know SNA, APPC, or LU 6.2.

Scenario: Using the Data Provider to Gain Access Host Files

With the Data Provider, you can gain access to file data on an IBM host from a Windows NT–based Web application. Suppose that you want to add content from a legacy file stored on an IBM mainframe or AS/400 computer to an ASP application running under IIS. ASP can be used to interpret user requests and format the return of data to the user via Web pages. The Data Provider can process calls from the IIS environment and pass data returned from the mainframe environment to IIS.

This scenario requires six main steps:

- Step 1 (setup and configuration): Configuring the OLE DB/DDM Driver.
- Step 2 (design time): Defining the application requirements.
- Step 3 (design time): Writing the application.
- Step 4 (design time): Testing the application.
- Step 5 (deployment): Deploying the application components.
- Step 6 (post-deployment): Maintaining the application.

Step 1: Configuring the Data Provider

To develop an application using the Data Provider, you must meet the following system installation requirements:

- Microsoft Windows NT Server 4.0 or Windows NT Workstation 4.0 or later updated with Service Pack 3 or later.
- Microsoft IIS 4.0 or later. This includes ADO 1.5, the ActiveX Data Objects release supported by the Data Provider.
- Microsoft Windows NT Client for SNA Server 4.0. Configure it to connect to SNA Server 4.0.

Additionally, the following packages must be installed and configured:

- Microsoft OLE DB Provider for AS/400 and VSAM.
- Microsoft OLE DB Provider for AS/400 and VSAM snap-in for Microsoft Management Console (MMC). Configure the DDM service for the target host and PC locale. Optionally, configure the Data Sources if you are not passing data source information through from ADO consumer application. Configure the mainframe data column description to OLE DB data type mappings.

Step 2: Defining Application Requirements

To accomplish this step:

- Compile a list of target host files, keys, and alternate index paths. Define the subset of records to be read from the target Web application.

- Specify the ADO objects, methods, properties, and collections supported by the Data Provider, to be used in the application.

- Consider using **Recordset.Filter** to define recordsets based on logical search criteria and to search for records based on application program and user input.

- Use the ADO errors collection to produce errors in formats the program can respond to, avoiding passing unnecessary error conditions to the Web browser.

- Use either the automatic AS/400-to-OLE DB data transformation, or a custom mapping using a DDM service host data column description file.

- Decide whether or not to map Windows NT logon user IDs obtained from the Web browser to host user IDs automatically.

- Choose a deployment option and decide whether to run the DDM service on the computer running SNA Server or the computer running Windows NT Client for SNA Server 4.0.

Step 3: Writing the Application

To accomplish this step:

- Write scripts to gain access to ADO 1.5 from an ASP page in a language that supports referencing of Automation objects, such as VBScript or JScript.

- Cast data to match the OLE DB and host data types. Refer to the recordset schema to determine which host data types are supported. Ensure that the host data is valid before writing to the host files, especially if a host application concurrently gains access to host data files.

- Check the syntax of supported OLE DB methods and properties. Pay special attention to the connection string and the **Recordset.Open** parameters. These are unique to each OLE DB Provider.

- If appropriate, use the MS$SAME placeholder to pass the user ID and password to the SNA Server host security feature.

- Program some loops to ensure that target recordsets contain data before passing recordset methods to allow for delays caused by network conditions and the remoteness of target hosts.

Step 4: Testing the Application

Test the new application to make sure that:

- The ASP pages run correctly.

- There are clean communications between ADO and the DDM Service on the Windows NT side. Consider starting the DDM Service on Windows NT automatically to ensure the timely availability of a PC-to-host connection with minimal session startup time.

- There are reliable, efficient operations between DDM Service and the host by way of SNA Server. Consider keeping the connection between SNA Server and the host connection active to reduce session startup time.

- There is proper data display in the Web applications. Ensure the data integrity of host files, because there can be a loss of precision when you move data from the host to the PC and back again.

Step 5: Deploying Application Components

Before deploying the application, the following packages must be installed on each production computer:

- Microsoft Windows NT Server 4.0 updated with Service Pack 3, or Windows NT Workstation version 4.0, updated with Service Pack 3.

- Microsoft Windows NT Client for SNA Server 4.0.

- Microsoft IIS 4.0.

- OLE DB Provider for AS/400 and VSAM.

- The ASP pages requesting data from the legacy files.

- DDM Service running with Windows NT Client for SNA Server 4.0 or SNA Server. To improve responsiveness, consider starting the DDM Service automatically when the system restarts to improve responsiveness.

Step 6: Maintaining the Application

If you modify the ASP scripts, you need to re-test the application using the following guidelines:

- Test the application fully if you add new scripts or script fragments to existing ASP pages that request data from new data sources.

- If the target host data files are restructured, or new host tables are added, these changes need to be incorporated into the Web application by modifying ADO methods and creating new recordsets as needed.

- If the host connectivity changes, you should verify the Windows NT Client for SNA Server 4.0 configuration or the Data Provider data sources.

Replicating Legacy Databases

Much of the data stored in systems resides in relational databases. In addition to gaining access to legacy data in place on the host, you can replicate database tables from a legacy application to SQL Server.

Why Replication?

Legacy database replication is a conversion process that copies, reformats, and migrates database tables for use in relational databases running under Windows NT 4.0. Using data replicated from a legacy database, developers and systems engineers can:

- Integrate the legacy data with data from the Windows NT side. If the data is replicated for storage in an Windows NT–side database, IIS 4.0 connects Internet or intranet clients to dynamically created Web pages retrieving the data through ODBC.

- Readily subject the data to new business logic. For new processes involving the database, developing in Windows is less costly than the development of legacy systems.

- Manage the data efficiently. Windows NT Server 4.0 with IIS provides a common set of system management tools, database management tools, Web application servers, and transaction servers.

Replicating DB2 Tables using the Host Data Replicator

The HDR (Host Data Replicator) is a database replication software product that copies pre-defined data from IBM DB2 database tables to Microsoft SQL Server database tables. It can do so on demand, at a scheduled time, or according to a recurring schedule. HDR has the capability to reverse the process as well, replicating SQL Server tables for use in a DB2 database.

HDR is composed of the data replicator service (a Windows NT operating system service) and Data Replicator Manager (a Windows NT operating system application for administration). The Data Replicator Manager has a user interface similar to those used by SQL Enterprise Manager and the scheduling portions of SQL Executive.

The HDR performs bi-directional full refresh replication. A complete "snapshot" of the source table is copied into the target database table. The target table has all its records overwritten each time replication occurs.

Replication Type

The Host Data Replicator performs bi-directional replication with full refresh. A complete "snapshot" of the source table is copied into the target database table using either BCP (when copying to Microsoft SQL Server) or ODBC "inserts." All of the records of the target table are overwritten each time replication occurs. Optionally, you can append data to the end of the existing table provided you do not change the table schema.

The following section outlines the types of replication supported by HDR.

Data Processing and Filtering:

- Replication of selected columns ("vertical partitioning").

- Replication of selected rows defined by SQL queries ("horizontal partitioning").

- Replication of selected columns from selected rows (combined vertical and horizontal partitioning).

- Construction of destination columns calculated ("derived") from source data.

- Use of SQL expressions to alter data in destination tables before or after replication.

- Change in column names, column data types, or column order between source and destination.

Scheduling

- Single replication on demand (repeatable at will, or through a programmatic interfaces such as SP_RUNTASK).

- Single replication at a pre-defined time.

- Recurring replication at pre-defined times.

Statistics

- Throughput for each replication operation.

- Number of bytes transferred for each replication operation.

- Elapsed time for each replication operation.

- Statistics are available through the Data Replicator Manager or Windows NT Performance Monitor.

Security

The Data Replicator Manager prompts the administrator to supply a valid Microsoft SQL Server account and password each time it establishes a connection to a Data Replicator Service. If a correct account and password are not provided, the Data Replicator Manager closes the connection, preventing administration of the associated service and its subscriptions. (A subscription is a description of a replication operation involving one source table and one destination table. A single Data Replicator Service can handle many subscriptions).

- For DB2: During subscription setup, an administrator must supply a valid DB2 account and password. HDR will also support the SNA Server version 3.0 Single Sign On option.

- Microsoft SQL Server destination table ownership can be defined during subscription setup. Access to replicated data is then controlled through normal Microsoft SQL Server security measures.

Performance

- Source table names can be filtered to reduce network traffic and improve performance during the setup of full refresh subscriptions in environments with large numbers of possible source tables.

- Connections to source and destination servers can be pooled to avoid performance costs of reestablishing connections unnecessarily. Pool sizes can be adjusted as needed.

- The Data Replicator Service caches subscription information to avoid the performance costs of obtaining the information from the data replicator control database when scheduled replication times arrive.

- HDR is a loosely-coupled product (meaning that it does not support a two-phase commit).

Supported Platforms:

HDR is supported on the following platforms:

- Microsoft SNA Server 3.0 or later.
- Windows NT Server 3.51 or later (Intel and Alpha).
- Microsoft SQL Server 6.5 or later.
- IBM DB2 including DB2 (MVS), DB2/VM (SQL/DS), DB2/400, and the common family (DB2/2, DB2/6000, and DB2/2 Windows NT through APPC).

Migrating Transaction Processes

Microsoft Transaction Server (MTS) is a transaction management server that provides reliable, secure transaction management for Web applications. The following section provides information that can help you plan a migration of transaction-driven applications from any legacy environment to the Windows NT 4.0 environment where transactions requested by IIS are managed by MTS.

Why Use Transactions?

Two changes in the use of information technology make the increased deployment of transaction management systems compelling for many organizations:

- The growing demand to use the Internet and intranets for exchanging secure information, including financial exchanges through online commerce.

- The increasing trend of running multiple reusable software components within one application, including components used to access databases.

A transaction is a multi-part update process in which the update is committed—made final—only if all of the parts of the transaction are completed successfully. An online transaction is an update process that is initiated and carried out over a data network.

The explosive growth of the Internet and organizational intranets has presented new opportunities for doing business over data networks. The elemental expression of doing business, the exchange of money for goods or services, requires updates to more than one database for each exchange.

Software design is increasingly shifting toward a component model in which applications are made up of many code segments operating independently of each other. Often, an application allows more than one component to concurrently update a database, or more than one database. Concurrent updates require a transaction manager to ensure transaction integrity while optimizing performance.

For more information, see Chapter 6, "Data Access and Transactions."

Migrating to Microsoft Transaction Server (MTS)

There is a growing need for transaction management on the Web, and there are many existing transaction systems on legacy networks processing business-critical data. Hence, many organizations need to manage transactions in both environments. One serious obstacle is that legacy transaction systems do not extend across boundaries, such as the boundary between SNA legacy networks and TCP/IP-based intranets with Windows NT–based servers. In other words, a legacy TP running under CICS or IMS cannot account for a database update on the Windows NT network. Additionally, the costs of development, hosting, and scaling up are higher in the legacy environment than on Windows NT–based networks.

The best solution is a Windows NT–based transaction management system that coordinates IIS-based Web transactions and legacy TPs. Any transaction can then involve updates of databases running under Windows NT, running under a mainframe TP, or both at once. Transaction processes can be selectively migrated to Windows NT–based database management software such as SQL Server, and any transaction processes left on the mainframe can be managed from Windows NT as well.

MTS Features and Capabilities

Microsoft Transaction Server (MTS) expands the capabilities of IIS to include Web-based transaction management. MTS is a component-based transaction management solution that provides a programming model, a run-time environment, and graphical server administration tools—everything required to design and develop a transaction application and migrate a legacy process to it. With MTS, Web developers using ASP can develop full transaction management capabilities for deployment on the Web.

By deploying MTS as your transaction management system, you can profit from the advantages of the Windows NT environment and migrate selected legacy transactional processes. In the meantime, MTS extends transaction management to include processes left running in the legacy environment.

In addition to full transaction monitoring and management, and the low cost of scaling up Windows NT–based systems and software, MTS offers advantages over its mainframe-based counterparts at design time and run-time, as well as for maintenance and administration.

MTS Design Time

The MTS programming model provides the framework for developing components that encapsulate business logic.

MTS fits perfectly in a three-tier programming model (see the sidebar, "Three-Tier Applications and Middleware"). MTS acts as middleware, managing the components which make it possible for a Web application to handle many clients. It also provides developers with a great deal of flexibility:

- The model emphasizes a logical architecture for applications, rather than a physical one. Any service can invoke any component.

- MTS connects requests for transactions (calls from ASP pages) to business logic and to database applications, so that you are not required to develop these processes.

- The applications are distributed, which means you can run the right components in the right places, benefitting users and optimizing use of network and computer resources.

Three-Tier Applications and Middleware

A three-tier application divides a networked application into three logical areas. Middleware, such as MTS, connects the three tiers.

Tier 1 handles presentation. In a Web application, data is requested by the browser and is sent there from the Web server for display.

Tier 2 processes business logic, meaning the set of rules for processing business information. In an IIS-based Web application, Tier 2 processing is carried out in IIS components.

Tier 3 processes the data—associated databases and files where the data is stored. In a Web application, Tier 3 consists of a back-end database management system or file access system with its associated data.

Three-tier systems are easier to modify and to maintain than two-tier systems because the programming of presentation, business logic, and data processing are separated by design. This architecture permits re-development to proceed in one tier, without affecting the others.

Middleware, such as MTS, manages the connections between the tiers, and makes efficient use of resources so that Web application programmers can concentrate on business logic. MTS can connect the browser request (Tier 1) to the business logic (Tier 2). In Tier 3, it can connect business logic to the databases and manage all activities of the transaction.

Application programming interfaces and resource dispensers make applications scalable and robust. Resource dispensers are services that manage non-durable shared state on behalf of the application components within a process. This way, you don't have to undertake traditional programming tasks associated with state maintenance.

MTS works with any application development tool capable of producing ActiveX dynamic-link libraries (DLLs). For example, you can use Microsoft Visual Basic, Microsoft Visual C++, Microsoft Visual J++, or any other ActiveX tool to develop MTS applications.

MTS is designed to work with a wide variety of resource managers, including relational database systems, file systems, and document storage systems. Developers and independent software vendors can select from a wide range of resource managers and use two or more resource managers within a single application.

The MTS programming model makes migration easier by making transaction application development simpler and faster than traditional programming models allow. For more information on developing MTS applications, see Chapter 6, "Data Access and Transactions."

MTS Run Time

The MTS run-time environment is a second-tier platform for running MTS components. This environment provides a comprehensive set of system services including:

- Distributed transactions.
- Automatic management of processes and threads.
- Object instance and connection pool management to improve the scalability and performance of applications.
- A distributed security service that controls object invocation and use.
- A graphical interface that supports system administration and component management.

This run-time infrastructure makes application development, deployment, and the management of applications much easier by making applications scalable and robust.

Overall performance is optimized by managing component instantiation and the connection pool. MTS instantiates components just in time for transactions, then purges state information from the instance when a transaction completes, and reuses the instance for the next transaction. For example, users can enter transaction requests from their browsers to an ASP page containing the code needed to call an MTS component. As these messages are received by MTS, the transactions are managed using components already instantiated. This minimizes the proliferation of object instantiation and connection-making that often inhibit the performance of systems supporting transactions.

MTS Administration Tools

MTS Explorer is a graphical administration tool used to register, deploy, and manage components executing in the MTS run-time environment. With MTS Explorer, you can script administration objects to automate component deployment.

Planning a Migration to MTS

As you migrate processes and databases from a legacy environment (TPs running under CICS on a mainframe) to MTS, TPs will continue to run on the mainframe for a while. To migrate to MTS:

- Use MTS and COM TI to extend transaction management to include all the parts of each transaction. This includes updates that take place on databases running under Windows NT, and updates that take place on the mainframe.

- Script the ASP pages so that IIS calls the MTS components that execute the transaction.

You can migrate parts of the legacy transaction infrastructure to SQL Server and use MTS to manage the parts of the transaction on the legacy host. All of the data can be accessed by IIS using ASP scripts.

Mapping Transaction Tasks to Windows NT–based Applications

The following table maps transaction-related functions to the applications used to support functions in the Windows NT environment.

Table 9.1   Transaction-Related Functions and Windows NT-Based Applications

Transaction-related task	Windows NT–based application
Manage transactions	Microsoft Transaction Server
Manage data resources	SQL Server 6.5
Call transactions from Web pages	Active Server Pages
Connect to a legacy network	SNA Server 4.0
Extend transactions to legacy TPs	COM TI

Resources

The following resources provide additional information on accessing legacy applications and data.

Web Links

http://www.microsoft.com/sna/
This Web site provides information about Microsoft SNA Server, the COM Transaction Integrator for CICS and IMS, the OLE DB Provider for VSAM and AS/400, and the Host Data Replicator.

Software Product Documentation

For information about Microsoft SNA Server, COM Transaction Integrator for CICS and IMS, OLE DB Provider for VSAM and AS/400, and the Host Data Replicator, see the SDK documentation included with Microsoft SNA Server 4.0.

C H A P T E R   1 0

Migrating Web Sites and Applications

10

Migrating from one Web server to another involves two main tasks: migrating configuration settings and migrating applications.

Of these two tasks, migrating applications is certainly the most potentially complex and difficult. Many applications are written to the CGI specification; quite often it makes sense to migrate these applications to an IIS technology such as the Internet Server API (ISAPI) or Active Server Pages (ASP).

As for migrating configuration settings, the IIS Resource Kit CD includes the IIS Migration Wizard to help with this task. The current version of the IIS Migration Wizard migrates settings from Netscape Enterprise Server versions 2.0 and 3.0.

The chapter begins with a discussion on how to migrate CGI applications. The next section describes migrating from Netscape Enterprise Server; it documents the configuration settings migrated by the IIS Migration Wizard and compares a sample ASP application to application written in Netscape LiveWire script. The final section of the chapter examines issues involved in migrating from Lotus Domino to IIS.

In this chapter:

- Migrating CGI Applications to IIS
- Migrating from Netscape Enterprise Server
- Migrating from Lotus Domino
- Resources

Migrating CGI Applications to IIS

As organizations move to deploy Web-based applications on Windows NT and IIS, they are naturally concerned about whether and how to migrate existing Web applications to IIS. Often, these applications have been built to the Common Gateway Interface (CGI) specification and take the form of scripts written in interpreted languages like Perl or Tcl, or monolithic executables written in C or C++. IIS fully supports both scripts and executables written to the CGI specification.

But IIS offers far more than just a hospitable environment for CGI applications. IIS provides both the Active Server Pages (ASP) scripting environment and the Internet Server API (ISAPI), which allow developers to write applications that are faster and more scalable than CGI applications on Windows NT. In addition, IIS provides some compelling application development features, such as script debugging and built-in database connectivity.

This section assumes the reader is familiar with Web-based applications and CGI. While several migration strategies are discussed, the focus is on migrating CGI applications to Active Server Pages.

Note This chapter is not a general-purpose guide to porting applications from other environments (such as UNIX systems) to Win32, nor is it a tutorial on all the development features within the Active Server Pages environment. For more information on developing with ASP, see Chapter 5, "Developing Web Applications."

Comparing CGI Applications to IIS Applications

As CGI developers are aware, a server responds to a CGI execution request from a client browser by creating a new process. That is, a new, separate process is created for every client request handled by a CGI application, even if a single client submits more than one request. At any given time, the server is supporting a separate process for every ongoing request. When a request is complete, the server must perform a series of steps to delete the process.

CGI was created for a UNIX environment where processes are the basic unit of operation and have less overhead than processes in Windows NT. In Windows NT, where threads are the basic unit of operation, processes have substantial overhead. Each process receives a private physical memory allocation, is granted space in the paged and nonpaged memory pools, and is protected by the Windows NT security model. In fact, every attribute that makes processes in Windows NT robust also makes them costly. Because each CGI request generates a new process, CGI applications have much higher overhead than ASP or ISAPI applications.

As a result, CGI performance is considerably reduced under Windows NT. Some benchmarks show that CGI applications run anywhere from three to five times slower than ISAPI applications and two to three times slower than ASP applications. For more information, see the "Web Application Performance" section in Chapter 3, "Capacity Planning."

CGI applications also scale poorly on Windows NT. Adding additional processing power or RAM typically does not allow a CGI application to support many more concurrent users. Therefore, if an application will be heavily used, there are strong reasons to move to a solution that uses ISAPI or ASP and components. ISAPI applications offer some performance advantages over ASP applications, but ASP applications can be developed much more quickly. The difference is comparable to the difference between developing in C or C++ and developing in Visual Basic.

Active Server Pages is an open, server-application environment in which you can combine HTML, server-side scripts, and reusable ActiveX server components to create dynamic and powerful Web-based business solutions. ASP enables server-side scripting for IIS with native support for both Visual Basic Scripting Edition (VBScript) and JScript. In addition to these native languages, the ASP environment supports any scripting language that conforms to the Active Scripting requirements. For example, there are Win32 implementations of the Perl, Tcl, and Python languages.

Unlike CGI applications, which cause a new process to be created with each execution request, ASP applications run on lighter-weight Win32 threads. IIS transparently and efficiently manages pools of such threads and allocates resources appropriately to service incoming requests.

ASP applications can be configured to run either *in process,* that is, within the IIS Web server process (for fastest execution speed), or *out of process,* isolated from the server process and running in their own processes (for maximum safety). Even when they are run as out-of-process applications, ASP and ISAPI applications typically execute much faster than CGI applications.

Developers are free to choose the level of process isolation appropriate for their needs. For example, while an application is under development, the developer may choose to run an application in its own memory space; when the application is in production, it can be run in process with the Web server.

Note Some developers are concerned that Active Server Pages requires them to support only one type of browser. But ASP pages contain server-side scripts that send HTML to the browser. The HTML they generate is completely under the developer's control. In no way does ASP tie the developer into supporting a particular browser.

Migration Strategies

There are several approaches to migrating an existing CGI application to the IIS environment.

Port the CGI Application to Win32

Although CGI applications are inherently inefficient under Windows NT, it is possible simply to port an application to Win32, leaving it as a straight CGI application. IIS supports CGI applications that expect to receive input via environment variables and the standard input stream, and expect to write output via the standard output stream. If your application can port to Win32, this may be all that is required.

If you port your CGI application, you should examine the code to see just how much of it is needed in the ASP environment—you may find that within the ASP environment, much of the application's code is unnecessary. This topic is further discussed in "Migrating to Active Server Pages" later in this chapter.

Because CGI applications do not scale well on Windows NT, simply porting an application to the Win32 environment is not a good idea if the application needs to support many concurrent users (or "hits"). The best way to build a scalable application is to use Active Server Pages and components.

If your current application is a script make sure you have a Win32-compatible version of the script interpreter available. The following Web sites provide Win32 implementations of Perl, Tcl, and Python:

Perl: http://www.activestate.com/

Tcl: http://sunscript.sun.com/

Python: http://www.python.org/windows/

Migrating Perl Scripts

The ActiveState Tool Corporation provides three options for running Perl scripts on Windows NT: Scripts can be run as CGI executables (Perl for Win32), as DLLs within the IIS process (Perl for ISAPI), or within the ASP environment (PerlScript). The ASP environment provides the best performance, but you may need to modify your scripts to run within it (for more information, see "Migrating to Active Server Pages" later in this chapter). If you want to migrate a script with minimal or no modification, Perl for ISAPI offers the best performance. The advantage of Perl for ISAPI is that a separate process is not created for every request, as is the case for CGI executables on Windows NT. For more information, see http://activestate.com/.

Port the CGI Application to an ISAPI DLL

If a CGI application has been written in C or C++, it may be feasible to convert it into an Internet Sever API (ISAPI) dynamic-link library (DLL). This would help the application's performance, and would begin to take advantage of some of the IIS application development features.

Usually, ISAPI application DLLs no longer read input from the standard input stream or write to the standard output stream but rather communicate through a data structure called the Extension Control Block (ECB).

IIS typically loads an ISAPI DLL the first time a request that calls the DLL is received; the DLL then stays in memory, ready to service other requests until the server decides it is no longer needed. IIS can also load ISAPI DLLs on startup and cache them for future use, thus enhancing performance.

Under IIS 4.0, an ISAPI DLL can be deployed by the developer or system administrator to run either within the IIS process or in its own process.

For more details on developing ISAPI applications, see the documentation in the Microsoft Platform Software Development Kit (SDK). The Platform SDK can be obtained at http://www.microsoft.com/msdn/sdk/platform.htm.

Creating ISAPI DLLs also requires a thorough understanding of the Win32 programming environment, including thread management. For some useful information sources on Win32 programming, see the "Resources" section at the end of this chapter.

Port the CGI Application to Active Server Pages

When you port your application to Active Server Pages, you may be able to:

- Remove a significant amount of existing CGI code. The ASP environment provides much of the functionality for managing forms, output, and state.

- Speed up execution, because you avoid the excess overhead of process creation, as well as take advantage of such features as ODBC connection pooling.

- Create a more productive development environment, as you take advantage of the Microsoft Script Debugger and IIS application management features.

You can choose the scripting language used within an ASP page. If the CGI application is written in C or Java, it may be easiest to use JScript because of its syntactical similarity. If the CGI application you're porting is written in Perl, it may be convenient to use PerlScript.

In any case, consider using Visual Basic Scripting Edition (VBScript) for building ASP pages. Millions of developers use the Visual Basic language. Organizations that move to VBScript can take advantage of this synergy and may find they have many more resources available to support them.

Script interpreters for JScript and VBScript are included with IIS. Interpreters for PerlScript and other languages are available from third parties.

The following sections outline some of the tasks you may need to perform when moving CGI applications to the ASP environment.

Migrating to Active Server Pages

The first step in planning a migration is to examine the CGI application. Many developers find they can divide their existing applications into five major types of logic:

- Input processing (reading forms, environment variables, and decoding HTML)
- Business logic
- Database (or gateway) logic for connecting to external services
- Logic for maintaining state between forms
- HTML output logic for returning results to browser clients

A general discussion on how to handle each of these kinds of logic follows.

Input Processing

A great deal of CGI processing revolves around capturing the contents of HTML forms as presented to the standard input stream, then reformatting them, decoding the HTML, reading environment variables, and so on. Because this is one of the most tedious aspects of developing CGI applications, many developers have used third-party libraries and tools, such as the Perl utilities Cgi.pm or Cgi-lib.pl. In most cases, these utilities are unnecessary in ASP applications; the ASP environment takes care of most of these housekeeping tasks for you.

Accessing Form Input and Decoding HTML

One of the major differences between CGI applications and ASP applications is how form input is handled. Accessing form data from an ASP page is much simpler than from a CGI application.

A CGI application written in Perl receives form input from a POST request on the standard input stream using code such as:

```
$form_size = $ENV('CONTENT_LENGTH');
read( STDIN, $form_data, $form_size );
```

Note that this form data is encoded and must be translated. Using Perl, the translation code might look like this:

```
$value =~ s/%([0-9a-fA-F]{2})/pack("c",hex($1))/ge;
```

Once the form data is decoded, the developer can search for a form variable. Here is a typical Perl routine to parse form data and place it in a list:

```
sub get_form
{
    local (*FORM) = @_;
    local ( $env_string, @collection, $key_value,
                $key, $value );
    read (STDIN, $env_string, $ENV{'CONTENT_LENGTH'});
    @collection = split( /&/, $env_string );
    foreach $key_value (@collection) {
        ($key, $value) = split( /=/, $key_value);
        $value =~ tr/+/ /;
        $value =~ s/%([0-9a-fA-F]{2})/pack("c",hex($1))/ge;

        if (defined($FORM{$key})) {
            $FORM{$key} = join("\0",, $FORM{$key}, $value);
        } else {
            $FORM{$key} = $value;
        }
    }
}
```

Once the routine is in place, it can be called to parse the form. The following code calls the `get_form` routine and references a variable called `home_address`:

```
&get_form(*my_form);
print $my_form('home_address');
```

Fortunately, the ASP environment takes care of these form processing and decoding chores for you. In ASP, the content of an HTML form is made available as a *collection.* For developers familiar with languages like Perl or Awk, collections are analogous to "hashes" or "associative arrays." They are named lists of key/value pairs.

Form variables are included in the **Form** collection of the **Request** object.

Instead of referring to a form variable with a Perl construction like:

```
print $my_form('home_address');
```

you can refer to a form variable as shown in the following VBScript example:

```
MyAddress = Request.Form("home_address")
```

Here's the same instruction written in PerlScript:

```
$MyAddress = $Request->Form('home_address')
```

Remember, there is no need to parse the input, as was required in the CGI example, because the ASP environment takes care of it.

Although ASP applications do an excellent job of eliminating form processing drudgery, developers sometimes need access to the unprocessed input stream. The following VBScript fragment writes the unprocessed input stream back to the output stream:

```
Response.Write Request.Form
```

In addition to the **Form** collection, the **Request** object includes a collection called **QueryString.** This collection contains form elements sent in response to the GET method of the HTML <FORM> tag. The elements of the **QueryString** collection are accessed in the same way elements of the **Form** collection are accessed.

Often, quite a bit of CGI code is devoted to determining whether a given form variable exists within the QUERY_STRING environment variable or in the standard input stream. However, within the Active Server Pages environment, you can avoid testing many of these conditions simply by referring to a variable by name:

```
MyVariable = Request("home_address")
```

In this case the Web server will search the QUERY_STRING first, then the form, in order to find the correct variable. This feature may eliminate the need to rewrite code to search both the query string and the form.

If an application needs to encode URLs or HTML, you can take advantage of the built-in **HTMLEncode** and **URLEncode** methods of the **Server** object.

In many cases, developers migrating CGI applications find they can remove most of the third-party form decoding and processing utilities, as well as any homegrown generic form processing modules.

Environment Variables

CGI applications that inspect environment variables can continue to do so when converted to ASP. Environment variables are provided as part of the **Request** object's **ServerVariables** collection.

Whereas in a CGI application, you might access the SERVER_NAME environment variable with something like the following line of C code:

```
serverName = getenv( "SERVER_NAME" );
```

or the following line, written in Perl:

```
serverName = $ENV{'SERVER_NAME'};
```

in ASP, you can use the following instruction, written in VBScript:

```
serverName = Request.ServerVariables("SERVER_NAME")
```

You can iterate through collections such as **ServerVariables** in order to examine all the values they contain. The following ASP page written in VBScript generates an HTML table containing all the variables contained in the **ServerVariables** collection with their values:

```
<%@ LANGUAGE=VBSCRIPT %>
<html><body>
<table border=1>
<% for each name in request.ServerVariables %>
    <tr>
        <td><%= name %></td>
        <td><%= request.ServerVariables( name )%></td>
    </tr>
<% next %>
</table>
</body></html>
```

Business Logic

Once much of the "plumbing" is removed from a CGI application, some business logic that needs to be ported usually remains. There are at least two approaches to migrating business logic:

- First, the logic can be ported to the Active Server Pages scripting environment. In other words, logic written in C, C++, Perl and so on can be rewritten in a scripting language such as VBScript, JScript, or PerlScript. If an ASP scripting engine that supports the language currently used is available, then porting may be relatively simple.

- Second, if the business logic is extensive, requires more functionality than is available in a scripting environment, or is very general, then the logic can be encapsulated within a component.

Components can be written in any language that supports the Common Object Model (COM), including C, C++, Java, Visual Basic, Delphi, and even some implementations of COBOL.

Note Server-side components run completely within the server environment. Their use has no effect on whether an application can support a particular browser on a specific platform.

It is important to consider overall application architecture. Building a successful and scalable distributed application, where application logic can reside on a Web client, a Web server, and on other back-end servers (such as databases) requires a careful separation of the application's functionality into logical groups of services, or "tiers."

For more information on designing and building Web applications using components, see Chapter 5, "Web Application Development." For references to additional information, see the "Resources" section at the end of this chapter.

External Gateway and Database Logic

CGI applications were originally created to allow Web clients access to applications outside the Web itself. Although the majority of existing CGI applications interface with databases of some sort, many CGI applications are used to provide services such as page counters, or to access services such as electronic mail servers. This section describes techniques for accessing databases and other external services through ASP.

Databases

ActiveX Data Objects (ADO) is a highly efficient database access method that can be used within the Active Server Pages environment. ADO is included with IIS on the Windows NT 4.0 Option Pack.

ADO exposes an object model to abstract the ideas of connecting to and executing commands against a remote database. The database need not support Structured Query Language (SQL), but a database-specific piece of software called an *OLE DB Provider* is required. If your database vendor supplies an Open Database Connectivity (ODBC) driver for your database, you can use a provider for ODBC data sources supplied with IIS.

Perl developers commonly access a database using a package like dbperl or the more current DBI package. No special package is required within the ASP environment. For example, the following simple ASP page written in PerlScript dumps the contents of a table called Orders using the ODBC datasource ADOSamples:

```
<%@ LANGUAGE=PerlScript %>
<html>
<body><p>

<%
    $Conn = $Server->CreateObject("ADODB.Connection");
    $Conn->Open( "ADOSamples" );
    $RS = $Conn->Execute( "SELECT * FROM Orders" );
%>

<TABLE BORDER=1>
<TR>
<%
    $count = $RS->Fields->Count;
    for ( $i = 0; $i < $count; $i++ ){
        %><TD><B><%= $RS->Fields($i)->Name %></B></TD><%
    }; %> </TR> <%
    while ( ! $RS->EOF ) {
        %> <TR> <%
        for ( $i = 0; $i < $count; $i++ ) {
            %><TD VALIGN=TOP>
            <%= $RS->Fields($i)->value %></TD><%
        };
        %> </TR> <%
        $RS->MoveNext;
    };
    $RS->Close;
    $Conn->Close;
    %>
</TABLE>
</BODY>
</HTML>
```

ADO is designed to be highly efficient in a multithreaded environment, where many concurrent instances of the ADO code execute simultaneously. Thus, ADO is ideal for Web server environments, particularly when they need to scale up to many concurrent users.

An additional benefit to working within the ASP environment is the ability to take advantage of the services of Microsoft Transaction Server (MTS). MTS is an integral part of the ASP environment. MTS not only provides support for process isolation, as discussed above, but also provides a simple way for developers to build scalable Web applications based on components. MTS takes care of all the plumbing issues, including transactions, connection management, and thread management, thus freeing the developer to concentrate primarily on building business logic.

For more information on ADO and MTS, see Chapter 6, "Data Access and Transactions," as well as the Transaction Server Web site at http://www.microsoft.com/transaction/.

More general information on ADO, ODBC, as well as Microsoft's overall data access strategies can be found at http://www.microsoft.com/data/.

The Perl-based DBI package and documentation, including ideas for porting existing DBI code to the Win32 platform, can be found at http://www.hermetica.com/technologia/DBI/.

Electronic Mail

Many CGI applications exist just to format RFC-822 e-mail messages for delivery to a mail server such as sendmail. This functionality can be reproduced easily within the ASP environment.

Note that IIS includes an SMTP Service and exposes all of its functionality through the Collaboration Data Objects (CDO) object model. Once the SMTP Service is properly installed and configured, an e-mail message can be scripted as simply as shown in the following ASP script, written in JScript:

```
<% @language=JScript %>

<%
    var msg;
    msg = Server.CreateObject("CDONTS.NewMail");
    msg.From = "someone@microsoft.com";
    msg.To   = "someone@microsoft.com";
    msg.Subject = "Test message";
    msg.Body = "This is a sample message.";
    msg.Send();
%>
```

Page Counters

Many of the CGI applications available on the Internet are page counters. Although many of these counters can continue to be used, the IIS Resource Kit CD supplies a **PageCounter** object that efficiently records hits into a disk-based hit-count data file. The developer can easily query the component in order to display the hit count or build a more elaborate display.

The following ASP page, written in PerlScript, demonstrates the use of the page counter component supplied with IIS 4.0:

```
<% @language-PerlScript %>

<html>
<body>
<%
    $counter = $Server->CreateObject("MSWC.PageCounter");
    $hits  = $counter->Hits;
%>

You are visitor number <%= $hits %> to this page.

</body>
</html>
```

The File System

Quite a few CGI applications need to interact with the file system. There are several approaches to accessing the file system from within the ASP environment.

The easiest method is to use the **FileSystemObject** and **TextStream** objects. These objects provide high level access to the file system. For example, the following ASP page, written in VBScript, creates a text file, and writes the contents of the environment variable SERVER_NAME to its own line:

```
<% @language=VBScript %>
<html>
<body>

<%
    dim objFS, objFile, append

    append = 8
    set objFS  = Server.CreateObject("Scripting.FileSystemObject")
    set objFile = objFs.OpenTextFile("c:\servlist.txt", append, True )
    objFile.WriteLine Request.ServerVariables("SERVER_NAME")
    objFile.Close
%>
Done
</body>
</html>
```

If the supplied **FileSystemObject** and **TextStream** objects do not meet your needs, file system access can be encapsulated with an ActiveX component.

Maintaining State

There are several schemes commonly used in CGI applications for maintaining state information about the client session on the Web server. Some of these involve scripts that save and restore data from server-side text files. Some involve embedding state in the client side HTML (in, say, hidden form fields). Some CGI applications even maintain state by setting themselves up as "mini Web servers" for the duration of the session, intercepting incoming HTTP requests.

Many Web developers have moved to using browser-based cookies for storing state information.

Active Server Pages provides built-in state management using session variables. When a client first connects to the application, a "session cookie" can be sent which identifies the new session. As the browser accesses other pages in the application, the cookie is retrieved by the system and is used to manage state.

All this is transparent to the Web developer. The developer has access to the **Session** collection of variables. For example, consider an ASP page in which the user's login name is retrieved and assigned to a session variable:

```
Session("login_name") = Request.Form("login_name")
```

The value of login_name will be available to all other pages within the application, until the session times out (the default is 20 minutes, but is configurable) or is explicitly abandoned.

Output Handling

A key difference between ASP applications and CGI applications is that in an ASP page, the developer can weave industry-standard HTML with scripting code to deliver the appropriate HTML to the client.

Many CGI applications emit HTML using the output facilities of the language they're written in. For example, a simple Perl-based CGI application might look like this:

```
#!/usr/local/bin/perl

print "Content-type: text/html", "\n\n";
$server_name = $ENV('SERVER_NAME');
print "<html><body>Your server name is ", $server_name;
print "</body></html>";

exit(0);
```

Note that the HTML is embedded within the print function. Here is the corresponding ASP page, with code written in VBScript:

```
<html>
<body>
Your server name is <%= Request.ServerVariables("SERVER_NAME") %>
</body>
</html>
```

Note that the entire page is just simple HTML, except for the construct

```
<%= Request.ServerVariables("SERVER_NAME") %>
```

which is a VBScript expression.

You can use both HTML and server-side script code within the same page to combine the most powerful elements of both environments.

Some applications need to specify HTTP header information, rather than using the default MIME type of text/html. In the ASP environment, this can be accomplished by using the **ContentType** property of the **Response** object. For example, the following instruction sets the content type to "text/plain":

```
<% Response.ContentType = "text/plain" %>
```

Many Perl-based CGI applications use the freely available Cgi.pm or Cgi-lib.pl modules. These tools assist the CGI developer tremendously in formatting HTML output, as well as performing other tasks.

For example, the following script uses Cgi.pm to generate a form that collects the user's address; once the form is submitted, the script redisplays the form with the address beneath it:

```
use CGI qw(:all);

print header;
print start_html('Enter your address'),
    h1('Enter your address'),
    hr,
    p,
    start_form,
    table(
        Tr(td("Street"),td(textfield('street'))),
        Tr(td("City"), td(textfield('city'))),
        Tr(td("State"), td(textfield('state'))),
        Tr(td("Zip"), td(textfield('zip')))
    ),
    submit,
    end_form,
    hr;

if (param())
{
        print
            "Street is: ", param('street'), p,
            "City is: ", param('city'), p,
            "State is: ", param('state'), p,
            "Zip is: ", param('zip'), p,
            hr;
}
```

This script provides a convenient way to lay out a form if you aren't able to generate the HTML as part of the source code. The drawback to these sorts of utilities is that they require the developer to master a "pseudo-HTML" dialect in order to generate the page.

The corresponding ASP page (with script written in VBScript) looks almost exactly like the actual HTML page that will be sent to the browser.

```
<html>
<head><title>Enter your address</title></head>
<body>
<h1>Enter your address</h1>
<hr>
<p>
<form method=post>
<table>
    <tr><td>Street</td><td><input name="street"></td></tr>
    <tr><td>City</td><td><input name="city"></td></tr>
    <tr><td>State</td><td><input name="state"></td></tr>
    <tr><td>Zip</td><td><input name="zip"></td></tr>
</table>
<input type=submit>
</form>
<hr>

<%  if Request.Form.Count > 0 %>

Street is: <%= Request.Form("street") %> <p>
City is:  <%= Request.Form("city")  %> <p>
State is: <%= Request.Form("state") %> <p>
Zip is:  <%= Request.Form("zip")  %> <p>
<hr>

<% end if %>

</body>
</html>
```

The freedom to use authentic HTML as part of the application code is a benefit that cannot be overemphasized. This feature allows the developer to emit any HTML that the client browser supports, whereas utilities like Cgi.pm are necessarily limited by the tags they have chosen to implement. As new developments such as Dynamic HTML (DHTML) come along, tools like Cgi.pm have to be modified, perhaps heavily, to support new tags or other new client-side features.

In addition, Web designers and staff other than programmers can author in pure HTML. Using a special HTML dialect prevents these users from being able to modify the generated HTML.

Summary

Developers often find, after examining their CGI application and removing code that is not required within the ASP environment—form processing, environment variable processing, e-mail manipulation, database handling, state management, and most importantly, output processing—that they are left with much smaller applications to migrate. Migration is usually very manageable. As a result, developers are free to concentrate on business logic, rather than building software infrastructure.

Migrating from Netscape Enterprise Server

The IIS Migration Wizard, included on the IIS Resource Kit CD, migrates Web server settings, the virtual directory structure, and user accounts from Netscape Enterprise Server (NES) version 2.0 or 3.0 to IIS. This section describes which settings the IIS Migration Wizard migrates and which ones it does not. The section also provides information on how settings are migrated and on the differences between configuring NES and IIS. The last part of this section walks through a sample Active Server Pages application and compares it to a Netscape LiveWire application.

> **Note** For instructions on using the IIS Migration Wizard, see the online Readme file included on the IIS Resource Kit CD.

Definition of Terms

Here are some essential terms used in Netscape Enterprise Server with explanations of their equivalents in IIS.

- **Hardware virtual server** In Netscape, a "hardware virtual server" is a site with a separate IP address; the term implies a number of Web sites on a single computer, each with a separate IP address. IIS supports this way of running multiple sites, but does not employ a special term for these sites.

- **Software virtual server** In Netscape, a "software virtual server" is a site that may share an IP address with one or more other sites. In IIS, you can assign any number of sites to a single IP address, but no special term is employed to describe them.

- **Multiple instances of the server**   This method of hosting multiple Web sites on one computer can be employed if:

  - The operating system does not have strong thread support.

  - The operating system does not allow a single process to schedule threads on more than one processor.

  - Multiple instances of the server provide full process isolation, protecting a Web site from failure should another site on the same system crash.

  It is not appropriate to run multiple instances of IIS, because IIS running on Windows NT Server offers thread support across multiple processors, full configuration of each site hosted by the server, and process isolation for applications.

- **Server Manager**   Server Manager is the Netscape Enterprise Server administration tool. The IIS equivalent is Internet Service Manager.

Netscape Enterprise Server Administration Settings

This section lists Netscape Enterprise Server (NES) administrative settings as they are displayed in the NES Server Manager user interface and indicates whether, and how, the IIS Migration Wizard migrates those settings. Each heading within this section corresponds to a settings tab within the NES Server Manager.

Server Preferences

In IIS, administrative settings are called *properties* and can be set on the server, site, directory, or even file level. Most of the NES settings listed in this section apply to the site level. In IIS, you can view and change properties in the Internet Service Manager. To view site properties, right-click a Web site in the Internet Service Manager and select **Properties** from the menu. For more information, see "Server Administration" in the Windows NT 4.0 Option Pack online documentation.

Table 10.1   NES Server Preferences

Setting	Migrates	Comment
On/Off	No	In IIS, you turn a site on or off by using Internet Service Manager.
Restore Configuration	No	Backup configurations are not migrated, but IIS supports configuration backup.
Maximum simultaneous requests	Yes	To view this setting, right-click a Web site, choose **Properties**, and select the **Web Site** tab. The setting appears in the **Limited To** box.
Enable DNS	No	In IIS, you can restrict access by domain name. This feature can have a significant negative effect on server performance, however.
HTTP Persistent Connection Timeout	Yes	To view this setting, right-click a Web site, choose **Properties**, and select the **Web Site** tab. The setting appears in the **Connection Timeout** box.
MIME Types	Yes	To view these settings, right-click a Web site, choose **Properties**, select the **HTTP Headers** tab, and choose the **File Types** button.
Server Name	Yes	The setting is migrated to a host header name. To view this setting, right-click a Web site, choose **Properties**, select the **Web Site** tab, and choose the **Advanced** button.
Server Port	Yes	To view this setting, right-click a Web site, choose **Properties**, and select the **Web Site** tab. The setting appears in the **TCP Port** box.
Bind To Address	Yes	To view this setting, right-click a Web site, choose **Properties**, and select the **Web Site** tab. The setting appears in the **IP Address** box.
MTA Host and NNTP Host	No	IIS includes an SMTP and an NNTP service. These services make it easy to set up a self-contained Web site that sends and receives e-mail and posts information to news groups via Active Server Pages. The SMTP service supports one mailbox for this purpose. The NNTP service makes it is easy to build and host an NNTP site.
Error Responses	Yes	In cases where the custom error page is a standard HTML page, you need only copy the file to the IIS system to complete the migration. In the case of CGI custom errors, you need to test the CGI scripts after moving them to IIS.

continued

Setting	Migrates	Comment
Dynamic Configuration Files	No	In IIS, you can select individuals or groups and classify them as "Web site Operators." They do not have to be Windows NT Administrators, and have limited authority to administer the site. To access this feature, right-click a Web site, choose **Properties**, and select the **Operators** tab.
Restrict Access	No	Restrictions by IP address are not migrated because they are defined differently on IIS. To access this feature, right-click a Web site, choose **Properties**, select the **Directory Security** tab, and choose the **Edit** button within the **IP Address and Domain Name Restrictions** box.
Convert 2.0 ACL file	Not applicable	No settings to migrate.
Encryption	No	You need to use the IIS Key Manager to generate a request for a certificate and then apply that certificate to the server. You can then establish your encryption settings.

Programs

The settings in this section deal with Web applications. IIS supports CGI applications, but since CGI applications don't run efficiently in the Windows NT environment, you should consider converting them into Active Server Pages (ASP) or ISAPI applications. For more information, see "Migrating CGI Applications to IIS," earlier in this chapter.

For information on configuring CGI applications to run on IIS, see the topics under "Configuring Applications" in the "Server Administration" section of the IIS online documentation.

IIS supports VBScript and JScript within the ASP environment.

Table 10.2   NES Programs Settings

Setting	Migrates	Comment
CGI Directory	Yes	NES CGI directories are given Execute permission in IIS.
CGI File Type	No	
Query Handler	No	
WAI Management	No	This setting has to do with IIOP; IIS uses the COM and DCOM object models.
Java	No	The Java virtual machine is already enabled on IIS, so there is no need to migrate this setting.
Server Side JavaScript	No	IIS includes server-side support for JScript and VBScript. There is no need to migrate a switch setting for these languages.
WinCGI Directory	Yes	NES WinCGI directories are given Execute permission in IIS.
ShellCGI Directory	Yes	NES ShellCGI directories are given Execute permission in IIS.

Server Status

The settings in this section primarily have to do with server logging. For more information on logging, see "Logging Web Site Activity" in the Windows NT 4.0 Option Pack online documentation.

Table 10.3   NES Server Status Settings

Setting	Migrates	Comment
View Access Log	Not applicable	No settings to migrate. For log file analysis, use Microsoft Usage Import and Report Writer, included with the Windows NT 4.0 Option Pack as part of Site Server Express. For enhanced reporting, purchase Site Server.
View Error Log	Not applicable	No settings to migrate. When running IIS, you can view errors in the Windows NT Event Viewer.
Monitor Current Activity	Not applicable	No settings to migrate. To monitor server activity on IIS, use the Windows NT Performance Monitor to evaluate performance and resource consumption.

continued

Setting	Migrates	Comment
Archive Log	Not applicable	No settings to migrate. When you set your logging preferences on IIS, you can use Windows NT Backup or other third-party backup tools to archive the log files and remove them from the server as appropriate.
Log Preferences	Yes	Basic log file settings are migrated, but due to differences in logging methods, you should review the settings created for you in IIS to make sure they are optimal for your new environment.
Generate Report	Not applicable	No settings to migrate. Usage Import and Report Writer, included with the Windows NT 4.0 Option Pack, is the preferred tool for IIS log analysis.
SNMP Sub-Agent Configuration	No	

Configuration Styles

The settings under this heading are not migrated to IIS. IIS includes support for property inheritance, which achieves much the same result as configuration styles. Within the Internet Service Manager, you can right-click the server and set global properties for the WWW Service. Every new Web site created on the server inherits the server's global properties. Similarly, when you set properties for a Web site, directories created for the site inherit the site's properties.

Content Management

The IIS Migration Wizard migrates most of the NES settings listed in this section.

Table 10.4   NES Content Management Settings

Setting	Migrates	Comment
Primary Document Directory	Yes	
Additional Document Directories	Yes	
Index Filenames	Yes	See the "Home Page/Index File" setting below.
Directory Indexing	Yes	If you have selected "Simple" or "Fancy" directory indexing, the IIS Migration Wizard sets the **Directory Browsing Allowed** setting. To view this setting, right-click a Web site, choose **Properties**, and select the **Home Directory** tab.
Home Page / Index File	Yes	If a home page is listed, it is migrated to IIS as the default document name, listed ahead of any documents listed as index file names (according to the Index Filenames setting also listed in this table). If no home page is listed, any specified index file names are set as the default documents.
Default MIME Type	No	
Parse Accept Language Header	No	Microsoft Index Server, included in the Windows NT 4.0 Option Pack, can interpret this header in order to determine the language in which a query is being written.
URL Forwarding	No	
Hardware Virtual Servers	Yes	Migrated as a component of ServerBindings. See the "Definition of Terms" section earlier in this chapter for an explanation of how IIS implements hardware virtual servers.
Software Virtual Servers	Yes	Migrated as a component of ServerBindings. See the "Definition of Terms" section earlier in this chapter for an explanation of how IIS implements software virtual servers.
International Characters	No	When using Active Server Pages, you can specify the character set by using the **Response.Charset** property.

Continued

Setting	Migrates	Comment
Document Footer	Yes	A document footer can be specified for the entire IIS server, for a single Web site, or for a directory. To view this setting in the ISM, right-click either the server, a Web site, or a directory; choose **Properties** from the menu, and select the **Documents** tab.
		The IIS Migration Wizard does not move document footer files, but once a file is copied into the appropriate directory, IIS can begin using it immediately.
Parse HTML	Not applicable	IIS uses Active Server Pages rather than SHTML. Pages written using this technique should be rewritten as ASP pages using JScript, VBScript, or other supported script languages.
Cache Control Directives	Not applicable	Caching is handled differently in IIS. The default for HTML pages is to allow them to be cached by proxy servers. The default value for ASP pages is "private," meaning they cannot be cached. With IIS, you can use the **Response** Object to control whether a proxy server will cache the page.

Web Publishing

Web publishing settings are not migrated. These features can be supported with client-side development and management tools such as Microsoft FrontPage (a member of the Microsoft Office family), Visual InterDev™, and Microsoft Content Analyzer (included in the Windows NT 4.0 Option Pack; a more full-featured version is available as a component of Microsoft Site Server).

Agents and Search

Agents and Search settings are not migrated. Microsoft Index Server is the tool used to index and search Web sites maintained on IIS. This tool, included in the Windows NT 4.0 Option Pack, is easy to install and configure. For information on Microsoft Index Server, see the Windows NT 4.0 Option Pack online documentation.

Auto Catalog

Auto Catalog settings are not migrated. As with Agents and Search settings, IIS uses Microsoft Index Server to build a searchable catalog of information about the content of the Web site.

Moving User Accounts to IIS

You can port your user account database from Netscape Enterprise Server (NES) 3.0 to the Windows NT user account database. You begin the process by exporting your users from NES 3.0 to an LDIF-formatted file. The IIS Migration Wizard uses that file to create another intermediary file. Next, copy this file to the Windows NT server and use it as input to the AddUsers utility, which is included on the IIS Resource Kit CD. AddUsers, as its name promises, adds users to the Windows NT user account database. It will still be necessary to set users' attributes and groups. The passwords for the imported users will default to blank with an immediate expiration. When a user first logs on, the user will be required to enter a new password.

For more information on using the IIS Migration Wizard to import users to Windows NT, see the IIS Migration Wizard documentation on the IIS Resource Kit CD.

Note The IIS Migration Wizard cannot migrate users from Netscape Enterprise Server 2.0.

Migrating to Active Server Pages

Active Server Pages (ASP) is the recommended choice for writing applications to run on IIS. This section describes a sample ASP application that accesses a database, and compares aspects of its code to the VideoApp sample LiveWire application included with Netscape Enterprise Server 3.0. For more information on developing applications in IIS, see Chapter 5, "Developing Web Applications."

Development Tools

Microsoft Visual InterDev is recommended for creating IIS Web applications. A major advantage to using Visual InterDev is that it handles a lot of database programming chores for you. When you want to add a database connection to your project, a couple of mouse clicks do the job. If you want to build an ASP application that lists records from a database and provides buttons to navigate through the database, Visual InterDev provides design-time ActiveX Controls that make this a trivial effort. It also provides access to database design tools and SQL query building tools that make working with a database much easier.

For more information on Visual InterDev, visit http://www.microsoft.com/vinterdev/.

IIS also includes Microsoft Script Debugger. This tool, included in the Windows NT 4.0 Option Pack, supports the usual debugging activities, including the setting of break points, discovery of variable values, setting variables, and so on.

A number of third-party tools, such as HomeSite, are available for Active Server Pages development. For information on HomeSite, visit http://www.allaire.com/.

Dagwood: A Sample Application

The Dagwood sample application keeps track of items neighbors might borrow from you. The application allows the user to display a list of available items and borrow an item. The application works with a SQL Server database to retrieve lists of items, to record items being borrowed, and to record items being returned. The Dagwood application is available on the IIS Resource Kit CD, along with a Readme file with instructions on how to set up the application and try it out for yourself.

The first thing the Dagwood application does when it starts up is establish database connectivity via an ODBC Data Source Name (DSN). For information on using DSNs, see Chapter 6, "Data Access and Transactions" or the Windows NT 4.0 Option Pack online documentation.

Next, Dagwood sets a few essential session variables so that the rest of the Web pages in the application can access the database. In the following code sample, taken from the application's Global.asa file, several session variables are set. The `ASPsample_ConnectionString` value represents the string used to connect through the DSN defined for the database. The other variables represent other relevant database settings that can be used throughout the application. Global.asa is an excellent place to initialize useful application-wide variables. The variable `neighbor` holds the key to the Neighbor table, which stores information about the person logged on; the variable `item` holds the key to the Item table, where information about items that can be borrowed is stored.

```
<SCRIPT LANGUAGE=JScript RUNAT=Server>
function Session_OnStart() {
    //--Project Data Connection
        Session("ASPsample_ConnectionString") =
"DSN=Dagwood;Description=Database for sample Dagwood
application;APP=Microsoft (R) Developer Studio"
        Session("ASPsample_ConnectionTimeout") = 15
        Session("ASPsample_CommandTimeout") = 30
        Session("ASPsample_RuntimeUserName") = "sa"
        Session("ASPsample_RuntimePassword") = ""
        Session("neighbor") = 0
        Session("item") = 0
}
</SCRIPT>
```

Compare this sample with the code that would be needed to establish database connections in a LiveWire application. In sample LiveWire applications such as Netscape's VideoApp, a substantial amount of code is needed to create and manage connection pools. This code is not needed when using ODBC, because connection pooling is handled automatically. It's recommended that you avoid using connection-pooling code in your application and allow the ODBC driver to handle it for you. It is more efficient and easier to code as well.

As you plan the architecture of your Web applications, consider taking advantage of Microsoft Transaction Server (MTS), included with the Windows NT 4.0 Option Pack. This is the preferred method of managing the commitment of successful transactions and the rollback of failed ones. It allows you to avoid writing application-specific code for this purpose. In the simplest case, you need only include the instruction `<%@ TRANSACTION = Required %>` as the first line of an ASP page to take advantage of MTS.

MTS is used in the Dagwood application in Borrow.asp and in Return.asp, which update two separate tables as part of each transaction to borrow or return an item. Once you have assigned an MTS transaction to a page, all database activity on that page is transacted. If the script completes with no errors, updates are automatically committed to the database. If you abort the transaction using conditional code by calling the **SetAbort** method, the entire transaction is failed and all database activity is rolled back. In contrast, the VideoApp LiveWire application uses extensive code to manage transaction commitment and rollback. Custom transaction code is more complex, more difficult to maintain, more likely to fail, and less scalable than MTS.

The home page for the Dagwood application is Default.htm, shown in the following figure. This page is the central point from which the user can access all other Web pages in the application.

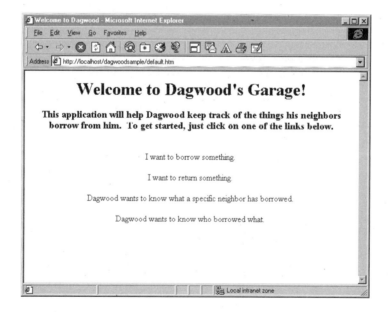

Figure 10.1   The Dagwood application's home page

The first thing a Dagwood user will likely want to do is borrow an item. To begin the process, the user clicks the **I want to borrow something** hyperlink on the Dagwood home page, which displays Type.asp, shown in the following figure.

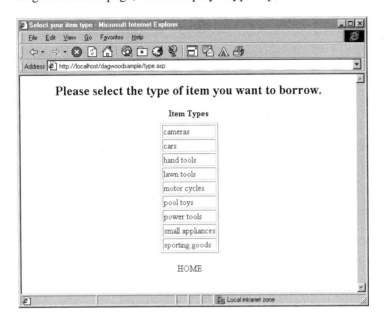

Figure 10.2   Type.asp

The Type.asp code is shown in the following listing. The code is heavily commented to explain what each instruction does.

```
<%@ LANGUAGE="JSCRIPT" %>
<HTML>
<HEAD>
<TITLE> Select your item type</TITLE>
</HEAD>
<BODY>
<CENTER>
<H2>Please select the type of item you want to borrow.</H2>
<%
// create database connection object
Conn = Server.CreateObject("ADODB.Connection");
// open the database connection
Conn.Open(Session("ASPsample_ConnectionString"));
// select records from the database
rsTypes= Conn.Execute("Select * FROM types Order by type");
// if there aren't any records
if (rsTypes.EOF)
```

```
        {
//      tell them the table is empty
            Response.Write('<b>Database contains no item types!</b>');
        }
        else
        {
//      There is at least one record, so build an HTML table for it
            Response.Write('<TABLE CELLSPACING=3 BORDER>');
            Response.Write('<CAPTION><B>Item Types</B></CAPTION>');
//      while we are not at end of file
            while (!(rsTypes.EOF))
            {
//          Write out each item from the database into the table
                Response.Write('<TR><TD><A HREF="Item.asp?type=');
                Response.Write(rsTypes("type").Value + '">');
                Response.Write(rsTypes("type").Value + ' </A> </TD> </TR>');
//          move to the next row in the database
                rsTypes.MoveNext();
//          go back to the top of the while loop
            }
//      we have reached EOF, so finish off the table
            Response.Write('</TABLE>');
        }
        %>
        <P><A HREF="default.htm">HOME</A></P>
        </CENTER>
        </BODY>
        </HTML>
```

Type.asp accesses a sample database and retrieves a list of the types of items that can be borrowed. In contrast to the LiveWire code in the VideoApp application, the use of session variables makes it possible to avoid building any constructs that require locking access to those variables. Also, because no code is used to support pooled connections, the database connection code is quite straightforward. A connection to the database is established, a session is opened, and records are retrieved from it. A new connection is created by the server only when needed. Where possible, the connection is drawn from a pool of connections managed by the driver. Once the execution of the page terminates, the database connection is automatically returned to the pool.

The user then sees the list of types of items available to be borrowed, and can select one of those types to see the list of items of that particular type available. Each type is formatted as a hyperlink to Item.asp. When the user clicks on a type, Item.asp is called and the type selected is passed to it. In the following figure, the user has chosen the "cameras" type, so the page displays a list of cameras available for borrowing.

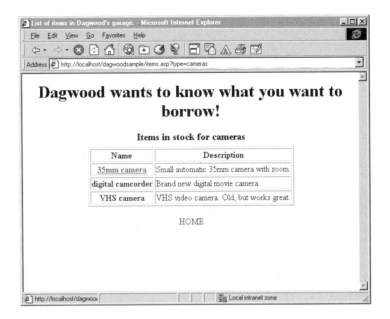

Figure 10.3   Item.asp

The source code for Item.asp is shown in the following listing. The script checks first to see whether the `type` variable has been passed to it. The `type` variable might not be passed if the user typed the page's URL for some reason and bypassed the Type.asp page that normally calls it.

```
<%@ LANGUAGE="JSCRIPT" %>
<html>
<head>
<title>List of items in Dagwood's garage.</title>
</head>
<body>
<CENTER>
<H1>Dagwood wants to know what you want to borrow!</H1>
<%
// If they got to this page without passing an item type
if (Request.QueryString().Count == 0)
{
//   tell them to pick an item and send them back
    Response.Write('<CENTER><A HREF="item.asp">');
    Response.Write('Please select an item type</A></CENTER>');
}
```

```
        else
        {
        // create database connection object
            Conn = Server.CreateObject("ADODB.Connection");
        // open the database connection
            Conn.Open(Session("ASPsample_ConnectionString"));
        // select records from the database
            rsItems = Conn.Execute("Select * FROM items WHERE qoh > 0 AND type =
        '"+Request("type")()+"' Order by i_name");
        //  If there aren't any rows in the table
            if (rsItems.EOF)
            {
        //      then tell them the table is empty
                Response.Write('<b>There are no items of this type.</b>');
            }
            else
            {
        //      There is at least one row, so build an HTML table for it
                Response.Write('<TABLE CELLSPACING=3 BORDER>');
                Response.Write('<CAPTION><B><FONT SIZE=+1>Items in stock for ');
                Response.Write(Request("type")() + '</FONT></B></CAPTION>');
                Response.Write('<TR><TH>Name</TH><TH>Description</TH></TR>');
        //      while we are not at end of file
                while (!(rsItems.EOF))
                {
        //          Write out each row from the database into the table
                    Response.Write('<TR><TH><A HREF="borrow.asp?item=');
                    Response.Write(rsItems("id").Value + '">');
                    Response.Write(rsItems("i_name").Value + '</A></TH>');
                    Response.Write('<TD>' + rsItems("description").Value);
                    Response.Write('</TD></TR>');
        //          move to the next row in the database
                    rsItems.MoveNext();
        //          go back to the top of the while loop
                }
        //      we have reached EOF, so finish off the table
                Response.Write('</TABLE>');
            }
        }
        %>
        <P><A HREF="default.htm">HOME</A></P>'
        </CENTER>
        </body>
        </html>
```

When the user selects an item from the list displayed, Borrow.asp is called and two variables passed to it, `item` and `neighbor`. Borrow.asp checks to see that these variables were in fact passed. If so, they are assigned to the appropriate session variables. The script uses these two values to assign a borrowed item to the user by recording that action in the Borrowed table. In addition, the script updates the quantity on hand (`qoh`) in the Items table to indicate that an item as been borrowed. Once the database tables have been updated, the script redirects the browser to Borrowed_confirm.asp, which displays the list of items currently on loan to the user, as shown in the following figure:

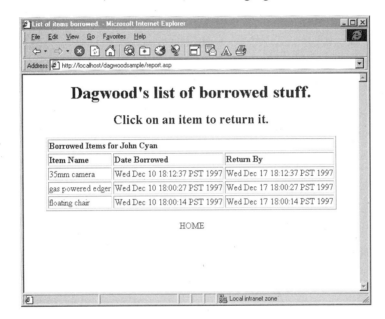

Figure 10.4   Borrowed_confirm.asp

The code for Borrow.asp is shown in the following listing:

```
<%@ LANGUAGE="JSCRIPT" TRANSACTION = Required %>
<!--#include file="adojavas.inc"-->
<%
// Server-side include gives us variables we can use for db access
// The include above can be found in the SDK that ships with the Option
Pack
// Create a string variable with the contents of the request string
mystring = new String(Request.ServerVariables("QUERY_STRING"));
//  check to see whether "item" is part of the request string
foundit=mystring.indexOf("item");
//  if it is, then "foundit" will have a value greater than -1
if (foundit > -1)
```

```
{
// because we found it, assign the request item to the session variable
    Session("item") = Request("item")();
}
// now look for "neighbor" in the request string
foundit=mystring.indexOf("neighbor");
// if it is, then "foundit" will have a value greater than -1
if(foundit > -1)
{
// we found it, so assign Request("neighbor") to the session variable
    Session("neighbor") = Request("neighbor")();
}
// if we didn't get a neighbor value, send the user to log on.
if(Session("neighbor") == 0)
{
// redirect the browser to a logon page.
    Response.Redirect("logon.asp");
}
else
{
// if we didn't get an item key, redirect the neighbor
// to the list of item types so he can pick one.
    if(Session("item") == 0)
    {
        Response.Redirect("type.asp");
    }
    else
    {
//      we know both the neighbor and the item so
//      let's put them down as borrowing an item
//      create the database object
        Conn = Server.CreateObject("ADODB.Connection");
//      create the recordset object
        RS = Server.CreateObject("ADODB.Recordset");
//      open the database
        Conn.Open(Session("ASPsample_ConnectionString"));
//      open the recordset to add a row to the "borrowed" table
        RS.Open("borrowed", Conn, adOpenKeyset, adLockOptimistic);
//      tell the database we are going to add a row
        RS.Addnew();
//      assign values to the columns in the row
        RS("neighbor") = Session("neighbor");
        RS("item") = Session("item");
//      some date logic so we can record the date
//      they borrwed the item (borroweddate)
```

```
//      and the date we would like to have it back (returnby)
        CurrDate = new Date();
//      the getVarDate method below puts the date into a format
//      that can be stuffed into a SQL Server date variable
        RS("borroweddate") = CurrDate.getVarDate();
        var ReturnDate = new Date();
        ReturnDate.setDate(CurrDate.getDate() + 7);
        RS("returnby") = ReturnDate.getVarDate();
//      assign a null value to the date returned
        RS("backdate") = null;
//      update the database
        RS.Update();
//      close our connection to the database
        RS.Close();
//      Now it's time to update the quantity on hand (qoh)
//      Get empty recordset
        RS.ActiveConnection = Conn;
        RS.Source = "SELECT * FROM items where items.id = " +
Session("item");
        RS.CursorType = adOpenStatic; // use a cursor other than Forward
Only
        RS.LockType = adLockOptimistic; // use a locktype permitting
insertions
        RS.Open();
        var return_qoh = 0;
        return_qoh = RS("qoh").Value;
        return_qoh = return_qoh - 1;
        RS("qoh").Value = return_qoh;
        RS.Update();
//      close our connection to the database
        RS.Close();
//      point the browser to a page that will confirm that
//      he has borrowed an item
        Response.Redirect("borrowed_confirm.asp");
    }
}
%>
```

The Dagwood application can also list items borrowed by various neighbors.
Users are able to return items and check them out again. When you are
comfortable with this example, you should be ready to begin the migration of your
LiveWire applications.

Migrating from Lotus Domino

This section describes how to migrate Lotus Domino Web sites and applications to IIS. It also describes different strategies for migration depending upon the given scenario.

This section doesn't cover migrating a Lotus Notes e-mail system to Microsoft Exchange Server. Nor does it cover migrating Lotus Notes applications to Microsoft Exchange Server, Microsoft Exchange Client, and Microsoft Outlook. For assistance in these scenarios, please consult the Lotus Notes to Microsoft Exchange Migration blueprint provided by Microsoft Consulting Services.

Migration Overview

The difficulty of migrating a Domino application depends on the complexity of the groupware facilities, application logic, and underlying services provided by the application. Domino is not only a Web server but also an integrated platform for workgroup applications. After migrating, Domino may still be required to provide services such as e-mail to Lotus Notes clients, unless the customer is also considering the migration of non-Web applications. Even in this case, a period of coexistence between Domino and IIS is still likely to be required during the migration.

Typical Migration Scenarios

The following are some scenarios that can prompt an organization to migrate Domino Web applications:

- Using IIS as the server for the corporate Internet Web site but maintaining Lotus Notes as their groupware platform.
- Using IIS as an Internet and intranet development platform, but still needing to access information from Lotus Notes databases.
- Migrating a Lotus Notes installed base to Microsoft Exchange Server and wanting to create Web applications.
- Wanting to create and extend Web applications using standard Internet development tools.

Migration Strategies

A Domino Web site is defined by one or more Lotus Notes databases that store the content and design of the site. Migration is typically done on an application-by-application basis.

Types of Applications

Typically, Domino Web applications fall into one of the following application categories:

- Applications based on Lotus Notes templates that include no special Web features and are just being shared to the Web. This type of application is not difficult to migrate because it typically doesn't include a lot of code, forms, views, or Navigators. Also, this type of application offers limited support for Web users and the functionality is very simple. The same type of application may have already been developed using Microsoft technology. The http://www.microsoft.com/intranet/ site includes many Web applications that can be customized or used immediately.

- Applications customized from Lotus Notes templates, or created with other tools, that don't have special Web features and are just being shared to the Web. This type of application offers a higher degree of complexity. The amount of code used in the application varies, but more forms, views, and Navigators are used. The number of Web users accessing the application may be lower than the number of Lotus Notes clients accessing it. Also, Lotus Notes clients will likely still access the application after migration, so special considerations have to be taken to make data accessible both to IIS and to Lotus Notes.

- Applications based on Lotus Notes templates with no special Web features and customized to incorporate special Web features. The application probably includes code for Lotus Notes clients and code for Web users. Lotus Notes clients may still need to access the application after migration.

- Applications based on Web-aware Lotus Notes templates (for example "Discussion" or "Doc Library for Notes & Web"). This type of application should not be too difficult to migrate. The templates usually don't include a large amount of code and tend to be simple. It's worth checking http://www.microsoft.com/intranet/ for comparable applications that run on IIS.

- Fully customized applications with special Web features and code. This type of application is typically based on Internet standards such as HTML and CGI. Some parts of the application may be reused after migration. Lotus Notes documents included in these applications tend to be more like HTML pages than typical Notes documents.

- Fully customized Web applications offering extended services like e-commerce with Domino.Merchant, Domino.Action, Domino.Broadcast, Domino.Doc or other products. This type of application requires more effort to migrate because the services it provides also have to be migrated.

You should analyze the business logic of each application and evaluate which components of the application can be reused. You can then redesign and develop the application using an architecture such as the three-tier model.

Elements of a Domino Web Site

Each Domino Web site includes at least one database that contains the following elements:

- Documents
- Forms
- Fields
- Views and folders
- Navigators
- Home page
- Links
- Formulas
- Agents and actions

Domino offers a completely different architecture from that of IIS. Every element of a Domino Web site is contained in a Domino database. Generally a Domino Web site migration involves:

- Data or document migration
- Application migration

Application migration is the most time-consuming task, and is made more difficult because of the differences between the Domino and IIS application development environments.

Document Migration

Domino documents can be migrated to HTML and Active Server Pages files if their content is static and similar to a Web page. If their content is rich and unstructured, they can be migrated to items in Microsoft Exchange folders. If their content is structured and text oriented, they can be migrated to SQL Server records. Many documents in a Domino Web site hold static content, which can be migrated to HTML and Active Server Pages rather than to Microsoft Exchange Server or Microsoft SQL Server.

HTML Pages

Some Domino documents include include HTML code and Internet components like Java applets, but are still saved to the Lotus Notes database proprietary format rather than as native HTML files.

There are no automation tools that can help the migration of Lotus Notes documents to standard HTML files, so the conversion must be done manually on a document-by-document basis.

Web Site Home Page

The Domino Web site home page is a good starting point for migrating Domino documents to HTML and Active Server pages. This page can be stored in the file system as an HTML file, or it can be stored in the Lotus Notes database as an About document, Notes document or Navigator.

The server document contains the Home URL field that stores the URL used as the site's home page.

HTML

Domino supports most HTML 3.2 tags. Lotus Notes documents are not pure HTML files, and there are several ways to incorporate HTML code into a Notes document. You need to be aware of where the HTML code comes from for every document.

In particular, check for:

- HTML formatting assigned to Notes documents with the form event "HTML Body Attributes."
- HTML code typed directly onto the form or document.
- Documents treated as pure HTML.
- Fields with HTML attributes.
- Existence of the field named HTML or $$HTMLHead that holds HTML code for the document.

Many Domino Web sites are created using a single form for Web pages, in which case the HTML code for every document is likely to be almost the same.

Java Applets

Java applets are supported in Notes applications. A Java applet can be included in a form to include the applet in each document created by the form, or it can be inserted into a document's rich text field to include it only in that document.

Applets usually reside in the file system; they can also reside on a Web server and be linked to it.

Using Microsoft Visual Interdev, Java applets can be added by using the FrontPage editor or by using the <APPLET> tag. The attributes of CODE, WIDTH, and HEIGHT are required.

The following example shows the syntax for setting attributes in the <APPLET> tag:

```
<APPLET
    ALIGN=LEFT|CENTER|RIGHT|TOP|MIDDLE|BOTTOM
    CODE=appletFile
    CODEBASE=codebaseURL
    HEIGHT=pixels
    HSPACE=pixels
    NAME=appletInstanceName
    VSPACE=pixels
    WIDTH=pixels>
<PARAM NAME=AttributeName VALUE=value...>
alternate HTML
</APPLET>
```

Object Store Migration

For documents that are more database-like, you need to decide whether the data contained in the Lotus Notes database should:

- Remain in the same database.
- Be migrated to a different database.
- Be synchronized between different systems.
- Not be migrated at all.

One of the main factors that will influence this decision is whether the data will still need to be accessed by Lotus Notes clients and whether the application is linked to other business processes that are not going to be migrated.

The Domino object store is a flexible container whose basic object is the document. A document can contain a wide variety of data types that range from simple text fields to rich text fields containing objects like documents and images. A Domino database often contains documents created by different forms.

The Domino object store is best suited for applications that handle unstructured data, and most Domino applications manage information of this type.

Maintaining Data in Lotus Notes Databases

The most common scenario for maintaining data in a Lotus Notes database is when an organization is building a Web site based on IIS and needs to integrate data contained in one or more Lotus Notes databases. The data is left in the Lotus Notes database so that Lotus Notes clients can access it, and there are no plans to migrate the application itself to Exchange and Outlook. In this case, the orgainization is not planning to migrate the actual application, but needs Web applications based on IIS to access the data contained on Lotus Notes databases.

Note that this configuration is suited only for certain types of applications. It works for applications that only need to retrieve public data or for applications where the identity of the user is not an issue. Security may be compromised because all the information will be stored in the Notes databases with permissions granted to the Notes user installed on the server running IIS.

Maintaining Data Both in Lotus Notes and in Microsoft Exchange Server or Microsoft SQL Server

You may want to choose to maintain data both in Notes and in Exchange or SQL Server when the Web application to be migrated will still need to be accessed by Lotus Notes clients. Synchronization between systems can be maintained for a period of time while the migration is taking place or it could be permanent. You need to decide what kind of database or object store best fits your needs. You can choose a relational database system like SQL Server or a more unstructured object store like Microsoft Exchange Server. The following table can serve as a guide to decide which system to use. Most Lotus Notes databases can be migrated smoothly to Exchange Server. Also, data contained in a Lotus Notes database can be separated—part of it can be migrated to SQL Server, and part of it to Exchange Server.

Table 10.5   Microsoft SQL Server and Microsoft Exchange Server Comparison

Microsoft SQL Server	Microsoft Exchange Server
Structured information—clearly defined tables, fields, and views	Unstructured information—different types of objects stored in the database
No rich text fields or rich text formatting	Rich text fields and rich text formatting
Table oriented	Document oriented
Very high performance	Messaging integration
	Threaded discussions
	Workflow functionality

There are several third-party tools that can either help synchronize Notes and other databases, or help to migrate from Notes to other databases.

- The Mesa Group offers a connection agent (CXA) that provides seamless coexistence and rapid migration between Lotus Notes databases and Microsoft Exchange public folders. CXA provides conversion and replication of information between groupware databases. It preserves elements like rich text, attachments, OLE objects, document links, custom properties, and discussion threading. For more information, visit Mesa's Web site at http://www.mesa.com/.

- Casahl Technology's Replic-Action for Microsoft Exchange 5.0, provides a high-performance tool for accessing, synchronizing, revising, and manipulating data on a client/server network. Replic-Action for Microsoft Exchange 5.0 allows you to replicate data between more than 40 databases, including Lotus Notes databases. For more information, visit Casahl's Web site at http://www.casahl.com/.

- Percussion Software's Notrix family of products provides a powerful set of data integration tools that facilitates the exchange of data between Lotus Notes databases and external data environments, especially relational database management systems. Microsoft SQL Server native access is provided. For more information, visit Percussion Software's Web site at http://www.notrix.com/.

Migrating Data to Microsoft Exchange Server or Microsoft SQL Server

If the Domino Web application to be migrated will be accessed only by Web browsers, then there is no need to maintain both the Lotus Notes application and a SQL server database or Exchange public folder. As soon as the Web application is migrated, users can point their browsers to the new Web site where the application is hosted. The third-party tools described in the previous section can be used to migrate data from one database to another. These tools are also helpful for migrating Domino applications that are not Web applications.

Not Migrating Data

For some types of applications, such as discussion databases, it isn't necessary to migrate information from the Lotus Notes database to another database engine. It's up to you to decide whether the information contained in the database is worth preserving on the other system.

Application Migration

Migrating applications is the most difficult migration task, partly because of the proprietary Domino scripting environment and the lack of tools to help automate the process of migration. Most of the time, a complete application redesign is needed. Some organizations use this redesign as an opportunity to reengineer their applications and implement architectures such as the three-tier model.

Database Access

Once a decision has been made about which databases or object stores are to be used by the new Web application and the data has been migrated or synchronized, you need to decide which database access method is going to be used by the Web application to access the information.

Visual Interdev provides an easy way to create data-aware Web pages with which you can perform standard database functions such as queries and updates. There are three key technologies that can be used to access databases from Active Server Pages:

- **Internet Database Connector (IDC)**   IDC is a built-in feature of IIS. You can use it to submit SQL statements to retrieve records from an ODBC-compliant database.

- **Remote Data Service (RDS)**   RDS is a set of ActiveX controls that can be placed on a Web page to enable client-side access to a database. When RDS controls are embedded in a Web page, they can retrieve, update, and create records on either an OLE DB or ODBC-compliant database. RDS accesses databases through ActiveX Data Objects (ADO).

- **ActiveX Data Objects (ADO)**   ADO is the latest data access model. ADO is a collection of automation objects that can retrieve, update, and create records in any OLE DB or ODBC-compliant database.

ADO is the recommended access method, because it is a newer technology that incorporates the functionality of the other two. For more information on database access techniques, see Chapter 5, "Data Access and Transactions."

These access methods apply to SQL Server, Lotus Notes databases, or any other ODBC-compliant database system. Exchange requires a different access method, using a technology called Collaborative Data Objects (CDO).

Lotus Notes Database

An ODBC driver is available for Lotus Notes (NotesSQL ODBC driver) with which you can open, query, and modify Lotus Notes databases. Any ODBC-compliant application can access a Notes database with this ODBC driver.

An ASP page can use ADO and the NotesSQL ODBC driver to access a Lotus Notes Database.

You must install the Lotus Notes client and the ODBC driver on the server that will be running Active Server Pages for this configuration to work. The Notes ID should not be password protected.

Microsoft SQL Server

Microsoft SQL Server also provides an ODBC driver that enables a Web application to access the databases. The following is an example of code generated by Visual Interdev in the Global.asa file to connect to a SQL Server database named PUBS. The Global.asa file holds event procedures that run when a Web application starts or ends or when a new session starts or ends.

```
</SCRIPT>
<SCRIPT LANGUAGE=VBScript RUNAT=Server>
Sub Session_OnStart
    '==Visual InterDev Generated - DataConnection startspan==
    '--Project Data Connection
        Session("PUBS_ConnectionString") = "DSN=SQL Server
database;Description=SQL Server PUBS
database;SERVER=myserver;UID=sa;PWD=;APP=Microsoft (R) Developer
Studio;WSID=WORKSTATION;DATABASE=PUBS"
        Session("PUBS_ConnectionTimeout") = 15
        Session("PUBS_CommandTimeout") = 30
        Session("PUBS_RuntimeUserName") = "sa"
        Session("PUBS_RuntimePassword") = ""
    '==Visual InterDev Generated - DataConnection endspan==
End Sub
</SCRIPT>
```

Microsoft Exchange Server

You can use Collaborative Data Objects (CDO) to create Web-based business applications that include Exchange Server technologies, such as messaging, scheduling, and groupware. CDO was known formerly as Active Messaging or OLE Messaging. It is designed to simplify the creation of applications that use messaging functionality.

CDO is made available through libraries that expose programmable messaging objects including folders, messages, recipient addresses, attachments, and other messaging components. By understanding the hierarchical structure of the object model, you can easily retrieve data from and add data to Microsoft Exchange Server.

CDO allows you to write server-side messaging applications based on Active Server Pages.

To access the Exchange information store, it's necessary to start a MAPI session. The **Session** object is at the top of the hierarchy of the CDO Model. The main children of the **Session** object are the **InfoStores** and **AddressList** collections, which contain objects like mailboxes, folders, and messages.

The following is an example of how to initiate a connection to a Microsoft Exchange Server using VBScript. This example creates a new session with the Exchange Server myserver and logs on as user administrator.

```
Set objOMSession = Server.CreateObject("MAPI.Session")
bstrProfileInfo = "myserver" & chr(10) & "administrator"'
objOMSession.Logon "", "", False, True, 0, True, bstrProfileInfo
```

The CDO rendering library makes it possible to call CDO objects from Active Server Pages and send the output to Web browsers in HTML format, easing the development of Web applications that access the Exchange information store.

Any Web application that needs to access the Exchange information store must call the CDO libraries from Active Server Pages. The CDO libraries are included on the IIS Resource Kit CD.

Forms and Fields

In Domino, a form is a framework for entering and viewing information in a database. A Domino form can contain:

- Fields that store data.

- Text labels or instructions.

- Subforms that store a collection of form elements you want to use on more than one form.

- Layout regions that combine graphics and fields in a way that affords greater design flexibility.

- Graphics that make forms easier to understand.

- Tables that summarize or organize information.

- Objects, file attachments, and links that extend the reach of Notes documents.

- Actions and buttons that perform functions automatically.

- Background color and graphics that enhance the look of a document.

Not all forms components are available to Web applications. Domino forms are translated to HTML forms by the HTTP server task when Web users access it.

HTML forms package the names and values of each control, and then send them to the location specified by the ACTION attribute. The location can be a CGI application, an ISAPI application, or an ASP page.

In the following example code, the form sends information to the file Events.asp.

```
<FORM ACTION=events.asp METHOD=POST>
```

CDO Web Forms

It is also possible to create Web forms by using CDO. With CDO, each page can contain a set of controls that provide nearly all the functionality offered by a form created with the Electronic Forms Designer (a tool for developing electronic forms for Exchange Server).

ASP pages are used to render messages and forms. These pages contain not only the CDO code that handles information received from users, but also the HTML code that interacts with users. This code can include input boxes, option buttons, and list controls that a standard message does not include.

Views

Views are the entry point for data stored in a Domino database. Users open a view to see a list of documents in the database and then open documents from there. Every Domino database must have at least one view.

Microsoft Exchange Server folders can also have views defined. Each view selects the items to be displayed to the user and the fields to be included in each column.

Folder views are stored as hidden messages in the folder and are accessible by anyone having Read access to the folder. All views must have the message class **IPM.Microsoft.FolderDesign.NamedView**.

The **View** collection object is used by the CDO rendering library to render a container object such as a public folder. The Web site http://www.microsoft.com/technet/appfarm/ contains examples of ASP applications that access Microsoft Exchange folders.

Navigators

Domino Navigators are roadmaps that direct users to a particular part of an application. Domino converts Navigators to HTML imagemaps. Some Domino documents may contain views and Navigators embedded into them.

Frames can provide the same functionality provided by Navigators. Frames divide the Web page into multiple scrollable areas, with each area defined by its own HTML file.

Programming

Domino offers the following ways to incorporate programming into a Web application:

- @functions
- @commands
- CGI programs
- Perl scripts
- Lotus Script

@functions and @commands

The @functions and @commands are intrinsic to the Domino architecture and application development environment. Any application logic provided by these features must be replaced by Active Server Pages scripting in languages such as VBScript or JavaScript, or by component objects called by an ASP page.

CGI programs

Because CGI programs are not stored in a Lotus Notes database, access permissions are handled by the operating system. Each CGI program used by a Domino Web application must be moved to IIS and tested. It is strongly recommended that CGI programs be migrated to Active Server Pages or ISAPI. Because CGI programs create a new process with every request, they are resource intensive and do not scale well. For information on migrating CGI applications, see "Migrating CGI Applications to IIS," earlier in this chapter.

It's a good idea to create a separate directory to install and configure CGI applications. The directory doesn't need to be named Cgi-bin. If the CGI programs are .exe files, the directory must have Execute permission. If the CGI programs are scripts, then the appropriate script interpreter must be installed.

Domino captures CGI variables by using fields in Notes documents with the same name as the CGI variable or by using the document context property in agent scripts.

Perl Scripts

Domino supports programs written in Perl. Perl programs are normally placed in the Cgi-bin subdirectory under the Domino directory. The environment variable PERLBIN stores the path of the Perl interpreter.

A Perl interpreter is available from ActiveState. For more information, visit http://www.activestate.com/.

Lotus Script

Lotus Script for form actions and buttons is not supported by Domino for Web users. Lotus Script is mainly used in agents for Web applications. Agents are stand-alone programs that perform specific tasks in a Lotus Notes database. Internet Information Server does not support Lotus Script.

Microsoft Exchange Server 5.5 includes a new feature called Microsoft Exchange Scripting Agent. This feature allows server-side scripting for the creation of event-driven agents. The scripts can be written in VBScript or JavaScript. It is also possible to create custom agents that are not programmed using scripting languages, but instead are compiled objects created in Visual Basic, Visual C++, Java, or any other programming language that supports COM (Component Object Model).

Resources

Web site information is current as of the date of publication, but is, of course, subject to change.

Tools and Applications

http://www.allaire.com/
Provides information on Allaire's HomeSite Web application development tool.

http://www.microsoft.com/data/
Microsoft's Universal Data Access Web site. Explains data access strategies.

http://www.microsoft.com/intranet/
The Microsoft Intranet Solutions Center site. Provides many Web applications that can be customized or used immediately.

http://www.microsoft.com/technet/appfarm/
The Microsoft Exchange Application Farm Web site. Provides sample ASP applications that access Microsoft Exchange folders.

http://www.microsoft.com/transaction/
The Microsoft Transaction Server Web site.

http://www.microsoft.com/vinterdev/
The Microsoft Visual InterDev site.

Component Development

http://www.microsoft.com/com/
The Microsoft Component Object Model site.

http://www.microsoft.com/dna/

The Windows Distributed interNet Applications Architecture (DNA) site. Provides information on Component Object Model (COM) development and Microsoft's distributed applications development model.

http://www.microsoft.com/msdn/

The Microsoft Developer Network site. Provides many useful resources for component developers.

http://www.microsoft.com/vbasic/docs/migr8/pre.htm

A Microsoft white paper, "Migrating Existing Information Systems to Component Architectures."

Scripting Languages

http://www.activestate.com/

ActiveState provides three Perl engines of interest to IIS developers: Perl for Win32, Perl for ISAPI, and PerlScript, an ActiveX scripting engine that allows the use of PerlScript code in an ASP page.

http://www.bio.cam.ac.uk/cgi-lib/

Provides information on the Cgi-lib.pl library.

http://www-genome.wi.mit.edu/ftp/pub/software/WWW/cgi_docs.html

Provides information on the Cgi.pm utility.

http://www.hermetica.com/technologia/DBI/

Provides a Perl-based DBI package and documentation, including ideas for porting existing DBI code to the Win32 platform.

http://www.python.org/windows/

Provides Python language products.

http://sunscript.sun.com/

Provides Tcl scripting language products.

UNIX Migration

http://www.cygnus.com/misc/gnu-win32/

Provides GNU development tools for Windows.

http://www.itribe.net/virtunix/

Provides Windows versions of popular UNIX tools.

http://www.mks.com/

Mortice Kern Systems makes the MKS Toolkit, which provides many utilities, such as htdiff, htsplit, url, and web, to help you automate Web development and maintenance tasks. The Toolkit includes a version of Perl, as well as Pscript, an ActiveX scripting engine that allows you to use PerlScript code in an ASP page.

Lotus Domino Migration

http://www.casahl.com/

Provides information on Casahl Technology's Replic-Action for Microsoft Exchange 5.0, with which you can replicate data between more than 40 databases, including Lotus Notes databases.

http://www.mesa.com/

Provides information on the Mesa Group's Lotus Notes and Microsoft Exchange conversion and coexistence tools.

http://www.notrix.com/

Provides information on Percussion Software's Notrix family of products—a set of tools to facilitate the exchange of data between Lotus Notes databases and other data stores.

A P P E N D I X   A

Using the IIS Resource Kit CD

A

The IIS Resource Kit compact disc contains samples, components, and utilities for Internet Information Server and the Windows NT 4.0 Option Pack. The IIS Resource Kit CD Setup program installs documentation for each application; this appendix summarizes the contents of the CD and provides installation instructions.

Installation

To install the applications on the IIS Resource Kit CD, place the compact disc in the CD-ROM drive. The Setup program will start automatically. During setup, you can choose to have the complete set of files copied to your hard disk, or you can customize your installation by selecting which items to install.

The contents of the Internet Information Server Resource Kit CD fall into three categories: ISAPI filters and applications, components, and utilities. During setup, the **Select Components** dialog box appears, which lists the three categories. To install everything, click **Next**. To select or deselect individual items to be installed, highlight the category and click **Change**. Check or clear each item, depending on whether you want Setup to copy it to your hard disk.

Resource Kit Support Policy

The software supplied in the *Internet Information Server Resource Kit* is not officially supported. Microsoft does not guarantee the performance of the *Internet Information Server Resource Kit* tools, response times for answering questions, or bug fixes to the tools. However, we do provide several ways for customers who purchase Internet Information Server or the *Internet Information Server Resource Kit* to report bugs and receive possible fixes for their issues. You can submit feedback on the *Internet Information Server Resource Kit* by sending e-mail to Rkinput@microsoft.com. This e-mail address is only for Resource Kit–related issues. For more general feedback on Microsoft Internet Information Server, send e-mail to Iiswish@microsoft.com.

ISAPI Filters and Applications

Internet Server Application Program Interface (ISAPI) filters and applications are DLLs written to the ISAPI interface. ISAPI is an API for developing filters and application extensions to IIS and other HTTP servers that support the ISAPI interface.

ISAPI filters can intercept specific server events before the server itself handles them. When a filter is loaded, it indicates what sort of event notifications it will handle. If these events occur, the filter has the option of processing the events, passing them on to other filters, or sending them back to the server after it has dealt with them. ISAPI filters run within the IIS process memory space.

ISAPI applications are called after the server handles a request. They can perform virtually any task a DLL can do. ISAPI applications can run in the same memory space as the IIS process or as separate processes.

The following section is an overview and brief description of the ISAPI filters and applications stored in the \ISAPI Filter folder of the IIS Resource Kit CD. Complete documentation for each filter and application is installed by the CD Setup program.

ASP Caching

The ASP Caching filter caches the HTML output of an ASP file. This allows a faster response for subsequent downloads of the same file. The speed gain depends on the page, according to how much processing the page would normally require.

Authentication Methods

The Authentication Methods filter is designed to change the authentication methods and order supplied to Internet Explorer by IIS. The filter is useful for authentication testing and for prioritizing the methods returned by IIS. This is achieved by catching the initial "401 Access denied" message that contains the list of supported authentication methods, and then modifying the message to contain a new list based on the virtual directory of the URL.

Cookie Munger

Cookie Munger is a filter that enables Active Server Pages to provide cookie functionality to browsers that do not support cookies or that do not accept them.

Distributed Authoring and Versioning

Distributed Authoring and Versioning (DAV) provides a means for publishing and accessing information on Web servers through the HTTP protocol. DAV includes the following features:

- Upload, rename, move, or delete files.
- Create, rename, delete, copy, or move directories.
- Set and retrieve properties on files and directories.
- Search for files based on their properties or text contents.

HTML Compressor

HTML Compressor dynamically compresses HTML as it is being sent to the browser.

IFilter Test Suite

The IFilter Test Suite calls **IFilter** methods and checks the returned values for compliance with the IFilter specification.

Index Server Filter for C and C++ Files

By using this filter, Index Server can index C and C++ source files. Instead of going through the Web server, the filter works with Srch.exe, a search utility for performing queries directly with Index Server.

ISpy

The ISpy filter is a tool for stepping through ISAPI filter notifications one at a time and examining (and modifying) any associated data. ISpy consists of an ISAPI filter DLL and a Win32-based front end. By using ISpy, an ISAPI filter developer can gain insight into the workings of IIS and better understand how to write an ISAPI filter.

W3Who

W3Who is a an ISAPI application that displays the current security context and session environment variables.

Components

The components on the IIS Resource Kit CD are COM objects that can be called from ASP pages or from ISAPI applications. The following section is an overview and brief description of the components stored in the \Component folder of the IIS Resource Kit CD. Documentation for each component is installed by the CD Setup program.

ASP to HTML

The ASP to HTML component can be used to gain much of the power of Active Server Pages, without the performance cost. Given a URL, the component can connect to the address and retrieve its properties. The document at the URL can also be saved to a local file. A typical use of this component would be to download ASP pages from your own server, let the server-side scripting occur, and save the resulting HTML files to your local hard disk. The HTML files can then be published on your Web site.

Collaborative Data Objects

Collaborative Data Objects (CDO) can be used to send mail and gain access to messages in an Exchange Server message store. Included with CDO is a collection of samples that show how to use CDO to create groupware applications. Also included is the HTML Forms Design Wizard and the FrontPage Discussion Wizard. With the HTML Forms Design Wizard, you can quickly create customized HTML forms based on the built-in forms included with Microsoft Outlook. With the FrontPage Discussion Wizard, you can create a discussion Web site, or add a discussion forum to an existing Web site, without writing any scripts.

Content Rotator

The Content Rotator component automatically rotates HTML content strings on a Web page. Each time a user requests the Web page, the Content Rotator component displays a new HTML content string based upon information that you specify in a Content Schedule file.

Because the content strings can contain HTML tags, you can display any type of content that HTML can represent: text, images, or hyperlinks. For example, you can use this component to rotate through a list of daily quotations or hyperlinks, or to change your text and background colors each time the Web page is opened.

Counters

The Counters component creates, stores, increments, and retrieves counters that you create. The counters persist until you remove them and can be accessed from any page on a site. Unlike a page counter (see "Page Counter" later in this section), counters do not increment automatically; they must be set programmatically.

HTML Table

The HTML Table component converts data stored in an ActiveX Data Objects (ADO) recordset into an HTML table.

Load Balancer

Load Balancer can be used with remote Performance Monitor statistics as a basis for software-based load balancing. The component continuously polls a user-defined list of servers for a specified Performance Monitor statistic and re-sorts the list based on the resulting values. The sort order can be specified as either ascending or descending depending on the nature of the statistic, at the programmer's discretion.

Page Counter

The Page Counter component provides the functionality of a basic page counter, sometimes called a "hit counter," which is used to track the number of accesses to one or more pages; that is, the total number of times that a page has been requested. The page counter writes its array of pages and corresponding hit counts to a text file periodically. The text file provides a persistent record of hit activity.

Permission Checker

The Permission Checker component can be used to check the access rights (for the current user) to a given file. You can use Permission Checker to exclude the items that are not accessible to the current user from the generated HTML page.

Registry Access

The Registry Access component is an ASP component that can be used to read and modify strings and numbers in the Windows NT registry. It can also be used to delete keys (and all associated subkeys and values) and to delete simple values, and it can be used to recursively copy keys. It will also work with registry keys on remote computers.

Status

The Status component returns server status information. Currently this server status is only available on Personal Web Server for Macintosh.

Summary Information

The Summary Information component can display the properties of a document (or directory of documents) in HTML format. For example, you can display the properties of a Microsoft Word or Microsoft Excel document (the information displayed by clicking **Properties** on the **File** menu of Word or Microsoft Excel).

Tools

The Tools component provides several utility methods:

- The **FileExists** method tests for the existence of a file specified in a URL.
- The **Owner** method checks whether the current user is the site administrator.
- The **PluginExists** method checks whether a specified Macintosh server plug-in exists.
- The **ProcessForm** method processes the contents of a form submitted by a visitor to the Web site.
- The **Random** method returns a random integer.

Tracer

The Tracer component is a profiler for ASP pages. Data can be output to a debug log or to a file. The data is formatted as a comma-separated list, so that it can be imported into a database or spreadsheet.

Utilities

The IIS Resource Kit utilities are applications that can be used in conjunction with IIS to extend or enhance the operations you might normally perform while administering and running your Web server. This section is an overview and brief description of the utilities stored in the \Utility folder of the IIS Resource Kit CD. Documentation for each utility is installed by the CD Setup program.

ADOSelect

ADOSelect is a simple ASP application that can be used to troubleshoot ADO connections to any ODBC-compliant data source.

ADSI Administration Scripts

The ADSI scripts are a set of VBScript and JScript files that automate many common Web server administration tasks (adding a new user, changing user properties, creating a Web site, and many more). For an overview of these scripts, and the Windows Scripting Host environment, see Chapter 7, "ISP Administration."

Backstab

Backstab is a multiplayer game written using ASP and Component Object Model (COM) technology. The user interface presented to player is a set of ASP pages. The game engine is a COM object that tracks game state. Backstab is an example of how multiuser transactional application functionality factors naturally into the ASP and COM application model.

Calendar

The Calendar application is an ASP script you can use to display the current day of the week, date, month, and year on a Web page.

COM Transaction Integrator for CICS and IMS

The COM Transaction Integrator for CICS and IMS creates components that provide an interface with mainframe-based applications. Running on Windows NT Server, components created with the Transaction Integrator appear as Automation servers that developers can easily add to their application. Behind the scenes, however, the Transaction Integrator functions as a proxy that communicates with an application program running on IBM's Multiple Virtual Storage (MVS) operating system. Applications that run in part on Windows platforms and in part on the mainframe are, by definition, distributed applications. COM Transaction Integrator for CICS and IMS supports all distributed applications that adhere to the Automation and distributed COM (DCOM) specifications, although not all parts of the application have to adhere to these standards.

FrontPage Index Server Query Wizard

The Index Server Query Wizard can be used to create new HTML search pages, IDQ query scripts, and HTX results templates. You can also use it as an IDQ editor for making changes to existing IDQ scripts by double-clicking them in the FrontPage Explorer.

IIS Host Helper Service

IIS Host Helper Service registers the host name specified for an IIS Web site. The host name is registered with NetBIOS on the local computer.

HTML Text Filter

The HTML Text Filter utility is a command-line tool that removes comments and extra white space from HTML files.

HTTPCmd

With HTTPCmd, you can execute HTTP requests at the command line. As input, HTTPCmd takes the name of an input file containing a full HTTP request. Some typical input files are provided as samples in the \Requests folder.

HTTPMon

The HTTPMon utility monitors and performs a statistical analysis of Web server activity.

IDC2ASP

By using the IDC2ASP utility, you can convert IDC/HTX projects to ASP pages. The IDC2ASP utility consists of a command-line utility and an ActiveX component. The component can be called from an ASP page or from executables created in any language that supports ActiveX, including Visual Basic, Visual J++, and Visual C++.

IIS Migration Wizard

The IIS Migration Wizard facilitates the migration of Web sites from Netscape 2.0 or 3.0 to IIS. The utility consists of a Perl module (the Scavenger) that runs on the source Web server, and an ASP application (the Migrator) that reads the data file and configures IIS on the target computer.

ISP Sign-up System

The ISP Sign-Up System provides an HTML interface for potential customers so that they can sign up for ISP services.

Javafy

The Javafy utility converts VBScript code to JScript.

JSAPI

JSAPI is a framework for creating ISAPI applications in Java using only native Java code with native Java data types. JSAPI encapsulates all the interactions between Java and C or C++ and COM, as well as the marshalling of different data types. JSAPI users only have to deal with native Java objects.

MetaEdit

You can use MetaEdit to edit the IIS metabase. It is similar to the Windows NT Registry Editor (RegEdit), but operates on the metabase instead.

Microsoft CDF Generator

Microsoft CDF Generator is a tool you can use for the creation of Channel Definition Format files (CDFs).

Microsoft Web Capacity Analysis Tool

The Microsoft Web Capacity Analysis Tool (WCAT) runs simulated workloads on client/server configurations. Using WCAT, you can test how IIS and your network configuration respond to a variety of different client requests. The results of these tests can be used to determine the optimal server and network configuration. WCAT is specially designed to evaluate how Internet servers running Windows NT Server and IIS respond to various client workload simulations.

MMC Snap-ins

The Microsoft Management Console (MMC) administration snap-ins for the Microsoft NNTP and SMTP Services included with IIS 4.0 allow administration from Windows NT Server computers only. With these extensions, you can administer these services from a remote Windows NT Workstation computer.

MTS Administrator (HTML)

MTS Administrator (HTML) is an HTML-based application with which you can administer Microsoft Transaction Server from a browser.

Orville

Orville is a Web application testing tool. It provides a way to implement an effective test plan for Web applications. Orville scripts can be recorded from a conversation between a Web browser, such as Internet Explorer, and a Web server. The browser, Orville, and the Web server can all be running on the same computer, or on different computer, depending on the tester's preference.

PerkMon

PerkMon is an application with which you can monitor Windows NT Server performance from any Java-enabled environment. PerkMon is designed to mimic Windows NT Performance Monitor (PerfMon), the standard monitoring tool for Windows NT Server.

Themes

Themes are sample style templates for Personal Web Server for Windows NT Workstation.

WebCheck

WebCheck monitors server activity and can send e-mail notification messages or log alerts to a database.

Xray

Xray is an object model viewer with which you can browse the methods and properties of any .tlb or .olb file.

APPENDIX B

ASP Standards

B

Standards for Active Server Pages (ASP) development promote:

- Script efficiency (fast application execution).
- Efficient use of server resources.
- Consistent styles and conventions.

Using ASP in IIS

To make the most efficient use of your server resources, you should use the .asp file name extension only for pages that contain scripts.

Writing Scripts for Browsers

When possible, write scripts to be executed by the browser, rather than the server. By using the client platform to perform tasks such as data validation, edit-checking, and selecting simple conditional output, you can reserve server resources for those tasks requiring ASP.

ASP Application Directory Structure

The directory and file conventions suggested in this section optimize ASP application directory structure for consistency, clarity, and ease of use.

The directories and files described are listed here:

/Application_Root

Default.htm

Global.asa

/Classes

/Content

/Media

/Themes

/Data

/DLLs

/Helpers (not in the Web site directories identifiable to users)

Application Root Directory

For readability and clarity, the application root directory should be named in a way that conveys what the site is about. For example, a site about financial research might be named /FinancialResearch or /FR. Avoid application root names that might be misidentified as standard subdirectories of a site, such as /Media or /Content. Also, avoid names that sound like part numbers or codes, such as /FR98346A.

While the site is being developed, the application root directory should be stored under /InetPub/Wwwroot.

The root directory of every application should contain at least these files:

- Default.htm
- Global.asa

Default.htm or Default.asp should be the default home page for the site, and the server default should be set accordingly. This combination enables users to find sites in your organization consistently, by typing the server address plus the application root directory name.

Global.asa contains scripts that affect the **Application** object and **Session** object. For example, Global.asa scripts make application- and session-scope variables available at startup. Global.asa should be present at the application root level for every ASP application.

/Classes Directory

The /Classes directory holds Java classes used by the application.

/Content Directory

The /Content directory holds all .htm files and all .asp files that may be run by a user of the site. The /Content directory has execute permissions. Keeping all scripted pages in this directory branch simplifies permissions management.

/Media A subdirectory of the /Content directory, Media should contain subdirectories for sounds, images, animation files, .avi files, and similar items. An /Images subdirectory should contain bullets, buttons, icons, and others that are used throughout the application independently of changing themes.

/Themes The /Themes directory is a subdirectory of the /Content directory. Establish a convention of using the /Themes directory to enable application-wide changes to the look of a site. The directory should contain style sheets, bullets, buttons, icons, rules, and similar items organized so that you can change the look of an application by changing any or all the theme-related items easily. Each item in the /Theme directory can be linked dynamically by setting an application variable to the image's virtual path. Themes are stored in Options.txt and assigned to the **Application** object in Global.asa.

/Data Directory

This directory should contain all database access information such as SQL scripts, file-based dataset names or other data needed by the application.

/DLLs Directory

This directory should contain ActiveX server components and Visual Basic 5.0 run-time DLLs, such as Vbrun500.dll and Msvbvm50.dll.

Helper Files

Helper files are include files or text files that make information available across the application. For security reasons the directory containing helper files should not be stored in the published Web space (the Web site directories identifiable to users).

File Name Extension Standards

This section suggests conventions for standardizing on file name extensions, accounting for the types of files containing scripts, or HTML and scripts (VBScript or JScript) together.

Extensions for Page Files

Standards:

- .asp—for pages containing ASP scripts
- .htm—for straight HTML pages

You must use the .asp extension for pages that contain ASP scripts. To save time and resources when serving pages, use the .htm extension for files that don't require server-side script execution.

Extensions for Included Files

Standards:

- .inc—for large amounts of data, with scripting, to be included in a page
- .txt—for text-formatted data files, without scripting, to be included in a page

For consistency, use include files to make specific information available to more than one referring page (changes to include files are distributed to all the pages that include them).

Connection Pooling

One of the potential bottlenecks in ASP application performance is connection management. If not managed properly, the opening and closing of connections can happen too frequently and can cause reduced server performance. Windows NT Server 4.0 features built-in support for connection pooling, achieving faster application performance and graceful timeout management with less coding effort.

To use ODBC connection pooling:

- Configure the driver for the database to which you are establishing a connection.
- Check the Windows NT registry to verify that Connection Pooling is on, and let it handle the connection logic.
- If Connection Pooling is off, use Regedit32 to turn it on in the Windows NT registry.
- Open individual connections—in your ADO code—just before you need data access on each individual page.
- Close your connections when the data access activities are complete.

Enabling connection pooling involves setting the **CPTimeout** property. For descriptions and examples on how to configure the **CPTimeout** property in the registry, see Chapter 6, "Data Access and Transactions."

Visual Basic Applications as DLLs

When you convert Visual Basic applications for use in ASP, they should be run as DLLs (components), rather than being converted to VBScript. Visual Basic DLLs will generally run more efficiently than scripts written in any scripting language. Encapsulate the Visual Basic code in DLLs and use **Server.CreateObject()**.

Visual Basic 5.0 should be used to create an ActiveX DLL that has its project properties set to Run in **Unattended Mode**, **Apartment Model Threaded**, and **Multi-instance**.

Object and Variable Initialization

The following discussion focuses on initializing and setting dimensions for objects and variables to achieve speed of execution and efficient use of server resources.

Application-Wide Scope for Convenience

Information stored in variables with application-wide scope is in memory and is cached for access by any page in the application. Establish a convention to give application scope to variables used often within an application if the values do not change frequently.

Whatever the potential benefits, use caution in deciding whether or not to give application scope to an object. It can potentially affect performance and decrease reliability (your application could hang). For best results, use application scope for objects with threading marked BOTH, aggregating the **FreeThreadedMarshaler**.

Declaring Objects with the <OBJECT> Tag

For objects that may or may not be used in an application, it's often most efficient to declare the objects without instantiating them until the need to use them arises (until they are referenced). To declare an object without actually creating it, use the <OBJECT> tag on the page instead of **Server.CreateObject()**.

Another advantage to bear in mind is that the <OBJECT> tag uses CLASSIDs, which are unique and tend to eliminate name collisions. The PROGIDs used by **Server.Create.Object()** do not force unique names, creating the possibility of name collisions.

Also, the <OBJECT> tag is supported in Global.asa and can be used to define scope using SCOPE or SESSION as values.

VBScript Conventions

The following suggested conventions apply to the development of ASP scripts written in Microsoft Visual Basic Scripting Edition (VBScript) and are designed to enhance consistency, performance, and reliability.

Comments in Scripts

Write consistent comment blocks near the top of each page listing, such as the file name, the group developing the file (not the person—e-mail should go to a group alias), the date developed, the HTML standard, and clear descriptions of all changes made.

Scripts that are commented out should be deleted unless they are placeholders, in which case they should be labeled as such.

Use comments to explain obscure or complex code. Do not leave a phrase such as the following without a comment:

```
If Err = -214983642 Then
```

Use comments to explain empty statements used as placeholders, as in this example:

```
If...Then...Else...Endif
```

Constant Names

To clearly distinguish constants from other elements, use all uppercase when naming them. An underscore can be used to separate terms when necessary.

Example:

```
Const MIN_QUAL = 25
```

Minimize Context Switching

For readability, try to minimize context-switching between HTML and scripts. When possible, use a few large blocks of script on a page instead of several scattered fragments.

Dictionary Object: Speed Access to Information

The VBScript **Dictionary** object enables fast lookup of arbitrary key/data pairs. Because the **Dictionary** object gives you access to array items by key, it is faster for finding items that are not in contiguous memory since you are specifying a key, rather than knowing where in the array the item is located.

Use the **Dictionary** object when you have set a high priority on fast searches of nonlinear data.

Delimiting Lines of Script for Readability

Lines of script should be blocked between a pair of delimiters, rather than written with delimiters on each line.

Instead of this:

```
<% strEmail = Session("Email") %>
<% strFirstName = Request.Form ("FirstName") %>
<% strLastName = Request.Form("LastName") %>
```

Do this:

```
<%
 strEmail = Session("Email")
 strFirstName = Request.Form ("FirstName")
 strLastName = Request.Form("LastName")
%>
```

For a single stand-alone line of script, keep the delimiters on the same line as the script.

Example:

```
<% strEmail = Session("Email") %>
```

If the line of script consists of an equal sign and a variable, make the equal sign part of the delimiter.

Example:

```
<%= strSubscrLName %>
```

Similarly, if the line of script specifies an ASP declarative, include the @ sign as part of the opening delimiter.

Example:

```
<%@ LANGUAGE = VBScript %>
```

Enable Session State Directive

Using the Enable Session State directive (set in Internet Services Manager) for your site enables the detailed tracking of user requests.

Save the resources used by IIS to process scripts for pages not using session state information by setting the Enable Session State directive to FALSE for those pages:

```
<%@ ENABLESESSIONSTATE = False %>
```

Language Default

Override the scripting language being used as the server's default language (VBScript) by using the @ language directive. For example, to ensure that the default language is JScript, put the following code at the top of each ASP page:

```
<%@ LANGUAGE = JScript %>
```

Layout Order of Scripts in ASP Pages

The following list summarizes the layout of VBScript scripts in an .asp file, from top to bottom.

- Specify language.
- Put **Option Explicit** statement.
- List function library includes.
- Declare page-scoped variables.
- Assign values to page-scoped variables.
- Code HTML and in-line scripting.
- List functions called by in-line scripts.

The first two script statements should specify declaratives and **Option Explicit** to force explicit variable declaration.

Inline scripts with HTML markup should call objects of functions placed at the bottom of the page. The inline scripts should be short and readable, even if this requires splitting out procedures to be placed at the bottom of the page.

Blank Lines in Files

In general, use blank lines sparingly. You should remove all blank lines at the beginnings and ends of files, but may want to include one blank line between statements, to increase readability.

Object and Procedure Call Names

To clearly distinguish object names and procedure calls from elements such as variables, begin each object name or procedure call with a verb. Use initial capitalization for each term within an object name or procedure call. The following list suggests some naming conventions that could be used to name objects for some typical activities.

Name	Function	Example
AddNew	add new records	**Customer.AddNew**
Update	edit records	**Customer.Update**
Remove	delete records	**Customer.Remove**
Get	return row from database	**Customer.GetNewest**
List	return multiple rows	**Customer.GetNew**

To limit criteria for methods that return information, use **From** and **For** with a method or function name.

Name	Function	Example
GetFor	returns criteria-based row	**Customer.GetForName**
ListFor	returns criteria-based multiple rows	**Customer.ListForPeriod**

Object Naming

As with variables and statements, used mixed case in naming objects, and in spelling out names of intrinsic objects. Capitalize the first letter of each term.

Use descriptive names for objects, even though this requires more characters per name.

The following example conforms to this convention (cnn prefixes an ADO connection variable, see "Variable Names" below):

```
Set cnnSQL = Server.CreateObject("ADODB.Connection")
Set cnnSQLServer = Server.CreateObject("ADODB.Connection")
```

These do not conform:

```
Set cnnS = Server.CreateObject("ADODB.Connection")
Set cnnsql = Server.CreateObject("ADODB.Connection")
```

Paths, using MapPath

Consider using **MapPath** instead of literal paths in ASP applications. The ASP **Server.MapPath** method allows you to physically relocate an ASP application without recoding scripts. This saves program modification and maintenance effort.

Performance is affected slightly, because every time you use **MapPath** in a script, IIS must retrieve the current server path. Consider placing the result of the method call in an application variable to avoid retrieving the server path.

Select Case Statement for Readability

For readability and efficiency, use the **Select Case** statement in place of **If...Else** to repeatedly check for the same variable for different values.

For example:

```
Select Case intYrsService
 Case 0 to 5
  strMessage = "You have ten days paid leave this year."
 Case 6 to 15
  strMessage = "You have fifteen days paid leave this year."
 Case 15 to 30
  strMessage = "You have twenty days paid leave this year."
 Case 30 to 100
  strMessage = "Will you never leave?"
End Select
```

Spaces in Scripts

To enhance script readability, use spaces consistently:

- Before and after operators, such as plus and equal.
- After commas, as when passing parameters.
- Exception: do not use spaces between arguments in ADO connection strings.

Statement Styles

Each scripting language has its own conventions for capitalization, indentation, and other style-related characteristics. Since VBScript is case-insensitive, capitalization conventions can be created to improve readability, as the following suggestions illustrate.

If...Then...Else...End If statements:

- Capitalize the first letter of If, Then, Else, and End If.
- Indent the clauses two spaces, or one tab.
- Put spaces at each end of an equal sign.
- Avoid using unnecessary parentheses.

Correct example:

```
<%
  If Request("FName") = "" Then
    Response.Clear
    Response.Redirect "test.html"
  Else
    Response.Write Request("FName")
  End If
%>
```

Similarly, capitalize the first letters of function and subroutine statements, and indent their definitions.

Example:

```
Sub SessionOnStart
  Set Session("MyId") = Request.ServerVariables(…)
End Sub
```

As with variable names, use mixed case, capitalizing the first letter in each term in a name. Avoid underscores.

For example, the second example is preferable:

```
first_name
FirstName
```

String Concatenation

For the sake of consistency and to achieve more self-documenting scripts, use the string concatenator (&), instead of a plus (+) sign.

String Function

Use the **String()** function to create a string consisting of repeated characters. Example: a string of non-breaking spaces ( ). The **String()** function is more readable and elegant than, for example: For I = 0 to 11 . . .

Case Values

Keep case consistent in both variable assignment and logical tests by using **UCase()** or **LCase()**. This is especially important when assigning and logically testing HTML intrinsic form controls, such as check boxes and radio buttons.

Trimming Values

Be consistent in trimming values. For example, consider always trimming values before putting them in state. This will eliminate errors in processing caused by inconsistencies in trimming schemes.

Variable Declaration

Declaring variables explicitly helps expose errors, such as misspelled variable names. To make code more reliable and readable use the **Option Explicit** statement in VBScript.

When you want to use strong variable typing, the logic should be programmed into a component built with a language that supports it, such as Visual Basic 5.0 or Visual J++. Loosely typed variables, such as Variants in VBScript, can affect performance, especially when mathematical computations are involved.

Variable Names for Consistency

For consistency in naming variables, use initial capital letters in variable names (do not capitalize prefixes).

To make the intended use of a variable clear to others reading your script, use three-character prefixes to indicate data type. Even though explicit typing is not supported in VBScript, the use of prefixes is recommended to denote the intended data type.

Table B.1   Suggested Prefixes for Indicating the Data Type of a Variable

Data Type	Prefix
Boolean	bln
Byte	byt
Collection object	col
Currency	cur
Date-time	dtm
Double	dbl
Error	err
Integer	int
Long	lng
Object	obj
Single	sng
String	str
User-defined type	udt
Variant	vnt
ADO command	cmn
ADO connection	cnn
ADO field	fld
ADO parameter	prm
ADO recordset	rst

To keep variable name lengths reasonable, use standardized abbreviations. For clarity, keep abbreviations consistent throughout an application, or group of related applications.

Instead of:

```
strSocialSecurityNumber
```

Use:

```
strSSN
```

Variable Scope for Performance

Use local scope (within subroutines and functions) for variables unless you have a compelling reason to use global scope. Local variables are resolved into table lookups when compiled, enabling fast execution at run time.

Declare global variables using the **Dim** statement before using them. This saves valuable first-use time by eliminating a search of the entire variable list.

HTML Conventions for ASP Pages

ASP applications serve dynamic information in standard HTML format. This means that you can customize information for a wide range of users.

Support Text-Only Browsing

Many users browse the Web in text-only mode in order to speed up the display of information to their browsers. To ensure that you present as much content as possible to these users, take the following steps to support text-only display:

- Include text-only navigation objects, such as menus.
- Include the alternative (ALT) parameter with each image tag to provide information about images.

  ```
  <IMG SRC="gravity.jpg" ALT="Picture of apple falling">
  ```

- When providing client-side imagemaps, add a text-only list of the mapped areas, with links to the information that would have been loaded if the user had clicked on a map link.

Checking HTML Files

You should check and debug your HTML code formally, using either a dedicated HTML checker or an HTML editor that includes a checker.

- Choose an HTML checker that helps enforce your HTML version standard.
- Debug each new HTML file as it is developed. Then debug your files again after each time they are modified.

To debug an HTML page that contains ASP scripts:

- Run the page that contains ASP scripts.
- View the source.
- Save the output, which is pure HTML.
- Run the saved output through an HTML checker.

This process is especially important for ASP pages that include forms. In these cases, HTML errors may corrupt the **Request** object sent from the browser to the server and cause a run-time error.

Using the 216-Color Palette

Color palette mismatches are ever-present concerns when you are creating images for a multi-platform Web. Even images in formats that require compact palettes, such as GIF (256 colors max), often display disparate colors when displayed on different platforms, such as Mac OS, Windows 95, and UNIX.

To ensure that your images display the same colors in different browsers on diverse platforms, use the 216-color palette—also called the safety pallete, or the 6x6x6 palette. This allows nearly as many colors as a GIF image can display, and displays consistent colors across systems.

Designing for Small Screens

Small-screen formats are still the standard for many users. Although larger formats are making progress, even 800 x 600 is too large to fit on millions of displays. For example, there are about ten million Macintoshes currently in use, many of which display 640 x 480 pixels.

To accommodate a broad spectrum of users, including those with small screens, design for 800 x 600 pixels.

For usability with small screens, keep the average line of text to approximately 12 words.

Displaying Standard Error Messages

For consistency and to make error messages informative, use standard **Response.Status** values, such as "401 Unauthorized – Logon failed" and other IIS standard responses in your pages. You can customize error messages in cases where additional information is needed.

Using Object Statements with Embed Statements

To use interactive objects delivered to multiple browsers you must code for browsers that do not support the HTML <OBJECT> tag.

To script the use of interactive objects, ActiveX Controls, or Java applets in HTML pages designed for a wide range of browsers:

- Use the <OBJECT> tag to place the object on the page.
- Add the <EMBED> tag to support browsers that do not support the <OBJECT> tag.
- Add a display object using the <NOEMBED> tag for browsers that cannot "play" the object.

The following example places a Shockwave control onto a page, and provides for the contingencies in the preceding sections:

```
<OBJECT ID="ShockedPMDauntless">
  CLASSID="foo"
  CODEBASE="http://www.fabrikam.com/marketing/movers/…"
  WIDTH=180 HEIGHT=120
  >
<PARAM NAME="swURL" VALUE="dauntless.dcr">
<EMBED SRC="dauntless.dcr" ALT="Movie of Fabrikam Dauntless model in
action" WIDTH=180 HEIGHT=120>
</EMBED>
<NOEMBED>
<IMG SRC="dauntless.gif" ALT="Picture of Fabrikam Dauntless model in
action" WIDTH=180 HEIGHT=120>
</NOEMBED>
</OBJECT>
```

APPENDIX C

Debugging Applications and Components

C

Debugging can be the most frustrating part of the Web application developer's job. Unlike desktop applications, which are self-contained, Web applications can be spread over several systems and frequently combine different programming languages and technologies. Although some application errors can be avoided with careful planning, others come about as unexpected side effects of complex component interactions. Tracking down these problems often requires the use of a variety of debugging and development tools.

This appendix contains authoring and debugging tips for Active Server Pages (ASP), as well as a section on setting up a debugging environment for ISAPI extensions and server-side components.

Active Server Pages

Because ASP pages often contain a mixture of HTML, server-side script, and components, problems can be difficult to track down. This section focuses on ASP script debugging, and covers three approaches to errors: avoidance, debugging, and script management.

Common Mistakes

Studies show that developers tend to make the same types of mistakes no matter what programming language they are using. Rather than spending a lot of time tracking down bugs, it is always easier to avoid creating them in the first place. This section cites common scripting mistakes that lead to bugs and suggests ways to avoid them.

Misspelling Variables

Most scripting run-time errors can be attributed to misspelled variables. VBScript automatically declares unrecognized variables, which can lead to subtle errors in your code. To avoid this problem, use the **Option Explicit** statement as the first line of script on every page. The **Option Explicit** statement requires variables to be explicitly declared with a **Dim** statement.

JScript has no counterpart to the **Option Explicit** statement. Unrecognized variables are automatically declared when they are defined. Some ASP methods, such as **Response.Write,** produce script errors when used with an undeclared variable. If a variable is declared, but not defined, it will return either "Undefined" or "NaN." (For more information, see the JScript documentation.)

Using an Object or Variable Out of Scope

A common problem is not understanding which objects are available in a given context. For example, you might attempt to set properties for a **Session** object in a client script, or attempt to use the Internet Explorer object model in a script running on a different browser.

Make sure that the objects you reference are available in the current scope. Be aware that objects (such as ASP built-in objects) are not an inherent part of a language such as VBScript; instead, they are part of the environment in which a script is running.

Not Using the Web Server to View ASP Pages

To view ASP pages in the browser, you need to request them from the Web server using the HTTP syntax. If you try to view them directly from the file system, the browser will either try to download the file, or will display the script without executing it. Other reasons for ASP pages not displaying properly: not having script (or execute) permissions set for the directory in which the page are stored, and not using the .asp extension when naming files.

Using the Scripting Language Inefficiently

Sometimes when developers are unfamiliar with a scripting language, they write code that fails to take advantage of the language's capabilities. Their code consequently runs more slowly than correctly implemented script. Likewise, if they don't understand the language conventions, they may inadvertently make syntax errors, such as using the wrong type of quotation marks to enclose string literals. This is an easy mistake to make when switching between languages such as Visual Basic and SQL.

Always seek to familiarize yourself with the native functionality, operators and conventions of the scripting language you are using.

Mixing Data Types

Because all ASP scripting variables are Variants (meaning, they can hold values of any type), you can easily assign inappropriate values to variables. For example, you could assign an object to a variable you intend to use for strings.

To help you remember what type of data a variable is supposed to contain, use a naming convention that will help you remember variable types. For a table of recommended variable names for VBScript, see Appendix B, "ASP Standards."

Misusing the Equal Sign

Visual Basic users expect the single "=" (equal sign) to evaluate the equality of the two operands. In JScript, however, the single "=" will assign the right-hand value to the left-hand operand. (JScript uses a double "=" to express equality.) Mistakenly using a single "=" in an expression will not only overwrite the left-hand value, it will cause the expression to evaluate to **True**. If this happens in an **If** statement, the inner logic is executed; in a **While** statement, it creates an infinite loop.

Remember that "=" is different than "==" in JScript. Additionally, don't forget to include the equal sign when using an *<%= expression %>* instruction.

Using Procedures Incorrectly

Not understanding when to use a function or procedure, or calling the incorrect function, is a common problem in any language. You can avoid using the incorrect arguments for functions, or passing arguments in the wrong order, by double-checking the function definition. Additionally, make sure that the function you are calling performs the task you want it to, check syntax for functions whenever using them, and avoid relying on default argument values.

Not Handling Errors

You should always check for unexpected user input, such as a string when prompted for a number, or a number value outside the bounds of what the program can use. Likewise, you must anticipate errors from within the program, and understanding the meaning of values returned by the functions you use.

To handle internal program errors in VBScript, you must use the **On Error Resume Next** statement. Without this instruction, the script will abort as soon as the error is detected, which prevents you from quietly handling errors with script. Here are a few precautions to keep in mind when using the **On Error Resume Next** statement:

- When debugging it is often necessary to disable error handling, since it will not be apparent where errors are occurring. Reenable it when you are finished debugging.

- Because you are resuming program execution at the next statement whenever an error occurs, you should avoid using script that may produce an error as the logic portion of an **If** statement, or the test of a **While** loop. If these statements cause errors, the inner logic of the **If** statement will not be executed, and the **While** loop will never complete.

Making Off-by-One Errors with Collections

Not all collections in VBScript begin with element 1. Some collections—the ADO **Fields** collection, for example—start at element 0. When looping through a complete collection, it is often safest to use the VBScript methods **LBound** and **UBound** to specify the starting and ending array indexes, respectively. Note that Microsoft's JScript also defines these methods on its **VBArray** object.

Forgetting Ending Braces, Delimiters, and Statements

The longer the script becomes, the more likely that the ending statement of a code block, such as **End If,** or an ending code delimiter (such as **%>**) can be overlooked. The result is often confusing and ambiguous script errors. To avoid this common problem, make a practice of typing the closing portion of a statement as soon as you type the opening portion.

Debugging ASP

Until the introduction of Microsoft Script Debugger, debugging ASP scripts often required lots of debugging output and an intimate knowledge of how the scripting language processed the code. The Microsoft Script Debugger makes debugging much easier.

Microsoft Script Debugger

You can use Microsoft Script Debugger to test scripts written in VBScript and JScript, as well as applications written in Java. You can also debug scripts in other languages, such as REXX or PerlScript, that support host-independent debugging.

Using Microsoft Script Debugger, you can:

- View the source code of the script you are debugging.
- Control execution line-by-line through the script.
- View and alter variable and property values.
- Set breakpoints, and view the call stack.
- Switch between threads of execution.

You cannot edit scripts being debugged, but you can save the script under a new name. When you have finished editing, you can load the new page in the browser.

You can use Script Debugger to debug both client-side and server-side scripts. Debugging must be enabled for each ASP application that you want to debug.

▶ **To enable debugging**

1. In Internet Service Manager, right-click an application virtual directory and click **Properties**.

2. On the **Virtual Directory** tab, click **Configuration**.

3. On the **Debugging** tab, select **Enable ASP server-side script debugging** and click **OK**.

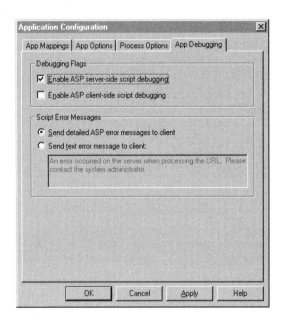

Figure C.1   Enabling ASP debugging from Internet Service Manager

To begin editing a document in Script Debugger, first open the **Running Documents** window (from the **View** menu) and double-click to open a document. Before you can open the script, it must be loaded locally in the browser, or in the ASP environment on the local Web server, if one is installed. Once the script is loaded, you can set breakpoints, and step through the application.

You can view and change the values of individual variables in the **Command** window when a script is running. To view a variable value, type a question mark (?) followed by the name of the variable, and press Enter. You can also evaluate simple numeric expressions using the "?" command form. To edit the value, type the name of the variable followed by an equal sign ("=") and a new numeric or string value.

Figure C.2 shows a typical debugging session:

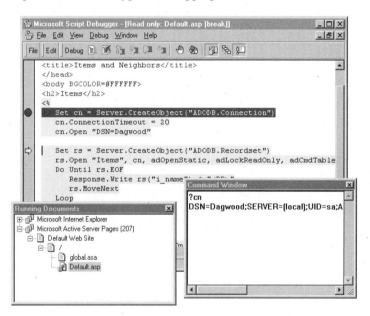

Figure C.2   Microsoft Script Debugger at work

For more information on Microsoft Script Debugger, see the online product documentation.

Script Debugger only works with scripts running on the local Web server. You cannot debug scripts running on remote Web servers. Because the script debugger interrupts script execution when it encounters an error, you won't want to enable script debugging on systems that are hosting applications critical to your business. For these systems, it is better to trace execution by using logs and output.

Debug Tracing

ASP debug tracing is limited to the following three methods:

- Liberal use of debug **Response.Write** statements throughout the code.

- **Response.AppendToLog** to write script values and events to the IIS Server log.

- A custom logging component to enable writes to the Windows NT System Event Log, database, or application-specific text file. (For example, see the Registry Access component included on the IIS Resource Kit CD.)

Implement debug tracing wisely. When you have to insert debug messages into your script, you should emphasize events that might enable you to reconstruct the flow through the code leading up to an error. Capture function calls and values of parameters. Log important values only; if you write too many messages, you can slow down the application considerably.

Try to make it easy to disable and enable debug tracing. For small projects, it's okay to comment out the debug trace statements that you want to disable. For larger projects however, you should encapsulate the debug trace code in a script or component function that can be enabled and disabled independently of the code.

Tracking Events in Global.asa

Debugging **Session** and **Application** events can be tricky, because you can't use the **Response.Write** method to display messages to the client browser. One useful technique is to use the **Scripting.FileSystemObject** to generate a simple log file with text messages indicating the success or failure of these events, as demonstrated in the following script:

```
<!--METADATA TYPE="TypeLib"
NAME="Scripting" FILE="C:\Winnt\System32\scrrun.dll"
UUID="420B2830-E718-11CF-893D-00A0C9054228" VERSION="1.0"
-->

<object ID="AppFileSystemObject" SCOPE=Application RUNAT=Server
    PROGID="Scripting.FileSystemObject">
</object>
```

```
<script LANGUAGE=VBScript RUNAT=Server>
Sub OutputDebugFile(ByRef strText)
    Dim ts
    Application.Lock
    Set ts = AppFileSystemObject.OpenTextFile(Application("DebugFile"),_
             ForAppending, True, TristateUseDefault)
    ts.WriteLine Now & ": " & strText
    ts.Close
    Application.Unlock
End Sub

Sub Application_OnStart
    '--- DebugFile must be defined before calling OutputDebugFile
    Application("DebugFile") = "c:\webs\appevnts.log"
    OutputDebugFile("Application Started")
End Sub

Sub Application_OnEnd
    OutputDebugFile("Application Ended")
End Sub

Sub Session_OnStart
    OutputDebugFile("Session Started: " & Session.SessionID)
    Response.Redirect "./end.asp" ' End Session (this creates a loop!)
End Sub

Sub Session_OnEnd
    OutputDebugFile("Session Ended: " & Session.SessionID)
End Sub
</script>
```

The preceding script writes notifications for the **Application** start and end events, and notifications for every **Session** start and end event.

Script Management

This section discusses some techniques to help you manage longer scripts, and minimize subtle errors in large projects.

Establishing a Library of Helper Routines

It's often a good idea to collect commonly used functions into one file and include that file in all pages that require those functions.

The included file can contain plain text, declare functions and subroutines with <SCRIPT> tags, or define variables and constants. To include the file, use a server-side include directive at the top of your file. Here is an example:

```
<!-- #include virtual="/MyRoot/include/funclib.inc" -->
```

Usually, included files are named with the .inc extension. Although this differentiates the file, it may pose a security threat if you have directory browsing enabled. The .inc extension is not normally script-mapped by IIS, and most browsers don't recognize it, so anyone who knows where to find the files can download and open them. You can prevent this from happening by either associating the .inc extension with Asp.dll in the script map (use the **App Mappings** tab of the **Application Configuration** dialog box), or by storing the included files in their own subdirectory and disallowing directory browsing and read access.

The entire text of the include file is incorporated into the ASP source file at the point where the include statement appears. Although there is technically no limit to the number of files you can include, each one adds to the size of the compiled ASP file—it's better to only include files that you know you will need.

Since all include files are processed before the script executes, you cannot dynamically decide which file to include. Also, you cannot use the include directive in Global.asa.

Using Dictionaries to Partition the Session Namespace

When used indiscriminately, the **Session** object is no better than a global data area. For large Web applications, the **Session** collection can become quite cluttered, increasing the likelihood that some part of the application may inadvertently make changes that have unexpected repercussions elsewhere. To avoid this situation, development teams must either use a naming convention that will decrease the chance of duplicate **Session** key names, or use other methods of storing session values.

One such method uses the **Dictionary** object to further partition the global session namespace. Like the **Session** object, the **Dictionary** object can store any number of values and keywords in an associative array. Disparate sections of the application can create individual **Dictionary** objects as necessary to contain local values, and store a single reference to their namespace in the **Session** object. Not only can groups of values be managed as a single entity, the **Dictionary** object makes it easy to free resources all at once when they are no longer required by the application. For more information on the **Dictionary** object, see the IIS online product documentation.

Improving Script Performance

Application scalability is never an accident. In all cases, high performance is a product of design and systematic performance tests and tuning. This section provides some tips for ASP application developers who want to improve the performance of their scripts.

ASP Performance Tips

Performance goals vary from application to application. You should set your goals to correspond with your expected user traffic. In general, you should aim for 20 pages or more per second with less than 30 percent CPU utilization, and response times of 10 seconds or less. The following list includes tips you can use to achieve your ASP performance objectives:

- Retrieving values from collections is relatively slow. Store retrieved values in local variables if you need to access them more than once.

- Avoid using server-side include directives to include large lists of constants. Use the new <METADATA> tag to import type-library constants into Global.asa.

- Avoid using **Server.CreateObject**. Use <OBJECT> tags instead.

- Group multiple **Response.Write** statements, and delimit them with one set of **<% %>** delimiters.

- Avoid redimensioning VBScript arrays.

- Use only one scripting language per page.

- Buffered responses (**Response.Buffer=True**) are faster than unbuffered ones. (Although they can appear less responsive.)

- Use **Response.IsClientConnected** during the processing of long scripts. This property determines if the client has disconnected from the server since the last **Response.Write**, and improves application responsiveness during times of peak usage.

- Use components to encapsulate business logic rather than complex script.

- Convert dynamic ASP output to static HTML using the ASP2HTM component wherever possible. (ASP2HTM is included on the IIS Resource Kit CD.)

- Store commonly requested, unchanging content in memory using an application-scope **Dictionary** object.

- Avoid using **Session_OnEnd** event procedures, if possible.

- Disable the **Session** object on a page-by-page basis with the **<% @ EnableSessionState=False %>** statement. This declarative allows ASP to process scripts concurrently, rather than sequentially.

- Write client scripts that don't require round-trips to the server. Distribute work to the client, such as form input validation. Use the Browser Capabilities component (**MSWC.BrowserType**) and customize client-side scripts to take advantage of the browser, incorporating such technologies as DHTML, client-side script, and ActiveX controls.

- Focus your optimization efforts on the most common paths through your site or application. You can determine user behavior with IIS service logs and the Usage Import and Report Writer component of Site Server Express.

- Set **Response.Expires** appropriately so that proxy servers can intelligently cache information that doesn't change often.

- Optimize the use of ADO **Connection** objects, with ODBC connection pooling and stored procedures. (See Chapter 6, "Data Access and Transactions.")

- Measure system performance with tools such as Task Manager, NetMon, and PerfMon. Measure Web capacity with WCAT. (See Chapter 3, "Performance Tuning and Optimization.") Profile portions of your ASP script with the ASP Tracer component.

The Tracer Component

The Tracer component is a rudimentary profiler for ASP pages. It acts as a stopwatch that can be started and stopped from within a script. It can be used to output debugging strings. The component can be instantiated on any page you want to profile. Here's an example of the ASP Tracer component at work:

```
<%
    Set trcr = Server.CreateObject("IISSample.Tracer")
    trcr.Name = "Default Trace"   '--- Give the tracer a name
    trcr.TimerStart                      '--- Start profiling
%>
<!-- Perform first script processing here -->
<%
    trcr.TimerSplit "Part I"      '--- Note time, and continue
%>
<!-- Perform more script processing here -->
<%
    trcr.Trace "Value: " & MyVal  '--- Output debug string
    trcr.TimerStop                       '--- Stop profiling
%>
```

Tracer output simply goes to the debug stream (using **OuputDebugString**), but you can easily modify the component to log to a file or whatever you choose. All output is formatted as a comma-separated list, so that it's easy to import into your favorite database or spreadsheet for manipulation.

Debugging ISAPI and Server Components

This section explains how to connect to running applications and use the debugger to step through the source code of your components, ISAPI filters, and extensions.

Disabling Debug Exception Catching

ASP experts should recognize the following error message:

```
Error 'ASP 0115'
Unexpected error
A trappable error occurred in an external object. The script cannot
continue running.
```

This error is caused by an access violation in a component process. The reason ASP is able to display a message is because the crash is detected by the built-in *exception handling* of the ASP process.

When you are debugging an application component, it is often easier to detect where faults occur when exception handling is disabled. You can disable exception handling by using the **Process Options** tab of the **Application Configuration** dialog box in Internet Service Manager. The **Process Options** tab appears either when editing global properties, which affect all in-process applications or when editing the properties of an application marked to run within its own memory space (out of process).

The extra overhead in system resources required to run an application in its own process is worth the added security of knowing a crash will not affect other applications. When you clear the **Enable debug exception catching** check box on the **Process Options** tab, ASP will not capture serious application errors. Instead, they will appear as faults in the isolated application process and components running in the same process.

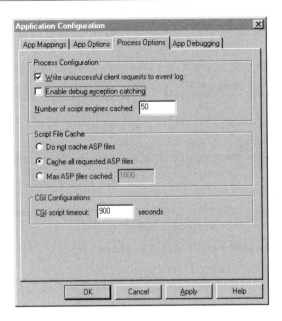

Figure C.3   The Process Options tab

Debugging Internet Information Server

Debugging IIS may be necessary should any of the following events occur:

- You receive ASP 0115 error messages from pages that call server-side components.
- IIS stops serving ASP pages.
- The Web service stops and clients cannot connect to the server.
- Inetinfo.exe causes the debugger (or Dr. Watson) to appear.
- Inetinfo.exe stops running for no apparent reason.

Establishing a Debugging Environment

There are several ways to establish an environment for debugging server components and ISAPI extensions. If you are using a debugging tool capable of attaching to a Windows NT process, you can use the tool to debug your component or extension. For example, if you are debugging an ISAPI extension with Microsoft Visual Studio you take the following steps:

1. Start the iisadmin process. This can be done from the command line with the command **net start iisadmin**. You can also use the Services application in Control Panel to start the IIS Admin Service, which will start the iisadmin process.

2. Run Visual Studio and select the **Attach to Process** command from the **Start Debug** submenu of the **Build** menu.

3. Click the **Show System Process** check box.

4. Select the inetinfo process from the list and click **OK**.

5. Start the w3svc service. This can be done from the command line with the command **net start w3svc**. You can also use the Services application in Control Panel to start the World Wide Web Publishing Service.

If the debugging tool you are using is not capable of attaching to a Windows NT process, you should take the following steps to establish an appropriate debugging environment.

1. Start the Services application in Control Panel.

2. Select the IIS Admin service and click **Startup**.

3. Select the **Allow Service to Interact with Desktop** check box and click **OK**.

4. Repeat steps 2 and 3 for all processes which run under the IIS Admin process, for example World Wide Web Publishing Service and FTP Publishing Service.

5. Use the Registry Editor to add a subkey named "Inetinfo.Exe" to the HKEY_LOCAL_MACHINE/Software/Microsoft/WindowsNT/CurrentVersion/Image File Execution Options key.

6. Add the following entry to this new key:
   Debugger = *DebuggerExeName* where *DebuggerExeName* is the full path to the debugger you are using.

When the World Wide Web Publishing Service is started, your debugger will run as well. You can now set appropriate break points in your ISAPI extension.

You won't be able to set breakpoints in a component's source code until the component has been loaded into memory. First, you will need to start Internet Explorer and view the ASP page containing the object. As soon as the page is loaded, you should be able to set breakpoints in your component. Click **Refresh** to view the page again, and trigger the breakpoints you selected. If the component cannot be loaded even once (for instance, if the fault occurs in component startup code), you will need to load the component DLL prior to starting the debugging session. (See step 11 in the section below.)

Running IIS as a Process

In some cases, you may not be able to use either of the two preceding procedures. If you have difficulty using these strategies, you can run IIS as a process (rather than as a service). This approach requires the establishing of Windows NT security privileges as well as making changes to the registry. It also disables your ability to run IIS as a service. This approach should be attempted only if the previous two strategies have failed.

1. Use the User Manager for Domains administration tool to add the "Log on as Service," "Act as part of the operating system," and "Generate security audits" rights on the local computer to the Windows NT account you will use when debugging the ISAPI extension.

2. Use the Distributed COM Configuration utility to change the identity of the IIS Admin Service to the user account you will use for debugging.

3. Use the Registry Editor to remove the LocalService keyword from all IISADMIN-related subkeys under HKEY_CLASSES_ROOT/AppID. This keyword may be found in the following subkeys:
   {61738644-F196-11D0-9953-00C04FD919C1} // IIS WAMREG admin Service
   {9F0BD3A0-EC01-11D0-A6A0-00A0C922E752} // IIS Admin Crypto Extension
   {A9E69610-B80D-11D0-B9B9-00A0C922E750} // IISADMIN Service
   The LocalService keyword may be found in additional subkeys of AppID.

4. Add LocalServer32 subkeys to all IISADMIN-related subkeys under the CLSID node of the registry. This will include subkeys corresponding to all of the subkeys you removed in the previous step. Set the default value of these new keys to *path*\inetinfo.exe -e w3svc. (*path* is normally C:\Winnt\System32\Inetsrv.)

5. Stop the WWW and FTP services from the Microsoft Management Console, or from the Services dialog box in the Control Panel.

6. Start Visual Studio and select the **Debug** tab in the Project Settings window.

7. Type **C:\Winnt\System32\Inetsrv\inetinfo.exe** in the **Executable for debug session** box.

8. Type **-e w3svc** in the **Program Arguments** box.

9. Select the **Link** tab in the Visual Studio Project Settings Window.

10. Enter the name and path of the ISAPI extension you are debugging in the **Output file name** box.

11. Optionally, add your component DLL to the list of additional DLLs that are loaded before the application starts. This will allow you to set breakpoints in component startup code.

12. Click **Go** to start the debugging session.

Note Additional instructions and two .reg files that automate the process of switching IIS between running as a service and running as a process are available in the SDK documentation included with IIS 4.0 on the Window NT 4.0 Option Pack.

Inability to Create Components

Sometimes the **Server.CreateObject** method fails and produces an "ASP 0177: Server.CreateObject Failed" error. This can happen even if the component works fine on the same computer in Visual Basic or using ASP on other computers.

One likely cause for this behavior is that the authenticated user does not have permission to invoke the COM object. In the simplest scenario, the authenticated user doesn't have access to the component DLL or executable. In many cases, however, the component depends on other DLLs that the authenticated user does not have permission to access. (Usually, a majority of users access a site anonymously, using the IUSR_*computername* account.)

To verify that it is a permissions problem, try invoking the component from another tool such as Visual Basic. This approach verifies that the component is registered properly on the server. If the component cannot be created from Visual Basic, you are probably not dealing with a permissions problem (the component may need to be registered).

If you believe you are dealing with a permissions problem, check permissions on the component and any dependent files such as other DLLs. If you still are unable to track down the problem, you may need to resort to a systematic permissions search.

Additional Resources

You can find more information on IIS debugging on the IIS Resource Kit CD, in the Chapter Samples\Appendix C directory.

Glossary

10BaseT

A variant of Ethernet that allows stations to be attached by a twisted-pair cable.

A

access control

Controlling who is allowed access to a computer's content and applications.

Access Control List (ACL)

The part of a security descriptor that enumerates the protections applied to a file or directory. The owner of a file or directory has discretionary access control of it and can change its ACL to allow or disallow access to others.

ACL

See *Access Control List.*

Active Group, The

A standards organization, under the auspices of the Open Group, which is an open, customer-driven steering committee responsible for the ongoing development and management of ActiveX technologies and licensing. For more information, see http://www.activex.org/.

Active Server

A collection of server-side technologies that are delivered with Windows NT. These technologies provide a consistent server-side component and scripting model and an integrated set of system services for component application management, database access, transactions, and messaging.

Active Server Pages (ASP)

A server-side scripting environment that runs ActiveX scripts and ActiveX components on a server. Developers can combine scripts and components to create Web-based applications.

ActiveX

An umbrella term for Microsoft technologies that enable developers to create interactive content for the World Wide Web. Also, a set of language-independent interoperability technologies that enable software components written in different languages to work together in networked environments. The core technology elements of ActiveX are the Component Object Model (COM) and the Distributed Component Object Model (DCOM). These technologies are licensed to the Open Group standards organization, and are being implemented on multiple platforms. See also *Common Gateway Interface (CGI)*; *Java*; *Component Object Model (COM)*; *Distributed Component Object Model (DCOM)*.

ActiveX Automation

A language-neutral way to manipulate an ActiveX component's methods from outside an application. ActiveX Automation is typically used to create components that expose methods to programming tools and macro languages. ActiveX Automation was previously called OLE Automation.

ActiveX component

A compiled software component based on the Component Object Model (COM) that encapsulates a set of business functionality. The functionality in an ActiveX component is accessed through ActiveX Automation interfaces. The ActiveX component can run either on a client computer or on a server computer, transparent to the calling application, using the Distributed Component Object Model (DCOM). ActiveX components can be driven by a scripting language such as Microsoft Visual Basic Scripting Edition (VBScript) or JScript. All Java applets running in the Microsoft virtual machine for Java are automatically ActiveX components and use the file name extension .class. ActiveX components that run within the calling application process use the extensions .dll or .ocx. ActiveX components that run outside of the calling application process use the extension .exe. See also *Component Object Model (COM)*; *Distributed Component Object Model (DCOM)*.

ActiveX Control

A compiled software component based on the Component Object Model (COM) that encapsulates a set of business or user interface functions. An ActiveX Control is used to provide user interface components and is designed to run on the client computer. ActiveX Controls can be embedded in Web pages for use over the Internet, as well as combined to create client/server applications that run over a corporate network. They can be created by a variety of programming languages from Microsoft or from third-party vendors. ActiveX Controls use the extension .ocx. See also *Component Object Model (COM)*.

ActiveX Data Objects (ADO)

A set of object-based data access interfaces optimized for Internet-based, data-centric applications. ADO is based on a published specification and is included with Microsoft Internet Information Server (IIS) and Microsoft Visual InterDev.

ActiveX object

An object that is exposed to other applications or programming tools through Automation interfaces.

ActiveX scripting

The act of using a scripting language to drive ActiveX components. ActiveX scripting is made possible by plugging a scripting engine into a host application. A scripting engine enables the processing of a specific scripting language such as Microsoft Visual Basic Scripting Edition (VBScript) or JScript. Examples of host applications that contain scripting engines are Microsoft Internet Explorer and Internet

Information Server (IIS) with Active Server Pages (ASP). See also *Active Server Pages (ASP)*; *ActiveX Automation*; *ActiveX component*; *scripting engine*; *script*.

ActiveX server component

An ActiveX component designed to run on the server side of a client/server application. See *ActiveX component*.

activity

A collection of Microsoft Transaction Server (MTS) objects that has a single distributed logical thread of execution. Every Microsoft Transaction Server object belongs to one activity.

Address Resolution Protocol (ARP)

One of the network maintenance protocols that is a member of the TCP/IP suite (not directly related to data transport). It is used to dynamically discover the low-level physical network hardware address that corresponds to the high-level IP address for a given host. ARP is limited to physical network systems that support broadcast packets. It is defined in RFC 826. See also *TCP/IP*.

ADO

See *ActiveX Data Objects*.

agent

The part of the system that performs information preparation and exchange on behalf of a client or server application. In Simple Network Management Protocol (SNMP), agent information consists of comments about the user, the physical location of the computer, and the types of service to report based on the computer's configuration.

aggregation

A composition technique for implementing component objects whereby a new object can be built using one or more existing objects that support some or all of the new object's required interfaces.

alias
A name that maps part of a URL to a physical directory on the server. In general, an easily remembered name used in place of an IP address, directory path, or other identifier; also called a friendly name. See also *hostname*; *virtual directory*; *virtual server*.

ALT string (for images)
An optional text string that an HTML author might include with an HTML IMG tag, which is used to describe the associated image. For example, for an image of a waterfall, the ALT string might read: "GIF image of waterfall." The ALT string allows people who use text-only browsers, or who have chosen not to download images, to know what the image depicts.

American National Standards Institute (ANSI)
ANSI serves as a quasi-national standards organization. It provides area charters for groups that establish standards in specific fields, such as the Institute of Electrical and Electronics Engineers (IEEE). Standards approved by ANSI are often called ANSI standards (for example, ANSI C is the version of the C language approved by ANSI). Additionally, ANSI is commonly used to refer to a low-level table of codes used by a computer. Most computers can choose among several different software code tables for deciding how to display information on a screen and how keys pressed on a keyboard appear as characters on a computer screen or printer.

American Standard Code for Information Interchange (ASCII)
A 7-bit character set widely used to represent letters and symbols found on a standard U.S. keyboard. By standardizing the values used for these characters, ASCII enables computers and computer programs to exchange information. The ASCII character set is the same as the first 128 characters (0-127) in the ANSI character set.

anchor
A source or target of a hypertext link. An anchor can be either a text or a graphic, and can occur anywhere on a Web page.

anchored graphic
A graphic, such as a button, that contains a link. See also *thumbnail*.

annotation file
For the File Transfer Protocol (FTP) service, a summary of the information in a given directory. This summary appears automatically to remote browsers.

anonymous FTP (File Transfer Protocol)
Anonymous FTP makes it possible for a user to retrieve documents, files, programs, and other archived data from anywhere in the Internet without having to establish a log on name and password. By using the special logon name of "anonymous," the network user will bypass local security checks and will have access to publicly accessible files on the remote system.

anonymous-only log ons
This feature allows remote access only by the IUSR_*computername* account. Remote users can connect to that computer only without a user name and password, and they have only the permissions assigned to that account.

ANSI
See *American National Standards Institute*.

apartment model multithreading
The Component Object Model (COM) supports a form of multithreading in Windows 95 and Windows NT called the *apartment model*. The apartment model is essentially a way of describing a thread with a message queue that supports COM objects. Apartment model multithreading enables multiple application threads—one for each apartment—that are managed by COM.

apartment thread

A thread used to execute calls to objects of components configured as "apartment threaded." Each object "lives in an apartment" (thread) for the life of the object. All calls to that object execute on the apartment thread.

API

See *Application Programming Interface.*

applet

An HTML-based program built with Java that a browser temporarily downloads to a user's hard disk, from which location it runs when the Web page is open.

application

A computer program such as a word processor or electronic spreadsheet; or a group of Active Server Pages (ASP) scripts and components that perform such tasks.

Application Programming Interface (API)

A set of routines that an application program uses to request and carry out lower-level services performed by a computer's operating system. Also, a set of calling conventions in programming that define how a service is invoked through the application.

application root

The root directory for an application; all directories and files contained within the application root are considered part of the application. Also called an application starting point directory.

argument

A constant, variable, or expression passed to a procedure.

array

A set of sequentially indexed elements having the same type of data. Each element of an array has a unique identifying index number. Changes made to one element of an array do not affect the other elements.

ARP

See *Address Resolution Protocol.*

ASCII

See *American Standard Code for Information Interchange.*

ASCII file

Also called a text file, a text-only file, or an ASCII text file, it refers to a file in the universally recognized text format called ASCII. An ASCII file contains characters, spaces, punctuation, carriage returns, and sometimes tabs and an end-of-file marker, but it contains no other formatting information.

associating

See *file name extension mapping.*

Asynchronous Transfer Mode (ATM)

A communications protocol defined for high-speed data communications.

asynchronous transmission

A form of data transmission in which information is sent one character at a time, with variable time intervals between characters; generally used in communicating by way of a modem. Because asynchronous transmission does not rely on a shared timer that would enable the sending and receiving units to separate characters by specific time periods, each transmitted character consists of a number of data bits (the character itself) preceded by a "begin character" signal, called the start bit, and ending in an optional parity bit followed by 1, 1.5, or 2 "end character" signals, called stop bits.

ATM

See *Asynchronous Transfer Mode.*

atomicity

A feature of a transaction that indicates that either all actions of the transaction happen or none happen.

attributes

Information that indicates whether a file is read-only, hidden, system, or compressed, and whether the file has been changed since a backup copy of it was made.

auditing

Tracking activities of users by recording selected types of events in the security log of a server or a workstation.

authentication

Verifying a user's identity based on user account information. A typical authentication method can involve prompting for user name and password.

authentication certificate

See *certificate, digital.*

authorization

In relation to computers, especially to remote computers on a network open to more than one person, the right granted to an individual to use the system and the data stored on it. Authorization is typically set up by a system administrator and checked and cleared by the computer. This requires that the user provide some type of identification, such as a code number or a password, that the computer can verify against its internal records. The terms permission and privilege are synonymous with authorization.

automatic directory listing

Providing a directory listing by default when a URL without a file name is received; also called directory browsing.

Automation

A technology that allows a client application to create and control an object by using the exposed object's properties and methods.

Automation object

An object that is exposed to other applications or programming tools through Automation interfaces.

B

bandwidth

The capacity of the transmission medium stated in bits per second (bps) or as a frequency (Hz). Generally, a higher bandwidth number indicates faster data-transfer capability. In communications, the difference between the highest and lowest frequencies in a given range. For example, a U.S. telephone line accommodates a bandwidth of 3000 Hertz (Hz), the difference between the lowest (300 Hz) and the highest (3300 Hz) frequencies it can carry. In computer networks, greater bandwidth indicates faster data-transfer capability and is expressed in bits per second (bps).

bandwidth throttling

Setting the maximum portion of total network capacity that a service is allowed to use. You can deliberately limit a server's Internet workload by not allowing it to receive requests at full capacity, to save resources for other programs such as e-mail.

Basic authentication

An authentication protocol supported by most browsers, including Internet Explorer. It is a method of authentication that encodes user name and password data transmissions. Basic authentication is sometimes called "clear text" authentication because the base-64 encoding can be decoded by anyone with a freely available decoding utility. Note that encoding is not the same as encryption. See also *challenge/response authentication; encryption.*

baud

Roughly the speed at which a modem transfers data. One baud is approximately equal to one bps, although baud rate and bps are not always synonymous. Bps is usually a more accurate measure of modem speed.

BIND

See *Domain Name System.*

binding

The way in which Microsoft Visual Basic for Applications (VBA) uses Automation to access objects in another application. See also *Automation*; *early binding*; *late binding*.

bits per second (bps)

The speed at which data bits are transmitted over a communications medium, such as a transmission wire or a modem. Common PC modem speeds are 28,800 and 14,400 bps.

Boolean

A type of variable that can have only two values, typically 1 or 0. Boolean variables are often used to express conditions that are either True or False. Queries with Boolean operators (And, Or, Not, and Near) are referred to as Boolean queries.

Boolean expression

An expression that evaluates to either True or False.

bps

See *bits per second*.

broken link

A reference to a resource that cannot be located, because the URL is not valid, the resource the link points to does not exist, or the server containing the resource is busy or having other technical difficulties.

browser

A client tool for navigating and accessing information on the Internet or an intranet. A browser interprets Hypertext Markup Language (HTML) and displays information on a computer screen. A popular example is Microsoft Internet Explorer.

bulk data encryption

The encryption of all data sent over a network.

business rules

The laws, regulations, policies, and procedures that a user encodes into a computer system. Also known as business logic.

bytecode

The executable form of Java code that executes within the Java virtual machine (VM). Also called interpreted code, pseudo code, and p-code.

C

CA

See *certificate authority*.

cache

A location for frequently-accessed files that are read from memory or a local disk, for faster access.

call

To transfer program execution to some other section of code, usually a subroutine, while saving the necessary information to allow execution to resume at the calling point when the called section has completed execution.

caller

A client that invokes a method of an object. An object's caller isn't necessarily the object's creator. For example, client A could create object X and pass this reference to client B, and then client B could use that reference to call a method of object X. In this case, client A is the creator, and client B is the caller.

Carrier Sense Multiple Access with Collision Detection (CSMA/CD)

The mechanism whereby hosts make sure the network is not being used before sending a packet. Collision detection means that the network can determine when this happens and provide corrective measures.

catalog agent
An automatic software program that periodically opens all files in a designated set of directories and indexes their contents; also called a link crawler.

certificate authority (CA)
An entity that issues, manages, and revokes certificates.

certificate, client
A digital certificate that functions in a way similar to a driver's license or passport. Client certificates can contain detailed identification information about the user and the organization that issued the certificate.

certificate, digital
An encrypted file containing user or server identification information, used to verify identity and establish a secure link; it is called a client certificate when issued to users, a server certificate when issued to a server administrator. See also *key pair*.

Certificate Revocation List (CRL)
A document maintained and published by a certificate authority (CA) that lists certificates that have been revoked by the certificate authority.

CGI
See *Common Gateway Interface*.

CGI (Common Gateway Interface) bin directory
The directory on a server where CGI script programs are stored. For Microsoft Content Analyzer, the location of the CGI bin directory is specified when the administrator uses the **New** command to map a site located on a local or networked file system.

CGI (Common Gateway Interface) script
A program that allows a server to communicate with users on the Internet. For example, when a user enters information in a form on a Web page, a CGI script interprets the information and communicates it to a database program on the server.

challenge/response authentication
An authentication method in which a server verifies user account information contained in a user's Web browser by means of a cryptographic exchange; actual passwords are never transmitted.

CICS
See *Customer Information Control System*.

class
In Microsoft Visual Basic Scripting Edition (VBScript), the formal definition of an object. The class acts as the template from which an instance of an object is created at run time. The class defines the properties of the object and the methods used to control the object's behavior. See also *Microsoft Visual Basic Scripting Edition*.

class factory
An object that implements the IClassFactory interface, which allows it to create objects of a specific class.

class ID (CLSID)
A universally unique identifier (UUID) that identifies a Component Object Model (COM) component. Each COM component has its CLSID in the Windows registry so that it can be loaded by other applications.

class restrictions
A general term sometimes used for access control by Internet Protocol (IP) address filtering and hostname filtering.

client

An application or process that requests a service from some process or component. A client facilitates a connection to server computers and manages and presents information retrieved from those sources. In a client/server environment, the workstation is usually the client computer. In referring to Component Object Model (COM) objects, an object that requests services from another object.

client certificate

A digital certificate.

client/server architecture

A model of computing whereby client applications running on a desktop or personal computer access information on remote servers or host computers. The client portion of the application is typically optimized for user interaction, whereas the server portion provides the centralized, multi-user functionality. See also *two-tier architecture*; *three-tier architecture*.

client tier

A logical layer of a client-server application that represents a local computer where browser software displays a Web page. See also *middle tier*; *data source tier*.

collision detection

See *Carrier Sense Mulitple Access with Collision Detection*.

COM

See *Component Object Model*.

commit

The phase in a transaction when all interactions are finalized and the persistent state of the underlying database is changed.

Common Gateway Interface (CGI)

A server-side interface for initiating software services. A set of interfaces that describe how a Web server communicates with software on the same computer. Any software can be a CGI

program if it handles input and output according to the CGI standard. CGI applications always run out of process. See also *gateway* and *server*.

Common Object Request Broker Architecture (CORBA)

An Object Management Group (OMG) specification for the interface definition between OMG-compliant objects.

communications protocol

A set of rules or standards designed to enable computers to connect with one another and to exchange information with as few errors as possible. Some communication protocols contain other protocols, such as hardware protocols and file transfer protocols. Examples include HTTP, TCP/IP, and SNA.

compile time

The time during which a program is translated from source language into machine language.

component

A discrete unit of code built on ActiveX technologies that delivers a well-specified set of services through well-specified interfaces. Components provide the objects that clients request at run time.

Component Object Model (COM)

The object-oriented programming model that defines how objects interact within a single application or between applications. In COM, client software accesses an object through a pointer to an interface—a related set of functions called methods—on the object.

concurrency

The appearance of simultaneous execution of processes or transactions by interleaving the execution of multiple pieces of work.

connected user

A user who is currently accessing one of the services of a Web server.

connection pooling
A performance optimization based on using collections of pre-allocated resources, such as objects or database connections. Pooling results in more efficient resource allocation.

content type
The type of file (such as text, graphic, or sound), usually indicated by the file name extension (.txt, .gif, or .wav, respectively).

control
In a graphical user interface (GUI), an object on the screen that can be manipulated by a user to perform an action. Perhaps the most common controls are buttons that a user can click to select an option, and scroll bars that a user employs to move through a document or position text in a window.

cookies
A means by which, under the HTTP protocol, a server or a script can maintain information on the client workstation. Cookies are small text files which are stored in the user's browser by the Web server. Cookies contain information about the user such as an identification number, a password, how a user shopped on a Web site, or how many times the user visited that site. A Web site can access cookie information whenever the user connects to the server.

CORBA
See *Common Object Request Broker Architecture*.

crawler
See *spider*.

CRL
See *Certificate Revocation List*.

CryptoAPI
See *Microsoft Cryptographic API*.

cryptography
A field science involving the transmission of information in an encoded form so that only an intended recipient can decode the information and reveal its meaning.

CSMA/CD
See *Carrier Sense Multiple Access with Collision Detection*.

cursor
A piece of software that returns rows of data to the application. A cursor on a resultset indicates the current position in the resultset.

Customer Information Control System (CICS)
A system from IBM that enables users working at remote terminals to enter transactions. These transactions can then be processed concurrently by business application programs. CICS includes facilities for building, using, and maintaining databases.

cycle
In logging, to close an existing log file and start a new one.

D

daemon
A networking program that runs in the background.

Data Encryption Standard (DES)
A type of encryption designed to protect against password discovery and playback. Microsoft Internet Connection Services for Remote Access Service (RAS) uses DES encryption when both the client and the server are using RAS.

datagram
A self-contained, independent entity of data carrying sufficient information to be routed from the source to the destination computer without reliance on earlier exchanges between the source and destination computer and the transporting network. See also *frame*; *packet*.

data provider
Software that implements OLE DB methods and interfaces.

data source
The name that applications use to request a connection to an Open Database Connectivity (ODBC) data source. It specifies the computer name and (optionally) database that the data source name (DSN) maps to. A system data source is a data source that is available to anyone using the computer. Data sources that will be used with a Web server need to be system data sources.

Data Source Name (DSN)
The logical name used by Open Database Connectivity (ODBC) to refer to the drive and other information required to access data. The name is used by Internet Information Server (IIS) for a connection to an ODBC data source, such as a SQL Server database.

data source tier
A logical layer that represents a computer running a Database Management System (DBMS), such as a SQL Server database. See also *client tier*; *middle tier*.

DCOM
See *Distributed Component Object Model*.

deadlock
A situation in which two or more threads are permanently blocked, with each thread waiting for a resource exclusively held by one of the other threads that is blocked. For example, if thread A locks record one and waits to lock record two, while thread B has locked record two and waits to lock record one, the two threads are deadlocked.

debugger
A software tool used to detect the source of program and script errors, by performing step-by-step execution of application code and viewing the content of code variables.

declarative security
In Microsoft Transaction Server (MTS), security that is configured with MTS Explorer to control access to packages, components, and interfaces by defining roles. See also *programmatic security*.

default document
The file sent by a Web server when it receives a URL that does not specify a file name. This document can be generated automatically by the server, or it can be a custom file placed in that directory by the administrator.

default gateway
In TCP/IP, the intermediate network device on the local network that has knowledge of the network IDs of the other networks in the Internet, so it can forward the packets to other gateways until the packet is eventually delivered to a gateway connected to the specified destination.

DES
See *Data Encryption Standard*.

design time
The time during which a user builds an application in the development environment by adding controls, setting control or form properties, and so on. In contrast, during run time, a user interacts with the application.

Design-time ActiveX Controls
Visual authoring components that help a developer construct dynamic Web applications by automatically generating standard HTML and scripting code. They are analogous to wizards. Design-time ActiveX Controls exist at design time, and not at run time.

developer isolation
A feature of some software that provides a way for an application developer to create and test scripts without a connecting to a Web server.

DHCP
See *dynamic host configuration protocol*.

DHTML
See *Dynamic Hypertext Markup Language*.

dial-up
A connection to a computer by telephone, through a modem.

Dial-up Networking
A component of Windows NT and Windows 95. Makes it possible for users to connect to remote networks such as the Internet or a private network.

digital signature
Part of a digital certificate containing an encryption key that uniquely identifies the holder of the certificate. See also *client certificate*; *key pair*.

directory browsing
A feature that automatically provides a default Web page of available directories and files to browsers that submit a URL that does not specify a particular file. See also *default document*.

directory replication
The copying of a master set of directories from a server (called an export server) to specified servers or workstations (called import computers) in the same or other domains. Replication simplifies the task of maintaining identical sets of directories and files on multiple computers, because only a single master copy of the data must be maintained. Files are replicated when they are added to an exported directory, and every time a change is saved to the file.

directory service
Middleware that locates the correct and full network address from a partial name or address typed into a dialog box. See also *middleware*.

disconnected recordset
A recordset in a client cache that no longer has a live connection to the server. If you need to do something with the original data source, such as

updating data, you need to re-establish the connection.

discovery mechanism
A way of finding other servers on the network.

Distributed Component Object Model (DCOM)
Additions to the Component Object Model (COM) that facilitate the transparent distribution of objects over networks and over the Internet. DCOM is part of the specification managed by the Open Group for deployment across heterogeneous platforms. See also *Component Object Model* and *the Open Group*.

distributed processing
The physical or logical distribution of software components, processing, data, and management of application software.

DLL
See *dynamic-link library*.

DNS name
See *domain name*; *Domain Name System*.

DNS name servers
In the Domain Name System (DNS) client/server model, the servers containing information about a portion of the DNS database, which makes computer names available to clients querying for name resolution across the Internet. See also *Domain Name System*.

DNS reverse lookup
Finding an IP address corresponding to a domain name.

DNS spoofing
Assuming the DNS name of another system by either corrupting a name-service cache, or by compromising a domain-name server for a valid domain.

domain

In Windows NT, a collection of computers defined by the administrator of a Windows NT Server network that share a common directory database. A domain provides access to the centralized user accounts and group accounts maintained by the domain administrator. Each domain has a unique name.

domain controller

For a Windows NT Server domain, the server that authenticates domain logons and maintains the security policy and the master database for a domain.

domain, Internet

The friendly name, such as microsoft.com, used for a site on the Internet. A fully qualified domain name (FQDN) also contains the name of the server; for example, samples.microsoft.com.

domain name

Part of the Domain Name System (DNS) naming structure, a domain name is the name by which a domain is known to the network. Domain names provide a text representation of a resource's IP address, using the unique name of the server computer, plus the kind of operation it is involved in, such as .com for a business or .edu for an academic institution. Domain names may have several parts, separated by periods. For example, www.microsoft.com is the domain name for the Microsoft site, where www.microsoft is the unique name for Microsoft's server on the World Wide Web, and com is the type of activity the company is involved with (in this case, a commercial business). See also *Domain Name System*.

Domain Name System (DNS)

A protocol and system used throughout the Internet to map Internet Protocol (IP) addresses to user-friendly names. Sometimes referred to as the BIND service in BSD UNIX, DNS offers a static, hierarchical name service for TCP/IP hosts. The network administrator configures the DNS with a list of host names and IP addresses allowing users of workstations configured to query the DNS to specify remote systems by host names rather than by IP addresses. For example, a workstation configured to use DNS name resolution can use the command **ping remotehost** rather than **ping 172.16.16.235** if the mapping for the system named "remotehost" was contained in the DNS database. DNS domains are not the same as Windows NT networking domains.

download

In communications, the process of transferring a copy of a file from a remote computer to the requesting computer by means of a modem or network.

DSN

See *Data Source Name*.

dynamic host configuration protocol (DHCP)

A standard protocol that assigns Internet Protocol (IP) configurations to computers. The DHCP-server computer makes the assignments, and the client computer calls the server computer to obtain the address.

Dynamic Hypertext Markup Language (DHTML)

A set of innovative features in Internet Explorer version 4.0 that can be used to create HTML documents that dynamically change their content and interact with the user. By using DHTML, authors can provide special effects on a Web page without relying on server-side programs.

dynamic-link library (DLL)

A feature of the Microsoft Windows family of operating systems that supports executable routines—usually serving a specific function or set of functions—to be stored separately as files with the extension .dll, and to be loaded only when called by the program that needs them. This saves memory during program execution and enables code reusability.

dynamic page

A Web page created automatically based on information provided by the user.

E

E-commerce

Electronic commerce. The process of buying and selling over the Web—often based on software products such as Microsoft Site Server, Enterprise Edition.

e-mail (electronic mail)

A system whereby a computer user can exchange messages with other computer users (or groups of users) through a communications network. E-mail is one of the most popular uses of the Internet.

early binding

Binding that occurs at compile time rather than at run time. See *binding*; *compile time*; *late binding*.

encapsulation

The technique used by layered protocols in which a layer adds header information to the protocol data unit (PDU) from the layer above. As an example, in Internet terminology, a packet would contain a header from the physical layer, followed by a header from the network layer (IP), followed by a header from the transport layer (TCP), followed by the application protocol data.

encryption

A way of making data indecipherable to protect it from unauthorized viewing or use, especially during network transmission or when it is stored on a transportable magnetic medium while it is being sent from computer to computer.

enterprise server

Refers to the server to which multiple primary domain controllers (PDCs) in a large organization or enterprise will replicate.

Ethernet

A 10-MBps standard for local area networks (LANs) initially developed by Xerox and later refined by Digital, Intel, and Xerox (DIX). All hosts are connected to a coaxial cable where they contend for network access using a Carrier Sense Multiple Access with Collision Detection (CSMA/CD) paradigm. See also *Carrier Sense Multiple Access with Collision Detection*.

event

Any action, often generated by a user or an ActiveX Control, to which a program might respond. Typical events include pressing a keyboard key, choosing a button by using a mouse click, and other mouse actions. Programmers write code to respond to these actions.

exception

An abnormal condition or error that occurs during the execution of a program and that requires the execution of software outside the normal flow of control.

executable program

A computer program that is ready to run. For example, a word processing program that a user does not have to alter before using it to create documents.

expires header

An expiration date or time for a file sent by a server; the expiration information is used by proxy servers and browser caches.

explore

To retrieve a resource by way of its URL. If the resource is a page that contains links to other resources, exploring the page also looks up the URLs for those linked resources. Microsoft Content Analyzer explores a resource when the user clicks the map object's question mark icon, or uses the **Explore** command.

extended partition

Created from free space on a hard disk, an extended partition can be subpartitioned into several logical drives. Only one of the four partitions allowed per physical disk can be an extended partition, and no primary partition needs to be present to create an extended partition. See also *logical drive*.

eXtensible Markup Language (XML)

A data format for structured document interchange on the Web. It is called the "extensible markup language" because it is not a fixed format like HTML. XML is designed to enable the use of SGML on the World Wide Web. XML is not a single markup language; it is a metalanguage that allows an author to design a markup language. A regular markup language defines a way to describe information in a certain class of documents (for example, HTML). With XML, authors can define their own customized markup languages for many classes of documents.

extranet

An intranet that can be accessed by selected outside (Internet) users.

F

failback

When the failed server node is fully restored to action.

failover

When one individual computer fails, another automatically takes over its request load. The transition is invisible to the user.

FAQ

See *Frequently Asked Questions*.

fault tolerance

The ability of a cluster to ensure that information is available to the user regardless of individual server failures. See also *replication* and *failover*.

file name extension mapping

Connecting all files with a certain file name extension to a program. For example, by a default setting in Windows NT Explorer, all .txt files are associated with Notepad.

file space

A term sometimes used for the file-directory tree of a server.

File Transfer Protocol (FTP)

The Internet standard high-speed protocol for downloading, or transferring, files from one computer to another.

filter

In Internet Information Server (IIS), a feature of ISAPI that allows pre-processing of requests and post-processing of responses, permitting site-specific handling of HTTP requests and responses.

filter, content

An Index Server component that is responsible for reading a document from the disk and extracting information. Typically filters are associated with particular document formats. For example, Microsoft Word documents have their contents extracted by a different filter than Microsoft Excel documents.

filtering, hostname

Allowing or denying access based on the hostname from which the browser is attempting access.

filtering, IP address

Allowing or denying access based on the Internet Protocol (IP) address from which the browser is attempting access.

finger

A program that displays information about a particular user, or all users, logged on to the local system or a remote system. It typically shows full name, the last time the user logged on, idle time, terminal line, and terminal location (where applicable). It may also display plan and project files left by the user.

firewall

A system or combination of systems that enforces a boundary between two or more networks and keeps intruders out of private networks. Firewalls serve as virtual barriers to passing packets from one network to another. See also *proxy server*.

footer

In Web publishing, a short addition to every Web page sent out by the server. See *server-side include*.

form

In Web publishing, a Web page or portion of a Web page that is filled out by the user and sent back to the server for processing.

FQDN

See *Fully Qualified Domain Name*.

frame

A frame is a datalink layer packet that contains the header and trailer information required by the physical medium. That is, network layer packets are encapsulated to become frames. See also *datagram*; *encapsulation*; *packet*.

Frequently Asked Questions (FAQ)

Usually a document containing questions and answers that address the basics. A visitor can find FAQs on many Web sites. An FAQ typically serves to introduce a visitor to the topic or subject of the Web site and to offer general guidelines about how best to use the site.

friendly name

A name that substitutes for an Internet Protocol (IP) address, for example, www.microsoft.com instead of an IP address such as 157.45.60.81.

FrontPage server extensions

A group of files installed on a Web server to give that server the ability to provide special Microsoft FrontPage functionality. With FrontPage server extensions, administrators can view and manage a Web site in a graphical interface. Also, authors can create, edit, and post Web pages to Internet Information Server (IIS) remotely.

FTP

See *File Transfer Protocol*.

Fully Qualified Domain Name

Also called Fully Qualified Hostname (FQHN). See *domain, Internet*.

G

gateway

A hardware or software device that directs network traffic. Conversion software that integrates dissimilar entities such as network protocols, software object models, or data storage devices.

GIF

See *Graphics Interchange Format*.

Globally Unique Identifier (GUID)

Identifiers (IDs) assigned to Component Object Model (COM) objects that are generated through a sophisticated algorithm. The algorithm guarantees that all COM objects are assigned unique IDs, avoiding any possibility of a naming conflict, even in distributed systems with millions of objects supplied by different vendors.

Gopher

An early Internet protocol and software program designed to search for, retrieve, and display documents from remote computers or sites.

graphical user interface (GUI)

A user interface that displays graphics and characters and which provides an event model for users to control the operating environment.

Graphics Interchange Format (GIF)

A computer graphics file format developed in the mid-1980s by CompuServe for use in photo-quality graphic image display on computer screens. Now commonly used on the Internet.

GUI

See *graphical user interface*.

GUID

See *Globally Unique Identifier*.

H

handshake

An informal term for the process in which two computers share information. For example, a security handshake involves the exchange of security tokens such as digital certificates.

header

An informational listing at the top of an HTTP request or response.

hit count

The number of times any given resource in a site is accessed by visitors. See also *usage data*.

home directory

The root directory for a Web site, where the content files are stored. Sometimes called a document root or Web root. In Internet Information Server (IIS), by default, the home directory and all its subdirectories are available to users. Also the root directory for an IIS service. The directory is accessible to the user and contains files and programs. Typically the home directory for a site contains the home page. See also *home page*.

home page

The initial page of information for a collection of pages. The starting point for a Web site or section of a Web site is often referred to as the home page. Individuals also post pages that are called home pages. See also *default document*.

host

Any computer that provides services to remote computers or users. A computer connected to a network.

hostname

The name of a computer connected to a network; also called sitename.

HTML

See *Hypertext Markup Language*.

HTTP

See *Hypertext Transport Protocol*.

hyperlink

Also called simply a link. A way of jumping from one place to another on the Internet. Hyperlinks usually appear in a different format from regular text. Users initiate the jump by clicking the link.

hypertext

Documents with links to other documents. Users click a link to display the other document.

Hypertext Markup Language (HTML)

A simple markup language used to create hypertext documents that are portable from one platform to another. HTML files are simple ASCII text files with codes embedded (indicated by markup tags) to indicate formatting and hypertext links. The formatting language used for documents on the World Wide Web. See also *Dynamic Hypertext Markup Language*; *Standard Generalized Markup Language*; *eXtensible Markup Language*.

Hypertext Transfer Protocol (HTTP)

The underlying protocol by which Web clients and servers communicate. HTTP is an application-level protocol for distributed, collaborative, hypermedia information systems. It is a generic, stateless, object-oriented protocol. A feature of HTTP is the typing and negotiation of data representation, allowing systems to be built independently of the data being transferred.

I

ICMP

See *Internet Control Message Protocol.*

IDC

See *Internet Database Connector.*

identities, multiple

A term sometimes used for multiple Web sites hosted on one computer; also called virtual servers or multihoming. See *Web site.*

IETF

See *Internet Engineering Task Force.*

imagemap

A bitmapped graphic image that links to multiple URLs by way of hotspots on the image. Users can click different regions of an imagemap to jump to different resources in the site. Imagemaps can be server-side or client-side. Server-side imagemaps map each URL on the server; they require server-side scripts. Client-side imagemaps, on the other hand, do not require mediating server-side scripts because the URL mapping is contained in an HTML file. Microsoft Content Analyzer recognizes client-side imagemaps and shows the links as children of the imagemap's parent page.

inheritance

Generally, the ability of a newly created object to automatically have, or inherit, properties of an existing object; for example, a newly created child directory can inherit the access-control settings of the parent directory. A programming technique

that duplicates the characteristics down a hierarchy from one class to another.

inline

A characteristic of how an image is specified in an HTML page, which indicates that the image is to be downloaded and displayed in the Web page.

in-process component

A component that runs in a client's process space. This is typically a dynamic-link library (DLL).

instance

An object of a particular component class. Each instance has its own private data elements or member variables. A component instance is synonymous with object.

instantiate

To create an instance of an object. The process of creating or activating an object based on its class.

Integrated Services Digital Network (ISDN)

An emerging technology that is beginning to be offered by most telephone service providers as a faster alternative to traditional modems. ISDN combines voice and digital network services in a single medium, making it possible to offer telephone customers digital data service and voice connection through a single "wire." A dial-up ISDN line can offer speeds up to 128,000 bps. A type of phone line used to enhance wide area network (WAN) speeds, an ISDN line can transmit at speeds of 64 or 128 kilobits per second. An ISDN line must be installed by the phone company at both the server site and the remote site. See also *bits per second.*

interactive application

A program written in Microsoft Visual Basic for Applications (VBA), C, Perl, or as a Windows NT batch file. The user usually initiates the program by clicking a hyperlink.

interface

A group of logically related operations or methods that provides access to a component object.

internal Web

An intranet; sometimes called an internal network, private network, local area network (LAN), or wide area network (WAN).

International Organization for Standardization (ISO)

A voluntary, nontreaty organization founded in 1946 which is responsible for creating international standards in many areas, including computers and communications. Its members are the national standards organizations of the 89 member countries, including ANSI for the U.S. See also *American National Standards Institute*.

Internet

Abbreviation for internetwork. A set of dissimilar computer networks joined together by means of gateways that handle data transfer and the conversion of messages from the sending network to the protocols used by the receiving networks. These networks and gateways use the TCP/IP suite of protocols. Originally part of the Department of Defense's Advanced Research Project Administration (DARPA).

Internet Control Message Protocol (ICMP)

An extension to the Internet Protocol (IP), ICMP allows for the generation of error messages, test packets, and informational messages related to IP. See also *Packet Internet Groper*.

Internet Database Connector (IDC)

IDC provides database connectivity between IIS applications and any ODBC-compliant database.

Internet Engineering Task Force (IETF)

A protocol engineering and development organization focused on the Internet. The IETF is a large, open international community of network designers, operators, vendors, and researchers concerned with the evolution of the Internet architecture and the smooth operation of the Internet. It is now under the auspices of the Internet Society, a non-governmental international organization for global cooperation and coordination for the Internet and its inter-networking technologies and applications. To read more about IETF, see http://www.info.isoc.org/.

Internet Network Information Center (InterNIC)

A coordinator for DNS registration of names in the .com, .net, .org, .edu, .gov, and .mil top-level domains. To register domain names and obtain IP addresses, contact InterNIC at http://internic.net.

Internet Protocol (IP)

The part of TCP/IP that routes messages from one Internet location to another. IP is responsible for addressing and sending TCP packets over the network. IP provides a best-effort, connectionless delivery system that does not guarantee that packets arrive at their destination or that they are received in the sequence in which they were sent. See also *packets*.

Internet Protocol (IP) Address

A unique address that identifies a host on a network. It identifies a computer as a 32-bit address that is unique across a TCP/IP network. An IP address is usually represented in dotted-decimal notation, which depicts each octet (eight bits, or one byte) of an IP address as its decimal value and separates each octet with a period. For example, 102.54.94.97.

Internet Server Application Program Interface (ISAPI)

An application program interface that resides on a server computer for initiating software services tuned for the Microsoft Windows NT operating system. It is an API for developing extensions to Microsoft Internet Information Server and other HTTP servers that support the ISAPI interface. See also *Application Program Interface*.

Internet service

Any protocol for transferring information over the Internet, except HTTP. The protocol is the first part of the full URL for a resource. Internet service types include Gopher, telnet, WAIS, NNTP, and FTP. See also *Hypertext Transfer Protocol*; *protocol*.

Internet service provider (ISP)

A public provider of remote connections to the Internet. A company or educational institution that enables remote users to access the Internet by providing dial-up connections or installing leased lines.

InterNIC

See *Internet Network Information Center*.

interoperability

The ability of software and hardware on multiple computers from multiple vendors to communicate meaningfully.

intranet

The application of Internet technologies on internal corporate networks. A TCP/IP network that can be connected to the Internet but is usually protected by a firewall or other device (for example, a corporate network).

IP

See *Internet Protocol*.

IP address

Internet Protocol address. A unique address that identifies a host on a network. It identifies a computer as a 32-bit address that is unique across a TCP/IP network. An IP address is usually represented in dotted-decimal notation, which depicts each octet (eight bits, or one byte) of an IP address as its decimal value and separates each octet with a period. For example: 102.54.94.97.

ISAPI

See *Internet Server Application Program Interface*.

ISDN

See *Integrated Services Digital Network*.

ISO

See *International Organization for Standardization*.

ISP

See *Internet service provider*.

J

Java

A derivative of the C++ language, Java is SunSoft's distributed programming language, offered as an open standard.

JavaBeans

An object model being developed by SunSoft that is targeted to interoperate with a variety of other object models, including Component Object Model (COM) and Common Object Request Broker Architecture (CORBA). See also *Component Object Model; Common Object Request Broker Architecture*.

Java Database Connectivity (JDBC)

Data access interfaces based on ODBC for use with the Java language.

JavaScript

A scripting language that evolved from Netscape's LiveScript language and was made more compatible with Java. It uses an HTML page as its interface. See also *JScript*.

Java virtual machine

A system that runs Java programs.

Joint Photographic Experts Group (JPEG)

A widely accepted international standard for compression of color image files, sometimes used on the Internet.

JPEG

See *Joint Photographic Experts Group*.

JScript

The Microsoft open implementation of JavaScript. JScript is fully compatible with JavaScript in Netscape Navigator version 2.0.

just-in-time activation (JIT)

The ability for a Microsoft Transaction Server (MTS) object to be activated only as needed for executing requests from its client. Objects can be deactivated even while clients hold references to them, allowing otherwise idle server resources to be used more productively.

K

Kbps

Kilobits per second.

Kerberos

The basis of most of the distributed computing environment (DCE) security services. Kerberos provides for the secure use of distributed software components and is based on symmetric key cryptography. See also *cryptography*; *encryption*.

key

In the Windows NT registry, a folder that appears in the left pane of a Registry Editor window. A key can contain subkeys and value entries. For example: Environment is a key of HKEY_CURRENT_USER.

key pair

The combination of private and public encryption keys that provides verification of the source of data sent across a network. See also *client certificate*; *digital signature*; *session key*.

keyword

A significant word, which is used for content indexing; see also *noise word*. In programming, a word reserved for a command or other program instruction.

keyword index

A file of significant words appearing in documents; used for keyword searches.

L

LAN

See *local area network*.

late binding

When Visual Basic for Applications (VBA) has to look up an object and its methods and properties each time it executes a line of code that includes that object. See also *binding*; *early binding*.

latency

The state of being latent, or to lie hidden; not currently showing signs of existence. Sometimes attributed to the time taken to retrieve pages from the World Wide Web.

LDAP

See *Lightweight Directory Access Protocol*.

Lightweight Directory Access Protocol (LDAP)

A protocol used by some directory services.

link

See *hyperlink*.

load balancing

When a server cluster shares the information requests equally over all of its active nodes. This can be done either statically, by loading all the content and all of the metabases onto all of the nodes and then routing the requests equally, or dynamically by having a central hard disk containing the content and routing the nodes to it dynamically as the request load varies.

local area network (LAN)

A group of computers and other devices intended to serve an area of only a few square kilometers or less and connected by a communications link that enables any device to interact with any other on the network. Because the network is known to cover only a small area, optimizations can be made in the network signal protocols that permit data rates up to 100Mbps. See also *Ethernet*; *token ring*.

local group
For Windows NT Workstation, a group that can be granted permissions and rights only for its own workstation. However, it can contain user accounts from its own computer and (if the workstation participates in a domain) user accounts and global groups both from its own domain and from trusted domains.

localhost
A placeholder for the name of the computer on which a program is running.

log file
The file in which logging records are stored. This file can be either a text file or a database file.

logging
Storing information about events that occurred on a firewall or network.

logical drive
A subpartition of an extended partition on a hard disk. See also *extended partition*.

LU 6.2
A type of preset unit that supports communication between programs in a distributed processing environment.

M

Mail or Messaging Applications Programming Interface (MAPI)
An open and comprehensive messaging interface used by programmers to create messaging and workgroup applications—such as e-mail, scheduling, calendaring, and document management. In a distributed client/server environment, MAPI provides enterprise messaging services within Windows Open Services Architecture (WOSA).

main thread
A single thread used to run all objects of components marked as "single threaded." See also *apartment thread*.

management information base (MIB)
Software that describes aspects of a network that can be managed by using the Simple Network Management Protocol (SNMP). The MIB files included in Windows NT can be used by third-party SNMP monitors to enable SNMP monitoring of the WWW and FTP services of Microsoft Internet Information Server (IIS).

MAPI
See *Messaging Applications Programming Interface*.

marshaling
The process of packaging and sending interface method parameters across thread or process boundaries.

master properties
In Internet Information Server (IIS) and Personal Web Server (PWS), the properties of specific files and directories, including access controls and other options.

Mbps
Megabits per second.

MD5
An encryption method used on the Internet.

message passing
A method for processes running in parallel to interact with one another.

message queuing
Server technology that developers can use to build large-scale distributed systems with reliable communications between applications that can continue to operate reliably even when networked systems are unavailable.

meta-authoring environment
A term sometimes used for the process of both authoring Web pages and setting up a Web site.

metabase

A structure for storing Internet Information Server (IIS) configuration settings; the metabase performs some of the same functions as the system registry, but uses less disk space.

metadata

Data used to describe other data. For example, Index Server must maintain data that describes the data in the content index. This data that Index Server maintains is called metadata because it describes how data in the index is stored.

method

A procedure (function) that acts on an object.

MIB

See *management information base*.

Microsoft Cryptographic API (CryptoAPI)

An application programming interface providing services for authentication, encoding, and encryption in Win32-based applications.

Microsoft Network, The (MSN™)

An online service that offers a free Internet site to all Internet users. Subscribers can also use proprietary information and obtain Internet access.

Microsoft Transaction Server (MTS)

Combines features of a transaction-processing monitor and an object-request broker.

Microsoft Visual Basic for Applications (VBA)

The development environment and language found in Visual Basic that can be hosted by applications.

Microsoft Visual Basic Scripting Edition (VBScript)

A subset of the Microsoft Visual Basic language, VBScript is implemented as a fast, portable, lightweight interpreter for use in World Wide Web browsers and other applications that use ActiveX Controls, OLE Automation servers, and Java applets.

middle tier

Also known as application server tier. The logical layer between a user interface or Web client and the database. This is typically where the Web server resides, and where business objects are instantiated. The middle tier is a collection of business rules and functions that generate and operate upon information. They accomplish this through business rules, which can change frequently, and are thus encapsulated into components that are physically separate from the application logic itself. See also *client tier*; *data source tier*.

middleware

Network-aware system software, layered between an application, the operating system, and the network transport layers, whose purpose is to facilitate some aspect of cooperative processing. Examples of middleware include directory services, message-passing mechanisms, distributed transaction processing (TP) monitors, object request brokers, remote procedure call (RPC) services, and database gateways. Microsoft Transaction Server (MTS) is middleware.

MIME mapping

See *Multipurpose Internet Mail Extension mapping*.

mirror set

A fully redundant or shadow copy of data. Mirror sets provide an identical twin for a selected disk; all data written to the primary disk is also written to the shadow or mirror disk. The user can then have instant access to another disk with a redundant copy of the information on the failed disk. Mirror sets provide fault tolerance. See also *fault tolerance*.

modem

Modulator/demodulator. A communications device that enables a computer to transmit information over a standard telephone line.

multihomed host
A host which has a connection to more than one physical network. The host may send and receive data over any of the links but will not route traffic for other nodes. See also *host*; *router*.

Multipurpose Internet Mail Extension (MIME) mapping
A way of configuring browsers to view files that are in multiple formats. An extension of the Internet mail protocol that enables sending 8-bit based e-mail messages, which are used to support extended character sets, voice mail, facsimile images, and so forth.

multi-tier architecture
Also known as three-tier architecture, multi-tier architecture is a technique for building applications generally split into user, business, and data services tiers. These applications are built of component services that are based on an object model such as ActiveX.

multithreading
Running several processes in rapid sequence within a single program, regardless of which logical method of multitasking is being used by the operating system. Because the user's sense of time is much slower that the processing speed of a computer, the impression of multitasking appears simultaneous, even though only one task at a time can use a computer processing cycle.

N

name resolution
The method of mapping friendly names to IP addresses. See also *friendly name*.

Network News Transfer Protocol (NNTP)
The protocol used to distribute network news messages to NNTP servers and to NNTP clients (news readers) on the Internet. NNTP provides for the distribution, inquiry, retrieval, and posting of news articles by using a reliable stream-based transmission of news on the Internet. NNTP is designed so that news articles are stored on a server in a central database, thus users can select specific items to read. Indexing, cross-referencing, and expiration of aged messages are also provided. Defined in RFC 977.

network sniffer
A hardware and software diagnostic tool that can also be used to decipher passwords, which may result in unauthorized access to network accounts. Cleartext passwords are susceptible to network sniffers.

NNTP
See *Network News Transfer Protocol*.

node
A computer that is attached to a network; also called a host. Also, a junction of some kind. On a local area network, a device that is connected to the network and is capable of communicating with other network devices.

noise word
An insignificant word, such as *the*, *and*, or *be*, ignored during indexing; also called an ignored word.

NTLM challenge response authentication
See *challenge/response authentication*.

O

object
In object-oriented programming, a variable comprising both routines and data that is treated as a discrete entity. An object is based on a specific model, where a client using an object's services gains access to the object's data through an interface consisting of a set of methods or related functions. The client can then call these methods to perform operations.

Object Linking and Embedding (OLE)

A set of integration standards to transfer and share information among client applications. A protocol that enables creation of compound documents with embedded links to applications so that a user does not have to switch among applications in order to make revisions. OLE is based on the Component Object Model (COM) and allows for the development of reusable, plug-and-play objects that are interoperable across multiple applications. This has been broadly used in business, where spreadsheets, word processors, financial packages, and other PC applications can share and link disparate information across client/server architectures.

object-cache scavenger

The code that periodically scans the cache for objects to be discarded. It deletes from the cache files that have not been used recently and therefore are unlikely to be used again in the near future.

Object Management Group (OMG)

A vendor alliance formed to define and promote CORBA object specifications.

object orientation

Representing the latest approach to accurately model the real world in computer applications, object orientation is an umbrella concept used to describe a suite of technologies that enable software products that are highly modular and reusable. Applications, data, networks, and computing systems are treated as objects that can be mixed and matched flexibly rather than as components of a system with built-in relationships. As a result, an application need not be tied to a specific system or data to a specific application. The four central object-oriented concepts are encapsulation, message passing, inheritance, and late binding.

Object Request Broker (ORB)

Manages interaction between clients and servers including the distributed computing

responsibilities of location referencing as well as coordinating parameters and results.

octet

Eight contiguous bits, or a byte. The term was created because some computer systems attached to the Internet used a byte with more than eight bits.

ODBC

See *Open Database Connectivity*.

OLAP

See *Online Analytical Processing*.

OLE

See *Object Linking and Embedding*.

OLE Automation

See *ActiveX Automation*.

OLE DB

Data-access interfaces providing consistent access to SQL and non-SQL data sources across the enterprise and the Internet.

OMG

See *Object Management Group*.

Online Analytical Processing (OLAP)

A multi-dimensional database model used for decision support analysis and data warehousing.

Open Database Connectivity (ODBC)

An application programming interface that enables applications to access data from a variety of existing data sources standard specification for cross-platform database access.

Open Group, the

Consists of a number of standards organizations including The Active Group—responsible for managing the core ActiveX technology, X/Open, and OSF.

ORB

See *Object Request Broker*.

out-of-process component

An ActiveX component that runs in its own memory space, separate from a container application. Microsoft Transaction Server (MTS) enables components implemented as DLLs to be used out-of-process from the client by loading the components into surrogate server processes.

P

packet

A transmission unit of fixed maximum size that consists of binary information representing both data and a header containing an ID number, source and destination addresses, and error-control data. A piece of information sent over a network.

Packet Internet Groper (PING)

A command used to verify connections to one or more remote hosts. The **ping** utility uses the ICMP echo request and echo reply packets to determine whether a particular IP system on a network is functional. The *ping* utility is useful for diagnosing IP network or router failures. The term is also used as a verb. See also *ICMP*; *router*.

page

See *Web page*.

parity

Redundant information that is associated with a block of information. In Windows NT Server, stripe sets with parity means that there is one additional parity stripe per row. Therefore, you must use at least three, rather than two, disks to allow for this extra parity information. Parity stripes contain the XOR (the Boolean operation called exclusive Or) of the data in that stripe. Windows NT Server, when regenerating a failed disk, uses the parity information in those stripes in conjunction with the data on the good disks to recreate the data on the failed disk. See also *fault tolerance*; *stripe set*; *stripe sets with parity*.

parser, HTML

Software that interprets HTML tags; there are different HTML parsers for different versions of HTML and its extensions.

partition

A partition is a portion of a physical disk that functions as though it were a physically separate unit.

password authentication

See *authentication*.

path, physical

A universal naming convention (UNC) directory path. See also *path, relative*.

path, relative

A universal naming convention (UNC) directory path with placeholders, or wildcards, at some levels; relative path is also sometimes used to mean the physical path that corresponds to a URL.

path, URL

A term sometimes used for the full URL submitted to the server; a URL path may or may not include a specific file name.

PCT

See *Private Communication Technology*.

Perl

Practical Extraction and Report Language. A scripting (programming) language that is frequently used for CGI scripts. It is an interpreted scripting language. See also *script*.

permissions

The levels of file or directory access granted to users, such as read only or full control access. See *Access Control List*.

PGP

See *Pretty Good Privacy*.

PING
See *Packet Internet Groper.*

Point-to-Point Protocol (PPP)
A set of industry-standard framing and authentication protocols included with Windows NT Remote Internet Connection Services for Access Service (RAS) to ensure interoperability with third-party remote access software. PPP negotiates configuration parameters for multiple layers of the OSI (Open Systems Interconnection) model. The Internet standard for serial communications, PPP defines how data packets are exchanged with other Internet-based systems using a modem connection.

Point-to-Point Tunneling Protocol (PPTP)
The Internet can be used for low-cost, secure remote access to a corporate network with virtual private networking support on Windows NT. This new protocol works by using a local call to an Internet service provider to gain secure access to the corporate network using the Internet. PPTP, an open, industry standard, supports the most prevalent networking protocols—IP, IPX, and Microsoft Networking. Companies can use PPTP to outsource their remote dial-up needs to an Internet service provider or other carrier to reduce cost and complexity.

policies
Conditions set by the system administrator such as how quickly account passwords expire and how many unsuccessful logon attempts are allowed before a user is locked out. These policies manage accounts to prevent exhaustive or random password attacks.

port number
A number identifying a certain Internet application. For example, the default port number for the WWW service is 80.

PPP
See *Point-to-Point Protocol.*

PPTP
See *Point-to-Point Tunneling Protocol.*

Pretty Good Privacy (PGP)
A security application that uses public-key encryption.

Private Communication Technology (PCT)
A protocol, similar to SSL, used to establish a secure link. PCT can interact with a client supporting SSL, and offers an enhanced encryption algorithm negotiation and longer encryption keys. See also *Secured Sockets Layer.*

process
In Windows NT, an object consisting of an executable program, a set of virtual memory addresses, and a thread; in UNIX, a synonym for thread. See also *thread.*

process isolation
Running an application or component out of the server process.

program file
A file that starts an application or program. A program file has an .exe, .pif, .com, .cmd, or .bat file name extension.

programmatic security
Procedural logic provided by a component to determine if a client is authorized to perform the requested operation. See also *declarative security.*

properties, document
Information about a document and its physical location on a hard disk.

properties, link
Information about an HTML document and the full URL associated with it.

property
A set of characteristics of an object.

protocol
The method by which computers communicate on the Internet. The most common protocol for the World Wide Web is HTTP. Other Internet protocols include FTP, Gopher, and Telnet. The protocol is the first part of the full URL for a resource.

proxy
A software program that connects a user to a remote destination through an intermediary gateway.

proxy server
A proxy server acts as a go-between, conveying information from Web servers to client computers. It also provides a way to deliver network services to computers on a secure subnet without those computers having direct access to the World Wide Web. Thus, secure intranets can run a proxy server on their firewall computers. See also *firewall*.

public-key encryption
A security method that uses encryption and two keys, one public and the other private. RSA is an example of public-key encryption. Note that the keys are used to negotiate a secure link, not to encrypt data. See also *session key*; *RSA*.

Q

query form   An online form that the user fills out to search for information by keyword or concept; also called a search interface.

query restriction   What to look for in a search; a query restriction narrows the focus of a search. Also called a search expression or search string.

R

RAID
See *Redundant Array of Independent Disks*.

RAM
See *random access memory*

random access memory (RAM)
Memory that can be read from or written to by the computer or other devices. Information stored in RAM is lost when the user turns off the computer.

RAS
See *Remote Access Service*.

realm
A term sometimes used for domain, in this case to refer to user domains established for security reasons, not Internet domains. For password-protected files, the name of the protected resource or area on the server. If you try to access the protected resource while browsing, the name of the realm usually appears in the dialog box that asks for your user name and password.

redirection
The process of automatically redirecting a browser to a different file or directory that that specific in the original request.

Redundant Array of Independent Disks (RAID)
A method used to standardize and categorize fault-tolerant disk systems. Six levels gauge various mixes of performance, reliability, and cost. Windows NT includes three of the RAID levels: Level 0, Level 1, and Level 5.

registry
The Windows NT registry is a database repository for information about a computer's configuration. It is organized in a hierarchical structure, and is comprised of subtrees and their keys, hives, and value entries.

Remote Access Service (RAS)
A service that provides remote networking for telecommuters, mobile workers, and other remote users.

remote administration
Administering a computer from another computer over the network.

Remote Data Services
A Web-based technology that brings database connectivity and corporate data publishing capabilities to Internet and intranet applications.

Remote Procedure Call (RPC)
A widely used standard defined by the Open Software Foundation (OSF) for distributed computing. The RPC transport enables one process to make calls to functions that are part of another process. The other process can be on the same computer or on a different computer on the network.

replication
Copying from one server node to another of either content or the metabase, or both. This copying can either be done manually or automatically by using replication software. Replication is a necessary function of clustering to ensure fault tolerance.

Request for Comments (RFC)
The document series, begun in 1969, that describes the Internet suite of protocols and related experiments. Very few RFCs describe Internet standards, but all Internet standards are written up as RFCs. The RFC series of documents is unusual in that the proposed protocols are forwarded by the Internet research and development community, acting on their own behalf, as opposed to the formally reviewed and standardized protocols that are promoted by organizations such as ANSI.

resource dispenser
A service that provides the synchronization and management of nondurable resources within a process, providing for simple and efficient sharing by Microsoft Transaction Server (MTS) objects. For example, the Open Database Connectivity (ODBC) resource dispenser manages pools of database connections. See also *Open Database Connectivity*.

resource manager
A system service that manages durable data. Server applications use resource managers to maintain the durable state of the application, such as the record of inventory on hand, pending orders, and accounts receivable. The resource managers work in cooperation with the transaction manager to provide the application with a guarantee of atomicity and isolation (using the two-phase commit protocol). Microsoft SQL Server is an example of a resource manager.

RFC
See *Request for Comments*.

robot
A fast, automated program, such as a search engine, indexing program, or cataloging software, that requests Web pages much faster than humans can. When Microsoft Content Analyzer automatically explores a Web site, it operates as a robot. Other commonly-used terms for robot include crawler and spider. See also *explore*.

router
An intermediary device on a communications network responsible for making decisions about which of several paths each message will follow on a network or the Internet. To do this, a router uses a routing protocol to gather information about the network, and algorithms to choose the best route based on several criteria called routing metrics.

RPC
See *Remote Procedure Call*.

RSA
A public-key cryptography for Internet security. This acronym derives from the last names of the inventors of the technology: Rivest, Shamir, and Adleman.

run time
The time during which a program actually runs.

S

scalability
The capability to use the same software environment on many classes of computers and hardware configurations. While often associated with an evolution to large systems, larger organizations often have need for the same software service to be provided with good performance to both small and large groups of users.

scope
Defines the visibility of a variable, procedure, or object. For example, a variable declared as Public is visible to all procedures in all modules. Variables declared in procedures are visible only within the procedure and lose their value between calls.

script
A kind of program that consists of a set of instructions for an application or utility program. A script can be embedded in a Web page. See also *Common Gateway Interface*; *ActiveX*.

scripting engine
A program that interprets and executes a script. See also *script*.

SDK
See *Software Development Kit*.

search expression
See *query restriction*.

search interface
See *query form*.

search string
See *query restriction*.

Secure Sockets Layer (SSL)
A protocol that supplies secure data communication through data encryption and decryption. SSL uses RSA public-key encryption for specific TCP/IP ports. SSL is an alternative method to Secure-HTTP (S-HTTP), which is used to encrypt specific World Wide Web documents rather than the entire session. SSL is a general-purpose encryption standard. It can also be used for Web applications requiring a secure link, such as E-commerce applications, or for controlling access to Web-based subscription service.

semaphore
A locking mechanism used inside resource managers or resource dispensers. Semaphores have no symbolic names—only shared and exclusive mode access—no deadlock detection, and no automatic release or commit.

server
A term used for any of the following: a computer on a network that sends files to, or runs applications for, other computers on the network; the software that runs on the server computer and performs the work of serving files or running applications; or, in object-oriented programming, a piece of code that exchanges information with another piece of code upon request.

server certificates
Unique digital identifications that form the basis of a Web server's Secure Sockets Layer (SSL) security features. Server certificates are obtained from a mutually trusted, third-party organization, and provide a way for users to authenticate the identity of a Web site. The server certificate contains detailed identification information, such as the organization affiliated with the server content, the organization that issued the certificate, and a unique identification file called a public key. This means that server certificates assure users about the authenticity of Web server content, and that it is safe to establish a secured HTTP connection.

server cluster
A group of server computers that are networked together both physically and with software, in order to provide cluster features such as fault tolerance or load balancing. See also *fault tolerance*; *load balancing*.

server node
Each individual computer in a server cluster.

server process
A process that hosts Microsoft Transaction Server (MTS) components. A Microsoft Transaction Server component can be loaded into a surrogate server process, either on the client (local) or on another computer (remote). It can also be loaded into a client application process (in-process).

server-side include
A file or other object that is included with a page sent out by a Web server; a footer is an example of a simple server-side include.

service
In Internet Information Server (IIS), services that use the most common Internet protocols, HTTP and FTP; in Windows NT, a process that performs a specific system function and often provides an application programming interface (API) for other processes to call. Also, any process that runs continuously on a computer, even when the administrator is not logged on. See also *application*.

session key
A digital key that is created by the client, encrypted, and sent to the server. See also *certificate*; *digital signature*; *key pair*.

SGML
See *Standard Generalized Markup Language*.

shared property
A variable that is available to all objects in the same server process by way of the Shared Property Manager. The value of the property can be any type that can be represented by a variant.

Simple Mail Transfer Protocol (SMTP)
A protocol defined in STD 10, RFC 821, used to transfer e-mail on the Internet.

Simple Network Management Protocol (SNMP)
SNMP (RFC 1157) is the Internet's standard for remote monitoring and management of hosts, routers, and other nodes and devices on a network. A TCP/IP-derived protocol governing network management and monitoring network devices. A protocol for monitoring your network. See also *management information base*.

single-threaded control
A model in which all objects are executed on a single thread.

sitename
See *hostname*.

slow link
A modem connection, usually from 9,600 bps to 56,000 bps.

SMTP
See *Simple Mail Transfer Protocol*.

SNA
See *Systems Network Architecture*.

snap-in
Programs hosted in the Microsoft Management Console (MMC) to actually manage your server applications. In Internet Information Server (IIS) 4.0, Internet Service Manager and Microsoft Transaction Server (MTS) Explorer are implemented as snap-ins. When the administrator starts Internet Service Manager, an MMC console loads the Internet Services Manager snap-in. Administrators can manage IIS applications and MTS packages from a single console.

sniffer
See *network sniffer*.

SNMP
See *Simple Network Management Protocol*.

socket
A software object used by a client to connect to a server; basic components include the port number and the network address of the local host.

Software Development Kit (SDK)
A set of documents, samples, and tutorials that programmers can use to create new applications.

spider
A fast, automated program—such as a search engine, indexing program, or cataloging software—that requests Web pages much faster than human beings can. When Microsoft Content Analyzer automatically explores a Web site, it operates as a spider. Other commonly used terms for spider are "crawler" and "robot." See also *robot*; *explore*.

spoofing
Impersonating another person or computer, usually by providing a false e-mail name, URL, or IP address.

SQL
See *Structured Query Language*.

SQL Access Group (SAG)
A consortium of vendors established in November 1989 to accelerate the Remote Data Access standard and to deliver protocols for interconnectivity among multiple SQL-based software products.

SQL logging
Logging to a Microsoft SQL Server database instead of to a text file. See also *logging*.

SSL
See *Secure Sockets Layer*.

Standard Generalized Markup Language (SGML)
An ISO standard (ISO 8879.1986) which supplies a formal notation for the definition of generalized markup languages. It is an international standard for the definition of device-independent, system-independent methods of representing texts in an electronic form. SGML is a metalanguage, that is, a means of formally describing a language, in this case, a markup language. See also *Hypertext Markup Language*; *International Standards Organization*; *eXtensible Markup Language*.

stateful object
An object that holds private state accumulated from the execution of one or more client calls.

stateless object
An object that does not hold private state accumulated from the execution of one or more client calls.

static page
An HTML page prepared in advance of the request and sent to the client upon request. This page takes no special action when requested. See also *interactive application*.

stripe set
Refers to the saving of data across identical partitions on different drives. A stripe set does not provide fault tolerance; however, stripe sets with parity do. See also *fault tolerance*; *partition*; *stripe sets with parity*.

stripe sets with parity
A method of data protection in which data is striped in large blocks across all the disks in an array. Data redundancy is provided by the parity information. This method provides fault tolerance. See also *fault tolerance*; *stripe set*.

Structured Query Language (SQL)
The international standard language for defining and accessing relational databases.

stub

An interface-specific object that provides the parameter marshaling and communication required for an application object to receive calls from a client that is running in a different execution environment, such as on a different thread or in another process. The stub is located with the application object and communicates with a corresponding proxy that is located with the client that calls it.

subnet mask

A TCP/IP configuration parameter that extracts network and host configuration from an IP address.

System Data Source Name (DSN)

A name that can be used by any process on the computer. Internet Information Server uses system DSNs to access ODBC data sources. See also *Data Source Name.*

Systems Network Architecture (SNA)

Systems Network Architecture. A widely used communications framework developed by IBM to define network functions and to establish standards for enabling its different models of computers to exchange and process data. SNA contains separate layers. As changes occur in one layer, no other layer need be changed.

T

T1

A U.S. telephone standard for a transmission facility at digital signal level 1 (DS1) with 1.544 Mbps in North America and 2.048 Mbps in Europe. The bit rate is with the equivalent bandwidth of approximately twenty-four 56-Kbps lines. A T1 circuit is capable of serving a minimum of 48 modems at 28.8 Kbps, or 96 modems at 14.4 Kbps. T1 circuits are also used for voice telephone connections. A single T1 line carries 24 telephone connections with 24 telephone numbers. When used for voice transmission, a T1 connection must be split into 24 separate circuits.

T3

A U.S. telephone standard for a transmission facility at digital signal level 3 (DS3). Equivalent in bandwidth to 28 T1s. The bit rate is 44.736 Mbps. T3 is sometimes called a 45-meg circuit.

TCP/IP

See *Transmission Control Protocol/Internet Protocol.*

Telnet

A protocol used for interactive logon to a remote computer.

thread

The basic entity to which the operating system allocates CPU time. A thread can execute any part of the application's code, including a part currently being executed by another thread. All threads of a process share the virtual address space, global variables, and operating-system resources of the process.

three-tier architecture

Divides a networked application into three logical areas. The first tier handles presentation, the second processes business logic, and the third provides the data.

throttling

Controlling the maximum amount of bandwidth dedicated to Internet traffic on your server. This feature is useful if you have other services (such as e-mail) sharing the server over a busy link.

thumbnail

A small version of a graphic with a link to a larger version of the same graphic.

timeout

A setting that automatically cancels an unanswered client request after a certain period of time.

token ring

A token ring is a type of network with nodes wired into a ring. Each node constantly passes a control message (token) on to the next; whichever node has the token can send a message. Often, "token ring" is used to refer to the Institute of Electrical and Electronics Engineers (IEEE) 802.5 token ring standard, which is the most common type of token ring. See also *local area network*.

TP

See *transaction processing*.

transaction

A group of processing activities that are either entirely completed, or if not completed, that leave the database and processing system in the same state as before the transaction started.

transaction context object

An object used to allow a client to dynamically include one or more objects in one transaction.

transaction manager

A system service responsible for coordinating the outcome of transactions in order to achieve atomicity. The transaction manager ensures that the resource managers reach a consistent decision on whether the transaction should commit or fail.

transaction processing (TP)

The real-time handling of computerized business transactions as they are received by the system. Also called online transaction processing (OLTP) systems or transaction programs.

Transaction Server object

A COM object that executes in the Microsoft Transaction Server (MTS) run-time environment and follows the Transaction Server programming and deployment model.

Transmission Control Protocol/Internet Protocol (TCP/IP)

A communications standard for all computers on the Internet. On the sending end, TCP breaks the data to be sent into data segments. IP assembles

segments into packets that contain data segments, as well a sender and destination addresses. IP then sends packets to the router for delivery. On the receiving end, IP receives the packets and breaks them down into data segments. TCP assembles the data segments into the original data set. See also *packet*.

tree, directory

A conceptual model used to describe the directory structure of a file directory or a Web site.

two-phase commit

A protocol that ensures that transactions that apply to more than one server are completed on all servers or none at all. Two-phase commit is coordinated by the transaction manager and supported by resource managers.

two-tier architecture

See *client/server architecture*.

U

universal naming convention (UNC)

The naming convention used for physical directories.

upload

In communications, the process of transferring a copy of a file from a local computer to a remote computer by means of a modem or network. With a modem-based communications link, the process generally involves instructing the remote computer to prepare to receive the file on its disk and then wait for the transmission to begin.

Uniform Resource Locator (URL)

A naming convention that uniquely identifies the location of a computer, directory, or file on the Internet. The URL also specifies the appropriate Internet protocol, such as HTTP or FTP. A URL is usually preceded with *http://* such as in this fictitious URL http://www.example.microsoft.com/.

upload
In communications, the process of transferring a copy of a file from a local computer to a remote computer by means of a modem or network. With a modem-based communications link, the process generally involves instructing the remote computer to prepare to receive the file on its disk and then wait for the transmission to begin.

URL
See *Uniform Resource Locator*.

URL directory
See *virtual directory*.

URL mapping
A term sometimes used for the process of associating a URL with a physical directory; see *virtual directory*.

usage data
Information the administrator can import to tell how other people are accessing and using a site. Analyzing this data helps an administrator identify a site's most popular (or unpopular) areas and clarifies the most common navigational paths through the site. See also *hit count*.

Usenet
The most popular news group hierarchy on the Internet.

V

VBA
See *Microsoft Visual Basic for Applications*.

VBScript
See *Microsoft Visual Basic Scripting Edition*.

virtual directory
A directory name, used in an address, which corresponds to a physical directory on the server. See also *URL mapping*.

virtual document
A term sometimes used for a document created automatically in response to information provided by the user; also called a dynamic document. A virtual document is created only in answer to a browser request, and is not permanently stored in a physical directory. An ASP page is an example of a virtual document.

virtual machine
The mechanism the Java language uses to execute Java bytecode on any physical computer. The virtual machine (VM) converts the bytecode to the native instruction for the target computer.

Virtual Reality Modeling Language (VRML)
A language for coding three-dimensional HTML applications.

virtual server
When a single computer hosts several Web sites, it looks like several servers to a browser. These multiple Web sites on a single computer are sometimes called a virtual servers. Virtual servers are also known as webs, Web sites, and multiple identities.

volatile objects
Typically, files that the Web site administrator updates frequently.

volume set
A combination of partitions on a physical disk that appear as one logical drive. See also *logical drive*.

VRML
See *Virtual Reality Modeling Language*.

W

W3C
World Wide Web Consortium. Founded in 1994 to develop common standards for the World Wide Web. The W3C is an international industry consortium jointly hosted by the Massachusetts Institute of Technology Laboratory for Computer Science (MIT/LCS) in North America, by the Institut National de Recherche en Informatique et en Automatique (INRIA) in Europe, and by the Keio University Shonan Fujisawa Campus in Asia. Initially, the W3C was established in collaboration with CERN, where the Web originated, with support from DARPA and the European Commission. For more information, see http://www.w3.org/.

WAIS
See *Wide Area Information Server.*

Web application
A software program that uses HTTP for its core communication protocol and delivers Web-based information to the user in the HTML language.

Web page
A World Wide Web document. Pages can contain almost any kind of content, such as news, images, audio, and video.

Web server
In general terms, a computer equipped with the server software that uses Internet protocols such as HTTP and FTP to respond to Web client requests on a TCP/IP network.

Wide Area Information Server (WAIS)
A method for searching and retrieving information from databases available on the Internet.

Windows Internet Name Service (WINS) server
A server that uses the WINS protocol to map Internet Protocol (IP) addresses to user-friendly names. See also *Domain Name System.*

Windows Open System Architecture (WOSA)
Standards for creating cross-platform applications that use Windows services.

working directory
A term sometimes used to describe the directory in which the Web server software is installed.

working set
The RAM allocated to a process in the Windows NT operating system.

WOSA
See *Windows Open System Architecture.*

World Wide Web (WWW)
The most graphical service on the Internet, the Web also has the most sophisticated linking abilities. Also called the Web or WWW. A set of services that run on top of the Internet, providing a cost-effective way of publishing information, supporting collaboration and workflow, and delivering business applications to any connected user in the world. The Web is a collection of Internet host systems that make these services available on the Internet using the HTTP protocol. Web-based information is usually delivered in the form of hypertext and hypermedia using HTML.

X

XML
See *eXtensible Markup Language.*

Index

Update *your* Resource Kit.
And your expertise.

Here's good news exclusively for owners of the MICROSOFT® WINDOWS NT® SERVER RESOURCE KIT, Version 4.0. These two CD-ROMs provide you with an inexpensive way to update your kit with the latest information, tools, and utilities. You get 14 completely new tools, more than 18 updated and enhanced tools, and hundreds of megabytes of valuable information directly from TechNet. This is the second supplement to the kit—and an essential supplement to your knowledge and skills.

Microsoft Press

Certification
success
begins here.

U.S.A.   **$99.99**
U.K.   £93.99 [V.A.T. included]
Canada $140.99
ISBN 1-57231-710-8

This Microsoft Press® exclusive provides complete, self-paced training for support professionals preparing for the Microsoft® Certified Professional exam on Windows NT® Server 4.0 Enterprise Technologies. This fully self-contained kit offers everything you need for learning to design, implement, and support Microsoft Windows NT in a multidomain environment—step-by-step lessons, lab exercises, certification goals and objectives, and review material. The kit is based on the Microsoft Official Curriculum used in Microsoft Authorized Technical Education Centers around the world. Whether you are preparing for the exam or for your real-world job, MICROSOFT WINDOWS NT SERVER 4.0 ENTERPRISE TECHNOLOGIES TRAINING will be an essential part of your education.

Microsoft *Press*

Hands-on, self-paced training for supporting Internet Explorer 4!

Here's the ideal way for support professionals to prepare for success on the job *and* on the Microsoft® Certified Professional (MCP) exam. That's because this is Microsoft Official Curriculum—the only self-paced training that's adapted from the corresponding Microsoft-authorized instructor-led course. Here you'll master, at your own pace, the architecture and key features of the Microsoft Internet Explorer 4 suite of products. Through the accompanying labs, you'll gain hands-on experience installing, configuring, using, deploying, and supporting Internet Explorer 4 in a networked environment, with particular emphasis on intranet use. And as you prepare for the real world, you'll also get specific preparation for success on the MCP exam. All of which makes MICROSOFT INTERNET EXPLORER 4 TECHNICAL SUPPORT TRAINING the smart way to advance your career now and well into the future.

U.S.A.	**$49.99**
U.K.	£46.99 [V.A.T. included]
Canada	$71.99
ISBN 1-57231-828-7	

Microsoft®*Press*

The *professional's companion* to
Microsoft
Internet Explorer 4.

Microsoft Professional Edition

Covers Microsoft Internet Explorer 4 and Microsoft NetMeeting 2.1

Includes Microsoft NetMeeting 2.1

Microsoft
Internet Explorer
ResourceKit

Comprehensive Resource Guide, Tools, and Utilities for Internet Explorer 4

Microsoft Press

U.S.A.	**$49.99**
U.K.	£46.99 [V.A.T. included]
Canada	$71.99
ISBN 1-57231-842-2	

This exclusive Microsoft® collection provides complete technical information on Microsoft Internet Explorer version 4.0 for the network administrator, the support professional, and the internet service provider. The MICROSOFT INTERNET EXPLORER RESOURCE KIT gives you a technical resource guide packed with authoritative information and an indispensable CD-ROM containing Microsoft Internet Explorer 4, the Microsoft Internet Explorer Administration Kit, valuable utilities, accessory programs, and source code that help you save time and accomplish more—all of which makes it easier for you to deploy and support customized versions of Internet Explorer in your organization.

Microsoft®*Press*

MICROSOFT LICENSE AGREEMENT

Microsoft Internet Information Server Resource Kit

(Tools and Utilities Disc)

6. LIMITATION OF LIABILITY. To the maximum extent permitted by applicable law, in no event shall Microsoft or its suppliers be liable for any special, incidental, indirect, or consequential damages whatsoever (including, without limitation, damages for loss of business profits, business interruption, loss of business information, or any other pecuniary loss) arising out of the use of or inability to use the SOFTWARE PRODUCT or the provision of or failure to provide Support Services, even if Microsoft has been advised of the possibility of such damages. In any case, Microsoft's entire liability under any provision of this EULA shall be limited to the greater of the amount actually paid by you for the SOFTWARE PRODUCT or US$5.00; provided however, if you have entered into a Microsoft Support Services Agreement, Microsoft's entire liability regarding Support Services shall be governed by the terms of that agreement. Because some states and jurisdictions do not allow the exclusion or limitation of liability, the above limitation may not apply to you.

7. MISCELLANEOUS.

This EULA is governed by the laws of the State of Washington, U.S.A.

Should you have any questions concerning this EULA, or if you desire to contact Microsoft for any reason, please contact the Microsoft subsidiary serving your country, or write: Microsoft Sales Information Center/One Microsoft Way/Redmond, WA 98052-6399.

Si vous avez acquis votre produit Microsoft au CANADA, la garantie limitée suivante vous concerne:

EXCLUSION DE GARANTIES. Microsoft exclut expressément toute garantie relative au LOGICIEL. Le LOGICIEL et la documentation y afférente sont fournis "en l'état", sans garantie d'aucune sorte, expresse ou implicite, y compris, de manière limitative, sans aucune garantie de qualité, d'adéquation à un usage particulier ou de non-contrefaçon. Vous assumez l'ensemble des risques découlant de l'utilisation ou des performances du LOGICIEL.

Pas de Responsabilité pour les Dommages Indirects - Microsoft ou ses fournisseurs ne seront pas responsables en aucune circonstance pour tout dommage spécial, incident, indirect, ou conséquent quel qu'il soit (y compris, sans limitation, les dommages entraînés par la perte de bénéfices, l'interruption des activités, la perte d'information ou toute autre perte pécuniaire) découlant de l'utilisation ou de l'impossibilité d'utilisation de ce LOGICIEL ainsi que pour toute disposition concernant le Suport Technique ou la façon dont celui-ci a été rendu et ce, même si Microsoft a été avisée de la possibilité de tels dommages. La responsabilité de Microsoft en vertu de toute disposition de cette convention ne pourra en aucun temps excéder le plus élevé entre i) le montant effectivement payé par vous pour le LOGICIEL ou ii) US$5.00. Advenant que vous ayez contracté par entente distincte avec Microsoft pour un Support Technique étendu, vous serez lié par les termes d' une telle entente.

La présente Convention est régie par les lois de la province d'Ontario, Canada. Chacune des parties à la présente reconnaît irrévocablement la compétence des tribunaux de la province d'Ontario et consent à instituer tout litige qui pourrait découler de la présente auprès des tribunaux situés dans le district judiciaire de York, province d'Ontario.

Au cas où vous auriez des questions concernant cette licence ou que vous désiriez vous mettre en rapport avec Microsoft pour quelque raison que ce soit, veuillez contacter la succursale Microsoft desservant votre pays, dont l'adresse est fournie dans ce produit, ou écrivez à : Microsoft Sales Information Center, One Microsoft Way, Redmond, Washington 98052-6399.

MICROSOFT LICENSE AGREEMENT

Microsoft Internet Information Server Resource Kit

(Sampler Disc)

IMPORTANT—READ CAREFULLY: This Microsoft End-User License Agreement ("EULA") is a legal agreement between you (either an individual or a single entity) and Microsoft Corporation for the Microsoft software product(s) identified above which may include associated software components, media, printed materials, and "online" or electronic documentation ("SOFTWARE PRODUCT"). By installing, copying, or otherwise using the SOFTWARE PRODUCT, you agree to be bound by the terms of this EULA. If you do not agree to the terms of this EULA, do not install or use the SOFTWARE PRODUCT. If the SOFTWARE PRODUCT was purchased by you, you may return it to your place of purchase for a full refund.

The SOFTWARE PRODUCT is protected by United States copyright laws and international copyright treaties, as well as other intellectual property laws and treaties. The SOFTWARE PRODUCT is licensed, not sold.

1. GRANT OF LICENSE. This EULA grants you the following rights:

• **Software Product.** You may make and use an unlimited number of copies of the SOFTWARE PRODUCT solely in conjunction with licensed copies of Microsoft Internet Information Server for the purpose of designing and developing customizations for your Microsoft Internet Information Server configuration ("Solution") provided that: (a) you must not modify the SOFTWARE PRODUCT except as expressly provided below and (b) you must maintain the copyright notice on all copies of the SOFTWARE PRODUCT. You may not redistribute the SOFTWARE PRODUCT.

• **Documentation.** You may modify the documentation portion of the SOFTWARE PRODUCT ("Documentation") in order to customize it for use with your Solution. You may not distribute the Documentation as provided with the SOFTWARE PRODUCT.

• **Sample Code.** You may modify the portions of the SOFTWARE PRODUCT designated as "Sample Code" for your Solution. For purposes of this section, "modifications" shall mean enhancements to the functionality of the Sample Code.

Microsoft reserves all rights not expressly granted to you.

2. DESCRIPTION OF OTHER RIGHTS AND LIMITATIONS.

• **Limitations on Reverse Engineering, Decompilation and Disassembly.** You may not reverse engineer, decompile, or disassemble the SOFTWARE PRODUCT, except and only to the extent that such activity is expressly permitted by applicable law notwithstanding this limitation.

• **Rental.** You may not rent or lease the SOFTWARE PRODUCT.

• **Software Transfer.** You may permanently transfer all of your rights under this EULA, provided you retain no copies, you transfer all of the SOFTWARE PRODUCT (including all component parts, the media and printed materials, any upgrades, this EULA and, if applicable, the Certificate of Authenticity), and the recipient agrees to the terms of this EULA. If the SOFTWARE PRODUCT is an upgrade, any transfer must include all prior versions of the SOFTWARE PRODUCT.

• **Support Services.** Microsoft may, but is not obligated to, provide you with support services related to the SOFTWARE PRODUCT ("Support Services"). Use of the Support Services is governed by the Microsoft policies and programs described in the user manual, "online" documentation, and/or other Microsoft-provided materials. Any supplemental software code provided to you as part of the Support Services shall be considered part of the SOFTWARE PRODUCT and subject to the terms and conditions of this EULA. With respect to technical information you provide to Microsoft as part of the Support Services, Microsoft may use such information for its business purposes, including for product support and development. Microsoft will not utilize such technical information in a form that personally identifies you.

• **Termination.** Without prejudice to any other rights, Microsoft may terminate this EULA if you fail to comply with the terms and conditions of this EULA. In such event, you must destroy all copies of the SOFTWARE PRODUCT and all of its component parts.

3. COPYRIGHT. All title and copyrights in and to the SOFTWARE PRODUCT (including but not limited to any images, photographs, animations, video, audio, music, text and "applets," incorporated into the SOFTWARE PRODUCT), the accompanying printed materials, and any copies of the SOFTWARE PRODUCT, are owned by Microsoft or its suppliers. The SOFTWARE PRODUCT is protected by United States copyright laws and international treaty provisions. Therefore, you must treat the SOFTWARE PRODUCT like any other copyrighted material except that you may either (a) make one copy of the SOFTWARE PRODUCT solely for backup or archival purposes, or (b) install the SOFTWARE PRODUCT on a single computer provided you keep the original solely for backup or archival purposes. You may not copy the printed materials accompanying the SOFTWARE PRODUCT.

4. U.S. GOVERNMENT RESTRICTED RIGHTS. The SOFTWARE PRODUCT and Documentation are provided with RESTRICTED RIGHTS. Use, duplication, or disclosure by the Government is subject to restrictions as set forth in subparagraph (c)(1)(ii) of the Rights in Technical Data and Computer Software clause at DFARS 252.227-7013 or subparagraphs (c)(1) and (2) of the Commercial Computer Software—Restricted Rights at 48 CFR 52.227-19, as applicable. Manufacturer is Microsoft Corporation/One Microsoft Way/Redmond, WA 98052-6399.

5. NO WARRANTIES. MICROSOFT EXPRESSLY DISCLAIMS ANY WARRANTY FOR THE SOFTWARE PRODUCT. THE SOFTWARE PRODUCT AND ANY RELATED DOCUMENTATION IS PROVIDED "AS IS" WITHOUT WARRANTY OF ANY KIND, EITHER EXPRESS OR IMPLIED, INCLUDING, WITHOUT LIMITATION, THE IMPLIED WARRANTIES OR MERCHANTABILITY, FITNESS FOR A PARTICULAR PURPOSE, OR NONINFRINGEMENT. THE ENTIRE RISK ARISING OUT OF USE OR PERFORMANCE OF THE SOFTWARE PRODUCT REMAINS WITH YOU.

6. LIMITATION OF LIABILITY. To the maximum extent permitted by applicable law, in no event shall Microsoft or its suppliers be liable for any special, incidental, indirect, or consequential damages whatsoever (including, without limitation, damages for loss of business profits, business interruption, loss of business information, or any other pecuniary loss) arising out of the use of or inability to use the SOFTWARE PRODUCT or the provision of or failure to provide Support Services, even if Microsoft has been advised of the possibility of such damages. In any case, Microsoft's entire liability under any provision of this EULA shall be limited to the greater of the amount actually paid by you for the SOFTWARE PRODUCT or US$5.00; provided however, if you have entered into a Microsoft Support Services Agreement, Microsoft's entire liability regarding Support Services shall be governed by the terms of that agreement. Because some states and jurisdictions do not allow the exclusion or limitation of liability, the above limitation may not apply to you.

7. MISCELLANEOUS.

This EULA is governed by the laws of the State of Washington, U.S.A.

Should you have any questions concerning this EULA, or if you desire to contact Microsoft for any reason, please contact the Microsoft subsidiary serving your country, or write: Microsoft Sales Information Center/One Microsoft Way/Redmond, WA 98052-6399.

Si vous avez acquis votre produit Microsoft au CANADA, la garantie limitée suivante vous concerne:

EXCLUSION DE GARANTIES. Microsoft exclut expressément toute garantie relative au LOGICIEL. Le LOGICIEL et la documentation y afférente sont fournis "en l'état", sans garantie d'aucune sorte, expresse ou implicite, y compris, de manière limitative, sans aucune garantie de qualité, d'adéquation à un usage particulier ou de non-contrefaçon. Vous assumez l'ensemble des risques découlant de l'utilisation ou des performances du LOGICIEL.

Pas de Responsabilité pour les Dommages Indirects - Microsoft ou ses fournisseurs ne seront pas responsables en aucune circonstance pour tout dommage spécial, incident, indirect, ou conséquent quel qu'il soit (y compris, sans limitation, les dommages entrainés par la perte de bénéfices, l'interruption des activités, la perte d'information ou toute autre perte pécuniaire) découlant de l'utilisation ou de l'impossibilité d'utilisation de ce LOGICIEL ainsi que pour toute disposition concernant le Suport Technique ou la façon dont celui-ci a été rendu et ce, même si Microsoft a été avisée de la possibilité de tels dommages. La responsabilité de Microsoft en vertu de toute disposition de cette convention ne pourra en aucun temps excéder le plus élevé entre i) le montant effectivement payé par vous pour le LOGICIEL ou ii) US$5.00. Advenant que vous ayez contracté par entente distincte avec Microsoft pour un Support Technique étendu, vous serez lié par les termes d' une telle entente.

La présente Convention est régie par les lois de la province d'Ontario, Canada. Chacune des parties à la présente reconnaît irrévocablement la compétence des tribunaux de la province d'Ontario et consent à instituer tout litige qui pourrait découler de la présente auprès des tribunaux situés dans le district judiciaire de York, province d'Ontario.

Au cas où vous auriez des questions concernant cette licence ou que vous désiriez vous mettre en rapport avec Microsoft pour quelque raison que ce soit, veuillez contacter la succursale Microsoft desservant votre pays, dont l'adresse est fournie dans ce produit, ou écrivez à : Microsoft Sales Information Center, One Microsoft Way, Redmond, Washington 98052-6399.

Register Today!

Return this
Microsoft® Internet Information Server Resource Kit
registration card for
a Microsoft Press® catalog

U.S. and Canada addresses only. Fill in information below and mail postage-free. Please mail only the bottom half of this page.

1-57231-638-1   ***MICROSOFT® INTERNET***   *Owner Registration Card*
INFORMATION SERVER RESOURCE KIT

_____

NAME

_____

INSTITUTION OR COMPANY NAME

_____

ADDRESS

_____

_____

CITY   STATE   ZIP

Microsoft Press
Quality Computer Books

For a free catalog of
Microsoft Press® products, call
1-800-MSPRESS

BUSINESS REPLY MAIL
FIRST-CLASS MAIL   PERMIT NO. 53   BOTHELL, WA

POSTAGE WILL BE PAID BY ADDRESSEE

MICROSOFT PRESS REGISTRATION
MICROSOFT® INTERNET INFORMATION
SERVER RESOURCE KIT
PO BOX 3019
BOTHELL WA   98041-9946